Causal Attribution

For Claudia

Causal Attribution

From Cognitive Processes to Collective Beliefs

Miles Hewstone

Basil Blackwell

Copyright © Miles Hewstone 1989

First published 1989
First published in USA 1990

Basil Blackwell Ltd
108 Cowley Road, Oxford, OX4 1JF, UK

Basil Blackwell Inc.
3 Cambridge Center
Cambridge, Massachusetts 02142, USA

British Library Cataloguing in Publication Data
A CIP catalogue record for this book is available from the British Library

Library of Congress Cataloging-in-Publication Data
Hewstone, Miles.
Causal attribution: from cognitive processes to collective
beliefs/Miles Hewstone.
p.   cm.
Includes bibliographies and index.
ISBN 0-631-15818-9 – ISBN 0-631-17165-7
(pbk.)
1. Attribution (Social psychology) I. Title.
HM291.H5256   1989
302'.12–dc20

Typeset in 10½ on 12 pt Times by Joshua Associates Ltd, Oxford
Printed in Great Britain by Billing & Sons (Worcester) Ltd

The causes of events are always more interesting than the events themselves.

Cicero, *Ad Atticum*, Bk ix, epis. 5 (49 BC)

Contents

Preface

Like many other social psychologists, indeed social scientists, I have long been fascinated by common-sense explanations. This book reflects my own ten-year involvement with attribution theory, a relationship that began with my doctoral dissertation and went on to include empirical studies, conceptual papers and two edited books (Hewstone, 1983a; Jaspars et al., 1983a). Much of that work was published in collaboration with Jos Jaspars and we long planned to write a book on the topic together. Tragically, Jos died, quite unexpectedly, in 1985, leaving European social psychology without one of its most brilliant protagonists. It was one of the reviewers of my own edited volume who provided me with the stimulus to take up the idea of a monograph once again. Klaus Fiedler, reviewing the book in the *British Journal of Social Psychology*, remarked that the variety of theoretical perspectives on causal attribution was now quite bewildering to many scholars and students and there was a need for theoretical integration.

This monograph provides a brief introduction to attribution theory and a review of its major social psychological literature over a span of some 40 years. I then try to provide integration by using Willem Doise's notion of four *levels of explanation* that can be used in social psychological studies: intra-personal, interpersonal, intergroup and societal levels. My review draws attention to the great achievements, as well as the shortcomings, of attribution theory and research at each level and it reflects accurately the history of the field to date. There has been far more work on attribution in relation to social cognition and social interaction (much of it North American) and far less work on attribution in the context of intergroup relations and societal beliefs (much of it European). Doise's framework, however, does more than merely organize a review of the literature, it points the way towards integration of attribution research at the different levels.

I hope that the book will convince some critics that there is more to causal attribution than they perhaps thought and that the scope of research has been more social, and less artificial, than they may have feared. Of course, I would also be delighted if the book were to provide encouragement for future researchers and to strengthen the conviction that an attributional approach does have a future, as well as a distinguished past, in social psychology. Needless to say, I dearly hope that Jos would have approved of the final product; whatever its merits and demerits, this volume is a personal testimony to a true scholar, not forgotten.

List of figures

List of tables

Acknowledgements

Writing this book has been the most satisfying experience of my academic life. I owe a tremendous debt of thanks to the many people and organizations without whom it would not have been written when and in the form that it was.

First, the people: I am especially grateful to Klaus Fiedler, Frank D. Fincham, John H. Harvey and Stephen J. Read, who each read large chunks of the first draft, commented extensively and provided yet more literature for me to read! The following friends and colleagues also provided very useful comments on individual chapters: Garth J. O. Fletcher, Adrian Furnham, David L. Hamilton, Denis J. Hilton, Gustav Jahoda, Penelope J. Oakes, Bernadette Park, Teun A. van Dijk and Peter A. White. Many other colleagues provided useful comments in seminars that I gave, as the book took shape, at the Universities of Leiden, Kansas, California-Santa Barbara, Southern California, California-Los Angeles, Wales-College of Cardiff, and at the London School of Economics. My graduate students, M. R. Islam and Lucy Johnston, kindly prepared the index.

Second, the organizations: this book is very much the product of a wonderful year, both professionally and personally, that I spent as a Fellow at the Center for Advanced Study in the Behavioral Sciences, Stanford, California. In the beauty and tranquillity of that setting I was able to work intensively and without distraction, with lunch-time volleyball for letting off steam. I wish to acknowledge the bibliographic, typing, computing and editing help of Margaret Amara and Rosanne Torre, Virginia Heaton, Lynn Gale and Kathleen Much, respectively. I would like especially to thank Gardner Lindzey and Bob Scott for all that they did to make my time at the Center such a happy and productive one. I also gratefully acknowledge the financial support of the National Science Foundation (BNS-8700864) and the John D. and Catherine T. MacArthur Foundation, during the nine months of my Fellowship, and the Economic and Social Research Council for a

Personal Research Grant (G00242059) that enabled me to stay a full
year at the Center.

Last, but not least, I thank my loving wife, Claudia, to whom this
book is dedicated. Although we were separated by thousands of miles
for most of the year in which the book was written, she gave me her
usual unfailing encouragement and support. I only hope that the final
product goes some way towards justifying my absence.

1 Introduction

Common sense is not a matter of inexplicable or arbitrary assertions and the notion of cause which it employs, though flexible and complex, is governed by statable principles...

(Hart and Honoré, 1961)

This book is about common-sense explanations, as studied within the social-psychological framework of 'attribution theory'. It will quickly become apparent that the term *explanation* is used in a broad sense, as is '*causal attribution*'. This chapter begins, therefore, with a brief, comparative analysis of how the term *explanation* has been used in different disciplines, and how different philosophers have conceived of causal explanations.[1] The second part of the chapter considers the intellectual ancestry of attribution theory and gives an overview of the book.

EXPLANATIONS IN SCIENCE, HISTORY AND COMMON SENSE

Passmore (1962) has usefully compared explanations in the three domains of science, history and common sense. Beginning with scientific explanation, he notes that a restricted and restrictive notion of cause has often been used: 'the scientific assumption has been that explanation always consists in using a general law as a means of explaining the behaviour of a particular case or kind of case' (p. 110). In contrast, historians have used the word *explanation* almost as liberally as the layperson. Passmore sharpens the comparison by considering three requirements that should be satisfied by a good explanation: it should be *intelligible*, *adequate* and *correct*. These criteria, he argues, are applied with varying degrees of severity in scientific, historical and common-sense explanations.

An explanation is *intelligible* if it refers to some familiar type of causal connection. As Passmore points out, no explanation is intrinsically intelligible, and over historical time explanations wax and wane in their acceptability (for example, psychosomatic and witchcraft explanations, respectively). This criterion is useful in drawing our attention to the interpersonal nature of explanation (see chapter 5), and to the obvious fact that explanations are related to social and collective beliefs (see chapter 7).

Adequate explanations are subsumed under intelligible ones; according to Passmore, every adequate explanation is intelligible, but not all intelligible explanations are adequate. Passmore defines an explanation as adequate if the connection between the explanation and the event to be explained is 'strong' enough (p. 112). Although vague, this criterion again has relevance for a social-psychological approach. Passmore proposes that everyday requests for explanation are typically 'polite rather than searching' (p. 112); this proposal leads to the interesting question of *when* people's criteria for adequate explanations become more or less strict (see chapters 3 and 4), and again to the role of interpersonal concerns in the type of explanation people feel it is necessary to give (chapter 5).

As adequacy entails intelligibility, so is adequacy entailed by *correctness*, the third criterion. Passmore argues that, in everyday life, we generally presume that an adequate explanation is correct. Unlike scientists, historians and laypersons do not usually search for strictly necessary and sufficient conditions, or for more general explanations. However, if attribution theorists are going to talk about 'errors' in the way people attribute causes, as they certainly have done, then they would do well to operate with some criterion of correctness, just as Passmore does.

Using these three criteria, Passmore distinguishes between science, on the one hand, and history and common sense on the other. This is an interesting conclusion, given the body of attribution research built on Kelley's (1967) idea that laypersons perceive causes in a manner similar to the scientist's (see chapters 2 and 4). Of more relevance here, however, is the fact that Passmore has outlined these three general criteria of explanations, which will be useful throughout the book. The next problem to tackle is what we mean by causal explanations.

EXPLANATIONS IN TERMS OF CAUSE

As Fischhoff (1976) has noted, psychologists – especially those interested in attribution theory – should read some philosophy. Many, perhaps most, of us lack a training in the conceptual analysis that characterizes philosophy, but we can benefit from the attention philosophers have devoted to such questions as what is 'behaviour' (Dretske, 1988), what is an 'event' (Pachter, 1974), what is a 'disposition' (Rozeboom, 1973) or, the focus here, what is a 'cause'? It is, to say the least, ironic that an idea so fundamental to attribution theory – the concept of causality – has received so little attention in the social-psychological literature (Shaver, 1981).

The classic approach is that of David Hume. His prototypical example of causality was one billiard ball striking another – the collision is followed by movement of the previously stationary ball, but is not seen as producing it. Many definitions of cause are to be found in Hume's work, but perhaps the clearest is the following:

> A cause is said to be an object followed by another, and where all the objects similar to the first are followed by objects similar to the second, where, if the first object had not been, the second had not existed. (Hume, 1748/1975, pp. 76–7)

Hume's causality is typically referred to as 'constant conjunction' (e.g., Ayer, 1980, p. 68), and the definition above certainly conveys the meaning of covariation between cause and effect, which is fundamental to Kelley's (1967) theory of causal attribution.

John Stuart Mill's (1872/1973) conception of cause has significantly influenced attribution theory, via Kelley's (1967) theory (see chapter 2). Mill wrote that the cause 'is the sum total of the conditions positive and negative taken together ... which being realized, the consequent invariably follows' (quoted by Davidson, 1967, p. 692). A key issue here, as Davidson noted, is whether the true cause must include all the antecedent conditions that were jointly sufficient for the effect. Mill argued that what people ordinarily call the cause is *one* of these conditions, arbitrarily selected, which becomes inaccurately labelled 'the cause'. Anyone seriously interested in the layperson's causal explanations should question whether this selection is, indeed, arbitrary. As Collingwood has pointed out, with an illuminating example, the selection is by no means arbitrary:

> If my car 'conks out' on a hill and I wonder what the cause is, I shall not consider my problem solved by a passer-by who tells me that the top of a hill is further away from the earth's center than its bottom, and that consequently more power is needed to take a car uphill than to take her along the level. All this is quite true; what the passer-by has described is one of the conditions which, together, form the 'true cause' of my car's stopping; and he has 'arbitrarily selected' one of these and called it the cause, he has done just what Mill says we always do. But now suppose an A.A. man comes along, opens the bonnet, holds up a loose high-tension lead, and says 'look here, sir, you're running on three cylinders.' My

problem is now solved. I know the cause of the stoppage. It is *the* cause, just because it has not been 'arbitrarily selected'; it has been correctly identified as the thing that I can put right, after which the car will go properly. (Collingwood, 1938/1961, pp. 305–6)

As the preceding example makes clear, we now need to ask how common-sense explanations distinguish between the cause and mere conditions. This question has been brilliantly attacked by the legal philosophers Hart and Honoré (1956/1961), whose work has only quite recently been drawn to the attention of social psychologists by Fincham and Jaspars (1980).[2] Hart and Honoré's interest in the common-sense notion of causation lies in the claims that the courts apply precisely this notion, and that the sitting judge answers questions of causation *as* an ordinary person. To distinguish between the cause and mere conditions, Hart and Honoré use two factors or contrasts, 'These are the contrasts between what is abnormal in relation to any given subject-matter and between a free deliberate human action and all other conditions' (1956/1961, p. 332). Pre-dating social psychological conclusions by about 30 years (e.g., Hastie, 1984; Weiner, 1985a), Hart and Honoré identify unusual occurrences (e.g., accidents, catastrophes) as the major instigators of causal explanations in ordinary life and in the law. As laypersons we acknowledge that certain conditions necessary for an outcome are simply normal conditions and we look for the condition that 'made the difference' (p. 334) between the disaster and the normal event:

> Thus anyone who asks what is the cause of a railway accident would assume until corrected that the train was moving at normal speed, carrying a normal weight, that the driver stopped and started, accelerated and slowed down at normal times. To mention these normal conditions would obviously provide no explanation of the disaster, for they are also present when no disaster occurs; whereas the mention of [a] bent rail does provide an explanation. Accordingly, though all the conditions mentioned are equally necessary, the bent rail is the cause and the others are mere conditions. It is the bent rail we say which 'made the difference' between disaster and normal functioning. (Hart and Honoré, 1956/1961, p. 334)

Some similar ideas have also been put forward by Mackie (1974), with reference to the idea of a 'causal field' (a notion introduced by J. Anderson, 1938). In Mackie's words, 'Both cause and effect are seen as differences within a field; anything that is part of the assumed (but commonly unstated) description of the field itself will, then, be automatically ruled out as a candidate for the role of cause' (Mackie, 1974, p. 35). Such ideas are of obvious relevance to attribution theory, but have only recently received attention by social psychologists (e.g.,

Einhorn and Hogarth, 1986; Fincham and Jaspars, 1980; Hastie, 1983).

In particular, Hart and Honoré's approach should appeal to social psychologists because it is eminently practical. It takes account of social context, and it acknowledges that the selection of normal and abnormal conditions will very often depend on the practical purposes of the search for a causal explanation. Unlike Collingwood (1938/1961), they do not argue that what is selected as a cause is always something that may be controlled or operated by human agency. They do, however, note the appeal of common-sense explanations that stop at a human action or omission (as opposed to some abnormal physical condition or event). In many cases, 'we press on for the more satisfying explanation in terms of human agency. At the common-sense level, once we have reached this point, we have reached an explanation with a special finality and usually do not press further for a causal explanation of a deliberate human action.' (Hart and Honoré, 1956/1961, p. 335). This view is remarkably similar to some of the ideas put forward by Heider (1944) and, as we shall see, the 'finality' of personal causes has remained a central issue in attribution research. In sum, the conceptions of cause put forward by Hart and Honoré, and by Mackie, seem much closer to common sense than the definitions of Hume and Mill (see Hilton, 1988, for a more detailed discussion).

THE STUDY OF EXPLANATIONS IN PHILOSOPHY AND PSYCHOLOGY

So far I have highlighted some of the contributions philosophers have made to the study of explanations. The selection has, of course, been limited and unrepresentative, because I am no philosopher and my primary concern is the social-psychological approach to causal attribution. Furthermore, P. A. White (1989) has argued that psychological research on causal inference and attribution has been predominantly influenced by regularity-based theories (e.g., Hume's) and that other philosophical theories (such as generative or productive relations, e.g., Harré and Madden, 1975) have had little or no impact on the field. White makes a convincing case for introducing a broader selection of philosophical approaches into the psychology of attribution, but this potential research is beyond the bounds of the present volume (see P. A. White, 1988a).

Even though philosophers have clarified our concepts, their contributions are tangential to the present approach. As Simon (1968) has pointed out, questions raised by philosophers in relation to causation are purely logical; they do not necessarily parallel the beliefs of the layperson. For example, R. Martin (1972) has noted that in both historical writings and everyday conversations two or more causes of an event are often mentioned, one of which is said to have been 'a more important cause'. Martin reports that philosophers have debated the propriety of 'weighting' causes, but for the researcher interested in lay explanations such debate is essentially irrelevant. What matters is what people think and believe, as Shaver has argued: 'An individual's perceptions of the causes of events may or *may not* follow the rational guidelines explicit in philosophical discussions. Asking how people *do* identify and understand the causes of actions is different from asking how such enquiries *should* proceed' (1981, p. 332). Accepting this viewpoint, some of the major antecedents of a social-psychological, or subjective, approach to causality are noted below.

ATTRIBUTION THEORY: AN ACKNOWLEDGEMENT OF ANCESTORS

Psychological interest in causality extends back far beyond attribution theory. According to the phrenologists Gall and Spurzheim, 'causality' was one of two 'reflective' intellectual powers (the other was 'comparison') that were located in the centre of the forehead (see Spurzheim, 1934 edn). More recently, Piaget (1930) studied the development of the idea of causality in children, and their use of causal language. But Michotte (1946/1963) really pioneered the psychological study of causality.

Michotte took issue with Hume's claim, that we have no 'direct impression' of the influence of one physical event on another. He argued that Hume's method, the 'analytical' observation of colliding billiard balls, only allowed for recognition of a succession of movements. What differentiated Michotte's work from Hume's (and what took nearly two centuries to be acknowledged) was that Hume's analytical mode of observation dissected the phenomenal world into pieces, and obscured the most interesting psychological facts. In contrast, Michotte's studies on the apparent movement and collision of geometrical shapes revealed that it was possible to experience causality directly: 'certain physical events give an immediate causal impression, and ... one can "see" an object *act* on another object, *produce* in it certain changes, and *modify* it in one way or another' (Michotte, 1946/1963, p. 15).

Michotte's experimental studies attempted to produce systematic combinations of movements involving several objects, and to discover which conditions brought about an impression of causality in his experimental subjects. These conditions included the length and direction of the moving objects' trajectories, the duration of contact between the objects, and the absolute and relative velocities of the two objects (Michotte, 1952). Through careful experimentation Michotte was able to show that perceivers can and do distinguish between qualitatively different kinds of effects. In what he called 'l'effet déclenchement' (the launching effect), one object was seen to trigger the movement of a second object, which then appeared to move of its own accord; in 'l'effet entraînement' (the 'entraining' effect), the first object was seen to encounter, push and then carry along the second object. In sum, Michotte revealed that it was possible to experience phenomenal causality directly and that this process was subconscious and perceptual, rather than conscious and inductive. The tension between 'simple' and 'complex' models of the attribution process continues to characterize attribution research, as will be seen in chapter 4. If all this seems far removed from *social* psychology, it is worth recalling the earliest research by Heider, the founding father of attribution theory. Like Michotte, he studied the perception of causality induced by the movement of simple geometric shapes (Heider and Simmel, 1944; see also Kassin, 1982), but of course for Heider this was merely a beginning, whereas for Michotte it was the end in itself.[3]

The psychological ancestry of attribution theory seems direct, obvious and acknowledged, but the same cannot be said for the influence from other social sciences. This oversight may be due partly to the perennial problem of interdisciplinary myopia and partly to the original publication of work in distant countries, sometimes in different languages. Before reviewing attribution theory in the following chapters, however, it is worth noting two early contributions of a more sociological nature, which seem to share the same basic concerns as attribution theory.

Billig (1982) has pointed out that Burke's *A Grammar of Motives* (1962) begins with the same question that underlies the study of causal attribution: 'What is involved when we say what people are doing and why they are doing it?' (p. xv). Burke was concerned with the attribution of motives, which he studied in the form of legal judgements, poetry, fiction, political and scientific works, news and bits of gossip. He used five key terms to name what took place (the *act*), the background situation (the *scene*), what person or kind of person performed it (*agent*), what means were used (*agency*), and why it took place (*purpose*). Burke contrasted two possible explanations of action, one focusing on an agent's dispositions (the 'scene-agent ratio') and the other on the situational factor (the 'scene-act ratio'). This distinction parallels that between personal and situational attributions, which is so central to attribution theory. Other than this similarity, however, Burke's 'dramatism', as he calls it, is closer to Harré's (1977) 'dramaturgical' approach to accounts of action than to mainstream attribution research (see Overington, 1977).[4] Burke does, however, represent a 'narrative' orientation towards social knowledge (exemplified in discourse, stories and historical accounts) that complements the 'paradigmatic' orientation (characterized by content-free propositions and formal, abstract principles) that has dominated research on attribution (see Zukier, 1986).

A far more obvious attributional ancestor is Ichheiser, even though he rejected an empirical psychology based on data collection and experimentation (M. Jahoda, 1983) and has been described as 'more sociologist than psychologist' (Rudmin et al., 1987, p. 173). As Rudmin et al. have argued, Ichheiser's work on 'misinterpretations' (1943, 1949, 1970) maps directly onto subsequent work in attribution theory, as can be shown with two examples.[5] First, as perceivers, we have a tendency to overestimate personal factors and underestimate situational factors. Supporting this 'misinterpretation', Ichheiser argued that we tend to overestimate the unity of personality, over-looking inconsistent information once an impression has been formed, and underestimating our own role in the situation in which we observe others. This general idea clearly foreshadowed L. Ross's (1977) influential work on the 'fundamental attribution error'. In contrast to subsequent work, Ichheiser emphasized that this was a collectively conditioned misinterpretation of personality, not a personal 'error', and one that was a consequence of the social system:

> We all have the tendency – conditioned ... by the ideology of our society – to interpret in our everyday life the behavior of individuals in terms of specific personal qualities rather than in terms of specific situations. Our whole framework of concepts of 'merit' and 'blame', 'success' and 'failure', 'responsibility' and 'irresponsibility', as accepted in everyday life, is based on the presupposition of personal determination of behavior (as opposed to the situation or social determination of behavior). (Ichheiser, 1943, p. 151)

This societal approach to attribution has received little attention, but it constitutes an important approach to attribution and is dealt with later in this volume (chapter 7). Ichheiser also identified a second mis-interpretation, the tendency to misattribute ability (or lack of ability) on the basis of the success (or failure) of an outcome. This misattribution serves to enhance the self-esteem of those who are favoured. Here Ichheiser's work previewed the later literature on attributions for success and failure (e.g. Heider, 1958; Weiner, 1986).

It should be clear from these two examples that Ichheiser made an early contribution to attribution theory, albeit one that has been largely overlooked by social psychologists. As the sympathetic historical review by Rudmin et al. concludes: 'Although Ichheiser cannot challenge Heider's place as the "father" of attributional social psychology, he might be considered a long lost "rich uncle", waiting to be discovered and welcomed home' (1987, p. 175).

OVERVIEW OF THE BOOK

The following two chapters review social-psychological work on causal attribution, beginning with the major theories and then grouping subsequent progress under the headings of some of the main questions attribution research has asked and, at least partly, answered. The remainder of the book devotes a chapter to each of the four main levels of analysis at which causal attribution has been, and should be, studied in social psychology.

This format is based on Doise's book, *Levels of Explanation in Social Psychology* (1986), in which he distinguished four kinds of explanation in social psychological studies. The *intra-personal* level (I) is limited to psychological or intra-personal processes that deal with how individuals organize their perception, evaluation and behaviour in the social world. The emphasis is on how (i.e., the mechanisms by which) individuals process information. A prototypical example of attribution work at this level is Kelley's (1967) analysis of variance model of how individuals process information to arrive at a cause (see chapter 4). The *interpersonal* level (II) concentrates on the dynamics of interpersonal processes within a given situation. The individuals occupy essentially equal positions and are considered as interchangeable actors. The research on actor-observer differences in attribution, based on Jones and Nisbett's (1972) hypothesis, is a prototype of this level of analysis (see chapter 5). The *intergroup* level (III) studies the effects of social categorization on attribution, and specifically whether identical behaviours or outcomes are explained differently as a function of targets' and perceivers' group memberships (see chapter 6). Taylor and Jaggi's (1974) study of Hindu perceivers' attributions for positive and negative acts by Hindu and Muslim targets is a proto-typical study at this level. Finally, the *societal* level (IV) studies the beliefs that are shared by large numbers of people within a society. A prototypical study is J. G. Miller's (1984) analysis of cross-cultural patterns of attribution.[6]

Doise identified a dominant tendency in social-psychological research, both European and North American, to limit the analysis to Levels I and II (see also Doise, 1980). The reference list for this volume verifies the truth of this claim for attribution research. Doise notes, however, that, in general, European social psychology differs from its American counterpart in its attempts to introduce Level III and IV analyses into both theory and research (see Jaspars, 1986). Some earlier publications (Hewstone and Jaspars, 1982a, 1984), have used the term 'social attribution' to describe attribution research at Levels III and IV. Although this work did successfully extend the scope of attribution research, I have come to regret my own usage. My subsequent thinking and research, as well as conversations with colleagues, have led me to view all four levels as social, albeit in different ways.

There are many ways in which the term 'social' could be used in relation to attribution (cf. Lukes, 1975):

1 Attribution is social *in origin* (e.g., an attribution may be based on social information, or influenced by social interaction).
2 Attribution is social *in its reference or object* (e.g., an attribution is made for an event involving a person, rather than physical objects, or for a social outcome, such as unemployment).
3 Attribution is social in that *it is common to the members of a society or group* (e.g., members of different groups or societies may share different explanations for the same events).

Although the third criterion is limited to work covered in chapters 6 and 7, the first two criteria are broad enough to embrace studies reported throughout the book. Using Doise's levels, both writer and reader are forced to consider the breadth of attribution theory and research, and thus to confront what Doise calls the 'master problem' of articulating, or integrating, the different levels of analysis.

I attempt to integrate throughout the volume, as points of overlap become evident; my main conclusion, however, may as well be stated at the outset, because it has influenced both my decision to write the book, and the manner in which I have tried to present it. I believe that a social-psychological approach to causal attribution should deal with, and integrate, phenomena at all four levels; the analysis should be psychological *and* social.

2 Classic Theories of Causal Attribution

There is occasions and causes why and wherefore in all things.

(Shakespeare, 1564–1616)

INTRODUCTION

This chapter and the following one present a selective review of attribution theory and research which, as Kelley and Michela (1980) have noted, has primarily been carried out within social psychology, with a focus on the perceived causes of other people's behaviour. The amount of published work has now reached monumental proportions; Pleban and Richardson (1979) recorded that attribution research accounted for 11 per cent of all published social-psychological research, and Kelley and Michela's computer-assisted search yielded more than 900 relevant references for the ten year period of their review. No one can read all this literature and still have time to think and write; as Heider himself noted in an interview, 'keeping up with all the literature on attribution is difficult' (1976, p. 14). For comprehensive reviews the reader is referred to the *Annual Review* chapters by Kelley and Michela, and by Harvey and Weary (1984), the *Handbook* chapter by Ross and Fletcher (1985) and a number of edited volumes (Harvey et al., 1976, 1978a, 1981; Harvey and Weary, 1985; Hewstone, 1983a; Jaspars et al., 1983a).

The present chapter is more modest in its aims. It gives a fairly detailed summary of the three main theories of causal attribution because, as several authors have noted (e.g., Jones and McGillis, 1976; Kelley and Michela, 1980) these theories have provided, directly or indirectly, the major conceptual advances in the field. This is not to devalue the contributions of others (e.g., Bem, 1967, 1972; Schachter, 1964), but as Kelley and Michela noted, neither theory was originally put forward specifically as an attributional analysis. In this respect,

Jones's (1985a) distinction between 'attribution theories' and 'attributional approaches' is useful. The former address themselves to testing particular theoretically-derived hypotheses, but the latter can more accurately be described as 'attribution-based research' (Jones, 1985a, p. 92). The present work focuses on attribution theory, rather than attributional approaches, with an emphasis on attributions for the behaviour of others, as studied in social psychology. The most obvious areas that are deliberately excluded, or mentioned only in passing, are the development of attributions (e.g., Fincham, 1983; Kassin, 1981), responsibility attribution (e.g., Fincham and Jaspars, 1980; Shaver, 1985), and applications of attribution theory (e.g., Antaki and Brewin, 1982; Frieze, Bar-Tal and Carroll, 1980). Rather than attempt to include all this work, the present chapter centres on the three major theories and the following chapter looks at some fundamental questions concerning attribution, on which a stance needs to be taken at the beginning of this volume.

'PHENOMENAL CAUSALITY' AND THE 'NAIVE ANALYSIS OF ACTION'

Heider's 'naive psychology' attempted to formulate the processes by which an untrained observer, or *naive psychologist*, makes sense of the actions of others. These ideas were set out in two landmark publications – an article (Heider, 1944) and a monograph (Heider, 1958) – each of which deserves attention.

Heider's article 'Social perception and phenomenal causality' (1944) introduced the two key notions of 'unit formation' and persons as the 'prototype of origins'. Unit formation referred to the process whereby origin (cause) and effect, actor and act, were seen as parts of a causal unit. Heider, influenced by Wertheimer's (1923) principles of perceptual organization, was particularly interested in the varying degrees of similarity between the two parts of the unit. Thus, factors such as similarity and proximity were seen as determining the locus of attribution. If two events were similar to each other, or proximate, then the one was likely to be seen as the cause of the other. Heider referred to Zillig's (1928) series of experiments in which a 'bad' act was more easily connected with a 'bad' person than a good one. In fact, Zillig included no attributional dependent variables; as will be seen in chapter 6, however, there is powerful evidence for the existence of intergroup biases in causal attribution. A further consequence of the link between actor and act is their mutual influence, which Heider referred to as 'the influence of causal integration on the relations between parts' (1944, p. 363). He argued that acts became infused with characteristics of the person to whom they were attributed.

Linking actor and act in this way, Heider noted that a 'person' attribution was more likely than a 'situational' one (see Ichheiser, 1949), because persons are seen as the 'prototype of origins' (1944, p. 359). Here Heider was clearly influenced by Fauconnet's (1928) legal-philosophical treatise on responsibility. Fauconnet identified the person as a 'first cause' (1928, p. 177), an interesting parallel with Hart and Honoré's description of explanations in terms of human agency as having a 'special finality' (1956/1961, p. 335). Heider argued that this tendency to perceive persons as origins influenced social perception in many ways; indeed, it led to 'an underestimation of other factors responsible for [an] effect. Changes in the environment are almost always caused by acts of persons in combination with other factors. The tendency exists to ascribe the changes entirely to persons' (1944, p. 361). Here Heider was referring to what has become known as the 'fundamental attribution error' (L. Ross, 1977).

Heider's monograph *The Psychology of Interpersonal Relations* (1958) has had a diffuse effect on the emerging field of attribution theory. Questions of attribution, however, were just one aspect of the naive, or common-sense, psychology in which Heider was interested. He believed that common sense was important for two main reasons. First, whether true or not, common-sense beliefs were assumed to guide behaviour; as Heider put it: 'If a person believes that the lines in his palm foretell his future, this belief must be taken into account in explaining certain of his expectations and actions' (1958, p. 5). Second, common-sense psychology was considered a 'valuable resource' (p. 95), not something to be sanctified (cf. Calder, 1977), but a body of knowledge from which scientific psychology could learn (see Fletcher, 1984).

In some ways the most interesting manner in which to examine Heider's influence is in the light of later theoretical developments, an approach that of course has the dangers of any 'Whig history'. I will therefore follow Ross and Fletcher (1985) in highlighting four central ideas in Heider's naive psychology, illustrating more liberally than they did with Heider's unique style of writing.

First, Heider proposed that causal analysis was in some respects similar to the perceptual process, as conceived in Brunswik's (1952) 'lens model'. An object 'out there' with objective properties constitutes the distal stimulus, but what is psychologically important is the proximal stimulus, the way the object appears to the perceiver. For social perception, Heider suggested that the important distal stimuli were dispositional properties linked to the proximal act; these often referred to psychological states. He argued, further, that these invariant dispositional properties were needed to explain the behaviour of others and render the perceiver's world stable, predictable and controllable. As Heider wrote:

> It is an important principle of common-sense psychology, as it is of scientific theory in general, that man grasps reality, and can predict and control it, by referring transient and variable behavior and events to relatively unchanging underlying conditions, the so-called dispositional properties of his world. (Heider, 1958, p. 79)

This activity, fundamental to the naive analysis of action, introduces Heider's second major contribution, the crucial distinction between personal and situational causes (see also Lewin, 1951; Murray, 1938; Rotter, 1954, 1966). Heider illustrated this distinction in an often-quoted passage:

> In common-sense psychology (as in scientific psychology) the result of an action is felt to depend on two sets of conditions, namely, factors within the person and factors within the environment. Naive psychology also has different terms to express the contributions of these factors. Consider the example of a person rowing a boat across a lake. The following is but a sample of expressions used to refer to factors that are significant to the action outcome. We say, 'He is *trying* to row the boat across the lake', 'He has the *ability* to row the boat across the lake', 'He *can* row the boat across the lake', 'He *wants* to row the boat across the lake', 'It is *difficult* to row the boat across the lake', 'Today is a good *opportunity* for him to row the boat across the lake', 'It is sheer *luck* that he succeeded in rowing the boat across the lake'. These varying descriptive statements have reference to personal factors on the one hand and to environmental factors on the other. (Heider, 1958, p. 82)

This distinction opened the way for Weiner's (1986) extensive research on attributions for success and failure. Heider also addressed again the perceiver's tendency to ignore, partly or completely, situational factors when explaining behaviour. As Heider put it, 'behavior in particular has such salient properties it tends to engulf the total field' (1958, p. 54). The third contribution can be seen as a refinement of the personal-situational dichotomy. Heider suggested that personal dispositions were more readily inferred for intentional than unintentional actions. He put forward three criteria for making inferences about intentionality: *equifinality* (whether action is goal-directed rather than means-centred), *local causality* (whether people are seen as agents of an action, rather than passive recipients of environmental forces) and *exertion* (people are presumed to try harder to achieve intended effects or goals; see Heider, 1958, p. 101). These criteria have, however, had little impact on subsequent research, although the attribution of intentions is central to Jones and Davis's (1965) theory, as discussed below.

Heider's fourth central idea was his answer to the question of why we sometimes attribute effects to the person, at other times to the object, and at still other times to mediating conditions (1958, pp. 68–9). He identified three relevant pieces of attributional information – 'factors within the perceiver', 'properties of the object' and 'mediating conditions' – and proposed J. S. Mill's method of difference (which he called the covariation principle) as a canon for making an attribution in such circumstances. Later, Kelley (1967) formalized these ideas, as discussed below.

These four contributions go some way towards illustrating the extent to which Heider's insights provided the blueprint for succeeding theories. Although his approach has been described as phenomenological (Shaver, 1975), Heider himself has rejected this label (Heider, 1976). As Weary et al. (1980) have argued, Heider was more interested in the antecedent conditions of perception and in causal analysis than in the perceptual experience. Whatever label is applied to Heider's work, his bequest is massive. As Jones wrote in a retrospective review of Heider's monograph, 'There is little question that Fritz Heider can rightly be called the father of both balance and attribution theories ... no reader of Heider's 1944 article on phenomenal causality and his 1958 book can doubt his clear paternity of the attributional approach' (1985b, p. 215).

CORRESPONDENT INFERENCE THEORY

As Heider reported, the criterion of intentionality is critical to personal causality. The direct lineage from Heider to Correspondent Inference Theory (Jones and Davis, 1965) was made explicit in Jones's statement that the theory 'attempted to formalize some of Heider's attributional ideas' (1985a, p. 90).

According to this theory the goal of the attribution process is to infer that observed behaviour and the intention that produced it *correspond* to some underlying stable quality in the person, or actor. The aim of Correspondent Inference Theory is 'to construct a theory which systematically accounts for a perceiver's inferences about what an actor was trying to achieve by a particular action' (Jones and Davis, 1965, p. 222). The central concept of the theory, the correspondent inference, refers to the perceiver's judgement that the actor's behaviour is caused by, or corresponds to, a particular trait (note, however, that Howard, 1985, has identified at least four different conceptions of 'correspondence' in the later paper by Jones and McGillis, 1976). Thus underlying dispositions are directly conveyed in behaviour, or, as Jones put it, 'the heart is on the sleeve' (1979, p. 108). A simple example of such an inference would be to ascribe someone's hostile behaviour to the trait 'hostility'. There are two main stages in the process of inferring personal dispositions: the attribution of intention, and the attribution of dispositions.

Attribution of intention

The perceiver's first problem is to decide which effects of an observed action, if any, were intended by the actor. To infer that any of the effects of an action were intended, the perceiver must believe that the actor *knew* the consequences of his action, and that he had the *ability* (e.g., the physical strength) to perform the action. According to Jones and Davis's theory, the perceiver processes information backwards from effects, through action, to inferences about knowledge and ability (see figure 1, which is to be read from right to left). What Jones and Davis left out of their figure, however, was *perceived freedom of choice*. Environmental constraints were certainly not ignored by Jones and Davis and led to some interesting and unexpected results.

Attribution of dispositions

The perceiver can begin this stage of the attribution process by comparing the consequences of chosen and non-chosen actions. The 'non-common effects principle' is used: a perceiver makes a correspondent inference when the chosen action has a few relatively unique or non-common consequences. In Jones and Davis's original example,

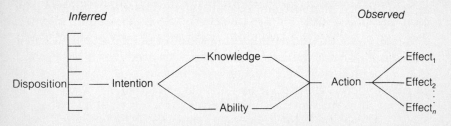

FIGURE 1   *Attribution of dispositions from observed action (from Jones and Davis, 1965, p. 222)*

effects common to the universities of Harvard and Yale (e.g., both Ivy League schools, both located in New England) could hardly be decisive in determining a young psychologist's choice between them. Of much more use would be distinctive differences between the universities (e.g., proximity to New York; their orientations towards teaching and research). These predictions have generated little research, but have received some empirical support. Newtson (1974) found that fewer non-common effects resulted in more confident and more extreme inferences about an actor. Ajzen and Holmes (1976) demonstrated that the attribution of a behaviour to one of its effects was a linear function of uniqueness, being highest when the effect was unique and decreasing as the effect was common to one, two or three alternative behaviours.

The perceiver's beliefs about what other people would do in the same situation ('social desirability') are also relevant. Correspondent inferences are stronger when the consequences of the chosen behaviour are socially *un*desirable. Jones and McGillis (1976) have modified this aspect of the theory to argue, more generally, that only behaviours that disconfirm expectancies are truly informative about the actor. When people say what is expected of them in a particular situation, or while playing a particular role, then we learn little about them. This hypothesis was supported in Jones, Davis and Gergen's (1961) study in which subjects judged candidates being interviewed for the job of either a submariner or an astronaut. The behaviour of candidates who presented themselves as fitting the desired type (i.e., they were 'other directed' for the submariner's job, 'inner directed' for the astronaut's job) was judged relatively uninformative about the individual's personal characteristics. In contrast, when the candidates answered questions in a manner inconsistent with the role expectations (expectancy-disconfirming or out-of-role behaviour), inferences about their personality were stronger and made with more confidence (see also Steiner and Field, 1960). Jones and McGillis also distinguished between perceivers' expectancies based either on prior experience of and information about the specific actor or target ('target-based') or on the target's membership in a particular class, category or social group ('category-based').

Biases in the correspondent inference process

The greatest contribution of research based on this theory was to open up the area of biases in attribution. Anticipating later work, two kinds of bias can be distinguished. First, Jones and Davis identified two *motivational* biases, as they moved away from rather neutral explanations for the behaviour of others, to include personal involvement in another's actions. The 'hedonic relevance' of an action was used to refer to the positive and negative effects of an actor's choice for the perceiver. The more hedonically relevant the action is to the perceiver, the more likely she or he is to make a correspondent inference (Jones and De Charms, 1957) and to make an extreme (positive or negative) judgement of another person (Chaikin and Cooper, 1973). In Jones and De Charms's manipulation of hedonic relevance, the failure of an experimental accomplice at a task either prevented the other group members from winning a monetary reward (high hedonic relevance), or had no effect on their outcomes (low hedonic relevance). The accomplice was rated as being less competent and less dependable when his failure affected the other group members. Thus the increase in hedonic relevance led to an increased correspondence between the observed failure and the attributed disposition of incompetence (see also Gergen and Jones, 1963).

The variable of 'personalism' was introduced to distinguish between cases where an actor's behaviour has general (positive or negative) relevance, and those where the behaviour is directed towards the perceiver. For example, our evaluations of another person are even more extreme, especially in a negative direction, if we feel that his or her behaviour was aimed at us personally. There has been little research on personalism (Enzle et al., 1980; Potter, 1973), but Heider (1976) later referred to a phenomenon called 'target attribution', by which he meant the tendency to think that people do things because of oneself. As he mentioned, and we all know, this is especially true of the person who falls in love; taken to clinical extremes, it is what we call paranoia.

Shortly after the publication of Jones and Davis's (1965) paper, Maselli and Altrocchi (1969) added two conditions that they thought were important in facilitating the attribution of intent: power and intimacy. These two conditions are linked, respectively, to hedonic relevance and personalism. The acts of people who are more powerful are more hedonically relevant, Maselli and Altrocchi argue; and in intimate relationships not only does one find extreme attributions, but they may result in extreme consequences (see chapter 5).

If we turn to *cognitive* bias, it is significant that in their 'ten year anniversary' return to Correspondent Inference Theory, Jones and McGillis (1976) concentrated exclusively on purely cognitive aspects of information-processing, and explicitly ignored the potential impact of motivational effects on attribution. The one cognitive bias that dominates this approach is the underestimation of situational factors.

This effect is illustrated in an experiment by Jones and Harris (1967). In this study, American college students were presented with another student's short written speech either for the Castro government in Cuba (unexpected behaviour) or against it. Subjects were told that some targets had chosen which side to support (choice conditions), and others had been required to argue their position (no-choice condition). Subjects then rated what they felt was each person's true attitude towards Castro. The most important, and unexpected, finding was that even in the no-choice condition, subjects tended to attribute attitudes consonant with the speech. They seemed to attach too little weight to the situation (the no-choice instructions) and too much weight to the person. Snyder and Jones (1974) found that even when the subjects themselves had previously been required to write such an essay, they still succumbed to the bias. Not surprisingly, this phenomenon has generated a large amount of research and has moved beyond the confines of the original theory. For this reason it is covered in the following chapter in the section on attributional biases.

Critical issues relating to Correspondent Inference Theory

Although experimental studies have, as indicated, yielded some support for Correspondent Inference Theory, four main limitations should be noted.

1   The theory argues that attribution of intention must precede a dispositional inference. Yet some dispositions are defined in terms of unintentional behaviours, e.g., carelessness, clumsiness and forgetfulness (Eiser, 1983a). For this reason, the theory is applicable only to 'actions', which have some element of choice, and not to 'occurrences' which may be involuntary (Kruglanski, 1975).

2   The theory does not provide an accurate description of the way people actually make attributions. Subsequent research has indicated that perceivers tend to attend to occurrences, not 'non-occurrences' (see Nisbett and Ross, 1980, chapter 5; L. Ross, 1977, pp. 196–7), and that they tend thereafter to seek out further instances of the same behaviour (e.g., Snyder and Swann, 1978a). This is an important and complex issue, which is dealt with in more detail in chapter 3. Nevertheless, the claim that perceivers typically pay much attention to non-chosen behaviours and their consequences should be viewed with caution.

3   Although behaviour that disconfirms expectancies is obviously informative, expectancy-confirming behaviour can also be so. As

Crittenden (1983) has pointed out, Correspondent Inference Theory, with its emphasis on the informational value of unexpected behaviour, fails to explain how people infer the dispositions of others with whom they have repeated, routine interactions. It is also evident from the studies of intergroup attribution reviewed in chapter 6, that behaviour that is expected of certain people (e.g., outgroup members) does generate strong person attributions, just because the behaviour fits the stereotype.

4   Finally, nearly all of the original studies based on, or co-opted by, the theory did not include causal attributions among their dependent measures (e.g., Jones and De Charms, 1957; Jones and Harris, 1967; Steiner and Field, 1960).[1] Although these studies may have, or seem to have, implications for causal attribution, it should not be assumed that processes of dispositional and causal attribution are similar. More recent research from a cognitive perspective (e.g., Bargh, 1984; D. L. Hamilton, 1988; see chapter 4) suggests that trait attributions (i.e., descriptions) are more spontaneous, and involve less thought and effort, than causal attributions (i.e., explanations) and the two types of judgement should therefore be kept conceptually distinct (see also Trope, 1986; Wetzel, 1982).

Correspondent Inference Theory has been critically evaluated, and has declined as a primary focus of research (see Antaki, 1984; cf. Howard, 1985), but it has proved most useful as a 'rational baseline model' (Jones and McGillis, 1976, p. 404) against which actual attributions could be compared. As such, it provided a firm basis for further theorizing (e.g., Jones, 1979; Jones and Nisbett, 1972; L. Ross, 1977), which led to systematic analysis of biases in how people make causal attributions. To conclude, both its weaknesses and its strengths have been accurately recognized by its proponents:

> It does not summarize phenomenal experience; it presents a logical calculus in terms of which accurate inferences could be drawn by an alert perceiver weighing knowledge, ability, non-common effects, and prior probability. But the role of the theory has been as much to identify attributional bias as to predict precisely the course of the social inference process. (Jones and McGillis, 1976, p. 404)

This epitaph serves to explain why the theory receives the attention it does here, but is not explored further in the following pages.

COVARIATION AND CONFIGURATION

Kelley's (1967, 1972a, 1973) contribution to attribution theory began with the question of what information is used to arrive at a causal attribution. He outlined two different cases that depend on the amount of information available to the perceiver. In the first case the perceiver has information from multiple sources and can perceive the covariation of an observed effect and its possible causes. In the second case, the perceiver is faced with a single observation and must take account of the configuration of factors that are plausible causes of the observed effect. The theories of covariation and configuration will be dealt with in turn.

Covariation

In outlining attribution in the case of covariation, Kelley built onto Heider's proposals that: (1) understanding of the distal environment was gained by means of a causal analysis that is 'in a way analogous to experimental methods' (Heider, 1958, p. 297); and (2) social perception was similar to a naive 'factor analysis' (1958, p. 66). Kelley was also influenced by Duncker's proposal that cause and effect analysis was achieved by a pseudoscientific 'abstracting induction' (Duncker, 1945, p. 64). Kelley presented the covariation principle as a naive version of J. S. Mill's method of difference: 'The effect is attributed to that condition which is present when the effect is present and which is absent when the effect is absent' (Kelley, 1967, p. 194).[2] Kelley based his model on the analysis of variance (ANOVA) statistical technique, which examines changes in a dependent variable (the 'effect') when the independent variables (the 'conditions') are manipulated. Kenny (1985) has recently commented on the wide-ranging use of ANOVA in social psychology, arguing that it is no longer merely an analytical tool but has become the framework in which we think about theoretical and research issues. He also noted (admittedly with hindsight), 'It was only a matter of time before someone proposed that the naive social psychologist uses analysis of variance to make sense out of social reality' (p. 489).

According to Kelley, the perceiver's purpose, like the scientist's, is to separate out which effects are to be attributed to which of several possible factors. At this stage the reader may contrast the parallel Kelley drew between the layperson and the scientist, and the distinction Passmore (1962) drew between scientific explanations and those

in history and common sense (see chapter 1). However, Kelley used the
ANOVA as a *model*, arguing only that, 'The logic of the [layperson's
causal] analysis is obviously akin to that employed in analysis of
variance' (1967, p. 195). He underlined the limits of this analogy in a
later publication: 'In an earlier paper, I argued that people often make
causal attributions *as if* they were analyzing data patterns by means of
the analysis of variance' (1972a, p. 151). As will be seen, although the
lay and scientific conceptions of cause clearly differ, the analogy
proved fruitful for theory and research.

   The essence of the ANOVA model can be demonstrated most
clearly by considering an example sentence from L. McArthur's
(1972) study: 'John laughs at the comedian.' This outcome could be
caused by something in the person (John), the circumstances (e.g., the
occasion on which the outcome occurred), the entity or stimulus (the
comedian), or some combination of these factors. The independent
variables constitute the three possible ways of examining variations in
effects (see figure 2): (1) over persons (from which *consensus* information is derived), (2) over time/modalities (from which *consistency* is
derived), and (3) over stimuli (from which *distinctiveness* is derived).

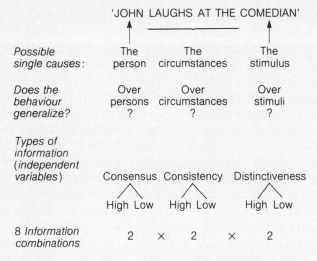

FIGURE 2   *The analysis of variance model of covariation*
   Note   *An explanation for a simple sentence of this type can be generated by identifying each possible single cause (person/circumstance/
stimulus), asking whether the behaviour generalizes across persons,
circumstances and stimuli, and thus specifying the level of information in
each case (after Kelley, 1967; McArthur, 1972)*

The dependent variable is, of course, whether the effect occurs or not. The covariation principle suggests that the effect is seen as caused by the factor with which it covaries. Thus if only John laughs at the comedian (low consensus), he has done so in the past (high consistency), and he also laughs at all other comedians (low distinctiveness), then the effect is seen as caused by something in the person (John). In fact, Kelley's one explicit prediction based on these three informational variables referred to entity attribution: 'External attribution . . . is made when evidence exists as to the (high) distinctiveness, consistency and consensus of the appropriate effects' (1967, p. 196).

McArthur (1972) provided the first real test of the ANOVA model by assigning high or low values to each of the three information variables and thus generating eight (2 × 2 × 2) informational configurations. This study produced results apparently consistent with the model, confirming that consensus, distinctiveness and consistency did indeed affect the attribution of causality in the way predicted by Kelley and in line with the covariation principle (e.g., Hansen, 1980; Major, 1980; Pruitt and Insko, 1980; Ruble and Feldman, 1976; Smith and Miller, 1979a; Zuckerman, 1978; see Kassin, 1979, for a review). Later conceptual analysis modified Kelley's model, however, as will be spelled out in chapter 4. For the present, it is useful simply to note some of the main issues arising in relation to the ANOVA model.

Critical issues relating to the covariation principle

1   The covariation principle is limited as a basis for scientific inferences of causality (see Hilton, 1988). This principle actually allows causal relationships that are spurious – as statistics books remind us, correlation does not necessarily imply causation. Nor does causation necessarily imply correlation; for example, we all know that sexual intercourse is the cause of pregnancy, but the two are not, in fact, highly correlated (see Einhorn and Hogarth, 1986). As Shaver (1981) has pointed out, distinguishing truly causal conditions from covarying but noncausal ones is an important attributional as well as philosophical problem (see chapter 1; and Shaver, 1985).

2   In the type of experiment used to collect the relevant data (e.g., McArthur, 1972), subjects are provided with 'pre-packaged' covariation information that, under normal circumstances, they might neither seek out, nor use. There is less support for the covariation principle when perceivers have to extract or abstract consensus, distinctiveness and consistency information from the normal flow of events (see Stevens and Jones, 1976; Tillman and Carver, 1980). Zuckerman

(1978) has also reported that the impact of the information variables on causal attribution depends on the type of behaviour involved; impact is clearer for occurrences than for actions.

3   The preceding limitation is made more serious by the fact that people are not always very skilled at assessing covariation between events (see Alloy and Tabachnik, 1984; Crocker, 1981). Their performance depends a good deal on whether they have the right theory concerning the data in question (see the need to integrate covariation and configuration, below).

4   Although subjects' attributions may appear *as if* they used the covariation principle, their actual information-processing may be completely different from Kelley's model. Just because people's attributions fit the ANOVA framework does not mean that they are doing anything like the ANOVA in their heads. The fascinating question of the cognitive processes involved in causal attribution must be deferred until chapter 4. There it will be seen that quite simple models of causal analysis also exist. For example, Nisbett and Ross (1980) have suggested that people may select causes on the basis of such obvious criteria as their similarity to effects, and their perceptual salience with respect to other causal candidates and the background.

Configuration

Another drawback of the covariation model is that it requires multiple observations yielding consensus, distinctiveness and consistency information. Although Kelley maintained that the detailed process implied by the ANOVA model was appropriate in some cases, he described it as a 'full dress causal analysis . . . an idealized model and not descriptive of most everyday, informal attributions' (1972a, p. 152). Even if a complete analysis seemed justified or required, the perceiver might lack the information, time or motivation to examine multiple observations. In these cases of incomplete data, Kelley argued, attributions are made using 'causal schemata'. These schemata are beliefs or preconceptions, built up from experience, about how certain kinds of causes interact to produce a specific kind of effect:

> A causal schema is a general conception that a person has about how certain kinds of causes interact to produce a specific kind of effect. Each schema can be described in terms of a hypothetical matrix of data that summarizes the attributor's beliefs and assumptions about the distribution of the effect over various combinations of the causal factors. (Kelley, 1972a, p. 151)

Kelley outlined two main types of causal schema from which others could be generated.

One of the simplest causal schemata is the multiple sufficient cause (MSC) schema. It conveys the idea that an effect occurs if *either* cause A *or* cause B is present, or when *both* are present (see figure 3). Kelley also put forward two attributional 'principles' that accompany the causal schemata. The MSC schema is associated with the 'discounting principle': given that different causes can produce the same effect, the role of a given cause in producing the effect is discounted if other plausible causes are present. This principle is illustrated in Thibaut and Riecken's (1955) study, showing that a high status person's compliance with a request was generally attributed to an internal cause, but a low status person's compliance was attributed to an external cause. The presence of one cause (e.g., the situational pressures on a low status person to comply) makes any inference regarding the other cause ambiguous (see also Kassin et al., 1980; Kruglanski et al., 1978).

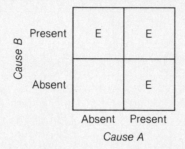

FIGURE 3   *Causal schema for multiple sufficient causes (from Kelley, 1972a, p. 152, © 1972 Lawrence Erlbaum Associates, Inc., reprinted by permission of the publisher and author)*

Kelley also proposed an 'augmentation principle': the role of a given cause is augmented if an effect occurs in the presence of an inhibitory cause. The augmentation principle applies to both the MSC and the more complex multiple necessary cause (MNC) schemata.[3] According to the MNC schema, several causes must operate together to produce the effect (see figure 4).[4]

Part of the appeal of causal schemata is that they permit the perceiver to predict effects from the presence or absence of certain causes; and, given an effect, the perceiver can generate inferences about its underlying causes. Kun and Weiner (1973) provided subjects with information concerning success and failure outcomes at tasks that

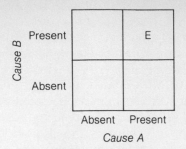

FIGURE 4   *Causal schema for multiple necessary causes (from Kelley, 1972a, p. 156, © 1972 Lawrence Erlbaum Associates Inc., reprinted by permission of the publisher and author)*

varied in their perceived levels of difficulty. Subjects later made attributions concerning the certainty of the presence/absence of *either* high or low ability, *or* high or low effort, given knowledge about the presence/absence of the other of these two causes. The results supported Kelley's (1972a) hypothesis that the MSC schema would be evoked to explain common events, and the MNC schema would be evoked to explain unusual or extreme events. Success at an easy task and failure at a difficult one were ascribed to only one cause, but success at a difficult task and failure at an easy one were generally attributed to multiple causes (see also Cunningham and Kelley, 1975; but cf. Surber, 1981).

According to Kelley, there are several other kinds of causal schema available to the layperson; they are important for three main reasons: (1) they help the perceiver to make attributions when information is incomplete; (2) they are general conceptions about causes and effect which may apply across content areas; (3) they provide the perceiver with a 'causal shorthand' for carrying out complex inferences quickly and easily (Fiske and Taylor, 1984).

Critical issues relating to causal schemata

The apparent advantages of causal schemata notwithstanding, some issues still require theoretical and empirical attention.

1   Fiedler (1982) has argued that the existence and functioning of causal schemata, although intuitively plausible, have not yet been successfully demonstrated. He criticized research such as Kun and Weiner's (1973) for being artificial and merely descriptive (but cf.

Shaklee, 1983), and for having a built-in device for finding a causal schema in any kind of attribution by the subject. Thus different responses are seen as evidence of the use of different kinds of schemata, although there is no way of knowing that a schema was used at all. Here it might be useful to return to Kelley's original formulation. In a sense Kelley anticipated Fiedler's criticism, because he noted that his figures illustrating the MSC and MNC schemata (see figures 3 and 4, above) were 'merely rearrangements' (1972a, p. 158) of each other, and that both were related to the compensatory schema. Kelley also, however, referred to a number of possible measures for the identification of schemata, for example, selective attention, long-term retention and ease of learning information (see DeSoto, 1960; DeSoto et al., 1968). Subsequent research has not followed up these interesting suggestions.

2   Fiedler (1982) also criticized the abstract, content-free conception of schema. In Bartlett's (1932) earlier sense of the term, and more recent work (e.g., Fiske and Taylor, 1984), a schema represents organized knowledge, based on cultural experience and not just an abstract relation between cause and effect. This richer interpretation of schema is taken up in the 'knowledge structure' approach to attribution presented in chapter 4.

3   Finally, one might ask whether the notion of a causal schema is still an overly complex model of common-sense attribution. Kelley himself acknowledged that it might be: 'As in the earlier use of the analysis of variance as a model of the layman's attribution processes, the present paper runs the danger of confusing his attributional concepts and procedures with the sophisticated and complex procedures that scientists have laboriously evolved' (1972a, p. 171). Here I would defend Kelley's conception and his analysis. He did not assume that the lay attributor explicitly thinks about causal problems in incomplete data matrices. He did, however, suggest that lay people respond to information '*as if* [they] are using matrix-like schemata. But strictly speaking, the data matrices are our means for summarizing [their] activities, for thinking about them, and for making predictions about [their] use of information under various conditions' (p. 171). There is, then, a discontinuity between a descriptive model and a heuristic one, and causal schemata have a primarily heuristic value.

COVARIATION AND CONFIGURATION: AN INTEGRATION

In spite of the critical issues raised by this discussion, both covariation and configuration notions are central to attribution research, but they need to be integrated. Lalljee (1981) has characterized Kelley's conception of the naive scientist as that of the 'inductivist', approaching nature with no theories, counting instances of events in particular classes and under different conditions, and drawing conclusions. Yet Kelley noted very early that 'interpretation of a given covariation analysis often depends upon the perceiver's prior causal attributions' (1972b, p. 3). For example, Golding and Rorer (1972) showed that suppositions about the causes of specific behaviour led observers to see nonexistent covariation in data, and to overlook true covariation. Since then, there has been extended discussion of whether attributions are 'data driven' (by covariation) or 'theory driven' (by configuration) (e.g., Nisbett and Ross, 1980). Important questions still remain, such as when pre-existing beliefs are finally modified by new data, rather than imposing themselves on the data (Kelley and Michela, 1980). Such questions will have to be taken up in chapter 4, because this area is one of the most fascinating, but complex, in attribution theory. In general, there seems to be an interaction between data and expectations, with preconceptions influencing not only how, but what, data are processed (Alloy and Tabachnik, 1984). As Ross and Fletcher concluded:

> Not only are attributions theory driven, in the sense that covariation information is utilized according to causal schemata, but the observations of the underlying data patterns themselves are also powerfully influenced by the attributor's *a priori* causal theories. (1985, p. 82)

To conclude, building onto Heider's (1958) notions of experimental analysis and the distinction between internal and external causes, Kelley contributed an elegant and sophisticated approach to the attribution process. In addition his models of covariation and configuration were set out in such a way as to generate empirically testable hypotheses. As Jones later wrote, it was above all Kelley's formalizations that 'began to generate momentum for the attributional approach' (1985a, p. 90).

THEORIES OF CAUSAL ATTRIBUTION: A SUMMARY

The three theories outlined above – those of Heider, Jones and Davis, and Kelley – are generally considered the major contributions in the field. They ushered in the 'halcyon days' of attribution theory (Hewstone, 1983b) and, to borrow a phrase from Lukes (1975), since then they have all been paid the tribute of unrelenting criticism. At this stage the reader might reasonably expect some integration between the theories. Like Fiske and Taylor (1984), however, I prefer to argue that each theory has made a unique contribution, and each seems to offer insights about specific attributional problems. Jones and McGillis (1976) have made an ambitious attempt at integration. They rightly draw parallels between Correspondent Inference Theory and the covariation principle (e.g., between category-based expectancies and consensus), but their own 'integrated framework' is overly complex. They even admit that the sequence from observation to inference in their flow-chart model (see p. 415) 'is not expected to bear much of a relationship to the phenomenology of a naive perceiver' (p. 414). Perhaps for this reason their model has received little empirical attention, and the quest for a general theory of attribution has faded (but see Medcof, in press).

To summarize, it can at least be said that the three theories converge on a few specific and general themes: Generally, they highlight mediation between stimulus and response, active and constructive causal interpretation, and the perspective of the naive scientist or layperson (Fiske and Taylor, 1984; Taylor, 1981). Specifically, the theories all address the kinds of information that people use to determine causality, the kinds of causes that they distinguish, and the rules they use for going from information to inferred cause (Passer et al., 1978). Most important, all share a concern with common-sense explanations and answers to the question 'why?' Based on the rich, descriptive work of Heider, the theories of Jones and Davis and then Kelley ambitiously attempted to formalize the common-sense rules people might be using to make causal attributions. They answered many questions and raised a great deal more. The next chapter reviews the progress that has been made in answering these questions.

3 Attribution Theory and Research: Fundamental Questions

'I wish he would explain his explanation.'

Lord Byron (1818)

INTRODUCTION

This chapter deals in some detail with five fundamental questions concerning causal attribution. As will be seen, great progress, both theoretical and empirical, has been made in understanding what attributions are, how to measure them, when they are instigated, to what extent they are systematically biased and, finally, the closely related questions of what functions they serve and what consequences they entail.

THE NATURE OF CAUSAL ATTRIBUTION

The structure of perceived causality

Internal vs external attribution. As was noted above, in Heider's (1958) original formulation potential causal factors were thought of as internal to the actor (e.g., ability, effort, intention) or external to the actor (e.g., task-related factors, luck). This distinction is fundamental to attribution theory and research on the structure of perceived causality. It is, however, neither without problems nor without alternative schemes for specifying the nature of common-sense causal attributions.

It is first necessary to clarify Heider's distinction, because in different parts of his book he used rather different examples. In the passage quoted earlier to illustrate the distinction (Heider, 1958, p. 82; see chapter 2), the contrast is simply between 'personal' and 'environmental' factors. In an earlier passage (and consistent with his emphasis on dispositions), however, Heider wrote that 'behavior can be accounted for by *relatively stable traits* of the personality or by factors within the environment' (p. 56). Given the way subsequent researchers have used the distinction, it is more accurate to refer to it as an internal-external one, and thus to avoid the confusion of internal, or personal, with 'dispositional' causes. It is quite clear that internal or personal causes are not necessarily dispositional and, as Ross and Fletcher have pointed out, 'episodic causal attributions' (1985, p. 95) such as emotions, temporary beliefs or intentions, are quite common in everyday life (e.g., Darley and Goethals, 1980; Elig and Frieze, 1975). This clarification also has the advantage that the present argument can proceed without a detour to discuss the common-sense view of dispositions, about which there is some debate (see Fletcher, 1984).

Although the internal-external distinction is important, four major problems threaten its use and value (Miller, et al., 1981):

1 The hydraulic assumption. Heider (1958) proposed a hydraulic relation between internal and external causality. The more a person was seen as causing an action, the less the environment was perceived as causal (and vice versa). Heider is by no means the only scholar to have assumed a negative correlation between internal and external attributions (see Lane, 1962; cited by Tyler and Rasinski, 1983). This view suggests that a single-cause measure can be used, such as a rating scale labelled internal (personal) causality at one end and external (situational) causality at the other end (e.g., Nisbett et al., 1973, Study 3). Or an index can be computed by subtracting the external from the internal score (e.g., Storms, 1973). There is, however, almost no evidence of the putative negative correlation from studies using separate scales to assess internal and external causality. The correlations are sometimes positive or only nonsignificantly negative, irrespective of whether the data were collected in the laboratory (e.g., Taylor and Koivumaki, 1976) or in field surveys (Tyler and Rasinski, 1983). On the basis of these results, Solomon (1978) argued for the measurement of internal and external attributions on separate response scales (see also Furnham et al., 1983; Goldberg, 1981; Smith and Miller, 1982).

2 The categorical error. A number of researchers have noted that the categories of internal and external causality are very broad, containing a heterogeneous collection of attributions (see Lalljee, 1981; Lalljee et al., 1983). As Miller et al., 1981 point out, when categories are so broad they risk becoming meaningless, as well as leading to confusion. Some researchers have reported that many of

their subjects failed to understand the distinction and/or did not find it meaningful (Taylor and Koivumaki, 1976).

3   The teleological confusion. Statements that seem to imply external attributions can be rephrased as statements implying internal attributions (and vice versa; see L. Ross, 1977, p. 176). This problem is particularly evident where researchers have attempted to code attributions from free responses. Nisbett et al. (1973, Study 2) asked subjects to write brief paragraphs describing why they had chosen their college degree subject. A statement was coded as internal if it 'referred in any way to the person doing the choosing' (p. 158). Thus, 'I want to make a lot of money' was coded as internal, but 'Chemistry is a high-paying field' was coded as external. As Ross noted, an obvious criticism of this method is that the two types of statements contain similar information and in fact imply one another. This problem is illuminated by Grice's (1975) work on conversational rules, which pointed to the fact that in communication we try to avoid redundancy and hence refer to only one factor if it implies the presence of the other (see Hilton, 1988). It remains possible, however, that subtle grammatical differences do reflect the psychological reality of the internal-external distinction (Fletcher, 1983).

4   The validity issue. Miller et al. (1981) reported low convergent validity among three measures (open-ended, difference score and bipolar scale) of internal and external causality. This led them to argue that experimental subjects defined the two types of causality (at least in this study) quite differently from the researchers.

To the points above should be added the finding that people are more likely to employ combinations of both internal and external attributions under certain conditions: when striving for attributional accuracy (Kassin and Hochreich, 1977), and when explaining extreme events (Cunningham and Kelley, 1975) or complex interpersonal events (Bradbury and Fincham, in press, a). As Funder pointed out, 'Thoughtful lay perceivers and clinicians typically can and do combine both dispositional and situational influences on behavior into their explanations. Indeed, it is the ability to go beyond first-order situational or dispositional explanations that constitutes knowing someone well, or having a "deeper" understanding of his or her behavior' (1982, p. 217).

Beyond the internal-external distinction. The research reviewed above raises serious questions about the validity of the distinction between internal and external attribution. An improved and multidimensional approach to the structure of perceived causality has been developed over some years by Weiner and colleagues (see Weiner, 1979, 1983, 1985a, 1986). Weiner has developed a taxonomy of causes that specifies their underlying properties in terms of three dimensions. *Locus* refers to the familiar location of a cause internal or external to the person; *stability* refers to the temporal nature of a cause, varying from stable (invariant) to unstable (variant); and *controllability* refers to the degree of volitional influence that can be exerted over a cause. Causes can theoretically be classified within one of eight cells (2 locus levels × 2 stability levels × 2 controllability levels), although Weiner has cautioned that the exact meaning of a cause may change over time, perceivers and situations. Thus, for example, ability (normally thought of as internal/stable/uncontrollable) might be viewed as an unstable cause of achievement, if learning were expected to occur; similarly, luck (normally thought of as external/unstable/ uncontrollable) could be seen as an enduring personal characteristic of some people. The important point, Weiner argues (1985a), is that even though the interpretation of specific causal inferences may change, the underlying dimensions (i.e., locus, stability, controllability) are constant.

As will be seen later, Weiner has developed this approach into an important theory of achievement and emotion, but its value here lies in taking us beyond the simplicity of the internal-external distinction. For example, ability and effort might both be seen as internal causes of achievement, but ability is further classified as stable/uncontrollable, and effort as unstable/controllable. As a result, the attribution of a failure to lack of effort has implications different from those of an attribution to lack of ability. Lower future expectancies of success arise from lack of ability attributions (Weiner et al., 1976) which are stable, but the unstable lack-of-effort attribution may protect self-esteem, with its implication that the exertion of greater effort would result in success.

Weiner's three-dimensional structure has received strongest support from Meyer's (1980) factor-analytic study, which revealed that people's attributions for success and failure did reflect identifiable dimensions corresponding to those proposed by Weiner (see also Weiner, 1986). Other general dimensions have also been suggested – intentionality (Weiner, 1979), globality (Abramson et al., 1978) and excusability (de Jong et al., 1988) – but Weiner (1986) argues that these dimensions have failed to achieve the theoretical and empirical support of his three dimensions (but see Fincham et al., in press). Weiner's approach has also been supplemented by Russell's (1982) development of the Causal Dimension Scale. This measure requires subjects to rate their own attributions, subjectively, on the dimensions of locus, stability and controllability. Thus it assesses subjects' perceptions of causes in a particular situation, and deals with the problem of differences between the theoretical classification of causes and how subjects actually perceive them. In short, it translates subjects' causal *attributions* into causal *dimensions*, thus avoiding what Russell called the 'fundamental attribution research error', whereby attributions made by the subject are 'translated' into causal dimensions by the researcher. The scale consists of nine items, three for each of Weiner's dimensions (locus, stability and controllability), which enable the researcher to gain a better understanding of how the perceiver views ascribed causes. It would show, for example, when a perceiver views 'ability' as stable or unstable, or 'luck' as internal or external (see Russell et al., 1987).

Causal and other explanations in common sense

Shaver (1985) has recently drawn psychologists' attention to the detailed analysis of the concept of causality in philosophy. This section, rather than attempting to review this philosophical literature, focuses on the kinds of explanation that characterize common sense.

Causes and reasons.   The internal-external distinction has also been challenged by Kruglanski (1975), who sought to replace it with an endogenous-exogenous partition. He defined an endogenous attribution as an *end* in itself, and an exogenous attribution as a *means* that mediates a further goal. Using the distinction between (voluntary) actions and (involuntary) occurrences, Kruglanski argued that in explaining occurrences it was justifiable to distinguish between internal and external causality. But this was not the case for actions, because all actions are generally understood to be determined by the will, which is internal to the actor. Kruglanski suggested that actions were explicable only in terms of reasons or purposes (thus their explanation was teleological, rather than causal). Although Calder (1977) counter-argued that the internal-external and endogenous-exogenous distinctions were not conceptually distinct, Kruglanski's distinction received little attention, until the publication of a provocative article by Buss (1978).

Buss argued that attribution theory, as an attempt to explain how ordinary people explain behaviour by making attributions, had concentrated on *causal* attribution and completely neglected *reason* explanations (see Davidson, 1963; Peters, 1958; Winch, 1958).

Causes and reasons are logically distinct categories for explaining different aspects of behaviour. Buss defined a cause as 'that which brings about a change' and a reason as 'that for which a change is brought about' (1978, p. 1311). Like Kruglanski, he distinguished between actions and occurrences, but he went on to argue that actors and observers of behaviour differ in the explanations they could give for these events. Occurrences could be explained exclusively with causes, by both actors and observers; actions could be explained only with reasons by actors, but with causes *or* reasons by observers (Buss, 1979, later conceded that actors could offer causal, and not merely reason, explanations for actions).

Buss's article raised a number of interesting issues and resulted in a flurry of responses (Harvey and Tucker, 1979; Kruglanski, 1979; Locke and Pennington, 1982). First, Harvey and Tucker illustrated that Heider's conception of common-sense explanation was not entirely causal in nature (see Heider, 1958, p. 110; see also Jones and Davis, 1965, p. 222, p. 263). Second, and more generally, both Kruglanski and Locke and Pennington pointed out that 'reason' can be interpreted as a specific type of explanation, whereas 'cause' is normally interpreted as explanation in the generic sense. This is, in fact, the orthodox philosophical position, that reasons are but one kind of cause (see Davidson, 1963). At the same time, Locke and Pennington's excellent discussion pointed out that (a) we might try to go beyond an actor's reasons, and try to find a causal explanation for those reasons; and (b) if people act as they do because they have reasons for their action, those reasons can be treated as the cause of the behaviour (see Dretske, 1988).

What, then, is the outcome of this debate, and how does it relate to the internal-external distinction? Locke and Pennington argued that we can speak of 'psychological' and 'situational', but not internal and external, reasons. Psychological reasons refer to some feature of the agent, while situational reasons refer to some feature of the situation. Further, psychological and situational reasons are often (but not always) interchangeable. Now we can understand the problems encountered in trying to classify open-ended explanations as internal and external (e.g., Nisbett et al., 1973). 'I want to make a lot of money' is a psychological reason, and 'Chemistry is a high-paying field' is a situational reason. Locke and Pennington bring considerable clarity to this field by arguing for a three-tier division of causes into internal and external, internal causes into reasons and other internal causes, and reasons into psychological and situational reasons (but see McClure, 1984). Thus both the internal-external and the cause-reason distinctions are useful for attribution theory.

Excuses and justifications.   A quite different approach to common-sense explanations is provided by the study of 'accounts', initiated by Scott and Lyman (1968) and outlined at length in a later book (Lyman and Scott, 1970). Accounts are 'statements made to explain untoward behaviour and bridge the gap between actions and expectations' (Scott and Lyman, 1968, p. 46). Scott and Lyman drew a rather extreme distinction between accounts and explanations; the latter, they claimed, refer to statements about events where 'untoward behaviour' is not an issue, and does not have critical implications for a relationship. It we accept this distinction, then the study of common-sense explanations should include accounts when it is focused on untoward behaviour. In contrast to attribution theory's concern with the informational antecedents and rules of causal inference, the focus of accounts is on linguistic forms and was much influenced by the work of Austin (1962). Scott and Lyman emphasized that one must have the right 'style' to validate an account, and that an important aspect of account-giving is managing the impression one conveys to other people (Goffman, 1959). This approach is social because it underlines to whom an account is given, and with respect to what background expectancies an account is necessary.

Scott and Lyman's work again raises the distinction between attribution of causality and attribution of responsibility (Fincham and Jaspars, 1980), the latter having a distinct moral quality. The issue of responsibility underlies the main distinction Scott and Lyman made between 'excuses' and 'justifications'. With an excuse one admits a bad or wrong act, but denies responsibility; with a justification, one accepts responsibility, but denies the pejorative quality associated with it. Two published studies have shown that prison inmates' explanations for their violent behavior were far more likely to be justifications than excuses (Felson and Ribner, 1981; Henderson and Hewstone, 1984). Henderson and Hewstone analysed these explanations using both attributional and accounting coding-schemes. This analysis showed the importance of distinguishing between the attribution of causality and responsibility. The offenders did sometimes accept their ultimate causal role (self-attribution) but they could excuse this behaviour (e.g., claiming it was an accident) or justify it (e.g., through the norm of self-defence).

Responsibility also seems to underlie the distinction Antaki and Fielding (1981) drew between 'agency' and 'propriety' explanations. An agency explanation would be wanted if, say, someone was neutrally curious about a broken window and asked what had caused it. All that would be required would be an account of what agency had brought about the breaking of the window – one could say that the wind had caused it, or the thinness of the glass, or the fact that a brick had been thrown at it by a passer-by. An account of propriety, on the other hand, would not be so neutrally motivated; at issue would be not merely the cause of the breakage, but whether it was excusable or justifiable. Semin and Manstead (1983) have extended this line of work to a general theory of the 'accountability of conduct' which goes far beyond the present focus on causal, not responsibility, attribution. Although we should seek to maintain that distinction for reasons of theoretical clarity, it will become clear that as one attempts to analyse attributions in more social settings the participants do not merely explain, they also account for their actions in a variety of ways, that include especially excuses and justifications (e.g., Orvis et al., 1976).

Before concluding this section, I should note that Antaki and Fielding (1981) include 'description' as a pervasive form of explanation in everyday life. As Burke wrote, 'Men violently disagree about the purposes behind a given act, or about the character of the person who did it, or how he did it, or in what kind of situation he acted; or they may even insist upon totally different words to name the act itself' (1962, p. xv). Only recently has research attention been turned to the link between labelling and attribution (Howard and Levinson, 1985), yet descriptions have the power to summarize a whole state of affairs in a manner that explains what is going on. Consider the following passage from an English newspaper:

> What happened at the Libyan Embassy yesterday was bloody and barbaric because the people involved are bloody and barbaric. (*Daily Mirror*, 18 April 1984)

Calling the event 'bloody and barbaric' predisposes the listener to believe that the explanation is likely to refer to such traits. At the very least these examples show that description, labelling and explanation are closely related and that the consequences of the relation are of some practical significance.

Summary

The nature of causal attribution is adequately captured by the definition that 'It provides an answer to the question: what causes the observed behavior and its consequences?' (Jones et al., 1972, p. ix). That 'answer', however, might involve an analysis of perceived causality that goes beyond the internal–external distinction, which has been shown to have both methodological and theoretical limitations. In addition, we may make more sense of people's explanations, especially when given in social contexts, if we distinguish reasons from other internal causes, and acknowledge that, as accounts, common-sense explanations often serve to excuse and justify, and not merely to explain. These considerations notwithstanding, a detailed analysis of the moral and legal decision-making involved in responsibility attributions is beyond the scope of this book (see Fincham and Jaspars, 1980).

THE MEASUREMENT OF CAUSAL ATTRIBUTIONS

Closed- vs open-ended measures

The reader will have noted already the widespread use of rating scales in attribution research. This has the signal methodological advantage that such scales can be assumed to have interval properties, thus allowing for the use of parametric tests. Over-reliance on this approach, however, has led to the relative neglect of the way in which people normally explain events. Kelley and Michela argued that 'the central irony of attribution research is that while its central concepts concern the causal distinctions made by common people, these have been little investigated' (1980, p. 490); and Ostrom asked, 'What is the actual vocabulary of causality in common use and which terms occur with the highest frequency?' (1981, p. 418).

Although some researchers (e.g., the discourse analysts) would argue against content-analysis of open-ended responses, this strategy has provided some answer to the criticisms above. There have been free-response studies of causal attribution in a wide variety of domains, including interpersonal conflict (Orvis et al., 1976), political events (Antaki, 1985), and young children's explanations of actions and emotions (Lalljee et al., 1983). The most impressive body of research exists in the area of achievement attributions (e.g., Cooper and Burger, 1980; Darom and Bar-Tal, 1981; Frieze, 1976) where there is, at least, broad agreement over the main causes used to explain success and failure (i.e., ability and effort).

The most sophisticated studies compare open- and closed-ended measures statistically (Elig and Frieze, 1979; and Miller et al., 1981, discussed above; cf. Howard, 1987, for a similar study on attributions of blame). Elig and Frieze acknowledged that respondents might find open-ended questions easier and more natural to respond to, but referred to them as 'psychometrically inferior' (p. 623). They used the multitrait-multimethod approach to test the reliability of three main attributional measures: open-ended responses, scale ratings and ipsative percentage judgements.[1]

Subjects' perceptions of the validity of the three measures were also assessed. The results revealed that open-ended measures of causal attribution had poorer inter-test validity and reliability than structured response measures; that subjects disliked the percentage method; and that the rating scale method had both good inter-method correlations with the percentage measures and good face validity. Elig and Frieze concluded in favour of the rating scale method, but the value of open-ended measures should not be underplayed (see Maruyama, 1982). Such measures may be especially important at the pilot stage of research and are essential when one attempts to study causal attributions in a less simplistic manner, as will be seen below.

Perceived causal structures

Attribution theory's conception of causality has already been criticized, above, for its simplistic focus on the internal-external distinction. Its conception is also simplistic in the sense that it is static, although many events have both proximal and distal antecedents through which a chain of causes can be traced (Brickman et al., 1975; Vinokur and Ajzen, 1982). Kelley (1980) has also pointed out that perceivers become more aware of both spatial and temporal perspectives as they develop from childhood to adulthood. As researchers, we must therefore ask about the temporal structure of explanations. For example, why did a woman die? Because a policeman shot her; because she surprised the policeman; or because her brain was deprived of oxygen? If we follow Hart and Honoré (1959), there are rational limits to the pursuit of causal connections backwards and forwards in time – attribution researchers need to ask questions such as 'Where do perceivers stop their causal analysis?', and not only whether their analysis centres on internal or external causes. So far, we know that people do not generally trace causes beyond voluntary human actions performed by an adult, which were intended to bring about the outcome that occurred (see Fincham and Shultz, 1981). We also know that perceivers have a tendency to attribute greater causal significance to prior, as opposed to immediate, events: however, this generalization holds only when, judged in isolation, the two events (or causes) are perceived to have relatively equal impact on the outcome or effect (see Vinokur and Ajzen, 1982).

Kelley (1983) has recently extended the idea that causal explanations occur at various degrees of remoteness from a focal effect. He used the term 'perceived causal structures' to refer to the way people perceive the temporal flow of life's events to be ordered causally. According to Kelley, people's explanations for their marital separation (Fletcher, 1983), cardiac patients' perceptions of the causes of their heart attacks (Cowie, 1976), and policy makers' arguments (Axelrod, 1976) all reveal a temporally ordered causal structure. Kelley went on to specify some of the properties of these structures, using a set of five dimensions: simple-complex, proximal-distal, past-future, stable-unstable and actual-potential. There is an important, if subtle, distinction between 'perceived causal structures', as described, and 'the structure of perceived causality', as discussed in Weiner's work (see above). Weiner emphasized the causal dimensions in terms of which causes could be classified *by researchers*, but Kelley's approach leads us to explore the way in which 'the common person's understanding of a particular event is based on the perceived location of that event within a temporally ordered network of inter-connected causes and effects' (1980, p. 343).

Once researchers examine the sometimes complex structure of explanations, the inadequacy of simple dichotomies like internal vs external is revealed. Kelley wondered how the ordinary research participant could be expected to respond with ratings or rankings on a pre-prepared list of causes. He therefore argued for the development of techniques and procedures for identifying and characterizing causal structures, with a view to learning how causal analysis is represented in thought, verbal statements, imagery and so on (see Zullow et al., 1988, for a new technique for reliable content-analysis of verbatim explanations).

One such technique has been pioneered by Antaki (1986), who has tried to break down responses from unstructured interviews into causal structures. His criterion for a causal structure underlying an event was 'that set of causes elaborating the explanation of a given event through one or more paths' (p. 217). To follow his example, someone might see unemployment as having two causal paths – world recession and the policy of a political party – one of which is traced back to one prior cause (changes in patterns of world trade), the other branching into two causes (the appeal of policies to the electorate and the party leader's own economic beliefs). Interestingly, Antaki found single-cause explanations to be rare, although the majority of causal structures were not very complex (e.g., one path, with two steps; or two paths). Although Antaki's study is based on only eight highly intelligent and politically involved respondents, this type of research makes an original contribution to the analysis of perceived causal structures. One should, however, remain somewhat cautious, because the method employed was one of forced metacognition. Respondents were prompted to arrange causes in a structured explanation (although they chose the number of causes) which they might not have done spontaneously (this criticism also applies to related work, e.g., Lunt, 1988).

In summarizing the work on perceived causal structures, it seems reasonable to suggest that there are circumstances in which perceivers will attribute events to proximal and distal causes, which arc mentally structured. The analysis of attributions in close relationships will provide some further examples (see chapter 5), and will emphasize the need to proceed beyond single-cause explanations. As Pachter (1974) has argued, with reference to history, situations in which no single cause can be named are the rule, not the exception.

Individual differences in causal attribution

A complete discussion of how attributions are measured should also include attempts to develop scales, with appropriate psychometric properties, that measure individual differences in causal attribution. Two such scales are currently in use.

The Attributional Style Questionnaire (ASQ; Peterson et al., 1982; Seligman et al., 1979) treats attributional style as a personality characteristic, defined as 'a tendency to make particular kinds of causal inference, rather than others, across different situations and across time' (Metalsky and Abramson, 1981, p. 38; see Feather and Tiggermann, 1984; Sweeney et al., 1986, for references to other questionnaires). Attributional style plays a central role in the reformulated learned helplessness model of depression (Abramson et al., 1978; see below); it is conceived as a personality trait that mediates between negative events and depression. The ASQ assesses the degree to which individuals explain aversive events along three dimensions: internal-external; stable-unstable; and global-specific. A 'depressive attributional style' refers to the tendency to view aversive events as caused by factors that are internal, stable and global. Trait constructs like attributional style are only justified if most individuals are reasonably consistent in the kinds of causal attribution they make across situations. The value of the ASQ has, however, been questioned in two studies by Cutrona et al., (1985). They reported only modest evidence of cross-situational consistency of attributional style; it was not even the case that a small subset of individuals appeared to have a consistent attributional style (see also Arntz et al., 1985; Cohen et al., 1986).

A second, very recent, attempt to measure individual differences in causal attribution followed up the idea that individuals vary in the degree of complexity with which they make attributions. The Attributional Complexity Scale (ACS; Fletcher et al., 1986) is based on seven attributional constructs, each of which is viewed as varying along a simple-complex dimension: 'Level of interest or motivation'; 'Preference for complex rather than simple explanations'; 'Presence of metacognition concerning explanations'; 'Awareness of the extent to which people's behavior is a function of interaction with others'; 'Tendency to infer abstract or causally complex internal attributions'; 'Tendency to infer abstract, contemporary, external causal attributions'; and 'Tendency to infer causes operating from the past' (pp. 876–7). The development of the scale was based on the hypothesis that individuals who are more complex on one of the seven dimensions would also be more complex on others, for which Fletcher et al. reported evidence. They also argued, however, that attributionally 'complex' individuals could vary from simple to complex in their attributions (attributionally 'simple' individuals could not). Thus, as they concluded, 'individual differences form only part of the puzzle' (p. 882; see also Fletcher et al., in press).[2]

Attributional complexity would appear to be an interesting variable, worthy of future research; but together the ASQ and the ACS provide only limited evidence of cross-situational individual differences in causal attribution.

Summary

In general, there are clear advantages and disadvantages to the use of closed- and open-ended measures of attribution. There would seem to be no strong consensus for using one to the exclusion of the other, and each has a value in relation to specific problems. One shortcoming shared by all these methods, however, is that they explicitly request or elicit attributions from respondents. The next section begins by reviewing the evidence for 'spontaneous' causal attributions, which has helped to clarify the conditions under which causal attributions are instigated.

THE INSTIGATION OF CAUSAL ATTRIBUTION

'Spontaneous' causal attributions

Langer (1978) has argued that we know that people are capable of perceiving the world in cause-and-effect terms, but not how often, and under what circumstances, they do so. Her critique raised the question of how much thinking the ordinary attributor does, and she argued that much ostensibly thoughtful action was, in fact, 'mindless'. She proposed that, most of the time, people were not consciously seeking explanations, nor were they actively engaged in monitoring new information. Especially when performing familiar activities, people rely on well-learned and general 'scripts' (e.g., Abelson, 1981; Langer and Abelson, 1972). Langer concluded that attribution theorists may have presumed too much mental activity on the part of people engaging in many of their everyday activities (see also Thorngate, 1976, 1979). The upshot of this criticism is that laboratory experiments on causal attribution may have instigated processes that would not normally have occurred; causal attributions may have been *elicited* by procedures, rather than *emitted* by perceivers (Enzle and Schopflocher, 1978).

To answer this criticism, Weiner (1985a) reviewed all the available evidence for what he called 'spontaneous' causal thinking. He deliberately excluded all studies that had measured attributions obtrusively, and concentrated on three types of studies where normal (verbal) behaviour had been observed and coded:

1   Coding of written materials. For example, Lau and Russell (1980) content-analysed attributions in the sports pages of newspapers and found, as one would predict, that unexpected outcomes elicited a greater number of attempts at explanation than did expected results.

2   Experimental subjects' 'think aloud' responses during or after task engagement, and their reported thoughts. In an interesting applied study, Carroll and Wiener (1982) collected verbal protocols from parole decision-makers as they examined actual case-history material. They found that parole officers searched for the cause of the crime, primarily to determine the risk of the criminal to society.

3   Causal search inferred from cognitive processes. Pyszczynski and Greenberg (1981) presented subjects with information about an actor that confirmed or disconfirmed their expectations, and then gave them the opportunity to select a limited number of pieces of

information from a larger array. This study found that attribution-relevant information about an actor was most sought when prior expectations were disconfirmed. Relatedly, Hastie (1984) reported that an incongruent act was more likely to elicit an explanation as a sentence completion than was a congruent act (see also Clarey and Tesser, 1983; D. L. Hamilton, 1988).

An additional method for measuring spontaneous attributions has been introduced by Harvey et al. (1980). Subjects were shown videotaped episodes where actors engaged in various surprising, unusual or negatively valenced behaviours. Subjects were then asked to write down what they saw on the videotape and any thoughts and feelings they might have had while they watched it. These written reactions were then coded for attributions and revealed the presence of 'unsolicited' attributional activity.[3] Harvey et al. reported more unsolicited attributional activity for 'empathy' vs 'detached' set conditions, serious vs moderate outcomes and anticipated (vs no anticipated) future interaction. Although the idea of an 'incidental' attribution paradigm is attractive, some doubt exists as to whether this measure constitutes an index of *causal* attribution. Coding criteria referred to dispositional as well as causal attributions and the authors reported only the predominance of 'dispositional' over 'situational-circumstantial' attributions (approximately 85 per cent vs 15 per cent across four studies), *not* the amount of dispositional vs causal attribution.

Weiner concluded that there were two key factors in eliciting attributions: unexpected (vs expected) events, and nonattainment (vs attainment) of a goal. The importance of unexpected events is consistent with the theories of both Jones and Davis (1965) and Kelley (1967). Jones and Davis proposed that individuals were more likely to make correspondent inferences if an outcome was rare; for Kelley, low consensus led to a person attribution. This finding also fits with Langer's (1978) claim that people rely on scripts when performing familiar activities and that scripted actions do not require explanations (Lalljee and Abelson, 1983; see chapter 4). Newtson's (1976) research on the perception of ongoing behaviour revealed some consistent findings. He asked subjects to view a sequence of behaviour and press a button when, in a given action sequence, one meaningful action ended and a different one began. In one study, subjects who had viewed an unexpected action used significantly more units per minute than did subjects not exposed to such an event. More generally, Nesdale (1983) has distinguished between situation- and person-expectations which may have an interactive effect: for example, violations of person expectations instigated attributional processing especially when the observed behaviour was expected in the situation.

In attaching such importance to unexpected events, psychologists also agree with some philosophical analyses. As was seen in chapter 1, Hart and Honoré (1959) identified unusual occurrences as the major instigators of causal explanations, and argued that causes were conditions that 'made the difference' between a normal event and such an occurrence. Mackie (1965, 1974) emphasized the 'causal field' or context in which judgements of probable cause were made, arguing that judgements of causal relevance are generally related to the degree that a variable is a 'difference-in-a-background'. Thus factors that are part of some presumed background or causal field are judged to be of little or no relevance, but differences-in-a-background (e.g., unexpected events) arouse causal thinking. Thus psychologists and philosophers have both emphasized the deviation from a normal course of events as a condition for causal reasoning (see Einhorn and Hogarth, 1986; Jaspars, Hewstone and Fincham, 1983).

The second general triggering event identified by Weiner (1985a) was nonattainment of a goal (loss, defeat or failure). Thus, when someone fails a task (typically an academic achievement task), she or he is more likely to engage in attributional reasoning to explain this outcome than a success, especially when the failure is unexpected (e.g., Diener and Dweck, 1978; Wong and Weiner, 1981). Performing poorly on an ability-linked performance task is potentially threatening to an actor's self-esteem and therefore elicits a special sort of explanation (see Darley and Goethals, 1980).

Weiner's review suggests that spontaneous attributional thinking is important in everyday life, and that research has uncovered some of the factors that instigate explanations. There remain doubts about just how 'spontaneous' these attributions were (respondents were still asked to think) and current research is exploring social cognition and attribution in more naturalistic settings (see Fletcher et al., 1988; Ickes et al., 1986). Additional factors also deserve mention, although they have been identified using standard and obtrusive measures of attribution.

Other instigating factors

As Jones and Davis (1965) pointed out, perceivers are sometimes dependent on another person for positive or negative outcomes (hedonic relevance), and this situation can influence attributions. A number of studies have examined the effect of anticipated future interaction (e.g., Berscheid et al., 1976; Miller et al., 1978). Berscheid et al. found that males and females who were about to go on a date with a stranger were both more extreme and more confident in rating persons they anticipated dating than they were in rating persons they did not expect to date. In this study the instigation of attributions can be seen as based on another person's ability to control the perceiver's outcomes, although the dependent variables were dispositional, not causal, attributions. Subsequent research has shown that there is an increase in causal attributional activity following an experience of lack of control (Liu and Steele, 1986; Pittman and D'Agostino, 1985; Pittman and Pittman, 1980). More will be said about control, below, as one of the functions served by causal attributions. Now that more attention is paid to the relationship between cognition and affect (e.g., Bower and Cohen, 1982; Isen, 1984), one would expect research on the power of mood states to determine attribution. But the available literature is limited. Weiner (1986) has reported some influence of affect on his three causal dimensions – locus (Gollwitzer et al., 1982), stability (Brown, 1984), and controllability (Alloy et al., 1981). In addition, if a negative event occurs when people are already feeling dysphoric, they may assess the cause more negatively than if they had been in a happier mood. These negative causal attributions may then further exacerbate the depressive mood (Storms and McCaul, 1976).

Work by Schwarz and colleagues (Bohner et al., 1988; Schwarz, 1987; Schwarz and Clore, 1983) has shown that causal attribution is instigated by negative, compared with positive, events (see also Abele, 1985; Wyer and Carlston, 1979) and, furthermore, that the effects of unexpectedness and valence can be unconfounded, even if in everyday life they often are confounded. Schwarz's work also led to the interesting question of why people in a bad mood should seek explanations more than people in a good mood. Drawing on the wider literature relating cognition and affect, Schwarz suggests that individuals in good and bad moods are characterized by qualitatively different information-processing. For example, people in a good mood are less systematic information-processors. As Isen et al. (1982) noted, 'A person in a positive affective state who is asked to make a judgment or solve a problem will tend to reduce the complexity of the judgment or decision and engage in speedy, simplified kinds of processing' (p. 246).

Schwarz (1987) has suggested that causal thinking can attenuate the intensity of feelings and that increased attributional activity following negative events, or while in a bad mood, may be understood in these terms. As Abele (1985) put it, 'It seems to be necessary to spend some time reasoning about negatively experienced events' (p. 329), of which causal reasoning is only one part (see also Mikula and Schlamberger, 1985). These findings surely represent only a beginning, and at present there is much less evidence for the role of affect as an instigator of attribution, than as a consequence (see below).

Another way to approach the question of what prompts attributions is to ask when people are motivated to seek attributions. Here Kruglanski's (1988) theory of lay epistemology may be useful, although it is more directly concerned with when individuals generate hypotheses than with when they make attributions. Kruglanski uses the term *freezing* to refer to the point at which individuals stop generating hypotheses. He has argued (e.g., Kruglanski et al., 1983) that factors determining whether a belief will be frozen or unfrozen include the individual's *capacity* and *motivation* to generate alternative hypotheses. Capacity depends on a person's store of general or domain-specific knowledge and the availability of ideas in a person's mind. Motivation comprises three components: the 'need for structure' (e.g., some knowledge on a topic); the 'need for specific conclusions' (e.g., to maintain a specific belief); and the 'need for validity' (e.g., when the anticipated costs of a mistake are high). Unfortunately, although Kruglanski et al. have applied these ideas in a broad and heuristic manner to the field of social cognition, they have not yet received support from specifically attributional research.

The conversational approach

A quite different approach to the instigation of attributions involves looking at the conversational context in which attributions are made, by whom and to whom. Lalljee (1981) suggested that concepts from discourse analysis (Coulthard, 1975), ethnomethodology (Garfinkel, 1967) and speech-act theory (Austin, 1962; Grice, 1975) could be used. Lalljee proposed four general principles that might underlie the presentation of a particular explanation: (1) 'Assumptions concerning the knowledge of the other'; (2) 'The relationship between the inter-actors'; (3) 'Topic and activity implications'; and (4) 'Interpersonal consequences'. In other words, the same event might receive different explanations (or perhaps no explanation at all), depending on the conversational context. Relatedly, Tetlock (1983) has shown that 'accountability' to another person leads to more conceptually complex or multidimensional thinking, but only when that person's views are unknown.

The results of attributional work in this vein have been interesting, if not plentiful. Slugoski (1983) demonstrated that speakers followed the kinds of rules discussed by Grice (1975) and only offered explanations that were informative from the listener's point of view. Turnbull (1986; Turnbull and Slugoski, 1988) proposed that explanations were essentially contrastive, being sought only when there was a gap between what was expected and what actually happened (cf. Scott and Lyman's, 1968, definition of an 'account'). Finally, a study by Antaki and Naji (1987) revealed an effect that was almost the opposite (although not necessarily contradictory) to Turnbull's. They analysed tea-time and dinner-party conversations of a sample of middle-class British people. They found that speakers most commonly brought up for explanation some long-standing state of affairs. Antaki and Naji suggested that people want to bring up that kind of event for explanation because of an important interactional goal of conversation – underlining that what one is saying is sensible. Often we state a 'fact' that needs to be bolstered by some supporting evidence, and explanations can serve that function.

These kinds of studies point to the pragmatic nature of ordinary language – any utterance has a force and a set of implications that go beyond its face value (see Levinson, 1983). In explanations, as in other utterances, conversationalists each make use of the shared knowledge that the other person is known to have. Thus explanations can proceed more economically, and without the speaker spelling out details (Hewstone and Antaki, 1988). Very little of this research has been published within mainstream social psychology, or within the framework of attribution theory, yet it does provide valuable evidence about the role and nature of ordinary language explanations.

Summary

There is good evidence that causal attributions are prevalent, but not ubiquitous, social judgements. The main instigating factors identified are unexpected events, nonattainment of a goal, outcome dependence and, more tentatively, mood. Additional principles that govern the nature and presence of explanations in conversation have also been proposed and further instigating factors will be identified in subsequent chapters, including dissatisfaction in close relationships (see chapter 5), counterstereotypical behaviour by outgroup members (see chapter 6) and catastrophic societal events (see chapter 7).

BIASES IN THE ATTRIBUTION PROCESS

It was noted above that the theories of Jones and Davis (1965) and Kelley (1967) were primarily responsible for the upsurge of experimental studies of causal attribution. Both models of the attribution process tended to view the perceiver as a fairly rational person, and Kelley's (1967) ANOVA model was even given the status of a normative model that indicated how perceivers should make attributions (using consensus, consistency and distinctiveness, according to the covariation principle). It is sometimes forgotten, however, that Kelley, like Heider, and Jones and Davis before him, also acknowledged that 'attribution processes are subject to error' (1967, p. 219). Indeed, he devoted the final section of his article to the exposition of biases or departures from the models.

At the outset, I will argue that we are not justified in referring to such tendencies as errors. In fact, the term *error* should be reserved for 'deviations from a normative model' (Fiske and Taylor, 1984) or 'departures from some accepted criterion of validity' (Kruglanski and Ajzen, 1983). Such models or criteria are rarely available for attribution research. For this reason, the term *bias* should be used although in this book I will refer to terms such as 'error' and 'fallacy' where the original, if inaccurate, label has stuck. A bias occurs if the social perceiver systematically distorts (e.g., over- or under-uses) some otherwise correct procedure (Fiske and Taylor, 1984). As will be seen, such biases have generated an enormous amount of research and seem to provide a better descriptive analysis of causal attribution than do complex normative models.

This section deals, in turn, with three of the most central biases in attribution. They are important in the sense that they have attracted theoretical and research attention, but also because they are crucial to the issues covered in this volume. A strong statement of the importance of biases in social judgement was made by L. Ross (1977) and followed up by Nisbett and Ross (1980):

an increasingly important goal of contemporary research and theory, is not the logical schemata which promote understanding, consensus, and effective social control; instead, it is the sources of systematic bias or distortion in judgment that lead the intuitive psychologist to misinterpret events and hence to behave in ways that are personally maladaptive, socially pernicious, and often puzzling to the social scientist who seeks to understand such behavior. (Ross, 1977, p. 181)

A rather different view has been put forward by Funder (1987), who has argued that what have been termed 'errors' are largely a function of the laboratory context and might not result in 'mistakes' in the real world. Funder defines an error in the same way as Kruglanski and Ajzen (1983) and Fiske and Taylor (1984). But he defines a mistake as 'an incorrect judgment in the real world' (p. 76), which must be determined by different criteria and, indeed, is much more difficult to determine.

The 'fundamental attribution error'

> Changes in the environment are almost always caused by acts of persons in combination with other factors. The tendency exists to ascribe the changes entirely to persons. (Heider, 1944, p. 361)

Citing the work of both Heider (1944, 1958) and Ichheiser (1949), Ross defined the fundamental attribution error as, 'the tendency for attributers [sic] to underestimate the impact of situational factors and to overestimate the role of dispositional factors in controlling behavior' (1977, p. 183).[4] Note that in this definition dispositional attribution is *relatively* more important than situational attribution. In contrast, Nisbett and Ross defined the 'error' in an *absolute* sense as 'the tendency to attribute behavior exclusively to the actor's dispositions and to ignore powerful situational determinants of the behavior' (1980, p. 31).

The former definition is to be preferred, because the latter is simply not what the relevant studies show. Consider Jones and Harris's (1967) study, generally used as an illustration (see chapter 2). First, subjects were not even given an opportunity to attribute the speech-writer's pro- or anti-Castro position to the situation. Second, the results implied that subjects attached too little weight to the situation (the no-choice instructions) and too much weight to the person (the attitude expressed in the speech); but as attitude attribution was never maximal, one can reasonably infer that the situation *was* seen as influential, albeit relatively less influential than the person (see figure 5).[5]

Despite the debate over how to define the fundamental attribution error, there is a good deal of putative evidence (cited by Jones, 1979; Nisbett and Ross, 1980; Ross, 1977, 1978; Ross and Anderson, 1982) for the tendency it identifies. In addition to the work on attitude attribution, studies have reported the consistent failure of perceivers to make adequate allowance for the effects of social roles on behaviour. For example, Ross et al. (1977a) randomly assigned subjects in a quiz game to the roles of questioner and contestant, with the former told to set difficult questions for the latter. Both contestants and observers overlooked the advantages conferred by the role of the questioner (i.e.,

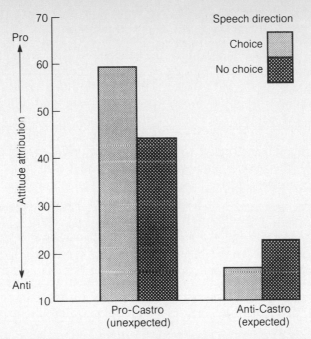

FIGURE 5 *Attitude attribution as a function of speech direction and freedom of choice (after Jones and Harris, 1967)*

choosing difficult questions from their areas of expertise) and rated the questioner much more knowledgeable than the contestant (see also Davies, 1985; Hui and Ip, 1989). In more applied settings, the fundamental attribution error seems to underlie the tendency to attribute the cause of road accidents to 'human factors', rather than the transport system or qualities of road vehicles (Barjonet, 1980). This bias may also be at work in foreign policy settings. Tetlock and McGuire (1986) noted, following Jervis (1976), that policy-makers tend to see the behaviour of other states as 'more centralized, planned and coordinated than it is' (1986, p. 265), and they tend to over-estimate the internal coherence of other states' foreign policy.

Defining and illustrating the fundamental attribution error are much simpler than explaining it. First, returning to Funder's (1987) criticism, one should ask what there is to explain. For both the Jones and Harris (1967) and the Ross et al. (1977) studies, Funder contends that the way in which subjects were given information (about the speech-direction and social role, respectively) would lead them to think that they were supposed to use that information, and to assume it to be diagnostic (see the above discussion of the 'conversational' approach to the instigation of attributions, and also Miller and Rorer, 1982). More persuasively still, Funder refers to research on the personality correlates of 14-year-olds who were *least* vulnerable to the role effect. They were independently characterized as the *least* socially competent and least well-adjusted (Block and Funder, 1986). As Funder argues, in many real-life situations people do say what they mean, and differences in apparent performance do, in fact, reflect differences in competence.

Notwithstanding the question of whether such data indicate an error or a mistake, it is instructive to consider some of the explanations put forward for the general phenomenon (see Reeder et al., in press). The major explanations derive from the intra-personal and societal levels, respectively. At the intra-personal level, one explanation is that the actor's behaviour is often more salient than the situation. As Heider (1944) noted, actor and act form a 'causal unit'; the perceiver focuses on the other person, not the situation, and he or she comes to be overrated as causally important. A general salience explanation is supported by Rholes and Pryor's (1982) demonstration that increasing the accessibility of situational constructs, by priming, increased the likelihood that situational factors would be considered in explaining a target's behaviour.

Another cognitive explanation refers to differential rates of forgetting for situational and dispositional causes. Moore et al. (1979) and Peterson (1980) have reported that self-attributions made some time after the behaviour in question tended to emphasize dispositional causes more, and situational causes less, than attributions made immediately. Miller and Porter (1980) revealed exactly the opposite finding, however, and Funder (1982) reported that shifts could occur in either direction, depending on the focus of information-processing that takes place immediately following the behaviour. While these studies may appear wildly inconsistent, this is not strictly true. The studies differed in terms of type of situation, type of attribution and method of data collection. There clearly is evidence of shifts in attribution over time, but these are not consistent enough to justify the 'dispositional shift' as a robust attributional phenomenon and as a complete explanation for the fundamental attribution error.

At the societal level, Higgins and Bargh (1987) have pointed out one obvious limitation of the cognitive-salience account – it fails to explain cultural and developmental differences. Thus J. G. Miller (1984) reported a developmental increase in reference to dispositional factors in an American sample, but an increase in reference to contextual factors in an Indian-Hindu sample. Studies have also shown that as children in a Western culture develop, they come to hold an increasingly dispositional view of the causes of behaviour (Higgins and Bryant, 1982; Ruble et al., 1979). Both findings strongly imply an explanation at the societal level. In addition, Jellison and Green (1981) proposed a societal norm for internality, so that internal attributions were viewed more favourably than external attributions (see also Beauvois and Dubois, 1988). This societal approach was emphasized by Nisbett and Ross:

> It is difficult to prove that people adhere to anything like an overarching 'general theory' of the relative impact of dispositional versus situational factors. There is reason to suspect, nevertheless, that a rather general, 'dispositionalist theory' is shared by almost everyone socialized in our culture. Certainly, it is part of the world view of the so-called Protestant ethic ... The 'dispositionalist theory', in short, is thoroughly woven into the fabric of our culture. (1980, p. 31)

This view is remarkably similar to that put forward by Ichheiser (1943; see chapter 1), but it was Nisbett and Ross's later emphasis on cognitive heuristics (1980, pp. 120–6) that was to influence later work (see chapter 4). If the actor's behaviour is salient, then actor-linked causes will be highly 'available' and may assume prominence in explanations over time. Or, since people's implicit theories give too much weight to dispositional causes of behaviour, then dispositional causes will be seen as 'representative' in explaining behaviour. Attributions can also be seen as strongly 'anchored' to person attribution, with insufficient adjustment for situational causality (Jones, 1979; Zuckerman et al., 1984). Such cognitive mechanisms may exaggerate societal-cultural tendencies, but should not lead us to ignore them (see chapter 7). One final influence noted by Nisbett and Ross also merits mention: linguistic factors. Although it is usually possible to describe both an action and an actor using near-identical terms (for example, we speak of generous/hostile actions or actors), the English language rarely allows us to label situations succinctly, using synonyms for action (for example, there is no word to describe the kind of situations that typically elicit generous/hostile behaviour). Linguistic factors in causal attribution have received little attention (e.g., Brown and Fish, 1982; Kanouse, 1972), but they are certainly worthy of closer attention (see below and chapter 4).

Notwithstanding the multiple explanations that have been reviewed, Harvey, Town and Yarkin (1981) posed the question, 'How fundamental is the fundamental attribution error?' (see also Harvey and McGlynn, 1982; Reeder, 1982). Three main areas of contention have arisen. First, there is the meaning of situational and dispositional attributions for both subjects (V. L. Hamilton, 1980) and researchers

(Funder, 1982; cf. the discussion of the internal-external distinction, above). Second, we have no criteria to justify the term 'error', although Funder (1982) has attempted to specify (admittedly extreme) cases in which personal or situational attributions might be identified as more reasonable. Third, under some circumstances people will overattribute another person's behaviour to situational factors: most notably, when behaviour is inconsistent with prior expectations (Kulik, 1983), and when attention is focused on situational factors that could have produced a person's behaviour (Ajzen et al., 1979; Quattrone, 1982a). In view of all these facts, we should probably start looking for a more modest label ('correspondence bias' is to be preferred; Gilbert and Jones, 1986). Yet this effect is nonetheless fascinating and one that exemplifies the social-psychological nature of attribution.

Actor-observer differences

The person tends to attribute his own reactions to the object world, and those of another, when they differ from his own, to personal characteristics in *o*. (Heider, 1958, p. 157)

In a bold statement, echoing Heider's, Jones and Nisbett proposed that: '*there is a pervasive tendency for actors to attribute their actions to situational requirements, whereas observers tend to attribute the same actions to stable personal dispositions*' (1972, p. 80; italics in original). Watson (1982) has provided the most comprehensive review of subsequent research, although he prefers the terms *self* and *other*, rather than *actor* and *observer*, because in many studies there is not, in fact, one person acting while another observes. Instead, experimental subjects are frequently asked to explain the behaviour of, or merely to describe, others who are absent. Watson has shown that there are four possible contrasts with which to test the effect predicted by Jones and Nisbett:

1 Self-attributions to situations vs self-attributions to traits;
2 Other-attributions to traits vs other-attributions to situations;
3 Self-attributions to situations vs other-attributions to situations;
4 Other-attributions to traits vs self-attributions to traits.

Watson pointed out, however, that many studies did not even collect all the data appropriate for such an analysis, let alone carry it out. His careful review revealed that there was an effect, but that it was confined to self-other differences in situational attribution (contrast (3), above): self-attributions to situations are higher than other-attributions to situations. Once again, there are competing explanations of this bias, three of which should be considered.

Information level. One hypothesis is that self-other differences arise from the greater amount of information available to the actors or self-raters. We should, after all, know more about our own past behaviour, and its variability across situations, than we know about the behaviour of others, and they know about our behaviour. Thus observers may assume more consistency of behaviour and infer dispositional causes. Several studies have shown that actors perceive more cross-situational variability in their behaviour and that observers make more trait attributions (e.g., Lay et al., 1974; Nisbett et al., 1973, Study 2). In addition, Nisbett et al. reported that as familiarity increased (i.e., length of acquaintanceship with the other person), so did situational attributions for the other's behaviour. The number of personal traits ascribed to others did not differ, however, with degree of acquaintanceship.

Perceptual focus. There has been far more research on the, admittedly more interesting, hypothesis that focus of attention explains actor-observer differences. An ingenious experiment by Storms (1973) followed up the most fundamental difference between self and other, the fact that they have, quite literally, different 'points of view'. Storms set up a getting-acquainted conversation involving two strangers, A and B, each watched by a separate observer, and each filmed by a videocamera. He hypothesized that it should be possible to change the way actors and observers interpret behaviour by changing their visual orientations: actors who come to see themselves should make more dispositional attributions about their own behaviour; and observers who come to see another aspect of the actor's situation should become more situational in attributing the actor's behaviour. The most interesting hypothesis was the predicted reversal of actors' and observers' attributions when subjects were shown a new orientation: actors' attributions became less situational, and observers' became more situational. It should be noted, however, that in all conditions person attribution was very high (another example of the 'fundamental attribution error'), and that the no video/control condition failed to show a difference in favour of situational attribution for actors (just as Watson, 1982, concluded).

Storms's findings have not always been replicated. It seems that the participant in the centre of the visual field (person A to the observer of A, and B to the observer of B) is rated as more causally important, but that this weighting does not always have a clear effect on dispositional and situational attributions (S. E. Taylor et al., 1979). Nevertheless Storms's findings underline the general point that methods exist for shifting the perspectives of actors and observers, and salience effects on the weighting of dispositional and situational attributions have been found in other studies too. For example, McArthur and Post (1977) had observers watch a conversation in which one conversant was made salient (e.g., by being illuminated with a bright light), while the other was non-salient (dim light). Observers rated the salient conversant's behaviour as more dispositionally, and less situationally, caused.

Several studies within the framework of objective self-awareness have investigated the consequences of viewing oneself as if from the perspective of an outside observer (e.g., Duval and Wicklund, 1972). Objective self-awareness has been manipulated by, for example, introducing a mirror or television camera into the laboratory. Heightened self-awareness tends to increase self-attributions (Duval and Wicklund, 1973), and to increase the predictive validity of dispositional self-attributions (Pryor et al., 1977; see Funder, 1982). Finally, observers' attributions have been made more situational through instructions to empathize with the actor (Brehm and Aderman, 1977; Gould and Sigall, 1977; Regan and Totten, 1975).

Motivational factors.   In their original statement, Jones and Nisbett (1972) also predicted that motivational factors might limit, eliminate or even reverse their proposed effect. Kelley and Michela (1980) reviewed the evidence for this explanation, but concluded that it was strongly supported only in studies using competitive experimental games (e.g., Snyder et al., 1976). A motivational explanation is, in any case, limited (as Ross and Fletcher, 1985, pointed out), because the actor-observer hypothesis includes neutral as well as valenced behaviours.

Linguistic factors.   Finally, Semin and Fiedler (1989) have turned their attention to the types of linguistic devices available to actors and observers. They showed that dispositionality (the 'enduringness' of a quality ascribed to a person) and how much a sentence reveals about a person varies systematically as a function of linguistic categories. Sentences constructed with 'descriptive action verbs' reveal least about a person and express the least enduring qualities of a person (e.g., 'John visited Mary'). Adjectives are the most informative about the subject and express the most enduring qualities (e.g., 'John is honest'). Semin and Fiedler replicated the study by Nisbett et al. (1973, Experiment 2) and supported their claim that actors and observers use different linguistic devices. Actor-attributors typically avoided statements about themselves in general and abstract terms which ascribed dispositional attributes to themselves in particular. When actors did use abstract terms, these occurred in sentences with interaction partners as the causal origin. In contrast, observer-attributors typically tended to describe actors with relatively more abstract terms that implied enduring, dispositional properties. These findings led Semin and Fiedler to conclude that what is generally regarded as the result of causal thinking or intra-individual cognitive processes is, in fact, a tendency determined by the social rules of language use.

The psychology of the processes that underlie self-other differences in attribution is fascinating (see Farr and Anderson, 1983), and their identification is of obvious significance to our everyday understanding of each other's actions. For example, self-other attribution differences have been shown to vary as a function of marital distress (Fincham et al., 1987a; see chapter 5). At present, the actor-observer or self-other difference is best understood in terms of perceptual salience, although categorical conclusions are unwise, in view of the widely different methods and measures used (see Watson, 1982). It would certainly appear incautious to assert that the attributions of actors are more accurate than those of observers, as Monson and Snyder (1977) have done. First, there are no criteria for accuracy. Second, as Locke and Pennington (1982) pointed out, even if actors are in a better position to know their reasons, because of motivational distortions they may be in a worse position than an impartial observer to know the other causes.

Self-serving biases

> That reason is sought that is personally acceptable. It is usually a reason that flatters us, puts us in a good light, and it is imbued with an added potency by the attribution. (Heider, 1958, p. 172)

The preceding treatment of actor-observer differences referred only in passing to research dealing with attributions for success and failure. The self-serving attribution bias refers to the fact that people are more likely to attribute their successes to internal causes such as ability, whereas they tend to attribute failures to external causes such as task difficulty. Kingdon (1967) provided a memorable example from the political world. He interviewed successful and unsuccessful American politicians about five months after a variety of elections and asked them to summarize the major factors (causes) that led to their victories or defeats over the years. The politicians attributed their wins to internal factors – their hard work, personal service to constituents, matters of campaign strategy, building a reputation and publicizing themselves. They attributed their losses to external factors – the party make-up of the district, the familiar name of their opponent, national and state trends, and lack of money. Kingdon labelled his findings the 'congratulation-rationalization effect' (p. 141). More generally, it is an example of the self-serving bias in attribution.[6]

Although the self-serving bias has been widely researched, its exact nature and explanation have aroused controversy. There are, in fact, two biases – a 'self-enhancing bias' (attributing success to internal, relative to external, causes) and a 'self-protecting bias' (attributing failure to external, relative to internal, causes). Miller and Ross (1975) claimed support only for the self-enhancing bias and they argued that it could be explained by cognitive factors, without recourse to motivational explanations. There were three strands to their cognitive, information-processing account: (1) people intend and expect to succeed rather than fail, and are more likely to make self-attributions for expected than unexpected outcomes; (2) people are more likely to perceive covariation between response and outcome if they are experiencing a pattern of increasing success, rather than constant failure; (3) people erroneously based their judgements of the contingency between response and outcome on the occurrence of the desired outcome, rather than the true pattern of contingencies.

More recent reviews have concluded in favour of motivational explanations. Zuckerman's (1979) systematic summary of the literature concluded that the need to maintain self-esteem directly affected the attribution of task outcomes. But he argued that the strength of this effect depended on factors including the extent to which self-esteem concerns were aroused in experimental subjects. He concluded that there are self-serving effects for both success and failure in most, but not all, experimental paradigms (see also Arkin et al., 1980a). Weary (Weary Bradley, 1978; Weary, 1980) proposed that positive and negative affective states produced by success and failure mediated subjects' causal attributions for their outcomes. She suggested different paths in relation to self-enhancing and self-protecting attributions. Self-enhancing attributions for success were mediated by, and served to maintain, relatively high levels of positive affect. Self-protecting attributions for failure were mediated by, and served to lessen, high levels of negative affect. More will be said about the affective consequences of attribution later in the chapter.

Weary also discussed self-serving attributions in the context of self-presentation. People may ascribe causality for outcomes in ways that avoid embarrassment and/or gain public approval. Thus studies have compared subjects' attributions under public vs private conditions (e.g., Greenberg et al., 1982; Weary et al., 1982), and with or without the use of the bogus pipeline (Riess et al., 1981). Some of the factors that influence the existence and choice of self-presentation strategies have been summarized in a taxonomy by Weary and Arkin (1981).

Perhaps the most important general issue raised by self-serving biases is whether, in fact, it is possible to distinguish between cognitive and motivational explanations. Various arguments have been raised against the purely cognitive account. Zuckerman (1979) argued that the cognitive explanations put forward by Miller and Ross (1975) actually contained motivational aspects; Tetlock and Levi (1982) described the cognitive research programme as so flexible that it could generate the predictions of virtually any motivational theory (see also Tetlock and Manstead, 1985). On the other hand, the most powerful argument against a purely motivational explanation is that motivational factors can have an effect on, and possibly via, information processing (see Hamilton and Trolier, 1986). For the present, it appears impossible to choose between the cognitive and motivational perspectives; both are surely correct (cf. Tomkins, 1981). As Ross and Fletcher concluded: 'People are both rational and rationalizers' (1985, p. 105) and, as Tetlock and Manstead (1985) argued, it is now time to abandon the quest for crucial experiments and to concentrate on the influence of both private and public identities on social behaviour. Whatever the explanation for this bias, it is one that evidently appears in interpersonal attributions (see chapter 5), and has also been extended to intergroup contexts (see chapter 6). As Pyszczynski and Greenberg (1987) have argued, the self-serving bias is likely to extend beyond causal attributions to the selection of hypotheses for testing, the generation of inference rules, the search for attribution-relevant information, the evaluation of accessed information, and the amount of evidence (confirmatory and disconfirmatory) that is required before an inference is made. As such it is surely one of the most pervasive biases in social cognition (for exceptions, among depressed samples, see Alloy and Abramson, 1979, 1982).

Summary

All three of these biases rely on the internal-external distinction, limitations of which were highlighted earlier: in the 'fundamental attribution error', internal attributions are held to be relatively more important than external attributions; the 'actor-observer' difference claims that actors' attributions are more external, and less internal than those of observers; and the 'self-serving' bias predicts that attributions for one's own success are more internal than external, while attributions for failure are more external than internal. These biases clearly do exist, but statements about how pervasive their effects really are depend on a systematic analysis of the relevant literature, as provided by Watson (1982) for the actor-observer effect, or Zuckerman (1979) for the self-serving bias. There is also a need for more research on how various biases are interrelated (e.g., Burger and Rodman, 1983), their interaction with contextual factors (Tetlock, 1983) and the behavioural consequences of attributional bias (Quattrone, 1982b).

The study of biases has been most influential in identifying what Taylor (1981) called the most severe problem faced by attribution theory – the mounting evidence that people do not use the kinds of formal, quasi-scientific processes laid down in the classic theories. Instead, they often make judgements quickly, on the basis of quite minimal information, and show clear biases of the type illustrated in this section (for further biases, see Fiske and Taylor, 1984). The tension between complex and simple models of social judgement and inference is fundamental, but not new. It can be found in the work of Heider (1944, 1958), Michotte (1946), Jones and Davis (1965) and Maselli and Altrocchi (1969). Nor is it unique to the study of causal attribution. Throughout the field of social cognition, researchers have distinguished between 'automatic vs controlled' processing (Shiffrin and Schneider, 1977), or 'heuristic vs systematic' processing (Chaiken, 1980; Petty et al., 1981). This issue will be examined in detail in chapter 4, which moves beyond the identification of biases to review our understanding of the cognitive processes underlying attributions.

FUNCTIONS AND CONSEQUENCES OF CAUSAL ATTRIBUTION

Functions of attribution

As Taylor (1981) has noted, the rise of cognitive social psychology embodied a movement away from motivation-based models of attitudes and behaviour. Thus it is not surprising to find that the original theories of attribution acknowledged motivational factors, and discussed the perceiver's needs and purposes (see Heider, 1958, p. 296; Jones and Davis, 1965, p. 220; Kelley, 1967, p. 193). Since then, there has been little explicit interest in the functions of attribution, although two reviews agreed in emphasizing three main functions (Forsyth, 1980; Tetlock and Levi, 1982):[7]

1   *The control function.* The motivation to achieve a degree of control over the physical and social world – especially understanding the causes of behaviour and events – is dealt with in a number of relatively early psychological writings (e.g., Kelly, 1955; White, 1959). Forsyth (1980) subdivided this function into explanation and prediction, referring to the central role of Heider's (1958) and Kelley's (1967, 1972b) work. The development of Kelley's work is especially interesting in this respect, as he changed his view of the lay person from 'pure scientist' to 'applied scientist':

> attribution processes are to be understood, not only as a means of providing the individual with a veridical view of his world, but as a means of encouraging and maintaining his effective exercise of control in that world. The purpose of causal analysis – the function it serves for the species and the individual – is effective control. (Kelley, 1972b, p. 22)

Thus common-sense explanations allow cognitive control of past and present events, as well as anticipating future occurrences (see Wortman, 1976). It is the control function of attribution that helps us to understand a wide variety of counter-intuitive attributional phenomena. Many of the studies referred to here used attributions of responsibility, rather than causality, but they do illustrate the general control function of explanations. For example, people derogate others who are victims of negative events (and see them as deserving such outcomes), in an attempt to maintain the belief that negative events will not happen to them personally (the 'just world hypothesis': see Lerner and Miller, 1978; Ryan, 1971). There is also evidence of 'primitive' self-attributions of blame by parents of children with leukaemia (Chodoff et al., 1964), cancer patients (Abrams and Fine-singer, 1953), and victims of accidents (Bulman and Wortman, 1977) and rape (Medea and Thompson, 1974). It seems that self-blame helps a person to understand an otherwise inexplicable event, and conveys the implication that he or she could act to prevent similar events from happening again (see Bains, 1983; Langer, 1975; Wortman, 1976).

Interestingly, Lefcourt's (1973) review reports that even if the perception of control is illusory, it can increase hope and enhance one's ability to cope with aversive stimuli. But the results are not clear-cut. Meyer and Taylor (1986) found that women who blamed themselves for having been raped actually recovered less well than did those who attached no blame to themselves. This latter position was also supported by Frey and Rogner's (1987) work on recovery from physical injury sustained in accidents. Patients who made high self-attributions tended to stay in hospital longer than those who made moderate or no self-attributions. Ratings of the healing process and subjective ratings of well-being followed the same pattern.

2   *The self-esteem function.* Few psychologists would disagree that positive self-esteem is essential to emotional well-being, and this function is exemplified in people's need to protect, validate or enhance their feelings of personal worth and effectiveness (see Greenwald, 1980). As shown in the previous section, evidence for this function comes mostly from studies that have compared self-attributions for failure and success. Attributions serve a self-esteem function to the extent that (in general) they are relatively internal for success and relatively external for failure (e.g., Weary, 1981; Zuckerman, 1979). Pyszczynski and Greenberg (1987) have recently reviewed the evidence linking attribution and self-esteem and concluded that there is clear evidence that the attributions people make for performance outcomes do indeed influence their self-esteem after such outcomes.

3   *The self-presentation function.* This function was illustrated above with reference to work on 'accounts' (Scott and Lyman, 1968) and in relation to self-serving biases. Individuals can potentially control the view that others have of them by communicating attributions that are designed to gain public approval and to avoid embarrassment (see Baumeister, 1982; Tedeschi and Riess, 1981).

There appears, then, to be some consensus about the main functions of attribution. Nevertheless, there are difficulties with a 'functional' perspective on attribution. First, separating motivational-functional and cognitive-information-processing explanations is difficult, perhaps impossible. Second, one should be extremely cautious of the 'strong' form of functionalism, which would propose that any individual pattern of attribution is 'explained by' the effects and consequences of the pattern. The 'weak' form of functionalism is much less contentious. It holds simply that theory and research may gain from a more detailed consideration of the functions fulfilled by common-sense explanations. Although I have proposed this latter view (Hewstone, 1983b), I now believe that much more has been, and will be, learned by studying the consequences, rather than the functions, of attribution.

Consequences of attribution

Kelley and Michela's (1980) review of the attribution literature drew a distinction between 'attribution theories' and 'attributional theories'. Attribution theories were concerned with the influence of antecedents (e.g., information, beliefs, motivation) on attributions (i.e., perceived causes); attributional theories were concerned with the link between perceived causes and consequences (e.g., behaviour, affect and expectancy). This distinction has, however, not generally been endorsed. For example, Harvey and Weary (1984) coined the term 'generic attribution theory' to convey a focus on all the segments of Kelley and Michela's general model, and Eiser (1983b) argued that there was no reason to favour the study of antecedents over consequences – both are important.

Detailed reviews of attributional consequences have been provided by Harvey and Weary (1984), and by Weiner (1986), including such topics as arousal effects, loneliness, helping and smoking cessation. No attempt will be made here to review all this work, much of which is concerned with the application of attributional ideas. Instead, this section selectively illustrates three consequences of causal attribution – cognitive-judgmental, behavioural, and affective – each of which is of importance to the social-psychological study of attribution. Each of these consequences is important in its own right, and I do not wish to argue for the primacy of behaviour, over cognition or affect. For those who do believe that behaviour is, ultimately, of most importance, it is worth reflecting on Kelman's (1958) analysis of social influence processes. Cognition, in the sense of 'internalization', can indicate a deep-seated change of views, and behaviour, in the sense of compliance, can be quite superficial.

Cognitive-judgemental consequences. Examples from three areas illustrate some of the consequences of causal attribution for cognitive information-processing and social judgement. The first area is *memory* for social information. A general question of interest here is the effect that making an attribution has on one's memory for the event that gave rise to the attribution. Wells (1982) concluded that memory was affected only if an unambiguous causal attribution was made (i.e., to the person or the situation). Interestingly, memories were not necessarily more accurate following an attribution, but, rather, included inferences based on the perceiver's attributions. Thus memory seemed to be 'reconstructed' using attributions. Research by Crocker et al. (1983)

also implicated the locus of attribution in relation to memory. Their first experiment examined recall for a target item as a function of whether the item was congruent or incongruent with an initial impression, and whether the item was attributed to a personal or situational cause. The incongruent target item was most likely to be recalled only in the person attribution condition. In the situational attribution conditions, the target was equally likely to be recalled whether it was congruent or incongruent. Finally, Hastie (1984) has also supported the general hypothesis that causal reasoning (instigated by the occurrence of an unexpected event) is at least one important determinant of the subsequent superior recall of that event (see also D. L. Hamilton, 1988).

Causal attributions also influence *belief perseverance*. Anderson et al., (1980) argued that attributions help to organize social information, but may become independent of the data on which they were originally based. They led subjects to believe that either a positive or a negative relationship existed between a trainee's preference for risky vs conservative choices, and his subsequent success as a firefighter. They then asked subjects to provide a one-page written explanation for this relationship. The results included a significant correlation between the presence or absence of general explanatory principles in subjects' explanations, and the degree of belief perseverance following debriefing. Kulik (1983) provided further, and more precise, data on how attributions lead to the perpetuation of social beliefs. He found that perception of the causal importance of situational factors was influenced by the degree to which an observed behaviour was consistent with prior beliefs about the actor. Behaviour that was consistent with prior conceptions was attributed to dispositional characteristics of the actor. Furthermore, situational factors that would in other cases be seen as compelling explanations were ignored in favour of dispositional factors as causes of expected behaviour. In contrast, inconsistent behaviour tended to be situationally attributed. Even settings normally considered to inhibit the observed behaviour were judged instead to be causal. Kulik pointed out that this confirmatory attributional tendency allowed the perceiver to dismiss the potential belief-altering implications of inconsistent or unexpected behaviour, and could thus impede change in negative beliefs about an outgroup (see chapter 6).

Attributions can also influence *judgements*, or decisions. That they do is clear from Carroll and Payne's (1976, 1977; Carroll et al., 1987) work on parole decisions, using both professionals and students. They argued that crimes attributed to internal and/or intentional (controllable) factors should lead to harsher evaluation and punishment than crimes attributed to external and/or unintentional (uncontrollable) causes. In addition, the estimated risk to society associated with a parole decision should depend on the stability of the perceived cause of the crime. A crime attributed to a stable cause should be associated with a high expectancy of future crime. According to Carroll and Payne's analysis, these three attributional dimensions (consistent with Weiner's, e.g., 1986, theory) affect the process of parole decisions in complex, but theory-consistent ways. The locus dimension (and to a lesser extent the controllability dimension) was related to evaluation (judgements of goodness-badness); the stability dimension was related to prediction (judgement of future acts); and both evaluation and prediction contributed to the parole decision.

Thus attributions have cognitive-judgmental consequences, although one should not rule out effects in the opposite direction. For example, memory can influence attribution (e.g., Moore et al., 1979), and the kinds of decision one (consistently) makes are likely to affect one's explanations.

Behavioural consequences. The hope that is held out for the behavioural consequences of attribution is clear from the increasing popularity of one therapeutic technique – 'attributional retraining' (Försterling, 1985, 1986, 1988). This technique has successfully related attribution to behaviour by inducing participants to alter their attributions for success and failure, and thereby to improve their performance. The aim of the technique, which owes much to Weiner's (1986) theory of attribution, is to make individuals more persistent in the face of failure, by changing their attributions of low ability to, for example, attributions of lack of effort (e.g., Dweck, 1975) or temporary external barriers (e.g., Wilson and Linville, 1985). Of more direct relevance to the present work is research on the behavioural consequences of attribution in social interaction (see Harvey and Weary, 1984). Two such studies by Yarkin, Harvey and Bloxom (1981) and Town and Harvey (1981) attempted to assess directly the role of causal attributions in mediating the relationship between information about, and social interaction with, another person. They also revealed the importance of the perceiver's 'cognitive set' concerning another person. Relatively positive sets about the other person (relating to mental health, or sexual orientation) were associated with positive attributions and approach behaviour; attribution was highly positively correlated with behaviour. These studies are, however, limited (as Harvey and Weary pointed out):

subjects interacted with an experimental accomplice, thus ruling out
the study of true interactions (i.e., how a person would respond to
certain patterns of attribution and/or behaviour).

The extensive literature on interpersonal expectancies and self-
fulfilling prophecies (e.g., Darley and Fazio, 1980; Jussim, 1986;
Miller and Turnbull, 1986; Snyder, 1984; see chapter 5) is obviously
important here. Snyder's work has been concerned with 'behavioural
confirmation', the idea that one's beliefs about another person might
influence social interaction in ways that cause the behaviour of that
person to confirm one's prior beliefs. Attributions seem to influence
whether such behavioural confirmation is internalized, and then
perseveres, beyond the boundaries of the specific context in which it
first occurred. Snyder and Swann (1978b) observed a series of dyadic
interactions. In the first interaction, one person (the 'perceiver') was
led to label the other (the 'target') as hostile or non-hostile. Acting
upon these beliefs, the perceiver treated the target as hostile or non-
hostile. The target then actually began to behave in a hostile (or non-
hostile) manner. In some conditions, the target was induced to regard
this behaviour as reflecting corresponding dispositions. When this was
the case, behavioural confirmation generalized, or persevered, beyond
the original interaction. In a second interaction, with a new partner, the
target behaved in a similarly hostile (or non-hostile) manner.

Such dynamic sequences of labelling-attribution-behaviour would
seem an essential characteristic of attributions in realistic, interpersonal situations. One could also hypothesize that, where perceivers
induce behavioural confirmation in other people, they themselves may
attribute the target's behaviour internally, and then generalize their
own behaviour towards other similar targets (e.g., members of the same
social category). These illustrations are no more than that; their aim is
simply to show that attributions can have interesting behavioural
consequences in social interaction. This topic will be examined in more
detail in chapter 5.

Affective consequences.   Interest has been growing in the affective
consequences of causal attributions, and the most important work
covers two topics: emotional reactions to success and failure, and
depression.

The major contribution in this area is Weiner's ambitious attributional theory of motivation and emotion, developed over a number of
years and with impressive empirical support (Weiner, 1979, 1982,
1983, 1985b, 1986). In his more recent writings, Weiner has argued
that how we ascribe causes can influence how we feel, but also that

some emotions can be elicited without intervening thought processes. At the same time, although he does not rule out the influence of emotional states on cognitive processes, Weiner sees the link from cognition to emotion as more typical. Considering five key emotions, anger, happiness, pity, pride and love (see Bottenberg, 1975; Davitz, 1969), Weiner (1986) argued that the first four could be accounted for from an attributional perspective.

Weiner has made an important distinction between two kinds of achievement-related affects: 'outcome-dependent' and 'attribution-linked' affects. Outcome-dependent affects refer to the very general, even 'primitive' emotions that are experienced following success and failure outcomes. These emotions include 'happy', following success and 'frustrated' or 'sad', following failure; they are labelled outcome-dependent because they depend on (non)attainment of a desired goal, not on causal attributions given for the outcome. Attribution-linked affects, in contrast, are influenced by the specific causal attribution for the outcome. Especially if an outcome is negative, unexpected or especially important, one makes causal attributions in order to make sense of it. According to Weiner, both causal attributions (e.g.. ability, effort) and their underlying causal properties (locus, stability, and controllability) generate more differentiated affects (e.g., 'surprise'). This view has recently been supported by Russell and McAuley (1986).

Weiner has also specified the roles of each of the three underlying dimensions for his general theory of motivation and emotion:

1   *Locus.* The main hypothesis is that success attributed internally (e.g., to personality, ability or effort) results in greater *self-esteem* (pride) than success attributed externally (e.g., to task ease, or good luck). It is also predicted that failure attributed internally will result in lower self-esteem than failure that is attributed externally (see Weiner et al., 1978, 1979). This relationship between locus and self-esteem is, of course, directly relevant to the self-serving bias. Yet, as Weiner (1986) has noted, researchers in that area have, surprisingly, seldom studied the putative link between attributions and feelings (Zuckerman's, 1979, review cites only two such studies: Nicholls, 1975; and Riemer, 1975; but see Pyszczynski and Greenberg, 1987).

2   *Stability.* The major importance of this dimension is in relation to (changes in) the *expectancy* of success and failure in the future (Weiner et al., 1976); although Weiner (1983) has suggested that stability may be linked to affective reactions such as 'hopelessness', when failure is attributed to internal and stable causes.

3   *Controllability*. This dimension relates to sentiment and evaluations of others. The main hypothesis is that if personal failure is due to causes perceived as controllable by others, then *anger* is elicited (see Averill, 1982, 1983). If negative outcomes for other people are due to causes perceived as uncontrollable, then *pity* is elicited.

On the basis of this research, Weiner has concluded confidently that 'some of the most common emotional experiences have activated structures of causality as their antecedents' (Weiner, 1986, p. 128). But the distinction between outcome-dependent and attribution-linked emotions remains tentative. McFarland and Ross (1982) led college students to believe that they had succeeded or failed on a test; their affective reactions were then factor analysed, yielding three factors – negative affect, positive affect and self-esteem. None of these affective reactions was independent of causal attributions (i.e., the emotions were attribution-linked); there was only rather weak evidence for outcome-dependent emotions from secondary analyses on each mood adjective separately. Overall, the results of available research suggest that, at least in achievement settings, affective consequences are determined primarily by attributions, although results do vary depending on factors such as the task and the subject population (see Russell and McAuley, 1986).

Perhaps the most serious affective consequence linked to causal attribution is clinical depression. In recent years there has been great interest in the study of depression from a social cognition perspective. Researchers have studied issues such as selective memories for negative information about the self (Derry and Kuiper, 1981) and the reliance of depressives on internal attributions for failure (Kuiper, 1978; Raps et al., 1982). The major focus of attributional research has been the reformulated learned helplessness model of depression (Abramson et al., 1978), which has already been referred to in the section on individual differences in attribution. Although, as noted above, there are problems in the measurement of attributional style, the reformulated learned helplessness model deserves closer attention.

The model states that the occurrence of uncontrollable negative events leads to depression via the expectancy that future outcomes are independent of one's responses; there is a 'noncontingency' between one's responses and desired outcomes. Abramson et al. proposed that it was people's understanding of the cause of current or past non-contingency that determined their expectations of future non-contingency and ultimately led to helplessness. They suggested that people who made internal, stable and global attributions for their negative outcomes, were *predisposed* to depression. Each of the three dimensions has been linked to particular kinds of consequences for the nature of helplessness. The more internal the cause, the lower the individual's self-esteem; the more stable the cause, the more chronic the helplessness deficits are expected to be; the more global the cause, the more the helplessness deficits are expected to generalize across situations.

Even if there are doubts about the consistency of a 'depressive' attributional style (Cutrona et al., 1985), and the theoretical basis of the globality dimension (Weiner, 1986), depression and causal attribution do appear to be related (see Robins, 1988). A recent meta-analysis of 104 studies by Sweeney et al. (1986) reported that, in particular, as attributions for negative outcomes became more internal, stable and global, depression increased; and the effect sizes were larger for psychiatric depressives than for two other groups (student-depressives and non-college-student-depressives). Yet the exact relationship between attribution and depression remains unclear. The reformulated learned helplessness model claims that a depressive attributional style predisposes individuals to depression, but this is by no means the only, or correct, direction of causality. Brewin (1985) has reviewed the available literature, using strict criteria for the relevance of studies. He compared five possible models ('symptom', 'onset', 'vulnerability', 'recovery' and 'coping'), each of which would be consistent with the finding of a simple positive correlation between attribution and depression. Brewin concluded cautiously in favour of the recovery and coping models. The recovery model predicts, simply, that once a person is depressed, attributions contribute to the chronicity of the condition. The more general coping model argues that an attributional style of internal, stable and global attributions for success (and the opposite for failure) encourages resistance to depression.

Attribution and depression do seem to be linked, but the status of the reformulated learned helplessness model is still contested (cf. Brown and Siegel, 1988; Coyne and Gotlib, 1983; Peterson and Seligman, 1984). Brewin's careful conclusions are the only ones justified at this juncture, but the area serves as a sober reminder of the importance and applicability of attributional ideas.

Summary

This selective review has highlighted three general functions (control, self-esteem and self-presentation) and consequences (cognitive-judgemental, behavioural and affective) of causal attribution. The selections made give some indication of the breadth and complexity of the area now infiltrated with attributional ideas. Although separate functions and consequences can be identified, it is also obvious that the interplay between them and other attributional phenomena is mutual. Thus mood may influence attribution but attributions also influence affect. If one takes a more flexible approach to social cognition (Showers and Cantor, 1985), attributions may also be chosen to maintain or alter a mood. In this way, for example, the self-esteem function, the affective consequences and self-serving bias are interrelated attributional phenomena. Finally, at the very least, the functions and consequences associated with attributions should serve to explain, and justify, why they have received the detailed research attention that they have.

CONCLUSION

This chapter has examined five fundamental questions concerning causal attribution. The breadth and depth of the field is now truly impressive. Thus, one can speak of it as 'still a highly fertile area of work' (Harvey and Weary, 1984, p. 453) or one of 'continued vitality' (Harvey and Harris, 1983). The extent of the field is partly due to what Jones has called the 'hospitality' of an attributional approach (1985a, p. 91), referring to the growing number of applications of attributional ideas, some of which were dealt with in the section on consequences. The breadth of research is also due to the fact, emphasized in this chapter, that attribution theory and research speak to some of the major questions in social psychology.

What is needed now is theoretical integration. At one level, this could take the form of an ambitious synthesis of existing attribution theories, a solution already eschewed earlier in this chapter. The remainder of this volume attempts a different kind of integration, bringing together attributional concepts under the four levels of analysis identified by Doise (1986) – intra-personal, interpersonal, intergroup and societal. This approach provides the challenge of exploring attribution theory in relation to four major fields of social psychology: social cognition, social interaction, intergroup relations and social representations. It also provides the opportunity to demonstrate that attribution theory is a truly social-psychological theory.

4   Intra-personal Attribution: Causal Logic, Cognitive Processes and Knowledge Structures

Attribution is part of our cognition of the environment. Whenever you cognize your environment you will find attribution occurring.

(Heider, 1976)

INTRODUCTION

This chapter looks at causal attribution from a cognitive or 'social cognition' viewpoint. Although the popularity of the cognitive approach to social psychology has grown in the last ten years, it can hardly be said to be new. Zajonc (1980) has argued that the vast majority of social psychological data are about *thoughts* – as judgements, beliefs, opinions, preferences, attitudes or attributions. As he pointed out, furthermore, cognition pervades social psychology at various levels – the level at which the problem is formulated, the level of methodology, and the level of theorizing (see also Markus and Zajonc, 1985). The influence of cognition at all three levels will certainly be clear in the following pages.[1]

This cognitive perspective notwithstanding, several authors have pointed out that the attribution literature has only recently confronted the issue of *process*, or processes (Hansen, 1985; Newcombe and Rutter, 1982a,b), although the terms have been used liberally. This belated development has been greatly influenced by the growth of interest in social cognition (e.g., Fiske and Taylor, 1984; Wyer and Srull, 1984). Yet there is more to a cognitive approach than simply the study of process, and one can usefully distinguish between the logic, process and content of causal attributions (Hansen, 1985), which topics form the three main divisions of this chapter. Causal *logic* refers to the concepts such as covariation and causal schemata that provide a rather formal approach to common-sense explanations. *Process* refers specifically to cognitive process and requires a more detailed analysis of how causal attributions are made. Causal *content* refers to the knowledge people use to answer causal questions; it is best understood by the term *knowledge structures* (Galambos et al., 1986), which, in this case, refers primarily to cognitive schemata of various types, especially event-schemata or 'scripts'.

I will review and evaluate the literature relevant to each topic and then assess its range of applicability. Taken together, this tripartite approach has considerably extended our knowledge of causal attribution; each component makes a unique, but limited, contribution to our understanding.

CAUSAL LOGIC

Covariation revisited

Kelley's (1967) covariation principle and his analysis of variance (ANOVA) model have already been introduced in chapter 2. This section re-opens the question of how attributions are made from multiple sources of information. The model of the layperson as scientist is first challenged, and then replaced with a model of the layperson as philosopher. Subsequently both models, however, must confront the reality of the layperson's shortcomings in actually perceiving covariation, a fact which suggests a quite different model of the layperson as hypothesis-tester.

The layperson as scientist. As noted in chapter 2, McArthur (1972) was the first to test Kelley's ANOVA model and report that consensus, distinctiveness and consistency influenced attribution in the way Kelley predicted. Person attribution was more frequent under low than under high consensus, under low than under high distinctiveness, and under high than under low consistency. Similarly, main effects for all three information variables were found on stimulus attribution. Stimulus attribution was more frequent with high than low consensus, high than low distinctiveness, and high than low consistency. Finally, on circumstance attribution, main effects for only two of the variables were reported. Circumstance attribution was greater under high than low distinctiveness information, and low than high consistency information. Despite the presence of interactions between the information variables, the attention of subsequent researchers has centred on McArthur's presentation of main effects and the percentage of variance in attributions accounted for by consensus, distinctiveness and consistency. In particular, consensus came to be seen as a relatively unimportant determinant of attribution.

The 'underutilization of consensus' quickly became established as a pervasive attributional bias and was linked to the so-called 'base-rate fallacy' in social judgement (Nisbett and Borgida, 1975; Kahneman and Tversky, 1973). This development at least led researchers to question how faithfully the layperson followed the scientific rules of the analysis of variance model. As it turned out, however, the appropriate question to ask was not *whether* consensus has an effect on attribution, but *under what conditions* (Ross and Fletcher, 1985). These conditions have now been delineated in two comprehensive papers that qualify any statements concerning a pervasive bias (Borgida and Brekke, 1981; Kassin, 1979). The conditions under which consensus has been used or sought include the following: when subjects are told that the sample on which consensus is based is a random sample (Wells and Harvey, 1977); when the social-group membership of the consensus sample is specified (Hewstone and Jaspars, 1983); when the information variables are presented in counterbalanced order (Ruble and Feldman, 1976); when social norms are not known (Hilton et al., 1988); and, perhaps most important, when expectancies are neutralized (see section below on causal schemata and covariation detection). One recent study that gave unexpected support to the role of consensus was that by Brewin and Furnham (1986). They reported that consensus was as strong a predictor of depression in undergraduate subjects as the number of distressing life events that subjects had experienced.

Although McArthur's (1972) study stimulated a great deal of further research (indeed, her study has now become a 'citation classic'), it also set the field back in understanding how perceivers might make attributions on the basis of covariation information.[2] The first goal of McArthur's study was to answer the question 'What causal attributions are facilitated by various combinations of consensus, distinctiveness and consistency information?' (p. 172). This goal suggested that she would follow Kelley in considering the three information variables together and her first predictions (derived from Kelley) did just that. Unfortunately, this analysis took second place to the main effects of the information variables on person, stimulus and circumstance attribution. These main effects then dominated subsequent research in such a way that some of the real insights of the ANOVA model were lost.

These insights are apparent only where predictions are tied to specific patterns of consensus, distinctiveness and consistency. Kelley, in both his first (1967) and later papers on attribution (1972a, 1973; Kelley and Michela, 1980), continued to discuss predictions from the ANOVA model at the level of *patterns* of consensus, distinctiveness and consistency. This approach is most clearly set out in a paper by Orvis et al., (1975). They considered the three configurations that McArthur found led to person (low consensus, low distinctiveness and high consistency), stimulus (high consensus, high distinctiveness and high consistency) and circumstance (low consensus, high distinctiveness and low consistency) attributions. Orvis et al. suggested that these patterns serve as prototypes or templates against which information is compared; each information variable would be considered in terms of the inferences it implied. It is obvious, however, that in some cases more than one cause is implied; for example, low consensus implies a person attribution, a circumstance attribution, or both. To circumvent this problem, Orvis et al. listed all inferences implied by each piece of information, and the attribution most frequently implied was then given as the predicted cause. If several causes were implied equally by the given information, then the combined attribution was predicted. For example, the combination of high consensus, low distinctiveness and high consistency would generate the following causal inferences: high consensus, stimulus; low distinctiveness, person; high consistency, stimulus and person. The result of this process is that stimulus and person are both implied twice and thus constitute the joint predicted cause.

The results of the Orvis et al. study are presented in table 1 in the format of the original article: for each information combination, the percentage of subjects making each of the seven possible attributions has been calculated. Orvis et al. presented the findings in columns of predicted and unpredicted results, on the basis of which they claimed that the findings 'conform quite well' (p. 612) to the predictions.[3] Nevertheless, a large percentage of responses fall in the unpredicted columns, a fact that raises obvious doubts about the model.

Orvis et al.'s model was also challenged by Smith and Miller (1979a), who replicated McArthur's (1972) study, and added response time measures to test the prediction that certain patterns of information would be easier to encode and process than others. If perceivers have stored only the three 'standard data patterns' (i.e., those for stimulus, person and circumstance attribution, respectively), then responses should be relatively fast to these patterns, but relatively slow to other patterns. In fact, Smith and Miller collapsed their data across information conditions, thus providing no fair test of the Orvis et al.

TABLE 1 Percentages of predicted and unpredicted attributions for eight information combinations

Information pattern			Study 1		Study 2	
Consensus	Distinctiveness	Consistency	Predicted	Unpredicted	Predicted	Unpredicted
High	High	High	s (69%)[a]		s (70%)	
High	High	Low	sc		sc	s (39%)
High	Low	High	ps (56%)		ps (31%)	p (43%), s (19%)
High	Low	Low	psc	c (48%)	psc	
Low	High	High	psc	p (35%), ps (18%), s (28%)	psc	s (31%)
Low	High	Low	c (54%)		c (54%)	
Low	Low	High	p (80%)		p (81%)	
Low	Low	Low	pc	c (37%)	pc	

[a] p = person, s = stimulus, c = circumstance. Attributions that were predicted but did not occur to a significant degree are listed in the predicted column without a percentage.

Source: based on table 2 in Orvis et al., 1975, © 1975 by the American Psychological Association, adapted by permission of the publisher and author.

model, but their data pointed to a quite different 'subtractive' model of attribution. They suggested that the perceiver might begin the task with a tentative three-component response and then engage in processing that leads to subtraction of components. Thus subjects took the shortest time to make the most 'complex' attribution ('person + stimulus + circumstance': 11.07 sec.) and the longest time for the 'simple' single-factor responses (e.g., *one* of 'person', 'stimulus' or 'circumstances': 13.71 sec.). Despite this innovative process analysis, doubts remain about Smith and Miller's conclusions. If patterns of information are linked to predicted attributions, then it makes no theoretical sense to collapse across conditions. In addition, the subtractive model might be an artefact of the method used. Subjects made their attribution by pressing response keys to stimuli presented on a screen. But they 'began each trial with three fingers of the preferred hand resting on the three keys' (Smith and Miller, 1979a, p. 1726). This starting position might possibly have led them to expect a three-key/three-component attribution, hence that response was fastest. In addition, as Hansen (1980) pointed out, the subtractive model relies on subjects' tendency to disconfirm, rather than confirm, their complex explanation for behaviour, a strategy that the problem-solving literature suggests is unlikely (e.g., Mynatt et al., 1977; Wason and Johnson-Laird, 1972).

The research considered so far has shown that experimental subjects *can* use consensus, distinctiveness and consistency information to make attributions, but by failing to specify the complete set of relations between the combinations of information and the possible causal attributions it has failed to do justice to Kelley's model. His model is analysed in more detail in more recent research.

The layperson as philosopher.   In opposition to the earlier analyses of the ANOVA model, a Logical Model has been developed (Hewstone and Jaspars, 1987; Jaspars, 1983; Jaspars et al., 1983b). This model is directly related to the original covariational definition of causality, yet does not require that the subject perform an intuitive ANOVA or its naive equivalent. Indeed, subjects are not presented with a complete data set necessary for such an analysis (Jaspars et al., 1983b; Pruitt and Insko, 1980). For example, subjects are not told whether the target behaviour occurs in the *joint* presence of other people and other stimuli. The Logical Model presents a method by which subjects may analyse covariation and identify the necessary and sufficient conditions for the occurrence of an effect. The model applies Mill's (1872/1973, book 3, chapter 3) method of difference (formalized by

Mackie, 1974) to persons, stimuli and circumstances by using consensus, distinctiveness and consistency as the relevant dimensions of generalization. The model also instantiates Mill's definition of a cause as the set of necessary and jointly sufficient conditions for the occurrence of an effect, thereby emphasizing combinations of necessary or sufficient conditions rather than single causal loci of persons, stimuli or circumstances.

The first step in the model is to suggest a way in which information, as presented in attributional vignettes, might be coded so that causal inferences can be derived from the encoded information. One can formalize the structure of a sentence such as 'John laughs at the comedian' in terms of B (behaviour), given a combination of s (stimulus/comedian), p (person/John) and c (circumstances/unspecified). The following three lines of the vignette are then coded for the presence and absence of the behaviour and of the circumstances, the person and the stimulus mentioned in the initial sentence.

Using this vignette coding, one can characterize each of the eight information combinations (see table 2). This coding can be easily understood when one considers that consistency, consensus and distinctiveness indicate whether the behaviour generalizes (B) or not ($\{B\}$) across other circumstances ($\{c\}$), persons ($\{p\}$) and stimuli ($\{s\}$), respectively (see Hewstone and Jaspars, 1987). Thus in the second row of table 2, $\{c\}$ denotes that the given circumstances are not present ('In the past ...'). Behaviour still generalizes (B) across circumstances under conditions of high consistency (columns 1, 2, 3 and 5) but not ($\{B\}$) under conditions of low consistency (columns 4, 6, 7 and 8). Similarly, $\{p\}$ in the third row indicates that the person is not present, with generalization across persons under conditions of high consensus (columns 1, 2, 4 and 6) but not under conditions of low consensus (columns 3, 5, 7 and 8). Finally, $\{s\}$ in the fourth row indicates that the stimulus is not present, with generalization across stimuli under conditions of low distinctiveness (columns 1, 3, 4 and 7) but not under conditions of high distinctiveness (columns 2, 5, 6 and 8). The Logical Model proposes that for each informational combination, the subject can ascertain whether the behaviour generalizes over circumstances, persons and stimuli. Thus the information contained in column 2 (for example, 'John laughs at the comedian; almost everyone laughs at the comedian (Cs); John does not laugh at almost any other comedian (D); in the past John has almost always laughed at the same comedian' (Cy)) indicates generalization over circumstances and persons but not stimuli (B, B, B, $\{B\}$).

The next stage of the model (see bottom part of table 2) is provided

TABLE 2 Logical Model of causal attribution

Informational combinations[a]

Vignette structure	1 Cs D̂ Cy	2 Cs D Cy	3 Ĉs D̂ Cy	4 Cs D̂ Cy	5 Ĉs D Cy	6 Cs D Ĉy	7 Ĉs D Ĉy	8 Ĉs D Ĉy
spc	B	B	B	B	B	B	B	B
sp(c)	B	B	B	{B}	B	B	{B}	{B}
s(p)c	B	B	{B}	B	{B}	B	{B}	{B}
[s]pc	B	{B}	B	B	{B}	{B}	B	{B}

Criteria of sufficiency and necessity

Causal locus	Su N	Su N	Su N	Su N	Su N	Su N	Su N	Su N
s	Su	[Su N]			N	N		N
p	Su		[Su N]		N		N	N
c	Su			[Su N]		N	N	N
sp	Su	Su	Su		[Su N]			N
sc	Su	Su		Su		[Su N]		N
pc	Su		Su	Su			[Su N]	N
spc	Su	Su	Su	Su	Su	Su	Su	[Su N]

Logical attribution								
	0	s	p	c	sp	sc	pc	spc

[a] B = behaviour, Cs = consensus, D = distinctiveness, Cy = consistency. Bars (e.g., Ĉs, D̂, Ĉy) denote low levels of information, curved brackets (e.g., {c}, {B}) indicate the absence of a factor; s = stimulus, p = person, c = circumstances; Su = sufficient condition, N = necessary condition; 0 = no prediction possible. A causal inference can be made in each case by establishing whether a particular condition (s, p, c, sp, etc.) is a sufficient and necessary [Su N] condition for the occurrence of the behaviour. If the behaviour occurs when a particular condition is present, the condition is a sufficient condition. If the behaviour does not occur when the condition is absent, the condition is coded as a necessary condition. If the behaviour occurs if and only if the condition is present, then the condition is both a necessary and sufficient condition for the behaviour to occur, and hence a causal attribution should be made to that causal locus. These conditions are indicated in square brackets in the lower part of the table.
Source: adapted from Hewstone and Jaspars, 1987, table 3, © 1987 by the American Psychological Association, reprinted by permission of the publisher and author.

by a fairly literal interpretation of the notion of causality suggested by Kelley as the basis for the attribution process. The subject considers for each of the causal loci (stimulus, person, circumstances and their possible combinations) whether it is present when the effect (behaviour) is present and absent when the effect is absent in the vignettes. In this way the subject might establish which condition is necessary and sufficient for the behaviour to occur. If the behaviour occurs when a particular condition is present, the condition is a sufficient condition. If the behaviour does not occur when the condition is absent, the condition is coded as a necessary condition. If the behaviour occurs if and only if the condition is present, then the condition is both a necessary and sufficient condition for the behaviour to occur, and hence a causal attribution should be made to that causal locus.

Table 2 presents the eight possible combinations of information for vignettes like those used by McArthur (1972) and the inferences that can be drawn according to the suggested Logical Model. For example, in column 2, the behaviour generalizes across circumstances (high consistency) and persons (high consensus) but not other stimuli (high distinctiveness). Working down the seven causal loci, one notes first that the stimulus is a sufficient condition for the occurrence of the effect: the behaviour occurs (B) when the stimulus is present (s) but not when it is absent ({s}). The high distinctiveness indicates that the stimulus is a necessary condition (see also columns 5, 6 and 8). In fact, because the behaviour occurs if and only if the stimulus is present, the stimulus is both a necessary and a sufficient condition for the behaviour to occur (there is laughter if and only if a certain comedian is present).

For the other causal loci in column 2, behaviour generalizes across both persons ('p') and circumstances ('c'), so they are neither sufficient nor necessary conditions. But the combinations of (a) stimulus and person and (b) stimulus and circumstances are sufficient conditions: the behaviour generalizes over circumstances when stimulus and person are present and over persons when stimulus and circumstance are present. But the behaviour does not generalize when only person and circumstance are present, so this causal locus is neither sufficient nor necessary. Finally and self-evidently, the stimulus/person/circumstance causal locus is sufficient. To summarize column 2: because only the stimulus (the comedian) is a necessary and sufficient condition for the behaviour (laughter), a causal attribution should be made to that causal locus. This prediction is indicated by the square brackets aligned with the stimulus in column 2.

The same rules of inference can be applied across the eight information combinations. Although in formal terms they may appear complex, they are in fact relatively simple for vignettes of the McArthur type, because the subject has only to verify which conditions are absent (i.e., {c}, {p}, {s}) when the behaviour is absent ({B}) in order to determine the cause of the behaviour. Thus in columns 2, 3 and 4, the stimulus, the person and the circumstances respectively are the single sufficient and necessary conditions. The subject's task is more complex in columns 5, 6, 7 and 8, where joint causes are implied, but the solution is still to link up the conditions that are absent when the behaviour is absent (e.g., stimulus/person for column 5). The reader can verify this reasoning by matching the symbol {B} in columns 2–8 with one or more of the symbols {c}, {p} and {s} on the left-hand side in the top half of table 2. Although all combined causes (with the exception of sp) were ignored by McArthur (1972), each one is the predicted causal locus for one information combination. This fact is made clear by arranging predicted attributions along the diagonal in table 2.

If the behaviour is indeed attributed to the condition that is present when the behaviour is present and absent when the behaviour is absent, the Logical Model makes unique predictions for each of the eight combinations of consensus, distinctiveness and consistency (if we take into account all possible interactions of stimulus, person and circumstances and allow for a no-response category). The no-response category is required for column 1, where the combination of high consensus, low distinctiveness and high consistency leads to the inference that each and every condition is sufficient for the occurrence of the effect (this is an interesting case to which I will return).

Although no one has actually suggested that common-sense causal attribution resembles in detail a mental calculus analogous to ANOVA or that lay people follow exactly the rational guidelines explicit in philosophical analyses of causality, the very use of such models demands adequate and accurate formalizations and tests. The Logical Model, based on the notion of causes as necessary and sufficient conditions, has refocused attribution theory on the concept of causality and demonstrated that subjects' attributions are often made to the causal locus that constitutes a necessary and sufficient condition for the occurrence of an effect. As noted above, this conception of causes as necessary and sufficient conditions is exactly what Mill had in mind and is also true to the original idea of Kelley's (1967) attribution theory.

The Logical Model thus makes theoretical, methodological and empirical advances over earlier interpretations of the ANOVA model when tested in detail against published data (Hewstone and Jaspars, 1987). The problem with such a model is that it may prove to be artificial and impossibly complex as a model of common-sense attribution. Indeed, Jaspars and I noted that the Logical Model has shortcomings as a process model of the layperson's causal attribution. Although the predictions from the model were confirmed to a large extent in the re-analysis of three published studies (Hewstone and Jaspars, 1983; Jaspars, 1983; McArthur, 1972; see also Hilton and Jaspars, 1987), it was also clear that experimental subjects made many attributions to conditions that were not predicted by the model. Further analysis showed that subjects did not apply the method of difference in a perfect, content-free fashion and that their criteria for causality (necessary, sufficient or necessary and sufficient conditions) varied with the locus of attribution (stimulus, person or circumstances).

The shortcomings of the Logical Model, as well as its insights, provided the starting point for Hilton and Slugoski's (1986) 'Abnormal Conditions Focus' model of attribution. Hilton and Slugoski started from a different philosophical-logical view of causality (Hart and Honoré, 1959; Mackie, 1974), which specifies two criteria for causality. According to Hart and Honoré, we select as a cause the necessary condition that is *abnormal* when compared with the background of the target event. The *counterfactual* criterion determines whether a factor is necessary or not for a given effect ('would the effect have happened in the absence of the condition?'). The *contrastive* criterion selects from the set of necessary conditions (by contrasting what is normal and what is abnormal) whether a condition is 'sufficient in the circumstances'; in Hart and Honoré's example of the train derailment (see chapter 1), the faulty rail (and not the train's speed or its load) is the abnormal condition.

Hilton and Slugoski first compared a 'default' version of the Abnormal Conditions Focus model with the Logical Model.[4] It is termed a default model because subjects' real-world knowledge plays no part in defining what constitutes an informative contrast and hence an abnormal condition. In this respect the default version of the Abnormal Conditions Focus model is very similar to the Logical Model. The difference between the models lies in the hypothesized method of drawing attributional inferences. The Logical Model, as seen above, posits the operation of formal inference rules. In contrast, the Abnormal Conditions Focus model proposes that subjects treat consensus, distinctiveness and consistency information as contrast cases that define the abnormal conditions facilitating the production of the event. The abnormal conditions are then treated as the causes of the event. Specifically, Hilton and Slugoski suggested that *low consensus* information ('hardly anyone else does it') identifies the target *person* as abnormal; *high distinctiveness* information ('the target person does it to hardly anything else') identifies the *stimulus* as abnormal; and *low consistency* information ('the target event has hardly ever happened before') identifies the present *circumstances* as abnormal. Hilton and Slugoski illustrated the functions of consensus, distinctiveness and consistency using the much-loved case of the man who suffers indigestion after eating parsnips (cf. Hart and Honoré, 1959; Mackie, 1974), showing how the definition of the abnormal condition depends on the nature of the contrast case(s) chosen to compare the target event against. The man's doctor would contrast the man with other patients (thus focusing on 'something about the man' as the abnormal condition), but his wife would contrast the man's reaction to his reactions after eating other vegetables (thus focusing on 'something about the parsnips' as the abnormal condition):

> From a disinterested point of view, we may wish not only to contrast the man with other men (consensus information) but also the parsnips with other vegetables he eats (distinctiveness information). We might also wish to contrast the current occasion on which the man eats parsnips with previous occasions on which he has eaten parsnips (consistency information). Assuming that the man always gets indigestion when he eats parsnips, the following pattern of information emerges:
>
> The man suffers indigestion after eating parsnips.
>
> Hardly anyone else suffers indigestion after eating parsnips.
> The man suffers indigestion after eating hardly any other vegetable.
> In the past the man has almost always suffered indigestion after eating parsnips.
>
> Given that the target event is thus compared along dimensions of consensus, distinctiveness, and consistency information, the abnormal conditions focus model would predict attributions to both the person (the man) and the stimulus (the parsnips) because both, respectively, are abnormal conditions in the context of the consensus and distinctiveness information supplied. On the other hand, the consistency information indicates that there was nothing abnormal about the circumstances (present occasion) when the man ate parsnips, consequently leading to the relegation of the present occasion to the status of a mere condition. (Hilton and Slugoski, 1986, p. 77)

Note that the designated cause (person-stimulus) is exactly what the Logical Model would have predicted (given low consensus, high distinctiveness and high consistency), but the logic of the Abnormal Conditions Focus model is much 'friendlier'.

Hilton and Slugoski have pointed to various advantages of the Abnormal Conditions Focus model over the Logical Model. Their model explains some of the response biases that result in deviations from the Logical Model's predictions and it can make predictions for the problematic high consensus, low distinctiveness, high consistency configuration (where the Logical Model makes no prediction). The main advantage of the Abnormal Conditions Focus model is sufficiently persuasive in itself: its rules are simpler than those of the Logical Model (one looks for the 'condition that makes the difference', not necessary and sufficient conditions) and thus more convincing as a representation of common-sense reasoning. Hilton and Slugoski also went further, to argue that the contrastive criterion of causal attribution interacts with real-world knowledge about normal states of affairs. Thus causal conditions could be selected that would not be identified by the Logical Model, with its content-independent and purely logical rules of inference.

Now that I have looked in some detail at three models – the ANOVA, the Logical Model and the Abnormal Conditions Focus model – it is useful to put differences between them into perspective. Hilton and Jaspars (1987) showed that all three models predict the same response to four configurations of information (see table 3, columns 2, 3, 6 and 7); the Logical Model and the Abnormal Conditions Focus model both differ from the ANOVA model in predicting responses to three configurations (columns 4, 5 and 8); and, finally, the ANOVA and the Abnormal Conditions Focus model both differ from the Logical Model in one case (column 1). The data support the Logical Model (and by implication the default Abnormal Conditions Focus model) over the ANOVA (see Hewstone and Jaspars, 1987), but it is clearly difficult to discriminate between the models in terms of predictions. Heuristically, the Logical Model highlights the fact that attributions should be linked to patterns of information and raises the important distinction between sufficient and necessary conditions. The Abnormal Conditions Focus model is to be preferred, however, for its parsimony. The logic of abnormal conditions is intuitively much closer to common sense than the science of the analysis of variance. Yet, although the Abnormal Conditions Focus model makes sophisticated sense of attributions in response to configurations of information, it is by no means clear that the layperson can accurately perceive such information, or indeed whether such information is sought as part of the process of common-sense attribution. These questions are taken up in the following two sections.

TABLE 3 Comparison of the ANOVA, Logical Model and Abnormal Conditions Focus model

	Informational combinations[a]							
	1	2	3	4	5	6	7	8
Model	Cs D̂ Cy	Cs D Cy	Ĉs D̂ Cy	Cs D̂ Ĉy	Ĉs D̂ Ĉy	Cs D Ĉy	Ĉs D Ĉy	Ĉs D Ĉy
ANOVA	sp	s	p	spc	spc	sc	pc	c
Logical Model	0	s	p	c	sp	sc	pc	spc
Abnormal Conditions Focus model	sp	s	p	c	sp	sc	pc	spc

[a] Predictions for the ANOVA model are based on Orvis et al., 1975. Cs = consensus, D = distinctiveness, Cy = consistency, s = stimulus, p = person, c = circumstances, 0 = no prediction possible.

Covariation detection: the layperson's shortcomings

There is no assumption as critical to contemporary attribution theory (or to any theory that assumes the layperson's general adequacy as an intuitive scientist) as the assumption that people can detect covariation among events, estimate its magnitude from some satisfactory metric, and draw appropriate inferences based on such estimates. (Nisbett and Ross, 1980, p. 10)

Given the importance of this assumption, the value of Kelley's covariation theory is, to some extent at least, dependent on the available evidence concerning the detection of covariation. Crocker (1981) has subdivided the task of covariation assessment into five separate steps of the normative or statistically appropriate model of how covariation judgements ought to be made:

1 Deciding how much and what kinds of data to collect.
2 Sampling cases.
3 Classifying instances as to the type of evidence (confirming or disconfirming cases).
4 Recalling the collected data and estimating the frequencies of each type of evidence.
5 Combining the evidence to make a judgement.

The research evidence suggests that the social perceiver is prone to bias on most of these steps (see also Alloy and Tabachnik, 1984; Nisbett and Ross, 1980) and that the most important factor influencing inaccuracy in covariation estimates is whether or not the perceiver has a theory or prior expectation about the relationship between the two covarying events (other key factors are the form in which the stimulus information is presented and the actual magnitude of the correlation present in the stimulus information; see Trolier and Hamilton, 1986). This question of the interplay between theory and data is best dealt with in relation to causal schemata (see below). What should be emphasized here is that most of the studies showing normatively correct causal inferences have used impoverished stimulus materials. The experimental subject has not been required to go through all the steps specified by Crocker, so that such research tends to inflate our judgements of the layperson's abilities (cf. Cordray and Shaw, 1978). As Fischhoff noted, one wonders whether the highly structured stimulus-and-response formats used in such research were 'not enough to get people on the road to reasonable inference' (1976, p. 436). For this reason it is instructive to turn to studies that relied less exclusively on structured, forced-choice response formats and to see what picture of the common-sense attributor emerges from them.

Covariation detection or hypothesis-testing? Lalljee (1981) has challenged Kelley's model of the naive scientist, not only because philosophers allow for concepts of causality other than that of covariation, but also because Kelley's scientist is only an inductivist: 'He approaches data with no theories, but counts instances of events in particular classes under different conditions and arrives at his conclusions from there' (1981, pp. 123–4). This criticism is, of course, unfair to the extent that Kelley's causal schemata function as theories, but Lalljee was nonetheless right to question whether consensus, distinctiveness and consistency work in the sense that Kelley proposed. Thus Lalljee suggested that although consistency and consensus information, for example, may influence attributions, they do not necessarily do so *because* they allow the perceiver to sort out questions of causality. To use one of his examples, an older person might explain the bizarre dress of a young person by saying, 'They all dress like that.' This statement may mean simply that the youngster in question is not atypical and therefore that his or her behaviour requires no explanation. It does not necessarily mean that the perceiver has used (high) consensus information, as Kelley proposed, to assess covariation of cause and effect. Lalljee also criticized the notion of consistency, arguing that this type of information could not be assessed purely by counting instances. What counts as 'doing something often' depends very much on the nature of the activity (in Lalljee's example, getting a divorce vs going for a walk).

Lalljee went on to argue that a possible alternative to Kelley's lay inductivist was provided by the notion that scientists are hypothesis-testers, rather than inductivists. This proposal led to the suggestion that the layperson too could be considered as a hypothesis-tester, confronting events with a set of plausible hypotheses and then attempting to choose between them. The questions then arise: do attributors seek out consensus, distinctiveness and consistency in order to make an attribution; or does such information itself guide the search for further information? Only a small number of studies have followed up these questions in relation to the covariation model, but their results are informative.[5]

Garland et al. (1975) examined the effects of person vs stimulus attribution on requests for consensus, distinctiveness and consistency information. They reported that requests for all three types of information were instigated by both types of attribution, but that only a small percentage (23 per cent) of all requests for information could be assigned to these three categories. Of these requests, most were made for distinctiveness (13 per cent), followed by consensus (7 per cent), then consistency (3 per cent). Major (1980) used a less stringent test. She presented subjects only with pre-attribution information relevant to Kelley's three types of information and allowed them to select information sequentially from an array in any order and then to stop collecting information when they wished. She reported that subjects acquired surprisingly little information before making an attribution and that early in the process most subjects sought consistency information, rather than consensus. The information-search process varied across the type of problem facing the perceiver, but consensus was generally acquired less frequently than, and subsequent to, consistency or distinctiveness. This order of information search is different from Garland et al.'s, but the methodology of the two studies was quite different.

Consistent with Major's finding that information search was restrained, Hansen (1980) suggested that perceivers bring to a 'causal quandary' naive causal hypotheses that serve as simplifying heuristics in the search for information on which to base an attribution. He presented evidence to support the theoretical position that information search followed a principle of 'cognitive economy'. Rather than search for information allowing for the disconfirmation of alternative explanations, perceivers seek information confirming their naive hypotheses. For example, subjects holding a hypothesis that behaviour was accounted for by a facilitative force within the actor (stimulus) sought to confirm the existence of such a force by gathering distinctiveness (consensus) information. In addition, perceivers were more confident when using information to make confirming rather than disconfirming inferences about causal forces. As Hansen put it, commonsense attributors are not 'lay Popperians' (cf. Popper, 1959).

The existence of a confirmatory bias in cognitive and social hypothesis-testing has been a topic of debate in social cognition. Although Snyder and Swann (1978a) claimed that there was a confirmatory bias in testing hypotheses about other persons (e.g., whether an extravert *was* extraverted), and certainly identified systematic patterns of information-seeking, it is not clear that they represent a confirmatory bias, as opposed to a preference for hypothesis-matching questions (see Hastie, 1983; Higgins and Bargh, 1987). At least as important is the tendency identified by Shaklee and Fischhoff (1982) for people to ascertain and clarify the role of one cause for an event without considering other possible causes. In general, however, there is support in the attribution literature for simplified patterns of information search. Hansen has pointed out that the cognitive economy of confirmatory bias is made explicit in formal information-processing models (e.g., Trabasso et al., 1971), which argue that conceptual disconfirmations require additional processing operations beyond those required for verification.

Finally, Lalljee et al. (1984) have presented evidence linking the processes of explanation and information search. They provided subjects with brief descriptions of hypothetical events; half the subjects were asked to write a number of common explanations and half the subjects wrote a list of questions to which they would like to know the answers if they were going to explain the event. Explanations and requests for information were then categorized. Lalljee et al. reported a strong correlation between the number of explanations and the number of questions falling into each category. As in Garland et al.'s (1975) research, requests for consensus, distinctiveness or consistency information were generally low (Studies 1 and 2) and such information was ranked less important than other questions (Study 3). Once again this research questioned the importance of consensus, distinctiveness and consistency information, and the variation in information search across different events suggests a role for the perceiver's background theories when events are explained. This point is returned to below, under the heading of knowledge structures.

Thus the few available studies of information acquisition in relation to causal attribution further question the causal logic implied by the model of attribution-by-covariation. I turn now to Kelley's causal schemata, a more simplified approach to the logic of common-sense attribution.

Causal schemata revisited

[T]he mature individual undoubtedly has acquired a repertoire of abstract ideas about the operation and interaction of causal factors. These conceptions afford him [or her] a solution to the need for economical and fast attributional analysis, by providing a framework within which bits and pieces of relevant information can be fitted in order to draw reasonably good causal inferences. (Kelley, 1972a, p. 152)

Kelley called these conceptions causal schemata. Although they represent a step in a less logical and more social direction, they are still highly abstract, content-free notions of the formal relations among causes and effects. Indeed, Kelley referred to them as assumed patterns of data within the complete analysis-of-variance framework and suggested that they provided people with very abstract notions of sufficiency and necessity in causal relations. These schemata and some related critical issues have been introduced in chapter 2. This section focuses on whether causal schemata influence the perception of covariation and whether the notion of content-free schemata is a realistic basis for common-sense attribution.

Causal schemata and covariation detection. Kelley himself posed the question, 'How do a priori causal beliefs affect the intake and processing of further information bearing on the attributional problem?' (1973, p. 119). This question has since been tackled by several researchers, who have arrived at somewhat different answers.

Nisbett and Ross (1980) emphasized that a priori theories or expectations could override observed patterns of covariation. They referred, for example, to Chapman and Chapman's (1969) work on illusory correlations and concluded that reported covariation reflected true covariation far *less* than it reflected theories or preconceptions of what associations 'ought' to exist. They noted that unexpected, true covariations *can* be detected, but that they tend to be underestimated and to be noticed only when the covariation is very strong (see also Crocker, 1981).

Alloy and Tabachnik (1984) contended that Nisbett and Ross had overstated their case for theories and that, in fact, assessment of covariation was influenced jointly by expectations *and* data. Alloy and Tabachnik suggested that people presented with a conflict between generalized beliefs and situational information generally make covariation assessments that are biased in the direction of their initial expectations. Belief-contradictory evidence can, however, 'pull' covariation assessment in the direction of current situational information, if it is sufficiently strong and salient. Thus the relative strength of the two sources of information determines the directional tendency and accuracy of perceived covariation.

With special reference to the use of covariation information in causal attribution, Alloy and Tabachnik noted that McArthur's (1972) study and its successors contrasted relatively strong situational information (consensus, distinctiveness and consistency) with presumably weak prior expectations. A fairer test of covariation vs configuration would allow for some influence of the perceiver's own beliefs. In the case of consensus information, Kassin (1979) has drawn a useful distinction between implicit and explicit consensus. *Implicit* consensus refers to beliefs about what others *would do* if they were present; *explicit* consensus refers to information concerning how a given sample of others *actually do* behave. Research has shown that people do sometimes have their own implicit consensus, based on their own behaviour (e.g., the 'false consensus effect': Ross et al., 1977b), characteristics of the target actor (e.g., 'target- and category-based expectancies': Jones and McGillis, 1976), or the situation (Lay et al., 1973). These expectancies can provide an initial basis for attributions and thus 'contaminate' manipulations of explicit consensus. This consideration suggested the need for a distinction between the two types of consensus, because Kassin (1979) maintained that where explicit consensus was discrepant with the perceiver's prior knowledge, or redundant with respect to it, then it would tend not to be used. In fact, McArthur's paradigm, with its impoverished information and syllogistic form, seems to direct subjects to the logical relations between information and possible causes so that they give little weight to implicit consensus even when it is introduced, and then only when explicit consensus is absent (Hewstone and Jaspars, 1988; but see Hilton and Knibbs, 1988).

In concluding, Alloy and Tabachnik (1984) disagreed with Nisbett and Ross's (1980) claims concerning the power of pre-existing theories. They reported that true-event covariation exerts an important influence on covariation judgements in the absence *or* presence of theories. They did, however, conclude that:

> Apparently, the causal attribution process is neither purely data based nor purely expectation based. Instead, the research and theory on people's use of covariation information in causal attribution indicates that there is an interaction between data and expectations with preconceptions serving to bias or distort presumably more rational or data based processing. (Alloy and Tabachnik, 1984, p. 119)

At the very least, then, the scientific model of attribution-by-covariation seems unrealistic for common-sense explanations involving any social content, unless they are given in the context of highly artificial experimental paradigms. This research underlines the importance of 'a priori causal beliefs' but says little about the nature of causal schemata. Are they really to be understood as abstract, content-free conceptions of cause-and-effect relations?

Causal schemata: the importance of content. According to Kelley (1972a), a schema provides a framework within which the perceiver can perform certain operations and their inverses. He called these operations the *implications* of the schemata, as when a perceiver draws an inference regarding cause A from information about the effect and cause B. Reeder and Brewer (1979) have developed this idea, using the term *implicational schema* to refer to a perceiver's prior conceptions about the categories of behaviour that are believed likely to occur given varying levels of a disposition. Strictly speaking, they presented a model of dispositional, not causal, attribution, but they made an important contribution by questioning the view that schemata were content-free. Indeed they started from the premise that the rules of inference for dispositional attribution may vary depending on the nature of the attribute to be inferred. They outlined three main types of 'implicational schemata', which refer to the perceiver's prior assumptions about the range of behaviour believed likely to occur, given different levels of a disposition (e.g., very friendly, quite friendly, very unfriendly).

The 'partially restrictive schema' conveys the idea that persons with an extreme disposition at one end of a trait dimension are not expected to behave in ways typical of the opposite end of the dimension. For example, if we are given information about someone's extremely friendly behaviour, then if this trait follows the partially restrictive schema, that same individual would not be expected to manifest extremely unfriendly behaviour. Moderate behaviours, in contrast, are less informative about the actor's disposition, because people with a variety of dispositional states might behave in this manner.

The 'hierarchically restrictive schema', in contrast, suggests that the range of behaviour at the upper extreme of a dimension is not restricted, but at the lower extreme it is. According to Reeder and Brewer, this schema is exemplified by dispositional attributions involving skill or ability. Very able people may experience a range of outcomes, depending on motivation and task demands, but people at lower ability levels are not expected to perform at a level above that of their aptitude. For example, information concerning a 'clever' person's failure does not disconfirm the attribution of ability ('even clever people fail sometimes'), but at the same time a 'stupid' person is not expected to succeed.

The third type of schema, the 'fully restrictive schema', implies a fairly inflexible link between dispositional level and range of possible behaviour. It refers to traits on which some persons are judged to have stable levels, but others are not. Reeder and Brewer suggested that dispositions such as preferences, values and personal styles may be conceived in terms of this schema. Thus, for example, 'neat' people are expected to be invariably tidy.

Reeder and Brewer put forward these implicational schemata to explain inconsistencies in the attributional literature, but they also reported evidence that dimensions such as extraversion-introversion, intelligent-unintelligent and skilful-unskilful operate in this manner (Messick and Reeder, 1974; Reeder and Fulks, 1980; Reeder et al.,

1977). Their findings caution against any view of general inference rules that apply across all content domains.

The same conclusion emerges from a scattered series of studies on the importance of linguistic content for causal attributions (see Fiedler and Semin, 1988; Hewstone, 1983c). These studies show that the language used to describe events frequently contains *implicit* attributions (Kanouse, 1972). This point was made by McArthur (1972), who reported that 'accomplishments' and 'actions' were attributed primarily to the person, and that 'opinions' and 'emotions' were attributed to the stimulus. These results are, however, subject to two qualifications. First, it is instructive to compare the percentage of variance in causal attributions accounted for by verb category in the control (45 per cent) and experimental (1 per cent) conditions (control subjects received only a simple statement – no consensus, distinctiveness and consistency information). Thus micro-linguistic effects may be due to highly impoverished stimulus materials. Second, such effects may reflect different patterns of attribution for the *event* described, rather than the verb itself (see Gilovich and Regan, 1986).

More recently, and more persuasively, Brown and Fish (1983) have proposed that a theory of psychological causality is implicit in natural language itself. They were interested in phrases such as 'Ted helps Paul' and 'Ted likes Paul' and whether subjects assigned greater causal weight to the subject of the sentence (Ted) or to the object (Paul). All of the verbs they used in their research (about 60) formed the basis for *derived adjectives* – help-helpful, like-likable, and so on. Thus a minimal answer to the questions of why 'Ted helps Paul' or why 'Ted likes Paul' is provided by their respective derived adjectives: because Ted is *helpful* and because Paul is *likable*. These two adjectives, in fact, illustrate an important difference between two types of adjective; *helpful* is attributive to Ted, the sentence subject, whereas *likable* is attributive to Paul, the sentence object. This fact suggests already a different implicit causal attribution in each case, for which Brown and Fish presented detailed evidence. Brown and Fish argued that verbs such as 'help' activate an 'agent-patient schema' (if 'S helps O', S is the agent and O is the patient) whereas verbs such as 'like' activate a 'stimulus-experiencer schema' (if 'S likes O', O is the stimulus and S is the experiencer). The agent in the former schema and the stimulus in the latter schema are regularly perceived as the causal origins of behaviour.

It is difficult to do justice to Brown and Fish's complex article in any summary, but its essence is captured in their own statement that 'adult native speakers of English think of causality in such inter-personal interactions as unequally apportioned between the interactants' (p. 270). Of course, their research is subject to the same qualifications as McArthur's – if subjects are presented with only a tiny amount of linguistic material, then linguistic factors are likely to assume prominence. Yet the generality of their basic findings across a large number of verbs, and in studies using various methods, is impressive (see Fiedler, 1978; Fiedler and Semin, 1988; Garvey and Caramazza, 1974; Van Kleeck et al., 1988; cf. Au, 1986). Several competing theoretical explanations for the implicit causality phenomenon have been reviewed by Fiedler and Semin (1988), who themselves have shown that interpersonal verbs that lead to opposite causal attributions are characterized by systematic differences in the behavioural context they imply (i.e., inferences about antecedent conditions and consequences of behaviour). As Fiedler and Semin point out, competent language users are normally unaware of the implicit knowledge conveyed by their choice of different verbs, but this fact may provide the basis for interpersonal misunderstandings and conflicts (see chapter 5).

The causality implicit in language is hard to deny. More generally, both the impact of causal schemata on perceived covariation and the evidence that *content* does have an impact on causal inference suggests that there is a need for a more content-oriented approach to schemata in studies of causal attribution. Given the reliance of many attribution studies on pencil-and-paper linguistic materials, the attention now being paid to linguistic factors is long overdue.

Summary

The research reviewed in this first part of the chapter has shown that, at best, subjects *can* use consensus, distinctiveness and consistency information to infer causality under conditions that provide them with the covariation information and little else, and that encourage them to behave quasi-logically. How subjects might process this information is now better understood, thanks to more sophisticated models of how specific causal inferences are related to specific patterns of information. These advances notwithstanding, research on covariation detection and information search raise grave doubts about whether common-sense attribution normally proceeds in any such fashion outside the laboratory. These doubts about the centrality of covariation are further reinforced by evidence that data-based covariation perception interacts with expectations. Finally, the treatment of such expectations as abstract relations between cause and effect, invariant across content domains, can be criticized. These different strands of research, although heavily influenced by Kelley's contributions to attribution theory, suggest two new directions, inspired by Nisbett and Ross's (1980) work on the intuitive scientist. The first is a more detailed analysis of the cognitive processes and 'judgemental heuristics' involved in less sophisticated modes of causal attribution. The second is a more detailed study of the 'knowledge structures' that are used in common-sense attribution. These two directions are followed up in the two following parts of this chapter.

COGNITIVE PROCESSES

As the first part of this chapter has shown, Kelley's naive scientist model of the layperson treated people *as if* they were fairly rational in their search for the causes of behaviour. Fiske and Taylor (1984) pointed out that this was a deliberate theoretical strategy designed to push a rational view of people as far as possible, in order to discover shortcomings in the common-sense attribution process. As Taylor (1981, 1982; Fiske and Taylor, 1984) has pointed out, however, the demonstrable inadequacy of the naive scientist model led to its replacement by a new metatheory driving the social cognition approach – the person as 'cognitive miser'. This new approach was intended to be more descriptive of what perceivers actually do, rather than prescriptive of what they should do. Its central idea is that people are seen as capacity-limited information-processors, who can deal with only a small amount of information at any time. Given these limitations, people use short cuts and adopt strategies to simplify complex problems of judgement, decision and attribution. These short cuts and strategies, generally referred to as *heuristics* (Tversky and Kahneman, 1974), produce quick and quite adequate solutions, rather than slow, normatively correct solutions. In short, people 'satisfice' (March and Simon, 1958) rather than optimize in their information-processing.

This part of the chapter follows the attempt to push attribution theory in a more cognitive direction, drawing on theory and methods from cognitive psychology. As Hansen (1985) has noted, in the light of social cognition research, issues such as the relative importance of consensus, distinctiveness and consistency seem superficial and esoteric, a question of more relevance to formal problem-solving. If there is to be a useful intra-personal approach to attribution, then it needs to focus on causal information-processing and to adopt a model of attribution that is compatible with existing theory in the field of social cognition.

Judgemental heuristics

Fischhoff (1976) was the first to refer to the rich (then possible) marriage between attribution theory (which deals with how people explain events) and 'judgement under uncertainty' (which deals with predictive inferences about unknown events). Fischhoff explicitly contrasted Kelley's intuitive scientist model of the lay attributor with Slovic and Lichtenstein's (1971) *doubts* as to whether people are intuitive statisticians. Full credit must be given to L. Ross (1977) and Nisbett and Ross (1980), however, for drawing the attention of social psychologists to the rich vein of research by Kahneman and Tversky (1972, 1973; Tversky and Kahneman, 1971, 1973, 1974) and its implications for social psychology. This contribution centres on three heuristics governing intuitive prediction and judgement: representativeness, anchoring/adjustment and availability. I will deal with them in this order, to highlight the most prominent link between heuristic research and causal attribution: the impact of salient information on attributions via the availability heuristic.

Representativeness.   According to the representativeness heuristic, an object is assigned to one conceptual category rather than another by virtue of the extent to which its main features *represent* or *resemble* one category more than another. Nisbett and Ross (1980, chapter 6), identified two distinct ways in which the representativeness heuristic may be said to underlie causal analysis. First, people may look for causes whose features match those of the effect. This strategy has been termed the 'resemblance criterion' or the search for causes that resemble the effect. Second, people may possess a causal model for effects of the general type they are trying to explain, then apply a 'causal theory' to the case at hand: they look for a causal factor that resembles the general type of causal factor specified in the model.

Nisbett and Ross gave some vivid anecdotes and some *post hoc* accounts of previous work to illustrate the representativeness heuristic in causal attribution. In addition, there is evidence that both children and adults assume that the nature of a cause often bears some resemblance to the nature of its effects (Regan et al., 1974; Shultz and Ravinsky, 1977). This heuristic will lead to erroneous causal attributions to the extent that true causes fail to match effects. As Einhorn and Hogarth (1986) pointed out, Pasteur's germ theory of disease must have seemed, at first, incredible to anyone using a simplistic resemblance criterion.

Anchoring/Adjustment.   For many kinds of judgements, people have to begin with some starting value and adjust this value in the light of subsequent evidence, before making a final judgement. As Tversky and Kahneman (1974) noted, however, there is a general failure to make necessary *adjustments* to initial judgements, and human beings are rather 'conservative' in integrating, or even attempting to integrate, new information. Jones (1979) used this heuristic to account, *post hoc*, for the phenomenon of 'overattribution' or the fundamental attribution error. He suggested that perceivers started with a hypothesis that behaviour reflected a correspondent disposition and failed to correct sufficiently for other personal and situational explanations for behaviour.

Availability. The availability heuristic refers, generally, to the tendency to judge events as frequent, probable or causally efficacious to the extent that they are readily *available* in memory. This heuristic is fallible because memorial availability is determined by many other, sometimes quite arbitrary, factors. Availability was used by Nisbett and Ross (1980) to explain both the fundamental attribution error and actor-observer differences – actors are an easily available explanation, and perceptually close to the action. This heuristic has also provided the starting-point for a whole series of studies on the tendency to assign visually salient causal agents a more causal role than non-salient agents (see below).

   These judgemental heuristics have generated an enormous amount of research in cognitive and social psychology, and the layperson's use of such automatic, nonreflective short cuts, rather than complex models, makes good intuitive sense. With reference to causal attribution, however, the first two heuristics have typically been used as *post hoc* explanations, and the heuristic approach is not without problems. As both Hastie (1983) and Sherman and Corty (1984) have noted, it provides a general understanding of human judgement, but it is too vague and difficult to test rigorously. In particular, it is often not clear which of the heuristics may have been used, or under which conditions its use is predicted. Only the availability heuristic has really generated testable attributional hypotheses, and this work has been closely tied to the topic of salience.

Salience

An appealing alternative to the scientific processes of attribution outlined earlier is that perceivers may, on many occasions, seek a 'single, sufficient and salient' explanation for behaviour (Jones and Davis, 1965; Kanouse, 1972). This is a view that returns attribution research to its earliest days, when both Heider (1944) and Michotte (1946) demonstrated that the perception of causality was heavily influenced by salient stimuli.

Elements that are salient have been described as having a Gestalt-quality of 'figure against ground'. Salience has then been used synonymously with Tversky and Kahneman's (1974) use of 'availability', to suggest some factor that is literally prominent in the perceiver's field of view, or that is easily retrievable from memory. This section critically reviews some of the relevant research, both within and beyond the ANOVA framework, and then compares the theoretical positions put forward to explain why salient features may influence judgements of causality.

Using McArthur's (1972) experimental paradigm, Pryor and Kriss (1977) manipulated the relative positions of the object and the person in simple sentences (e.g., 'John likes the car' vs 'The car is liked by John') and then tested effects of this order on the availability of information in memory. They found that salient elements were more prominent in memory than non-salient elements, as indicated by their shorter response times for recall (Experiment 1), and that salient elements were perceived as more causal (Experiment 2). Pryor and Kriss proposed that the salience of an element affects its availability in memory, which in turn mediates the attributions made to that element. As the recall and attribution measures were made in separate experiments, however, this study could not establish availability as a mediating process.

Another study using the ANOVA framework was reported by Ferguson and Wells (1980). They manipulated the cognitive accessibility of consensus, distinctiveness and consistency and measured the response times for subsequent attributions. Accessibility was operationalized by priming: observers of a videotaped interview were required to recall information that was either directly related to consensus, distinctiveness and consistency or unrelated. Subjects primed with the attribution-related information responded almost three times faster than did subjects primed with the unrelated information, although subjects' attributions were not affected by the priming manipulation. Ferguson and Wells suggested that all subjects used consensus, distinctiveness and consistency information, so there was no effect on attributions; but that because consensus, distinctiveness and consistency were primed in the attribution-relevant condition, those subjects responded more quickly. These results support the general finding that salient elements tend to influence attribution or, at least, attributional processing time. This study also raises the terminological issue of 'accessibility' (Tulving and Pearlstone, 1966) vs 'availability' (Tversky and Kahneman, 1973). As Higgins and Bargh (1987) put it, knowledge *availability* refers to knowledge that is stored in memory and could be used, whereas knowledge *accessibility* refers to the readiness with which stored knowledge is used. They suggested that Tversky and Kahneman's use of availability was actually closer to accessibility, although the former term is now more widely used in this literature.

Attributional research on salience has certainly not been restricted to McArthur's paradigm. Taylor and Fiske (1978) have reviewed evidence for attributional salience effects from a range of less artificial contexts. They called salience-based attributions 'top of the head' phenomena, because (1) they have little thought behind them; (2) they are responses to the first thing that comes to the perceiver's mind; (3) the perceiver has spent little time on the judgement; and (4) the perceiver has gathered little or no information beyond the immediate situation. Taylor and Fiske's overall argument is that point-of-view or attention determines what information is salient and that perceptually salient information is then over-represented in subsequent causal explanations. For perceivers who observe an interaction between two others, it is the actor who engulfs the visual field who is rated as more causal (1975; cf. Jones and Nisbett, 1972).[6] For perceivers observing a small group interaction, a 'solo' person (black/white/male/female) in an otherwise homogeneous group (in ethnicity and gender) was salient and was also perceived as disproportionately causal in the group's performance (Taylor et al., 1978). The solo person's ethnicity or gender is the basis for his or her distinctiveness, and that attribute will be highly available as an explanation for the solo's behaviour.

It has been predicted from the salience literature that observers attribute cause to the situation to the extent that it is salient and to an actor's disposition when the actor is more salient. For example, in studies by McArthur and Post (1977) one stimulus person was highlighted by being seated in a bright light or in a rocking chair. In their studies 1–3, a salient actor was viewed less situationally than a non-salient actor. A novel person's behaviour, however, was viewed more situationally than a non-novel person's, a finding that is inconsistent with Taylor et al.'s (1978) solo minority effect. Taylor and Fiske (1978) therefore noted the need to consider the salience of the actor's background as well as the actor's behaviour. In general, causality may be attributed to dispositions when attention is focused upon an actor, and to situational factors when the situation is salient, but the different manipulations and different dependent measures used in this research caution against strong conclusions.

As with the other two heuristics, the evidence for the use of the availability heuristic in attribution research has often been inferential, rather than direct. As Taylor (1982) has pointed out, there are at least three reasons for this vagueness: (1) studies have generally not been designed to examine availability *per se*; (2) measures of availability have differed across studies, sometimes using the speed of information retrieval (e.g., Pryor and Kriss, 1977), sometimes using the volume of recalled information (e.g., Ross and Sicoly, 1979); (3) conceptual ambiguity surrounds the use of the term *availability*. More work is needed on how, if at all, the availability heuristic influences attribution; these shortcomings of research have been explicitly challenged in process models of attribution.

Process models

In the last ten years or so, social psychologists have used a variety of sophisticated ways to examine attributional processing, all of which are attempts to sidestep a major methodological problem – the fact that we can never tap directly what is going on in the heads of our research subjects (Taylor and Fiske, 1981). Borrowing from cognitive psychology, social psychologists have begun to use measures such as visual attention, information search, memory and response time, as I have noted already in this chapter. More ambitious still are attempts to use these different measures to build process models. A process model is, simply, the description of everything that goes on in the subject's head, from start to finish of an experimental task. It is a statement of the presumed stages through which information is processed, such as encoding, storage, retrieval, recall and attribution. The aim of process analysis is to provide methodological precision, to specify the stages in social information processing and at what stage a given effect occurs. Two process models of salience-based attribution are now illustrated.

Smith and Miller (1979b) investigated salience in the context of McArthur's (1972) paradigm, using the same sentence-order manipulation of salience as Pryor and Kriss (1977). They measured both attributions and recall under conditions of 'extensive', 'moderate' and 'little' thought. Contrary to their predictions, the amount of thought engaged in by the attributor did not diminish the effect of salience. Thus they concluded that salience effects were not just a matter of making attributions without thinking (i.e., 'top of the head' phenomena). Rather, they appeared to be related to such cognitive processes as the way the stimulus sentence is initially perceived and encoded. Some indication of the process of these attributions was provided by the fact that salience affected both the attribution and the recall results, and by the significant partial correlations between the proportions of sentences recalled 'object first' and attributed to the object (these correlations, computed to control for differences in salience, information and experimental conditions, were, however, very small).

A second experiment showed that the effect of salience on attribution was significantly stronger after a delay than before. These findings led the authors to suggest that attributions were made as information was stored in memory – that is, attributional processing and recall both operate from a single internal, encoded representation of the stimulus sentence to which the subject refers in answering the questions posed by the experimenter. From this view, attributional processing or cause-inferring is intrinsic to the comprehension of sentences and therefore goes on all the time (see Kintsch, 1974).

This account of salience has been challenged by Fiske et al. (1982), who argued that such 'evidence' for simultaneous encoding was indirect. In Smith and Miller's first study, as noted, there was only a tiny relationship between recall and attribution; in their second study, the obtained relationships were not only small, but in a direction opposite to their theoretical predictions. Fiske et al. concluded that such effects did not suggest an integral relationship between recall and attribution. Their own research pointed to a quite different process model.

They identified two links in the process from salience to attribution. First, salient stimuli should attract attention, a prediction for which they cited strong evidence (e.g., Fiske, 1980; Langer et al., 1976). Second, stimuli that attract attention should have a strong impact on attribution, via processes of differential encoding and recall. The link between recall and attribution, however, is equivocal; since total volume of recall does not always covary with differential attention, recall may not be a necessary mediator of attribution. Fiske et al. proposed that salience effects on attribution might be mediated specifically by *visual* recall as opposed to verbal recall; or, even more specifically, by visual recall of information judged by the perceiver to be causally relevant (or 'representative'). These hypotheses were tested by having subjects watch a videotape of two persons (one of whom was made salient by assigning subjects to watch him) and then complete a variety of attributional- and recall-dependent measures.

Using structural modelling techniques in their first experiment, Fiske et al. revealed only weak evidence for the recall mediation hypothesis. Although there was a significant causal path from attention to visual recall, the crucial mediating path from visual recall to attribution was not significant. Their second experiment required subjects to indicate the extent to which items they recalled contributed to their causality ratings (positively, negatively or not at all). Their structural model again showed some effects of attention on recall, but no significant mediated effects. The only significant effect on causal attribution was a direct path from attention. This model with mediating paths was, however, still superior to the model of only the unmediated path from attention to attribution, leading Fiske et al. to conclude that they had 'strong evidence for a mediated model of salience effects' (p. 121). This conclusion appears unwarranted from the data, which fail to demonstrate convincingly how salience effects on attribution are mediated by recall.

The weak results reported by Smith and Miller (1979b) and Fiske et al. (1982), in their attempts to relate recall and attribution, can be understood in terms of Hastie and Park's (1986) distinction between 'memory-based' and 'on-line' social judgements. They noted that empirical studies have revealed no simple relationship between memory and judgement (including studies of causal attribution). They argued that direct relationships between memory and judgement should only be predicted for memory-based tasks, in which the subject must rely on the retrieval of relatively concrete evidence from long-term memory in order to make a judgement. No such relationship should be predicted in the more common on-line tasks, in which a subject forms, and sometimes revises, the judgement as information is encountered.

As Hastie and Park pointed out, many conditions are likely to instigate perception-based, on-line judgements and subjects make on-line judgements when they believe that a judgement is likely to be required at a later point in time. Without knowing subjects' expectations in Smith and Miller's experiments, it is impossible to know whether they made causal attributions spontaneously or whether they generated them on-line because they anticipated causal questions. Given the weak relationships between recall and attribution, it is reasonable to assume that causality was judged on-line, that is at the encoding stage. That is not to say, however, that causal attributions are always made automatically, a question to which I return at the end of this chapter.

The very different models put forward by Smith and Miller and by

Fiske et al. lead one to wonder whether process models do purchase methodological precision. Admittedly, as Fiske et al. acknowledged, some differences may be due to the very different types of experiment. For written materials of the McArthur type, perhaps causality is inferred at encoding; for live conversation Fiske et al. doubted that people invariably encode causality as a requirement for comprehension in ongoing observations. Aside from these modality effects, support claimed for two such different models illustrates some of the dangers of cognitive (process) analysis (see Fiske and Taylor, 1984, chapter 10; Taylor and Fiske, 1981). First, it is possible to specify any number of process models at different levels for a single phenomenon, and the process model can change depending on relatively minor factors. For this reason, measures such as response times are best used to rule out alternative models rather than to support a particular model. Second, by definition the attempt to measure cognitive process interferes with normal thinking. Measures such as recall and response times may not be informative about normal, extra-laboratory information use. Third, and consequently, there may be a trade-off between precision of measurement and generalizability of results. As Taylor and Fiske noted, 'Many cognitive process measurement techniques are more precise and more precisely understood than the social processes one is trying to test' (1981, p. 508).

Summary

The research reviewed in this section contributes a valid and distinct approach to causal attribution. With its theoretical basis in judgemental heuristics and the new methodological thrust offered by process models, the topic of salience has been fascinating but perplexing. On the one hand, there is evidence for salience effects on attribution from a wide range of circumstances and stimuli (e.g., Arkin and Duval, 1975; Duval and Duval, 1983; Duval and Wicklund, 1973; Taylor and Fiske, 1978). Further evidence that such effects are both robust and generalizable comes from unsuccessful attempts to place boundary conditions on them using distraction, general arousal and interest in the event to be explained (see Taylor et al., 1979). On the other hand, such strong manipulations in relatively artificial experiments may simply not generalize to more realistic contexts of attribution. Overall, this area represents a detailed attempt to explore the cognitive process of attribution in a descriptive fashion, thus turning attention away from the scientific model of earlier research. Its findings, however, lack consistency and conviction as a general model of the attribution process.

KNOWLEDGE STRUCTURES

In a well-known phrase Bruner (1957a) referred to the tendency of social perceivers to 'go beyond the information given'. A central aspect of social perception, he noted, was that people assimilate what they observe to pre-existing cognitive structures. Such structures have been encountered already in this and previous chapters, in the form of Kelley's (1972a) causal schemata. Although Kelley conceived of causal schemata as abstract, formal and content-free structures, he was also aware of the need for a more knowledge-based approach, stating that 'social psychologists must deal with the particular substance and content of thought, and not just with its form' (1973, p. 119). This part of the chapter reviews attempts to deal with social knowledge, beginning with the general notion of cognitive, as opposed to specifically causal, schemata. The second section looks in more detail at the most promising attempts to develop a knowledge-structure approach to causal attribution that deals with concrete explanations about specific actions in specific domains.

Cognitive schemata

Although the term *schema* has a relatively long history in psychology (e.g., Bartlett, 1932; Head, 1920; Piaget, 1958; see Brewer and Nakamura, 1984; Graumann and Sommer, 1984, for reviews), it has only quite recently assumed prominence in social psychology (e.g., Hastie, 1981; Fiske and Taylor, 1984; Taylor and Crocker, 1981), where it is the cornerstone of social cognition:

> Our knowledge about the social world is represented in cognitive structures called schemas. A schema is an abstract or generic knowledge structure, stored in memory, that specifies the defining features and relevant attributes of some stimulus domain, and the interrelations among those attributes. (Crocker et al., 1984, p. 197)

By storing knowledge about people and situations in this general form, social perceivers can make sense of new information by connecting it with their prior knowledge. As Fiske and Taylor (1984) pointed out, the schema concept reflects a concern with 'top down', 'conceptually based' or 'theory-driven' cognitive processes, focusing on the way people's prior concepts and theories influence how they view and deal with new information. 'Bottom up' or 'data-driven' cognitive processes, in contrast, imply that the data themselves shape people's theories. Fiske and Taylor emphasized the influence of schemata on three types of social information-processing: *perception* of new information, *memory* for old information and *inference* that goes beyond both. Relatedly, Wyer (1981) drew attention to two important, general consequences of schematic processing of presented information:

1 Features of the original information that are not encoded in the terms of the particular schema applied to it may be overlooked.
2 Features that were not specified in the original information, but are contained in the schema used to encode it, may be 'filled in'.

The likelihood of a given schema being used, for example to interpret ambiguous information, increases with the number of times it has been used in the past. The likelihood decreases with the time interval between prior use of the schema and presentation of the new information to be integrated (Srull and Wyer, 1979; Wyer and Srull, 1981).

Although the present focus, and indeed the vast majority of research, has been on the cognitive aspects of schemata, they also appear to be linked to affect. Fiske (1982) has provided evidence that affect is stored with the schema and is cued by fitting an instance (e.g., some person or event) to a schema; this issue will, however, not be taken up here, not least because the concern with schemata in attribution research has been purely cognitive.

Although it is argued that all schemata work in the simplifying manner described, it is useful to distinguish between types of schema. The most useful taxonomy of five types of social schemata has been put forward by Fiske and Taylor (1984): person-, self-, role-, event- and content-free-schemata, or procedural-schemata (cf. Hastie, 1981, and Wyer, 1981, for rather different taxonomies). Only two of these types, however, have had a real impact on the attribution literature: content-free- or procedural-schemata (e.g., Kelley, 1972a), discussed already, and event-schemata. The latter are best outlined in the context of the knowledge-structure approach to attribution, in which they constitute perhaps the central theoretical construct.

Knowledge-based causal attribution

The knowledge-structure approach. Although the schema notion may have put attribution research on the road to a more content-specific approach to explanations, its conceptual clarity is acknowledged to be weak (Taylor and Crocker, 1981). The nascent knowledge-structure approach to attribution (e.g., Abelson and Lalljee, 1988; Lalljee and Abelson, 1983; Leddo and Abelson, 1986; Read, 1987) has not tried to formulate abstract principles applying to all types of schemata, but rather to put forward a content-oriented approach (after Schank and Abelson, 1977). These researchers focus on particular schematic forms, each with its own particular contents, rather than on general schemata.

The starting-point for such an approach is the recognition that people's explanations of human behaviour depend on detailed social and physical knowledge. This fact is immediately clear from some of the favourite examples used by the knowledge-structure researchers:

1 'Anne walks in the front door and is greeted by her husband Dave. "The doctor thinks the operation will be quite expensive", says Anne. "Oh well," replies Dave, "there's always Uncle Henry." Dave then reaches for the telephone book.' (Read, 1987, p. 288; after Schank and Abelson, 1977)

2 'The Jewish Defense League sent a package of matzos to the Russian Embassy on Passover.' (Leddo et al., 1984, p. 934)

3 'Willa was hungry. She took out the Michelin Guide.' (Schank and Abelson, 1977, p. 71)

To understand any of these examples, we have to make various inferences (e.g., that Anne and Dave don't have the money, that this lack leads them to the goal of finding another source of money, and that Uncle Henry does have money; or that Willa wished to eat at a restaurant and that she looked in the Michelin Guide to obtain its address or telephone number) and build on our world-knowledge (e.g., the political relations between the Jewish Defense League and the Soviet Union). These inferences, which essentially provide an explanation for each event, may and probably do occur spontaneously at the time of input and may become part of the overall cognitive representation of the event. These simple vignettes pose a problem, however, for the classic theories of attribution (e.g., Jones and Davis, 1965; Kelley, 1967), which do not provide a sufficient analysis of either the knowledge or the cognitive processes involved in making the necessary inferences (Read, 1987). It certainly seems implausible that experimental subjects would seek out consensus, distinctiveness and consistency information in any of the three examples above; according to Leddo et al. (1984), in explaining such events subjects do a 'meaning analysis', not a covariation analysis. They use concrete, 'natural' knowledge structures particular to the events in question and ascribe goals to the actors involved.

The knowledge-structure approach does not deny that covariation analysis may sometimes be used (see Hilton and Knibbs, 1988), but it prefers to draw an analogy between the process of explaining events and the process of understanding events. This perspective draws heavily on Schank and Abelson's (1977) work on the comprehension of text and has a clear advantage over the covariation analysis, which ends with an abstract cause (e.g., 'something about the person' [John] caused him to laugh at the comedian). The knowledge-structure approach, in contrast, suggests that people's explanations will be quite concrete (e.g., 'John loves slapstick humour'). Certainly, people's ordinary language explanations are quite concrete and rest uneasily in the person-situation dichotomy (e.g., Lalljee et al., 1982; see chapter 2). People also give concrete explanations more quickly than abstract ones (Druian and Omessi, 1982; Smith and Miller, 1983, see below).

The knowledge-structure approach represents a general approach to social cognition, not just to causal attribution (see Abelson and Black, 1986). The fundamental principle of the approach is that knowledge is 'organized in chunks or packages so that, given a little bit of appropriate situational context, the individual has available many likely inferences on what might happen next in a given situation' (Abelson and Black, 1986, p. 1). As Read (1987) has shown, an important aspect of this approach is its emphasis on sequences of behaviour (see also Read et al., in press). Single actions rarely have a clear meaning outside of sequences of behaviour, and action must be 'embedded' in a coherent 'causal scenario' that relates an action to other actions, thus revealing its meaning. Read proposed that understanding and explaining a sequence of behaviour requires people to establish: (1) how the individual actions form a plan; (2) what the goals of the sequence are; (3) how that particular plan could achieve the person's goals; and (4) what conditions initiated the goal. In order to reason in this way, we must make inferences about people's goals and how their actions fit into a plan for achieving those goals. All this reasoning is intimately tied to social knowledge, because 'making these inferences requires detailed knowledge about the nature of human goals, the plans necessary to achieve those goals, personal relationships, stereotypes, and the characteristics of physical objects and their role in human goals and plans' (Read, 1987, p. 289).

In the most detailed exposition to date of the knowledge-structure approach to attribution, Read followed Schank and Abelson (1977) and focused on four main kinds of knowledge structures: scripts, plans, goals and themes. I will deal here only with scripts, which have the most general relevance for causal attribution (plans and goals, for example, would seem relevant only to intentional behaviour). Scripts, or event-schemata, are more or less stereotyped sequences of actions carried out in order to attain a goal in some situation (see Fayol and Monteil, 1988, for a review). A script (e.g., the 'restaurant' script) provides information about such matters as the typical goals, actors, roles, objects, location and sequence of actions for performing a given action. Thus the script enables the perceiver to fill in gaps in what is explicitly stated. For example, if an actor is described as having reached a certain point in the script (e.g., being handed a menu by the waitress), then it will be assumed that the actor must have performed the actions preceding that point (e.g., entering the restaurant and getting seated; Leddo and Abelson, 1986). Read also referred to Mackie's (1974) claim that people look for differences-in-a-background when explaining events; a script is a normal background against which unexpected events can be explained and different types of situations are perceived as having different causal structures (C. A. Anderson, 1983, 1985).

Constructive vs contrastive explanation. The importance of scripts for attribution is clear from the distinction between constructive and contrastive explanations (Lalljee and Abelson, 1983). In *constructive* explanation, the perceiver must embed the given event in an appropriately selected or constructed schema. In simple cases, one merely refers to an appropriate script. For example, 'Why did John 'phone the restaurant?' Answer: 'To get a reservation.' Read (1987) has dealt in detail with the construction of causal scenarios, and he argued that the way in which a script is used in explanation depends on whether one wants to explain the performance of the whole script, or just part of it. Performance of the whole script can be explained simply by referring to the goal of the script, or to events that would initiate that goal. Explaining a behaviour that is only part of a script depends on the arrangement of script actions in a goal-subgoal hierarchy. Actions within the script can be explained by reference to the subsequent actions or goals they enable.

In *contrastive* explanation the perceiver must account for a deviation from what normally occurs (cf. Mackie's, 1974, contrastive criterion of what *would* have happened if things had been otherwise). The perceiver must explain why something did *not* happen. For example, asking 'Why did George stay seated during the playing of the national anthem?' is equivalent to asking 'Why didn't he stand up?' In this case knowledge of the script provides a set of plausible hypotheses that can be tested (see earlier discussion of hypothesis-testing vs covariation models of attribution). Lalljee and Abelson (1983) set out three steps by which people make contrastive explanations: (1) establish what the expected action was; (2) embed this action in a typical script or plan sequence (by constructive explanation) that would have led up to the action; (3) try to identify the most likely failure that would lead to the unexpected action.

Leddo and Abelson (1986) have recently provided some experimental data on contrastive explanation. They noted that it is difficult to explain the *nonoccurrence* of expected events, because such events involve failures which themselves can occur in a large number of ways. They focused on how people selected among plausible causes of script or plan failure and reported two main conclusions. First, script failure (e.g., not eating, once one has reached a restaurant) was not likely to be ascribed to failure at some previous point in the script sequence. Second, failure explanations referred to events high in both 'centrality' and 'standardness'. Centrality refers to the degree to which an event is rated important to performing a script; standardness refers to the rating of the relative frequency of occurrence of the event in repeated performances of the script. Leddo and Abelson (1986) illustrated these dimensions for the 'library' script: 'Bill went to the library to check out a book. He left without the book he wanted.' The following four explanations for this event were generated by crossing high and low levels of centrality and standardness:

1 'The book he wanted was not on the shelf' (high centrality, high standardness).
2 'There was no one to inspect the books when he left the library' (low centrality, low standardness).
3 'Bill didn't get the call numbers of the book he wanted' (high centrality, low standardness).
4 'Bill didn't have his library card at check-out time' (low centrality, high standardness).

The first of these explanations was preferred by subjects.

Although research in this area is relatively recent, the principles of constructive and contrastive explanation seem to provide a neat approach to a variety of events and, moreover, one that does not make overly complex cognitive demands on the layperson.

Conjunctive explanations. The knowledge-structure approach has also thrown some light on the question of 'how much' explanation different events require. Leddo et al. (1984) examined this question in the light of the fact that many human actions are understood to have multiple reasons that can supplement each other (see Wilensky, 1983). They proposed that explanations for intentional acts might be regarded as better, or at least more 'complete', to the extent that they cite multiple goals. Thus subjects might succumb to the 'conjunction fallacy' (Tversky and Kahneman, 1983), by erroneously rating a conjoint explanation more probable than one of its component explanations, when the former seemed more complete and plausible.

Leddo et al. reported a high percentage of just such conjunction effects (see also Locksley and Stangor, 1984; McClure et al., 1989). For example, subjects rated more probable the conjoint explanation 'John wanted to attend a prestigious college and Dartmouth offered a good course of study in John's major', than the single explanation 'John wanted to attend a prestigious college.' In a second experiment this finding was replicated for 'completed' actions, but not 'failed' actions. As Leddo et al. pointed out, one thing going wrong is often explanation enough for an interrupted course of events. Although Zuckerman et al. (1986) have claimed that these results reflect a methodological artefact, they are intuitively compelling. In common-sense explanation we are more influenced by the extent to which a set of schematic causes matches the circumstances of an event, than we are worried about violating normative statistical principles. As the title of Leddo et al.'s paper puts it, there are cases 'when two reasons are better than one'.

Summary

In a very useful overview of schema theories, Abelson and Black (1986) noted three major presuppositions on which schema theories are based: the importance of top-down processing, the content-specificity of schemata and the flexibility of function of schemata. Whereas the first two characteristics are shared by the general approach to cognitive schemata, the knowledge-structure approach is alone in emphasizing the flexibility of function of knowledge structures. Abelson and his colleagues (Abelson and Black, 1986; Leddo and Abelson, 1986) have argued that it is both cognitively inefficient and implausible that specialized structures and processes should exist just to explain events. It makes more sense to think of explanation as part of the general process of understanding. From this perspective, explanation should be based on, not divorced from, world-knowledge, the kind of knowledge that artificial intelligence researchers find lacking in computers, but necessary if they are to be programmed to understand stories or even to explain events (e.g., Dreyfus, 1979; Minsky, 1975; Schank and Abelson, 1977).

This knowledge-structure approach offers yet another model of the lay attributor – not a naive scientist, quasi-logician or cognitive miser, but a 'story understander' (Read, 1987). This approach may still appear cognitively top-heavy, but it should be emphasized that attributions are seen in the context of real-world knowledge, knowledge that determines not only how attributions are made, but when. Thus Read has distinguished between two kinds of causal reasoning, implicit and explicit. *Implicit* reasoning occurs when an event fits easily into an existing knowledge structure, such as a script. An explanation is ready-made and requires no detailed construction of a causal scenario. *Explicit* reasoning, in contrast, is an active process of explaining and is more likely under conditions such as disconfirmation of an expectancy or nonattainment of a goal (see chapter 3). The final part of this chapter now considers this distinction in more detail and in more general terms, to ask what has been learned about the nature of causal attribution from the perspectives reviewed so far.

CAUSAL ATTRIBUTION FROM A COGNITIVE PERSPECTIVE

Up to this point, this chapter has shown that very different processes have been studied in the cognitive approach to attribution. At one extreme are the time-consuming, logical analyses that are probably feasible only for the perceiver faced with an important problem and no time-pressure. At the other extreme are attributions based on rapid cognitive processing, such as the perceived salience of stimuli against a background. Perhaps somewhere in between lies the more recent knowledge-structure approach that allows for both rapid, 'scripted', and more contemplative, 'unscripted', explanations and that treats real-world knowledge as a resource for efficient causal reasoning. This final part of the chapter deals with two emerging questions. First, to what extent are causal attributions best viewed as 'automatic' vs 'controlled' processes? Second, what are the limitations of a strictly cognitive approach?

Automatic vs controlled causal attribution

It was suggested in chapter 3 that causal attributions were instigated when an expectancy was violated, when a goal was not attained or, simply, when an explanation was explicitly requested. Since some attribution researchers adopted a cognitive perspective, however, a more sophisticated approach to this issue has been offered.

In cognitive psychology, or the study of information-processing, a distinction has been made between 'automatic' and 'controlled' processes (Schneider and Shiffrin, 1977; Shiffrin and Schneider, 1977). Taylor and Fiske (1978) suggested that there was also room for two different modes of processing *social* information. For example, they hypothesized that, with reference to salience phenomena, the search of the social environment was automatic, but that this was not necessarily true for the process of integrating acquired information to make a judgement.[7] Attributions, or indeed social judgements in general, are identified as automatic to the extent that they fulfil three criteria: (1) they occur without intention; (2) they occur without giving rise to awareness; (3) they occur without interfering with ongoing mental activity (Posner and Snyder, 1975).

Because so much attribution research has used verbal materials, attribution researchers have turned to the area of text comprehension in an attempt to understand better the nature of causal processing. Read (1987), for example, argued that many inferences about causal connections must be made automatically during comprehension, or the reader of text would simply fail to understand what was going on. He cited various sources on text comprehension to support this view (e.g., Bower et al., 1979; Trabasso et al., 1984). Furthermore, people have been shown to make similar causal and goal-based inferences when shown a videotaped sequence of actions, so these findings are not merely an artefact of mode of presentation (Lichtenstein and Brewer, 1980). It is necessary, however, to distinguish between types of attribution. As I have emphasized throughout this book, my topic is *causal* attribution. Yet some of the studies cited as evidence of spontaneous or automatic causal reasoning have measured trait or dispositional, not causal, attribution (e.g., Winter and Uleman, 1984; Winter et al., 1985). The importance of this distinction is made quite clear by the research of Smith and Miller.

Smith and Miller's (1979b) model of salience-based attribution has been discussed above. They argued that attributions can be made as information is stored in memory and that cognitive theory and research (e.g., Kintsch, 1974) support the idea that 'attributional (cause-inferring) processing is intrinsically involved in the initial comprehension of sentences and therefore that it goes on all the time' (p. 2247). Their later paper (Smith and Miller, 1983), however, provided a much clearer test of this hypothesis. They began by distinguishing the different types of inference used in attribution research – for example, causal judgements, trait judgements about an actor and judgements of the actor's intent. They then went on to assess which judgements mediate, and are mediated by, other judgements and thus to identify which inferences are made first. Once again, empirical estimates of the amount of processing time for different inferences were used in this research. The rationale for using response-time measures is simple (Hamilton, 1988). If the question corresponds to a process that occurs spontaneously during the initial comprehension of behaviour, then the answer to the question will be readily available and subjects' response time will be short. If, in contrast, the question asks about something not inferred from the comprehension stage, then the subject must retrieve the relevant information and make the inference before responding to the question; in the latter case the response time will be longer.

Smith and Miller reported that judgements of intention and trait inferences did not take significantly more time than a 'control' question concerning the actor's gender (see table 4). This finding suggested that these judgements may also be made during comprehension, or at least that they could be easily inferred. The slowest responses were to

TABLE 4   Response times to different questions in Smith and Miller's (1983) research

	Response time[a]	
Question	Study 1	Study 2
Gender	2.14	4.24
Intention	2.41	4.56
True trait	2.48	4.37
False trait	3.02	5.09
Person cause	3.42	5.68
Situation cause	3.80	6.05

[a] Response times are in seconds. In Study 1 responses indicate question-answering time, in Study 2 responses indicate time taken to read a sentence and answer a question about it.
Source: data drawn from Smith and Miller, 1983, © by the American Psychological Association, reprinted by permission of the publisher and author.

person-cause and situation-cause questions. Smith and Miller concluded that the 'basic' attribution (probably made during the initial process of comprehension) was a judgement of intention or a trait attribution or both (see Winter et al., 1985), *not* a person- or situation-cause. The longer response time for person- and situation-cause questions could also be due to the fact that people are not used to thinking about and answering questions in these terms. From these data causal processing does not appear to be automatic, at least if one adopts a strict, but theoretically sensible, distinction between trait and causal attribution. Like Hamilton (1988), I do not consider that the step of extracting dispositional properties for observed behaviour is itself an attributional inference. What occurs during the comprehension phase seems to be a simple trait inference, with no attempt to understand the causal basis of the behaviour.

Hamilton (1988) supported this conceptual distinction through his own research. He reported that for congruent behaviours, response times were lower for trait and intention questions than for person- and situation-cause questions. For incongruent behaviours, in contrast, response times for situation-cause and intention questions were lower than for trait and person-cause questions. According to Hamilton, what occurs during the comprehension phase for a congruent item is a trait inference, not a causal attribution. If subjects make a trait inference during the initial comprehension of an event, then this inference should facilitate answering the person attribution question. This is exactly what Hamilton found, and he suggested that the quick trait inference became the basis for a slower person attribution. As he noted, this result implies that the relation between trait inferences and causal attributional inferences is often the opposite of that proposed by Correspondent Inference Theory (Jones and Davis, 1965). The process seems to be from trait inference to person attribution, not vice versa. For an incongruent behaviour, however, a situational attribution is most often made (Crocker et al., 1983), and thus this response is faster for this question only to an incongruent item compared with a congruent one.

In sum, Hamilton contended that the attribution process is fundamentally different for congruent and incongruent behaviours. For congruent behaviours, extensive attributional thought is less likely to occur as the behaviour is attributed to a disposition that was inferred from the behaviour as it was comprehended. In this case trait attributions are spontaneous, occurring without much thought, although they are not necessarily automatic (see Bargh, 1984; Bassili and Smith, 1986). For incongruent behaviour, a more detailed causal analysis is spontaneously activated, requiring more time and effort on the part of the perceiver.

It is to the credit of the cognitive approach that it has supplied the techniques for permitting a more detailed and accurate view of the nature of causal attribution. Such an approach, however, has its limitations, and these should be honestly appraised before I conclude this chapter.

Limits to the sovereignty of social cognition

Ostrom, writing enthusiastically in the opening chapter of the *Handbook of Social Cognition* (Wyer and Srull, 1984), has argued for the 'sovereignty' of social cognition. He referred specifically to the relevance of cognitive psychology to the phenomena of social psychology and to the 'conceptual vocabulary' (p. 29) offered by cognitive processing models. I have tried to do justice to the strengths of a cognitive approach, but should such research really reign 'supreme'?

Taylor and Fiske (1981), in an excellent treatment of process analysis methodologies for attribution research, have underlined the need for methodological eclecticism or multiple measures of cognitive process. Such eclecticism is also necessary with respect to the *level* at which attribution research is conducted. These scholars also emphasized the need to study behaviour, and not just cognition, and to use techniques such as conversational analysis, interviews and ethnographic analysis. When one reflects on the cognitive-attributional literature, it is instructive to ask whether people really behave this way, entertain such thoughts and make such judgements outside the laboratory. White (1984) has contended that the primary orientation of the layperson is to the practicalities of living, and that we should therefore study topics such as self-presentation and interpersonal relationships, not just cognitive processes.

The social cognition approach to attribution is, then, ultimately limited in its conception of social psychology. The much-needed rigour of such an approach notwithstanding, our attempt to 'steal the clothes' of the cognitive psychologist may leave us naked as *social* psychologists. Thus one of the leading figures in cognitive psychology, as an invited discussant at a symposium on social cognition, referred to 'the extraordinarily narrow perspective from which scholars in this field approach their work' (Neisser, 1980, p. 602). My aim is not to endorse his sentiments but to warn that the social cognition view has its limits. It should not be allowed to constrain the breadth and uniqueness of a truly *social-psychological* approach to attribution.

CONCLUSION

This chapter has covered a great deal of ground in reviewing what has been one the most prolific areas of attribution research. It appears that, although experimental subjects are capable of quite sophisticated attributional information-processing under specified favourable conditions, this is not their normal mode of explanation. Judgemental heuristics, especially availability, provide a more reasonable model of common-sense attribution, and the use of process models in attribution research is an important development. These models, however, have yielded contradictory findings, so that even the causal impact of visually salient stimuli in artificial conditions has yet to be fully understood. The most general approach refers to knowledge structures and subsumes explanation under the topic of understanding. This approach argues convincingly for the identification of cognitive structures with flexibility of function and, via the notion of 'scripts', sensibly focuses attention on sequences of behaviour.

These three general approaches each proclaim a different model of the layperson as attributor – naive scientist, cognitive miser or story understander. I believe that each model receives some support in specific experimental contexts, but that each accounts for only specific empirical findings. For example, the knowledge-structure approach is not designed to explain the process of salience effects, and the heuristic approach seems to provide little help in understanding the inferences made in text comprehension. On the basis of this review I cannot conclude unequivocally in favour of one approach. I believe that it has been intellectually important and worthwhile to explore the full implications of a quasi-scientific or logical approach; the precision of the process approach has yielded a better understanding of the nature of causal attribution; and I contend that the study of knowledge-structures holds rich promise. The cognitive perspective reviewed here has made a major contribution in analyzing the causal attribution process in detail, including qualification of Heider's view that causal attribution is ubiquitous. The following chapters underline, however, that there is more to the study of causal attribution than the rigorous, precise but often artificial investigation of cognitive processes.

5 Interpersonal Attribution: From Social Interaction to Close Relationships

It is a special feature of social interaction that each participant is both a causal agent and an attributor.

(Kelley, 1972b)

Attributions are important in close relationships ... Highly interdependent persons often have occasion to wonder about the causes of events in their relationship – why their love life is not more satisfying, why their partner is so influenceable by his or her family, whether a hurtful act was intentional or accidental. In a close relationship, we often explain our own actions to our partner; we also often tell our partner why he or she acted in some particular way.

(Kelley, 1977)

INTRODUCTION

Despite the apparently obvious prevalence and significance of attributions in interpersonal encounters, research at this level has, surprisingly, lagged behind work on intra-personal attribution. In a paper entitled 'Attribution in social interaction', Kelley (1972b) noted a problem: most of the relevant studies included non-attributional dependent measures, permitting him only to infer a mediating role for attributions in interpersonal behaviour. More recently, as noted briefly in chapter 3, there have been calls for a 'conversational' approach to attribution, an approach that emphasizes the links between everyday communication and everyday explanation. Hilton (in press) has pointed to the parallels between Grice's (1975) four conversational maxims for ordinary conversation and the 'rules' of interpersonal explanation:

1 The maxim of quality (speakers should say something they know not to be false, and not say something for which they lack adequate evidence);

2 The maxim of quantity (speakers should make their contributions as informative as required for the purposes of the exchange, but not more informative than necessary);

3 The maxim of relation (speakers should be relevant);

4 The maxim of manner (speakers should avoid obscurity and ambiguity; they should be brief and orderly).

In each case the term 'speakers' could be replaced by 'attributors' and we should have a set of rules by which most of us are probably guided in our everyday explanations (see also Lalljee, 1981). As Hilton emphasized, causal explanation is both a part of communication and of social interaction:

> Causal explanation is first and foremost a form of social interaction. We speak of *giving* causal explanations but not perceptions, comprehensions, categorizations or memories. The verb 'to explain' is a three-part predicate: *Someone* explains *something* to *someone*. Causal explanation takes the form of a conversation, and is thus subject to the rules of conversation. (in press, MS p. 1)

Attribution is, then, part of 'the communication game' (Higgins, 1981; Higgins et al., 1981), where communication is conceived as a game in the sense that it involves social roles and purposive interpersonal behaviour on the part of both speakers and listeners. Burleson (1986) has also argued that the analysis of naturally occurring conversations can be an important source of information for studies of causal attribution.

These are intriguing ideas, yet they map the possible future, rather than the past, of research on interpersonal attribution. This chapter organizes the relevant theory and research into two main parts. The first part deals with attribution in social interaction, evaluating the evidence for attributional biases in interpersonal encounters and, in particular, examining how they are affected by factors such as evaluation and attraction (although much of the research on attributional biases has not focused on their interpersonal aspects, these biases do reappear in the later analyses of attribution in close relationships). I then consider the behavioural consequences of attribution in social interaction, highlighting the role of attributions in behavioural confirmation or self-fulfilling prophecies. The second part of the chapter focuses on attribution in close relationships, reviewing the nature and role of attributions in three broad realms: interpersonal conflict, marital satisfaction and relationship termination.

SOCIAL INTERACTION

Actors and observers

In the review of evidence for Jones and Nisbett's (1972) actor-observer hypothesis in chapter 3, a number of theoretical and methodological problems came to light. Before we can assert that actors tend to give more situational attributions and observers tend to give more personal attributions, we must examine three main problems. The first of these is purely methodological, but the remaining two are of fundamental importance in any attempt to generalize from Level I-type studies of divergent perspectives (where information-processing is the focus) to Level II situations, where the focus is on the dynamics of interpersonal processes within a given situation, in which the individuals occupy essentially equal positions (see chapter 1).

Methodologically, Watson (1982) has provided a critical review of the reliability, convergent validity and construct validity of measures used to test the actor-observer hypothesis. More immediately questionable is the conflation of trait and causal attributions, a looseness in terminology that I have criticized earlier. As Monson and Snyder's (1977) review noted, actor-observer differences have been investigated with reference to *causal identification* (e.g., Nisbett et al., 1973, Study 2), *inferences* about an actor's *traits* (e.g., Nisbett et al., 1973, Study 3) and *predictions* about an actor's future behaviour (e.g., Nisbett et al., 1973, Study 1). If the goal of research is to map the extent and limitations of actor-observer differences, then it is desirable to examine all three measures, but to report the results separately. But if the focus of research is causal attribution, as here, then trait inferences and predictions are, strictly speaking, irrelevant.

A second problem relates to experimental design. Monson and Snyder (1977) pointed out that some studies compared subjects' perceptions of their own behaviour with their perceptions of others (the 'common rater' procedural paradigm; e.g., Nisbett et al., 1973, Studies 2 and 3). Other studies compared subjects' self-attributions with those of outside observers (the 'common target' procedural paradigm; e.g., Nisbett et al., 1973, Study 1). As in Watson's (1982) usage, these two approaches can be termed *self-other* and *actor-observer*, respectively. Watson preferred the self-other distinction, because the actor-observer distinction implies a situation in which person A is acting while person B is observing. Although Watson was correct to argue that a true actor-observer interaction was not always present, it is probably the most relevant focus for a chapter on inter-personal attribution. Watson's methodological rigour notwithstanding, his preference for the self-other vs the actor-observer distinction had the unfortunate consequence of further de-emphasizing the fascinating question of how interactants explain their own and each other's behaviour in real social interactions.

A third criticism of actor-observer research drives right to the core of normal social interaction. According to van der Pligt, 'Most research in this area fails to distinguish between descriptive and evaluative aspects of attribution' (1981, pp. 98–9). He contended that the observer's evaluation of the actor and his or her behaviour does affect the attribution process and that actor-observer differences could be related to different evaluations of one's own and another's behaviour. Van der Pligt proposed, consequently, that attribution theory should incorporate the social desirability of the behaviour and the observer's attitude towards the person performing the behaviour.

In their original paper, Jones and Nisbett (1972) emphasized cognitive and perceptual factors in attribution and only touched on the possible effects of motivational variables on the tendency of actors and observers to engage in divergent causal attributions. They also suggested that the strongest support for their hypothesis would be found in cases where the act in question is neutral, affectively and morally, and the observer holds a neutral opinion towards the actor. In contrast, in situations where the act is negatively or positively evaluated by the observer, or the observer's relationship to the actor is not affectively neutral, the predicted actor-observer difference may not hold up.

There is evidence that the actor-observer effect is weakened when we have positive or negative, compared with neutral, outcomes. Positive outcomes are attributed more to persons, and negative outcomes are attributed more to situations (e.g., Taylor and Koivu-maki, 1976; Tillman and Carver, 1980). The evidence from studies manipulating instructions to empathize can also be understood in these terms. When actors are told to observe themselves as an observer might, they become more dispositional in their attributions; conversely observers induced to empathize with actors become more situational in their attributions (Gould and Sigall, 1977; Regan and Totten, 1975; Wegner and Finstruen, 1977).

The results for empathy manipulations suggest that there ought to be a link between attribution and attraction. The evidence on this question has been reviewed by Regan (1978). He proposed that when we already know something about the actor's dispositions, and like or dislike him or her, we may arrive at an attribution for that person's behaviour that is relatively consistent with our prior knowledge. This hypothesis was tested by Regan et al., (1974, Experiment 1), who manipulated liking for another person and assessed college students' perceptions of that person's skilled and unskilled performance on a task. These responses, however, can be considered only indirect causal attributions. Rather than asking for an explanation of the person's performance, Regan et al. asked subjects to judge on a rating scale how good a measure of abilities the task was (from accurate to inaccurate). Subjects judged the task to be a more accurate measure of ability for the two consistent conditions (liked person/skilled performance and disliked person/unskilled performance) than the two inconsistent conditions (liked/unskilled and disliked/skilled). The second study contained a more direct measure of causal attribution. Subjects named someone they liked and someone they disliked and were subsequently told that one of their nominees had been asked by an experimental accomplice to do a favour and had done so. Subjects were then asked to explain why the other person had complied, using forced-choice response measures that all contained the word 'because'. The results were clear: prosocial behaviour was attributed to internal causes if it was performed by a liked person and to external causes if performed by a disliked one.

Evaluation, then, would seem to be an important qualifier of the actor-observer hypothesis. It is, moreover, a likely characteristic of many, perhaps most, naturalistic interpersonal interactions. Other findings further bolster the suspicion that actor-observer differences may be less pervasive in natural settings than in laboratory encounters between strangers. The purported difference also disappears when observers anticipate discussing their attributions with another observer (Wells et al., 1977), or when they expect to interact, or think that they are currently interacting, with the actor (Knight and Vallacher, 1981).

What seems, most of all, to have been lost in actor- observer research is the central notion of perspective – 'a point in space/time from which events are viewed' (Farr and Anderson, 1983, p. 45; see Mead, 1927). That actors and observers do, at least sometimes, have different perspectives, and that these can be altered, was the important revelation of Storms's (1973) study (see chapter 3). More recently the importance of perspective has been demonstrated by Howe's (1987) study of observers' attributions for marital conflict. He asked college students to take the perspective of one participant – husband, wife or counsellor – while viewing three short videotapes, and then to explain what caused the observed argument. When subjects took the husband's perspective, they were more likely to attribute the cause to the wife, and less likely to attribute the cause to the husband. The reverse was true when subjects took the wife's perspective. When subjects took the counsellor's perspective, in contrast, their use of husband and wife attributions tended to fall in between the two extremes of subjects in the other perspective conditions. In addition, when taking the counsellor's perspective, subjects were more likely to attribute the cause to *both* husband and wife than they were when taking one of the spouse perspectives. Perspective is likely to influence, and be influenced by, evaluation. Both variables qualify actor-observer differences, yet are likely to be typical of naturalistic social interaction. Another characteristic of attributions in the course of everyday interaction is that they will, at least sometimes, serve a variety of personal and interpersonal functions. This topic is closely allied to another bias, that of self-serving attributions for success and failure.

Self-serving biases

I have already discussed self-serving attributions in the context of both biases in and consequences of attribution (see chapter 3). I argue now that self-serving attributions, in the most general sense of the term, illustrate the rich variety of interpersonal attribution.

Attributional egotism. Snyder et al. have defined attributional egotism as 'the tendency to take credit for good outcomes and deny blame for bad ones' (1978, p. 91). Once again, we should maintain a clear distinction between attributions of cause, traits, responsibility and blame. So many of the relevant studies have, however, used responsibility- or blame-dependent measures that I will include them, because the focus of the research is clearly on common-sense explanation and not on legal, moral and philosophical issues, such as whether laypersons follow a legal model of attribution (cf. Fincham and Jaspars, 1980; Shultz and Schleifer, 1983). The basic issue of self-serving biases, however, concerns whether individuals tend to make more flattering attributions following success outcomes than following failure outcomes (typically, flattering attributions are considered to be internal for success and external for failure, a view that is itself simplistic).

As in the case of actor-observer differences, issues of experimental design are again relevant. Self-serving biases in attribution have been investigated, and demonstrated, on a variety of tasks (see Zuckerman,

1979). Given the present focus on interpersonal attribution, I will follow Zuckerman in proposing that there are two possible tests of the self-serving hypothesis:

1   Within-subjects designs, i.e., comparisons of an actor's attributions about his or her own behaviour and that of another person (the 'self/other' paradigm);
2   Between-subjects designs, i.e., comparisons of an actor's and an observer's attributions for the actor's behaviour (the 'actor/ observer' paradigm). These two paradigms are, of course, the same ones noted for actor-observer differences, but here the focus is on comparing attributions for success and failure outcomes.

A further problem, which should now be obvious following the exposition of work by Weiner (e.g., 1986) and Russell (1982), is that the meaning of a performance attribution (e.g., ability, effort, luck, task) may vary greatly across both persons and situations. In certain cases, for example, attributions of effort may be treated as stable dispositions (e.g., Feather and Simon, 1973; Valle and Frieze, 1976) and task difficulty may be seen as an unstable factor (e.g., Deaux, 1976). A particularly interesting possibility for interpersonal attribution is that the *same* factor may be viewed quite *differently* for self and other. An appropriate technique to overcome this problem is Russell's (1982) Causal Dimension Scale, by means of which the investigator assesses directly how the attributor views the causes that he or she stated (e.g., Ronis et al., 1983; Russell et al., 1987). Unfortunately, this more detailed approach has rarely been used, so that in evaluating self-serving biases in interpersonal attribution one has to assume that the meaning of causal attributions was consistent with Weiner's model.

In the self-other paradigm, self and other work independently, cooperate on the same task or compete against one another. According to Zuckerman's (1979) comprehensive review, there is no clear evidence regarding the self-serving hypothesis from the 'independent' studies (e.g., Wortman et al., 1973), but there is some evidence from the 'cooperative' studies (e.g., Wolosin et al., 1973, Experiment 1), and the strongest evidence comes from the 'competitive' studies (e.g., Stephan et al., 1976). The results from the actor-observer paradigm, in contrast, were inconsistent and failed to support the hypothesis. One study, which further underlines the importance of perspective, did, however, show that observers who share a perspective with the actor made more flattering attributions about the actor's performance than observers who did not (Arkin et al., 1978).

Further evidence for self-serving biases in more social settings comes from studies of interpersonal attributions within small social groups. A series of studies by Schlenker and colleagues all used responsibility attribution as the key dependent measure and confirmed the hypothesis that group members would feel more responsible for their group's performance following group success than failure (e.g., Forsyth and Schlenker, 1977; Schlenker, 1975). A further series of studies revealed how interpersonal relations may influence attributional egotism. When subjects were allowed to communicate with one another in a group of peers, there was no egotism (e.g., Schlenker et al., 1976); egotism was stronger for individuals who enjoyed majority, compared with minority, status within a group (Schlenker and Miller, 1977a), and it appeared in low-cohesion, but not high-cohesion, groups (Schlenker and Miller, 1977b). Egotism can, however, give way to group-serving attributional bias, where the group is favoured over the self, especially when the group has some sense of history and future (see Taylor et al., 1983) and where group members' actions are interdependent (Zaccaro et al., 1987).

Overall, there is clear evidence of self-serving biases in interpersonal attribution, but the bias is by no means ubiquitous. Instead, performance attributions are influenced by the setting and seem tailored to fit the needs of specific social situations. This more strategic conception of interpersonal attribution is best seen in work that relates attributions to impression management or self-presentation.

Strategic self-presentation. Weary Bradley (1978) broadened the scope of self-serving biases in attribution by suggesting that they may be viewed as public self-presentations. The motivation to maximize public esteem, rather than to maintain or increase one's private self-esteem, could explain counter-defensive attributions if we propose that public-esteem needs might sometimes be best served by making self-attributions for negative, rather than positive, outcomes. For example, people might not want to accept undeserved credit for positive outcomes and to avoid credit for negative outcomes if they were aware that an unrealistically positive self-presentation could be invalidated by their own subsequent behaviour or by observers' present or future assessment of their behaviour. As Weary Bradley contended, the potential embarrassment resulting from such public invalidation would probably threaten their public image.

Self-presentation, or impression management, has been defined as 'the process of establishing an identity through the appearance one presents to others, ... the more or less intentional control of appearances in order to guide and control the responses made by others toward us' (Weary and Arkin, 1981, p. 225). Such self-presentation is aimed at establishing, maintaining or refining a view of the actor in the minds of observers (Baumeister, 1982). Although the importance of self-presentation in interpersonal behaviour has received close attention in recent social-psychological theorizing (e.g., Schlenker, 1980; Semin and Manstead, 1983; Tedeschi, 1981), it also has a long historical tradition (e.g., Cooley, 1902; Goffman, 1959; James, 1890; Mead, 1934; see Tetlock and Manstead, 1985).

The immediate value of such an approach to attribution was that it offered an explanation of counter-defensive, or apparently non-self-serving, attributions (see Ross et al., 1974), by comparing attributions in public and private settings. Under public conditions, people tend to make more internal attributions for negative outcomes than they do when their performance outcomes and attributions are more private (Frey, 1978; Weary et al., 1982). One should be cautious, however, in contending that public-private manipulations provide an effective means of distinguishing between intra-psychic and impression-management models of attribution (i.e., the self-esteem vs public esteem motive). As Tetlock and Manstead (1985) have argued: (a) it is reasonable to assume that public-private manipulations always have intra-psychic effects; and (b) not all impression-management explanations require that experimental findings occur only in public settings (some theories claim that people try to impress an internal audience).

Weary and Arkin (1981) have put forward a systematic analysis of self-presentation and attribution, by examining the effects of audience characteristics, task and attributional response factors, presenter characteristics and interaction goals. For example, public evaluation of a person's performance by a committee of prestigious individuals can moderate, or even reverse, self-serving tendencies (e.g., Arkin et al., 1980a, b; Greenberg et al., 1982). At least one explanation for why people may make counter-defensive attributions in more public settings is that they are aware of how other people respond to their strategic causal claims. Tetlock (1980) carried out a simulation of the study by Ross et al. (1974) and found that subjects more positively evaluated a teacher who had made counter-defensive attributions (i.e., had taken responsibility for pupil failure, but not pupil success) than a teacher who made defensive attributions. Thus what actors say about the causes of their own or personally related outcomes affects observers' evaluations of them.

Although the present focus is on causal attributions studied within social psychology, I should reiterate that other approaches and other disciplines have studied similar issues. In sociology there has been work on 'accounts' (Scott and Lyman, 1968), and social psychologists have also begun to pay more attention to 'excuses' (e.g., Snyder et al., 1983; Weiner et al., 1987) and, more generally, to what Semin and Manstead (1983) called 'motive talk'. The outcome of all this work is that our causal claims in interpersonal encounters appear to serve a communicative, informational function and provide a way to control observers' attributional conclusions about an actor (Forsyth, 1980).

The evidence so far rests on explanations given *after* a performance, but it has also been suggested that actors sometimes provide attributions *before* a performance, revealing a more subtle form of self-serving attribution. This proactive attributional bias has been termed 'self-handicapping' (Jones and Berglas, 1978), and it refers to 'an individual's attempt to reduce a threat to esteem by actively seeking or creating inhibitory factors that interfere with performance and thus provide a persuasive causal explanation for potential failure' (Arkin and Baumgardner, 1985, p. 170). The idea is to use extraneous causal factors to obscure the link between performance and evaluation, thereby mitigating the impact of failure. As Jones and Berglas put it, the self-handicapper 'reaches out for impediments, exaggerates handicaps, and embraces any factor reducing personal responsibility for mediocrity and enhancing personal responsibility for success' (1978, p. 202).

Arkin and Baumgardner (1985) have provided a detailed review, and an integrative model, of self-handicapping strategies and their motivational bases. There is evidence that people use attributional principles (such as Kelley's, 1972a, discounting and augmentation principles) to manipulate their image. For example, subjects who expect to fail on a task may take debilitating drugs or consume large quantities of alcohol in order to provide a self-serving explanation for their imminent failure (Berglas and Jones, 1978; Tucker et al., 1981). In a similar manner, lack of effort can serve as a useful 'impediment' to future poor performance and thus protect the actor against inferences of low ability due to his or her failure (Frankel and Snyder, 1978; Snyder et al., 1981).

It is worth emphasizing here that self-handicapping does not avoid *internal* attributions, but rather avoids *lack of ability* attributions. Once again, the inadequacy of basing the self-serving bias on the distinction between internal vs external attribution is apparent. People may hide behind the 'attributional shield of self-handicapping' (Berglas and Jones, 1978, p. 406), but they do not simply choose external vs internal attributions for negative outcomes, such as failure.

Furthermore, Jones and Berglas (1978) assert that not everyone self-handicaps, at least not systematically, and that this kind of strategy, ultimately self-destructive, characterizes only those who are abnormally concerned with their self-worth.

Egotism vs egocentrism.   Before we leave self-serving attributions, a final distinction must be made between two terms that have been used rather loosely and sometimes interchangeably. Greenwald (1980) distinguished between three cognitive biases associated with what he called 'the totalitarian ego': 'egocentricity' (perceiving the self as more central to events than it is), 'beneffectance' (perceiving the self as selectively responsible for desired, but not undesired, outcomes) and 'conservatism' (resistance to cognitive change).[1] The first of these biases is illustrated by what attribution researchers have called egocentric attributions (see below), attributions that are self-centred rather than based on outcome valence. The second bias is, of course, illustrated by self-serving attributions for success and failure, attributions that are, essentially, conceited. The third bias, not dealt with here, is exemplified by the anchoring or availability heuristic (see chapter 4).

The egocentric, or 'contribution', bias in attribution refers to the tendency for people to accept more credit or responsibility for a joint product than other contributors ascribe to them. The best evidence for this bias comes from a series of five studies by Ross and Sicoly (1979), who proposed that biased attributions of responsibility for a joint product could be due to an egocentric bias in availability of information in memory. If self-generated inputs were more available, then people would be more likely to claim more responsibility for a joint product than others would attribute to them. Ross and Sicoly also tried to identify which of four processes might be operating to increase the availability of one's own contributions – selective encoding and storage, differential retrieval, informational disparities or motivational influences. Ross and Sicoly's central hypothesis is phrased in terms of responsibility attribution, although the studies vary considerably in their dependent measures.[2]

Ross and Sicoly (1979, Experiment 1) asked 37 married couples to estimate the extent of their responsibility for each of 20 activities relevant to married couples (e.g., making breakfast, deciding how money should be spent, causing arguments). Results revealed an egocentric bias across the majority of both couples and activities, including negative activities. There was also a significant correlation between the tendency to recall self-relevant behaviours and the tendency to overestimate one's own perceived responsibility. This correlation is consistent with the hypothesis that egocentric biases in attribution are mediated by biases in availability; it provides a neat example of the desirable integration of Level I and Level II analyses.

Subsequent experiments investigated estimates of contributions to a joint experimental outcome (success/failure), a team's basketball game, a problem-solving session and an honours thesis. Ross and Sicoly concluded tentatively in favour of the differential retrieval hypothesis (subjects attempt to recall mainly their own contributions and inappropriately use the information retrieved to estimate their relative contribution), although they acknowledged that the evidence is suggestive rather than conclusive.[3] Most important for the present discussion, the evidence seems to contradict both the actor-observer hypothesis (that the responses of actors are more salient and available to observers than to actors themselves) and the self-serving hypothesis (that actors will take more credit than they are due only for positive outcomes). Ross and Sicoly suggested that the critical variable may be the extent to which the observer departs from a passive role and *interacts* with the actor. When, as in their five studies, people are involved in quite complex interactions, they alternate between the roles of speaker and listener, actor and observer, just as Kelley (1972b) noted in the epigraph to this chapter.

Burger and Rodman (1983) explicitly contrasted the egocentric bias and the actor-observer difference. They reported that in eight studies that obtained the egocentric bias, subjects were asked about events that either had occurred over a long period of time or had occurred a minimum of two days earlier. Burger and Rodman's own series of three studies revealed that the egocentric bias did not occur when subjects were asked for attributions immediately after task performance and in the absence of any self-awareness manipulation. This interaction of the egocentric bias with time should, they argued, have been predicted from the actor-observer literature. One's partner (the other/actor) is more salient during the course of interaction, but over time may appear to be less salient (see Moore et al., 1979).

More recently, research on egocentric attribution has investigated the attributions of marriage partners. Thompson and Kelley (1981) reported egocentric bias, but only for 14 of 36 activities investigated; Christensen et al., (1983) found an increasing tendency for couples to attribute responsibility for negative items to the partner as the length of the relationship increases. Fincham and Bradbury (in press) also reported egocentric bias among spouses, in a study using improved methodology (respondents were not forced to make a single, comparative judgement for a relationship event; they could assign equal contributions to an activity; and they were not asked specifically to think only of their own contribution). The evidence tended, however, to support an egocentric bias for negative events, but a 'partner-centric' bias for positive events, in a sample relatively high in marital satisfaction. Like Burger and Rodman, Fincham and Bradbury found only equivocal support for an availability explanation, so that future research is still needed on the conditions under which and the mechanisms by which the bias operates.

There is, then, overwhelming evidence for self-serving biases in interpersonal attribution, when that term is used loosely to encompass evidence of egotism, self-presentation and egocentrism. Broadly speaking, egotism is especially likely in competitive interpersonal contexts; self-presentation is typical of evaluative public settings; and egocentrism is most likely to occur when respondents are asked to recall behaviours first and then estimate their own and their partner's contribution. It should be noted that in each of Ross and Sicoly's (1979) studies subjects had to recall previous joint endeavours, a procedure that might be expected to favour the availability heuristic.

Interpersonal consequences of attribution

As Crittenden has succinctly stated, 'Attribution is a process that begins with social perception, progresses through causal judgment and social inference, and ends with behavioral consequences' (1983, p. 426). The relation between attribution and social interaction has been a topic of interest for many years (e.g., Kelley, 1972b), and most attribution theorists assumed, explicitly or implicitly, that attributions either had a direct effect on behaviour or, at least, mediated the relationship between other factors and behaviour. Yet, as Harvey and Weary (1984) have argued, surprisingly little research has examined directly the behavioural consequences of interpersonal attribution. In this section I deal first with studies on attribution and social interaction and then with the possible role of attributions in expectancy confirmation.

Attribution and social interaction.   A series of studies by Harvey and colleagues (Town and Harvey, 1981; Yarkin et al., 1981; Yarkin-Levin, 1983) all focused on how attributional activity might mediate between social perception variables and social interaction (see Kelley, 1972b; Kelley and Michela, 1980; Snyder, 1976). Town and Harvey (1981) investigated the sequence of forming impressions about a person, making attributions about that person and then behaving towards that person. As all three studies used essentially the same paradigm, I will describe it in some detail first. Male subjects first watched a four-minute videotaped social encounter in which the stimulus person (a female accomplice) disclosed either highly intimate or less intimate information. After observing the videotape, all subjects learned that they would interact with the person. They were given an attribution measure or a distraction task and then participated in a three-minute interaction with the woman. The main dependent measures were attributions made after watching the videotape and behavioural responses made during the interaction. Town and Harvey hypothesized that a desire for control would be evoked in subjects shown the highly intimate disclosure (in which the female accomplice revealed that she was becoming aware of personal homosexual tendencies). Control motivation was expected to influence both the amount and type of attributional activity and the valence of the behaviour. For the high self-disclosure condition the researchers predicted increased attributional activity (dispositional vs situational), to restore a sense of control, and negative behaviour towards the female accomplice; they further predicted that this behaviour would be correlated with the amount of unsolicited attributional activity (using the technique suggested by Harvey et al., 1980; see chapter 3).

The results revealed significant interactions between disclosure level and attribution for measures of eye contact and percentage speech duration (the number of seconds the subject spent talking, divided by the overall length of the conversation). The differences between high and low disclosure conditions for both behavioural measures were larger when the attribution measure, rather than the distraction task, was administered. The attribution condition differed from the distraction condition within the high, but not the low, disclosure conditions. Finally, the amount of attributional activity was significantly correlated with a combined behavioural index (eye contact, proximity and percentage speech duration) in both the high and low self-disclosure conditions; the correlation was negative in the former and positive in the latter. Thus the study showed a possible role for attributions in mediating between perceptions about another person and behaviour towards that person.

Hearing a woman express homosexual tendencies before interacting with her is equivalent to being provided with a powerful label, schema or 'set' (see Snyder and Uranowitz, 1978; but cf. Bellezza and Bower, 1981; Clark and Woll, 1981). Yarkin et al. (1981) investigated the sequence of receiving a cognitive set about, making attributions about and then behaving towards a person. A positive set portrayed the female accomplice as being psychologically healthy, a negative set portrayed her as psychologically unhealthy, and these conditions were compared with a 'no set' condition. In this study female subjects received the set *before* viewing the videotape, and the authors assumed that the set (like a hypothesis) would guide people in their observation of, attributions about and behaviour towards another person (see Snyder, 1984; Snyder and Gangestad, 1981). In addition, half the subjects completed an unsolicited attributional measure; the other half were given a distractor task after viewing the videotape and before interacting with the woman (the 'no attribution' condition).

Of most importance here, subjects in the positive set/attribution condition displayed longer durations of eye contact, engaged in a more positive conversation and spoke for a longer period of time than did subjects in the positive set/no attribution condition. In the negative set/ attribution condition, subjects displayed shorter durations of eye contact, engaged in more negative conversation and spoke for a shorter period of time than did subjects in the negative set/no attribution condition. There were also significant correlations between indices of the number of attributions and behaviour, in both the positive and negative set conditions, but not the no set condition. Significant correlations were also found for the relationship between the valence of attributions and behaviour in all three conditions. Overall, the correlational data showed a relatively strong relationship between attribution and behaviour (partial correlational analyses between set condition and behaviour, with attributional data partialled out, were not significant). In sum, although we do not know whether subjects would have engaged in attributional thought in the absence of a probe, the results of this study confirm that attributions can mediate between social perception and social interaction.

A final study in this series examined how anticipated interaction might affect both individuals' attributions about, and behaviour towards, another person (Yarkin-Levin, 1983). This study also asked whether the very act of writing one's thoughts (as in the two previous studies) might influence behaviour independently of the attributional content of the written thoughts. Some subjects were given the opportunity to write their thoughts retrospectively (attribution condition), and others were given no instructions about either thinking or writing their thoughts retrospectively (no instruction condition) or a distraction task.

The results were quite complex, but included replication of several effects obtained by Yarkin et al. (1981). Set manipulations had the predicted effects on attribution and behaviour (e.g., negative set-negative attribution-negative behaviour) and there was a significant relationship between the valence and number of attributions and behaviour. Of most theoretical importance, there were significant three-way interactions (anticipation condition × set × attribution/no instruction/distraction) for several measures, including duration of eye contact, positivity of the conversation and amount of time the subject spoke. The most pronounced attributional and behavioural responses (in all set conditions) occurred when the subjects anticipated interaction and wrote out their attributions.

Taken together, these three studies suggest that attributions can mediate between social perception and interaction. A question mark remains, however, concerning whether the unsolicited measure of attribution actually tapped causal, and not merely dispositional, attribution (see chapter 3). Hazlewood and Olson (1986) have argued that these studies merely examined subjects' personality trait judgements about the targets. They compared an explicitly *causal* attribution task with a condition in which no attribution question was asked, and found that covariation information (consensus, distinctiveness and consistency, patterned to imply a person or situation attribution) actually had a stronger impact on subjects in the no attribution condition (they used measures such as interpersonal distance, smiling and reported comfort during interaction). Thus it would be premature to conclude that *causal* attributions are necessary mediators of social interaction or, indeed, that they are always associated with more pronounced behavioural responses. Nonetheless, these studies made an important contribution in studying the link between attributions and social interaction, a link that had been largely overlooked.

Attribution processes in expectancy confirmation. Social scientists have long been fascinated by the way in which social perceivers label others, interact with them, instigate behaviour from them and interpret that behaviour (e.g., Merton, 1948); as Snyder put it, the way in which 'social beliefs can and do create their own social reality' (1984, p. 293). Not all analyses, however, have identified an attributional component to such instances of expectancy confirmation or self-fulfilling prophecy. Only those that have done so are of interest here, because they highlight the role of attributions in sequences of social interaction that tend to confirm a perceiver's initial expectations.

Darley and Fazio (1980, p. 868) analysed the social interaction process by identifying six steps in the sequence of interaction between a target and a perceiver:

1 Either because of past observations of another person or because of the categories into which he or she has placed the other, a perceiver develops a set of expectancies about a target person.
2 The perceiver then acts towards the target in a manner consistent with his or her expectancies.
3 The target interprets the meaning of the perceiver's action.
4 The target's response to the perceiver's action is based on this interpretation.
5 The perceiver interprets the target's action.
6 After acting towards the perceiver, the target interprets the meaning of his or her own action.

Darley and Fazio acknowledged that this sequence is arbitrary, in that step 1 may itself be a response to a previous step or may indeed represent the beginning of the interaction; as I have emphasized already, both participants in any interaction are, in reality, both target and perceiver. Yet Darley and Fazio were surely correct to argue that it is often useful and accurate to identify one person as the perceiver and another as the target – for example, when the perceiver has power over the target and interaction is, therefore, asymmetric. This power is exemplified in the idea (central to Merton's, 1948, 1957, definition of a self-fulfilling prophecy) that one person (the perceiver) can impose an expectancy on another person (the target) in such a way as to make the target behave in a fashion that confirms that expectancy. Thus, for Darley and Fazio, the self-fulfilling prophecy refers to 'the process by which the expectancies held by one individual about another alter the behaviors of that other in ways that observers would interpret as confirming the perceiver's expectancy' (1980, p. 869).

Darley and Fazio noted that most research has focused on the link between step 1 and steps 4 and 5. They concentrated on the intervening stages, thus studying in more detail the unfolding of a sequence from step 1 through step 5. Causal attributions, however, are most obviously important at steps 3, 4, 5 and 6, to which I direct attention.

Attributions at step 3 – how the target interprets the perceiver's action – can be thought of as complex and slow vs simple and fast. Darley and Fazio outlined four possible categories of attribution that might be used by the target: (1) dispositional characteristics of the perceiver; (2) attributions to the situation; (3) self-attribution; and (4) complex attributions (i.e., some combination of (1)–(3)). At step 4, the target's response will be affected by his or her attribution at step 3. For example, the target's response following a self-attribution may be quite different from that following an attribution to the perceiver's characteristics. Darley and Fazio pointed out that there has been little research on whether the target will accept or challenge the perceiver's impression (see Gurwitz and Topol, 1978). Another study, however, found that targets who were told that the perceiver held an expectancy about them were able to overcome this expectancy (Hilton and Darley, 1985). Presumably, informing the target in this manner may lead him or her to make an internal attribution to the perceiver.

The most obvious role for causal attributions is at step 5 – how the perceiver interprets the target's response – which Darley and Fazio considered separately for confirming, disconfirming and ambiguous behaviour. For confirming behaviour, the perceiver should, rationally, acknowledge his or her own role in eliciting the target's behaviour. But as noted earlier, observers (i.e., the perceiver as observer of the target) appear to underestimate the causal role of situational factors, at least when compared with actors, and thus the perceiver may tend to attribute the behaviour to the target, even ignoring compelling situational explanations (Kulik, 1983). For disconfirming behaviour, the role of attributions in belief perseverance is relevant (see chapter 3). The perceiver seems to interpret disconfirming behaviour by means of what Darley and Fazio called an 'impression-maintenance attributional bias' (1980, p. 876). An emphasis is placed on situational forces (e.g., Regan et al., 1974), even when such factors are normally considered to *inhibit* the observed behaviour (Kulik, 1983) and the behaviour is still seen as consistent with previous trait ascriptions (Bell et al., 1976; Hayden and Mischel, 1976). Ambiguous behaviour, too, is usually explained as consistent with the perceiver's initial expectancy (e.g., Duncan, 1976; see chapter 6).

Miller and Turnbull's (1986) review distinguishes between two kinds of distortion on the part of the perceiver. First, the perceiver's expectancies can influence the *encoding* of behaviour (e.g., Rothbart et al., 1979), leading perceivers to 'see' or attend to behaviour consistent with their expectancies, or to label behaviour in an expectancy-consistent way (Jones et al., 1984). Second (and the focus here), the perceivers' expectancies can influence how they *explain* behaviour. According to Miller and Turnbull, there are at least three reasons why perceivers might explain behaviours that they encoded as disconfirming their expectancies, in a way that made the behaviour appear consistent: (1) perceivers might discount the reliability or diagnostic value of the unexpected behaviour; (2) perceivers might attribute the unexpected behaviour of another to their own behaviour; and (3) perceivers might discount the unexpected behaviour by focusing on motives of concealment that they might attribute to the target.

Finally, how does the target interpret his or her own action? In Watson's (1982) specification of the actor-observer difference, actors tend (at least, compared with observers) to underestimate the power of situational forces and so may consider their own behaviour to be somewhat self-revealing. A second possibility noted by Darley and Fazio (1980) is that the target may polarize his or her attitude towards the perceiver. For example, after ascribing a perceiver's hostile behaviour to dispositional qualities in the perceiver, a target may come to confirm the perceiver's expectancy, at the same time confirming his or her own expectancies about the perceiver. A third alternative noted by Darley and Fazio has recently received some empirical support. The target, being behaved towards in a hostile manner, may infer something about him or herself. As Snyder and Swann's (1978b) research found, targets who were led to believe that their hostile response to a perceiver reflected their own negative disposition, acted in a hostile way towards a new partner. This behaviour is actually an extension of the classic self-fulfilling prophecy, by means of which the target internalizes the very qualities the perceiver expected. This process is used to dramatic effect in Max Frisch's play *Andorra*. The hero, Andri, is mistakenly identified as a Jew by the townspeople and is persecuted as a result. He eventually comes to see himself as a Jew, and interpret his behaviour in these terms, as he finally explains in a poignant confession to the priest:

> Ever since I have been able to hear, people have told me I'm different, and I watched to see if what they said was true. And it is true, Father: I am different. People told me my kind have a certain way of moving, and I looked at myself in the mirror almost every morning. They are right ... And I watched to see whether it was true that I'm always thinking of money ... and they were right again: I am always thinking of money.... And people told me that my kind are cowards. I watched out for this too.... I didn't want to admit what they told me, but it's true.... Now it's up to you, Reverend Father, to accept your Jew. (Frisch, 1961, p. 61)

The tragedy of the play, whose themes are the fallacy of anti-semitism and the power of the self-fulfilling prophecy, is that when the people finally find out that Andri is not a Jew, it is too late to save him. He has become their stereotype.

Darley and Fazio's analysis of the self-fulfilling prophecy assigns a central role to causal attributions. A more recent conception by Jussim (1986) is less attribution-centred, arguing that a variety of social-cognitive biases are relevant. At the same time, however, one of Jussim's examples constitutes a seventh step in Darley and Fazio's sequence. As a consequence of the types of perceiver attributions outlined above, certain behaviour may follow. For example, if teachers attribute high-expectancy students' failures to the situation, then they may attempt to alter the situation in order to allow the students to express their true ability. This explanation could contribute to the teachers' willingness to persist longer with high-expectancy students who are performing poorly (by repeating or rephrasing questions, providing clues and giving more time; e.g., Allington, 1980; Brophy and Good, 1970).

To summarize: Darley and Fazio have provided a persuasive theoretical account of the centrality of causal attribution to the expectancy confirmation process, although the evidence specifically for causal attribution is still rather sparse. Expectancies might just as well lead to self-disconfirming prophecies as to self-fulfilling prophecies (see Bond, 1972; Hilton and Darley, 1985; Ickes et al., 1982), but researchers have simply been more interested in studying the former, which are more socially divisive (see Miller and Turnbull, 1986). Even strong expectancies about another person can be disconfirmed when the other's behaviour is clearly inconsistent with the expectancy (see Swann, 1983), yet the questions remain of whether, and when, they will be disconfirmed (see Hilton and Darley, 1985, for a discussion in terms of interaction goals). In general, as Snyder has argued, the pattern of confirmatory attributions revealed here must 'tend to contribute to the perpetuation of any hypotheses that initiate them' (1984, p. 275).

Summary

The research considered so far underlines the importance of causal attributions in social interaction, and also emphasizes the difference between intra-personal and interpersonal attribution. At the interpersonal level, one has to consider different roles and perspectives (e.g., actors and observers) as well as how attribution is related to evaluation. The self is also of central importance; taking a broad view of self-serving biases, I have found the evidence for attributional egotism, self-presentation and egocentrism to be persuasive. Finally, attributions appear to mediate between social perception and social interaction, a role that assumes major importance in the form of a confirmatory attributional bias that can help perceivers, erroneously, to conclude that their expectancies have been confirmed in social interaction. These findings are, on the one hand, compelling, but on the other hand, disappointing; as Fincham wrote:

The investigation of attributions for interpersonal behavior constitutes a major portion of attribution research. In the vast majority of cases, however, judgments are made about a stranger or hypothetical other on the basis of highly restricted information and for the purpose of complying with experimenter instructions. Each of these characteristics casts doubt on the relevance of such research for understanding attributions in relationships. (1985a, p. 205)

With those caveats in mind, the remainder of this chapter is devoted to the issue of attributions in close relationships where, perhaps, the truly interpersonal nature of attributions is best exemplified.

CLOSE RELATIONSHIPS

Conceptual and methodological issues

Before evaluating the evidence for attributions in *close relationships*, we must first consider what is meant by that term and what methodological innovations may be required in studying attributions in relationships.

Relationships and their stages. Harvey has defined close relationships as 'relationships involving some extended period and a strong, frequent, and diverse interdependence in activities, thoughts, and feelings' (1987, p. 420; see Kelley et al., 1983). *Interdependence* is the key word here, and other scholars have also pointed out that it must be especially important to understand and explore the behaviour of others with whom one is closely and mutually dependent. According to Orvis et al. (1976), close relationships not only increase the importance of determining causes of other people's behaviour, but also increase the need to state clearly the reasons for one's own actions. Thus attributions in close relationships tend to be *communicated* and can fulfil a variety of purposes, ranging from attacking or influencing one's partner to defending or justifying one's own behaviour.

The study of close relationships is now receiving detailed, if overdue, attention in mainstream social psychology with research focused on the three core stages of relationships: formation, maintenance and dissolution (e.g., Argyle and Henderson, 1985; Brehm, 1985; Clark and Reis, 1988; Duck, 1984; Kelley, 1979; Kelley et al., 1983; Levinger, 1980). A number of attribution researchers have also proposed that attribution processes are integrally related to these stages or phases of a relationship. Fincham (1985a) has suggested that during the *formation* phase of relationships, attributions will help to reduce ambiguity and ease the processing of information about behaviour in the relationship. During the *maintenance* phase, attributional activity should decrease; the existence of stable conceptions (dispositional attributions) will increase predictability and reduce the need to make attributions. In the *dissolution* phase, attributions are again likely to increase and to be functional in helping partners to understand what is happening in the relationship. Harvey stated the argument for studying attributions with respect to relationship stages as follows:

> attribution is an ongoing, dynamic activity through the course of close relationships. The dynamism comes from the fact that the quality of the attributions must change as the relationship itself intensifies, falters, or is terminated. (1987, p. 424)

Given the fluctuations in relationships and their concomitant affective components, an obvious question is whether one can generalize from attributions between strangers (the typical laboratory study) to attributions in close relationships. Theoretically, generalization for phenomena like actor-observer differences must be cautious in view of the fact that attributions are influenced by factors that are endemic to relationships – such as expected future interaction (Knight and Vallacher, 1981) and the affect experienced by an attributor towards an actor (Regan et al., 1974). As Kelley noted, 'Whenever the observer departs from a passive role and actively attempts to control the actor, the Jones and Nisbett generalization probably tends to break down' (1977, pp. 96–7). Methodologically, generalization is complicated by the fact that the kinds of attributions made in close relationships may simply not be the same ones found in interactions between strangers. This point requires more detailed exposition.

The nature of attributions in relationships. Harvey (1987) has referred to the difficulty of coding complex attributions about relationships, because multiple causes and dimensions are often involved in respondents' free-response explanations. It makes intuitive sense that attributions that occur explicitly in close relationships will be about interactive causes; we therefore need sophisticated measurement and coding schemes, suitable for repeated use, that are tailored to this context. That demand may sound ambitious, but I believe that the relatively small band of researchers in this area have already responded constructively to the challenge.

Newman (1981a) has pointed out that the very categories of dispositional vs situational attribution (central to the actor-observer literature) were derived from situations in which the observers did not have ongoing relationships with the actors whom they observed.

Applied to relationships, such categories are problematic. At the individual level, attributions made to one's partner are external, but at the relationship level factors outside the relationship represent external attributions. Further, attributions to oneself or one's partner may be directed at the individual *or* may focus on the interaction between the couple. Newman calls the latter 'interpersonal attributions', attributions which focus on 'one's perception of self in regard to other' and 'other in regard to self' (1981a, p. 63). As Howe (1987) has argued, although both personal and interpersonal attributions ascribe cause to characteristics of one partner, the former focuses on general dispositions (e.g., 'He is a suspicious person'), and the latter points to personal characteristics of one partner directed towards the other partner (e.g., 'He is suspicious of me').

Fincham (1985a) has gone a stage further, contending that it is possible to distinguish between an interactive attribution that centres on the partner (e.g., 'She does not trust me') and one that is truly dyadic or relational (e.g., 'There is a lack of trust between us'). Significantly, the latter kind of attribution (implicitly acknowledged by Newman, 1981a) sees the relationship itself as a cause of the behaviour. As Bradbury and Fincham (in press, b) have pointed out, the implications of a focus on the dyad, rather than the partner in relation to the other, can be quite serious (compare 'We have disagreements because sometimes we don't take the time to listen to one another' and 'We have disagreements because he doesn't take time to listen to me'). Thus a more complete taxonomy of attributions in relationships would include internal and external attributions as well as interpersonal attributions and relationship attributions. As will be seen below, such detail has rarely been observed, but it is a mark of the more sophisticated studies.

An additional, now familiar, methodological problem concerns the variety of terms used to denote 'attribution' – perceived cause, responsibility, credit and blame. These terms have sometimes been used interchangeably (e.g., Sillars, 1981; Thompson and Kelley, 1981), but some researchers have also made a commendable effort to obtain ratings of several of these measures and then to assess their relative importance as mediators of other variables, such as marital satisfaction.

The remainder of this chapter reviews the evidence for, and impact of, attributions under three broad headings – interpersonal conflict, marital satisfaction and relationship dissolution – with a focus on heterosexual relationships and especially marriage. These headings suggest, but do not completely overlap with, relationship stages, because, for example, conflict could occur, or marital satisfaction could be an issue, at various stages in the life of a relationship. These three topics reflect, rather, broad areas of relationships in which attributions have received sustained attention and attribution theory has received considerable support.

Interpersonal conflict

Horai (1977) used the term 'attributional conflict' to denote disagreement by two or more parties over what causal explanation to adopt. Orvis et al. (1976) investigated differences in attributions between the members of 41 young, heterosexual couples (of whom 21 were dating and the rest were married or living together). The couples were asked to describe instances in which their explanations for the behavior of one member of the couple differed, so there was an explicit focus on attributional conflict.

The couples were asked to elaborate on examples that both partners had listed independently, and they completed the attributional questionnaire separately. They were asked to list examples of their *own* and their respective *partners'* behaviour and, in each case, to give their *own* and their *partners'* explanation. One of the strongest effects reported by Orvis et al., and the one on which I will focus, concerned whether the explanation was given by the person who performed the behaviour (the actor) or by the partner; they called these actor-partner differences. This comparison centres not on the two individuals' actual explanations for any given behaviour but, rather, for each behaviour, on the explanations that one (or the other) *says* the two of them gave.

Actors tended to emphasize external causes, temporary internal states, judgements of what is preferable or necessary, concern for the partner's welfare and both the intrinsic properties of the activity and its direct consequences. Partners, in contrast, tended to give explanations (quite negative in tone) couched in terms of the actor's characteristics, the actor's negative attitude towards the partner and the indirect consequences of the activity. Interestingly, the partners tended to see the particular action as part of a more general pattern of behaviour and their attributions implied relative stability, whereas the actors viewed it as a single incident, explained by unstable causes.

A similar pattern of results was reported in a study of the meaning given to various interpersonal attributions (Passer et al., 1978). Undergraduate students judged the similarity between the 13 categories of explanation obtained by Orvis et al., either from the perspective of the actor or from the perspective of the observer. In both

conditions the positive or negative attitude of the actor towards the
partner was a highly salient dimension (dimension 1 in figures 6 and 7).
In the actor condition, the second dimension contrasted intentional
with unintentional causes; in the partner condition the second
dimension contrasted the actor's traits with their states or circumstances. Kelley (1979) integrated the findings of this study with those of
Orvis et al. by locating both actor's and partner's preferred types of
explanation in the meaning space inferred from the similarity
judgements of uninvolved respondents. In figure 6 it can be seen that
the actor's preferred explanations imply, for the most part, a positive
attitude towards the partner and include both unintentional and
intentional causes. In figure 7, the partner's preferred explanations
imply either a negative attitude on the part of the actor, or negative
traits, or both.

There is clearly some similarity between actor-partner and actor-

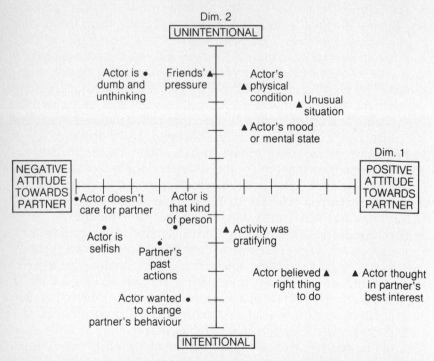

FIGURE 6   *Two-dimensional solution for 'actor' condition; the types of
explanations preferred by actors are indicated by triangles (from Passer et
al., 1978, © 1978 by the American Psychological Association, reprinted
by permission of the publisher and author)*

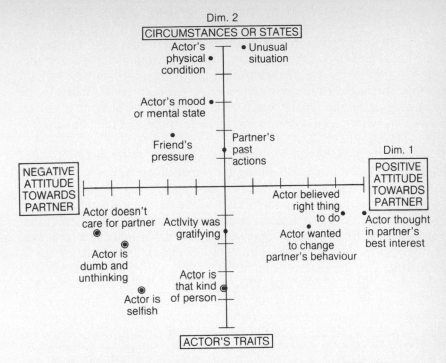

FIGURE 7 *Two-dimensional solution for 'partner' condition; the types of explanations preferred by partners are indicated by circles (from Passer et al., 1978, © 1978 by the American Psychological Association, reprinted by permission of the publisher and author)*

observer differences, but there is also a difference. Some of the explanations coded as 'internal' by Orvis et al. referred to causes within the partner that mediated between situational requirements and behaviour. In coding such explanations Orvis et al. reported that the boundary between the environment and the actor's state was blurred. The investigators also doubted whether Jones and Nisbett's (1972) informational-perceptual differences accounted for these actor-partner differences, preferring to emphasize the importance of evaluation (cf. van der Pligt, 1981). On the one hand, the actor was 'concerned about justification and exoneration'; on the other hand, the partner (a participant rather than a mere observer of negative behaviour) was 'concerned about its meaning, about redress or retribution, and about preventing its recurrence' (Orvis et al., 1976, p. 364). Unlike Jones and Nisbett, Orvis et al. stressed the links between attribution and communication. They suggested that their data 'reflect the consequences of a communication process' and speculated that 'communication about divergent causal interpretations of behaviour is a common and important part of the interaction within these couples' (p. 378). In addition to justifying and excusing actions, communicated attributions can help to maintain a relationship, by drawing attention to the basic understanding of behaviour, or its absence, within a relationship and feelings about that relationship (see also Newman, 1981a,b).

As Kelley (1972b) noted for actor-observer attributions in social interaction, each spouse plays the role of speaker and listener. Similarly, Fincham (1985a) argued that a given act by one spouse is simultaneously both a stimulus (if it is followed by a partner behaviour) and a response (if it follows a partner behaviour). It is therefore difficult, and arbitrary, to impose a linear cause-effect structure on such interpersonal interaction. This complex interdependence is illustrated by the example of a husband who says 'I withdraw because you nag', and whose wife retorts, 'I nag because you withdraw' (Watzlawick et al., 1967, p. 56). What may appear, superficially (or in the separation imposed by a coding scheme), to be two different one-way causal sequences actually represents a circular causal process; each partner's actions are both an effect of the other's prior behaviour and a cause of the other's subsequent behaviour (Kelley, 1977). Family theorists (e.g., Watzlawick et al., 1967) refer to such instances, where two people fail to agree on which act in a sequence is stimulus and which is response, as problems of 'punctuation'. If actor and partner cannot even agree on the true sequence of behaviour, then perhaps it is not surprising that they disagree in their causal attributions.

Although Orvis et al.'s study had a seminal impact on the direction of attribution research, its results are qualified in certain respects (see Fincham, 1985a; Howe, 1987). First, as these authors acknowledged, the coded explanations referred only to instances of attributional conflict. Furthermore, respondents were asked to list the causes of their own and their partners' actions, rather than the causes of the interactions between the two of them, a procedure that would seem to inflate personal attributions. Second, where multiple explanations were given, only the one defined as most prominent by the investigators was coded. Third, where a sequence of events was given, only the most immediate one was coded. Fourth, attributions such as 'My partner has a poor attitude about me' were coded as internal although, in the light of more recent research, such an attribution is clearly inter-personal. These limitations are perhaps most revealing to the extent that they set criteria for studies of attribution in close relationships, but they should also be borne in mind in extrapolating from this research and in judging its successors.

In contrast to the apparent ease with which Orvis et al. were able to examine attributional conflict, a subsequent study reported that couples were unaware of their actual attributional divergence. Harvey et al. (1978b, Study 1) asked 36 unmarried couples (who had been living together for at least six months and who had been chosen for their experience of relational conflict) to complete a questionnaire measuring their own attributions and predicted partner attributions concerning the sources of real conflict. Interestingly, in spite of evidence of attributional divergence, both males and females predicted that their partners would make attributions very similar to their own (i.e., they perceived convergence). Thus couples can be egocentric in their attributions and Harvey et al. suggested that this inaccurate view might become a major determinant of conflict in close relationships.

Once again, some qualifications to these findings should be stated. First, as Fincham (1985a) pointed out, Harvey et al. examined ratings of attributions for sensitive relationship conflicts (e.g., incompatibility of sexual relations, influence of possible alternative lovers), whereas Orvis et al. explicitly avoided them (because of concern about producing conflict). Second, although these couples were chosen for their experience of relational conflict, they turned out to be in highly satisfactory relationships. Thus ignorance of attributional divergence may be associated with greater relationship satisfaction.

Interpersonal conflict is not, of course, necessarily characteristic of, or restricted to, relationships within heterosexual couples. Sillars (1981, Study 1) asked 58 female and 51 male college dormitory residents to recall the most significant 'interpersonal problem' they had experienced with their room-mates. As in previous studies, there were again actor-partner differences. Respondents attributed more responsibility for the conflicts to their room-mates than to themselves. Responsibility attributed to a room-mate was also positively correlated with the perceived stability of conflicts; responsibility attributed to oneself was negatively correlated with perceived stability.

Sillars also measured three indices of conflict escalation and relationship deterioration – the perceived importance of conflicts, the frequency of conflicts with the room-mate and satisfaction with the room-mate – all of which were strongly and consistently associated with attributions. The pattern of results suggested that as conflicts intensified and relationship satisfaction declined, there was a decrease in self-attributed responsibility, an increase in other-attributed responsibility and an increase in the perceived stability of conflicts. Sillars also related attributions to respondents' reported conflict-resolution strategies. He found that respondents were more likely to report using 'integrative strategies' (defined as 'Explicit acknowledgement and discussion of conflict that sustains a neutral or positive evaluation of the partner and does not seek concessions', p. 290) when they perceived their partners to be more cooperative, attributed more responsibility to themselves and saw the conflict as less stable.[4]

In a second study, Sillars (1981, Study 2) followed up these ideas in a more naturalistic manner by videotaping 46 pairs of same-sex college students as they discussed problems they had experienced as room-mates. In this study there was no difference between the average responsibility attributed to self, compared with partner, but conflicts attributed to the partner were attributed to more stable factors (i.e., personality traits) than were conflicts not attributed to the partner. Unfortunately for a study of interpersonal conflict, 66 per cent of the respondents rated their satisfaction with their room-mates as 10 or more out of a possible 12 points, and actor-partner differences emerged only in dyads where both partners expressed moderate or low satisfaction. The conditions affecting actor-partner differences were, however, similar to those reported in the first study. As conflict increased in importance and frequency, and relationship satisfaction decreased, there was a decrease in self-attributed responsibility, an increase in other-attributed responsibility and an increase in the perceived stability of conflict.

Sillars reported that respondents who made internal attributions (more attribution to self than partner) differed from those who made external attributions in their use of 'avoidance', 'distributive' and 'integrative' strategies (in avoidance strategies 'Discussion is avoided to minimize negative reactions from the partner'; in distributive strategies there is 'Explicit acknowledgement and discussion of conflict that seeks concessions from the partner', p. 290). Self-attributed responsibility was associated with more integrative behaviour and other-attributed responsibility was associated with more avoidance and distributive behaviour.

Finally, Sillars analysed transition sequences to examine how an act by the partner was responded to by the actor. The results suggested that other-attributed responsibility led to reciprocation and conflict escalation in response to distributive acts, whereas self-attributed responsibility led to de-escalation and conciliation. As Sillars admitted, it is not possible to say whether conflict escalation produced changes in attributions, or vice versa, or whether both conflict escalation and attribution are symptoms of a third factor. Just as other researchers at the interpersonal level emphasized that attribution in interaction is a circular process, Sillars expected causal influence in both directions.

The three studies reviewed in this section, based on a variety of relationships (dating, living together, married and room-mates), provide initial evidence of the incidence and nature of attributions in interpersonal conflict and the association between attributions and other variables, such as relationship satisfaction and conflict-resolution strategies (see also Fincham et al., in press). As Fincham (1985a) has argued, however, it is important to distinguish between types of relationships (e.g., intimate-distant, equal-unequal) and, in particular, to distinguish between non-married and married couples, where legal obligations can change some aspects of relationships from voluntary to compulsory (see Lederer and Jackson, 1968). In view of these arguments, the following section concentrates solely on attributions in relation to marital satisfaction, a topic that has now stimulated a sizable body of theory and research.

Marital satisfaction

Distressed and non-distressed spouses. In recent years both practitioners and researchers in the area of marital therapy have drawn attention to the importance of causal attributions in marital dysfunction (Baucom, 1986; Fincham, 1985a). A first line of research was to compare the causal attributions made by distressed and non-distressed spouses. As Fincham (1985b) pointed out, an initial hypothesis (extending the self-serving bias) was that distressed spouses would attribute negative partner behaviour to internal causes, thereby accentuating the negative impact of such behaviours and maintaining marital distress. Non-distressed spouses, in contrast, would make external attributions for negative behaviour, thus minimizing its impact. It was similarly predicted that distressed spouses would make external attributions for positive partner behaviour, whereas non-distressed spouses would make internal attributions.

Some support for this simple internal–external hypothesis was claimed by Jacobson et al. (1985). Distressed and non-distressed marital partners engaged in a set of conflict-resolution tasks in the laboratory. Preceding one of these interactions, one of the partners was privately instructed to increase his or her positive (or negative) actions towards the other spouse. After the interaction, the other spouse completed a causal attribution questionnaire. As predicted, distressed couples rated negative spouse behaviour as more internal, whereas non-distressed couples did so for positive spouse behaviour. A similar result was also reported by Shields and Hanneke (1983), who found that wives attributed significantly more of their husbands' violence to internal causes than did the husbands.

Fincham and colleagues, however, reported no such differences in internal and external attributions between couples seeking therapy and happily married couples (Fincham et al., 1987b; Fincham and O'Leary, 1983). Fincham therefore augmented the simple locus dimension with stable-unstable, controllable-uncontrollable and global-specific ratings of perceived cause as well. This extension was suggested by the clinical observation that spouses presenting themselves for therapy often felt 'helpless' with respect to their marriages, believing that there was little they could do to change their partners' behaviour or improve the relationship. Seeing the parallel with learned helplessness, Fincham investigated the attribution dimensions that theoretically mediate learned helplessness (Abramson et al., 1978; see chapter 3). He predicted that spouses seeking marital therapy would make more spouse (external), global, stable and uncontrollable causal attributions for negative behaviours by the partner than would their non-distressed counterparts, and that the reverse pattern would be found for positive behaviours by the partner.

To test their predictions Fincham and O'Leary (1983) asked 16 happily married and 16 distressed couples (the latter were in marital therapy) to imagine that their spouses had behaved in a certain way. The subjects then named the major cause of six positive and six negative hypothetical behaviours by their spouses and rated each instance on the four causal dimensions – locus, stability, controllability and globality. Respondents also indicated the affective impact of the imagined behaviour and their most likely response to it. The results did not conform completely to the learned helplessness model, but there were significant differences between the attributions of distressed and non-distressed spouses. Distressed spouses rated the causes of negative behaviours as more global, whereas non-distressed spouses rated the causes of positive behaviours more global. The non-distressed spouses also rated the causes of positive behaviour more controllable. Overall, this study suggested a relatively minor role for attributions. Only for positive spouse behaviours did attribution ratings predict a significant portion of the variance in likely responses to behaviour, and the results of a path analysis suggested that the effect of attributions on likely behaviour was mediated by their impact on affect.

Given that the previous results might be restricted to hypothetical spouse behaviours, Fincham (1985b) asked a new sample of 37 couples (18 of which were in the early stages of marital therapy) to give their attributions, individually, for the two most important difficulties they experienced in their marriages. Respondents wrote down what they considered to be the major cause of the difficulties and then answered seven questions relating to the cause. These questions tapped perceptions of causal locus (in oneself, the spouse, the relationship, or outside circumstances), globality-specificity, stability and the extent to which the cause was due to the speaker's negative attitude or feelings towards them. A distressed spouse was more likely than a non-distressed spouse to see the partner, and the relationship, as the source of the marital difficulties; to perceive the causes of the difficulties as more global; and to see the causes as more reflective of the spouse's negative attitude towards the rater. This study thus extended and replicated the previous one, also clearly demonstrating the need to go beyond simple internal-external attributions.

The results so far can be summarized as follows. Happily married (or non-distressed) spouses tend to give their partners credit for positive behaviours by citing internal, stable, global and controllable factors to explain them. Negative behaviours, on the other hand, are explained away by ascribing them to causes viewed as external, unstable, specific and uncontrollable. As Holtzworth-Munroe and Jacobson (1985) noted, these attributions maximize the impact of positive behaviour and minimize the impact of negative behaviour; they can therefore be viewed as 'relationship-enhancing.' Distressed couples, in contrast, tend to give exactly the opposite pattern of attributions, which can be thought of as 'distress-maintaining' (see table 5).

Holtzworth-Munroe and Jacobson provided an important addition to this literature by investigating the frequency of 'attributional activity' in distressed and non-distressed relationships. They defined attributional activity as either the process of asking 'why?' questions (e.g., 'Why did he come home late?') or the outcome of such a process (e.g., 'He came home late because his boss kept him after hours.'). To measure unsolicited attributional activity, Holtzworth-Munroe and Jacobson used an indirect probe derived from work by Harvey et al. (1980; see chapter 3). The attributional thoughts coded were explicitly causal and not dispositional, and an attributional thought was defined as 'a statement that explained or explored the reasons *why* a spouse engaged in a behavior' (p. 1402).

Holtzworth-Munroe and Jacobson then compared 20 non-distressed and 20 distressed couples' attributions for 20 events from

TABLE 5   Relationship-enhancing and distress-maintaining attributions

	Type of partner behaviour	
Type of spouse	Negative	Positive
	(Relationship-enhancing)	
Non-distressed	External	Internal
	Unstable	Stable
	Specific	Global
	Uncontrollable	Controllable
	(Distress-maintaining)	
Distressed	Internal	External
	Stable	Unstable
	Global	Specific
	Controllable	Uncontrollable

Source: after Fincham et al., 1987a; Holtzworth-Munroe and Jacobson, 1985.

the Spouse Observation Checklist (Weiss and Margolin, 1977). The events consisted of five behaviours from each of four categories: frequently occurring positive events, infrequently occurring positive events, frequently occurring negative events, and infrequently occurring negative events. Distressed couples reported the highest number of attributional thoughts for frequent negative events, and they were more inclined towards attributional activity for such events than were non-distressed couples (see figure 8). For distressed couples, attributional activity was also least common in response to frequent positive behaviour on the part of the partner. According to Holtzworth-Munroe and Jacobson, the disinclination to explain a partner's frequent positive behaviour, and the heightened attributional activity for frequent negative behaviour, suggest that distressed spouses are more willing to focus their interpretation on the displeasing behaviours in which their partners engage, whereas they often ignore the implications of frequent and pleasing behaviour. As Bradbury and Fincham (in press, b) have pointed out, however, in comparing the occurrence of attributions for different types of events, one should take into account the base rates for those events. It could be, for example, that the base rate for 'frequent negative events' was different for distressed and non-distressed couples, thus obscuring a different ratio of attributions to behaviours for the two groups.

One of the most interesting findings reported by Holtzworth-Munroe and Jacobson was that distressed and non-distressed *wives* did not differ in their amounts of attributional activity, but distressed

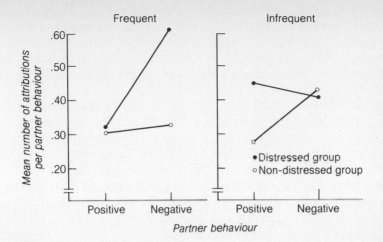

FIGURE 8 *Number of attributional thoughts as a function of marital satisfaction, behavioural frequency and impact of partner behaviour (from Holtzworth-Munroe and Jacobson, 1985, © 1985 by the American Psychological Association, reprinted by permission of the publisher and author)*

husbands reported significantly more attributional thoughts than did non-distressed husbands (within the distressed group, there was no difference between husbands and wives; within the non-distressed group, wives reported more attributional thoughts than husbands). Given that non-distressed husbands were particularly unlikely to engage in attributional activity, Holtzworth-Munroe and Jacobson speculated that 'Perhaps the role of married women in our culture produces a chronic attributional vigilance that obviates the need for enhanced mindfulness when displeasing or conflict-laden events occur ... men tend to ignore causal dynamics as long as the relationship is proceeding smoothly' (p. 1408). Holtzworth-Munroe and Jacobson found this fact interesting because it suggests that, at least for attributional activity, men rather than women may be the 'barometers' of relationship satisfaction. This view is in contrast to the claim that women tend to be the 'voice' of marital distress (Floyd and Markman, 1983).

With regard to the content of indirect, or unsolicited, attributional thoughts, non-distressed couples made a higher percentage of relationship-enhancing attributions than did the distressed couples, although all spouses' attributions for positive behaviours were more likely to be relationship-enhancing than were their attributions for negative behaviours. Spouses in distressed marriages produced significantly more distress-maintaining attributions for their partners' behaviour than did spouses in happy marriages. Spouses in both distressed and non-distressed relationships produced more distress-maintaining attributions for negative events.

In addition to their indirect probe measure of attribution, Holtzworth-Munroe and Jacobson also asked couples to nominate a primary cause of the event (i.e., a direct probe) and then to rate that perceived cause on 11 content dimensions. Responses to the direct probe were also coded as relationship-enhancing or distress-maintaining. For relationship-enhancing attributions, both distressed and non-distressed groups' attributions for positive behaviour were more likely to be relationship-enhancing than were their attributions for negative behaviours. For distress-maintaining attributions, spouses in distressed marriages produced significantly more distress-maintaining attributions for their partners' behaviour than did spouses in happy marriages. In addition, spouses in both distressed and non-distressed relationships produced more distress-maintaining attributions for negative events than they did for positive events.

There were also clear effects in the content dimensions. Non-distressed spouses were more likely than their distressed counterparts to attribute positive behaviours to their partners and less likely to attribute them to outside circumstances. They were more inclined to view such behaviours as intentional, voluntary and reflective of underlying personal traits; and they also perceived the causes as global and stable across time. In contrast, distressed spouses discredited their partners' positive behaviour by attributing it to circumstances or to the partner's state (as opposed to trait), by perceiving that the partner acted unintentionally and involuntarily, and by believing that the causes of such behaviours were unstable and specific. The opposite pattern of causal attributions was offered by non-distressed and distressed spouses for negative behaviours. Thus distressed couples' attributions for negative behaviour maximized the impact of these events by attributing them to the partner and his or her personal traits, seeing them as done intentionally and voluntarily, and perceiving them as being stable and global (cf. Camper et al., 1988).

Clearly, in its measurement of attribution by indirect and direct probes, as well as the content of attributions, Holtzworth-Munroe and Jacobson's study sets a new standard for research in this area (its results have recently been replicated for dating relationships by Grigg et al., in press). The same detailed study of the content of attribution dimensions characterizes research by Fincham et al. (1987a). Their first study investigated the attributions given by 44 married couples (of which half were in or seeking marital therapy) for a list of potential behaviours generated from the Spouse Observation Checklist (Weiss and Perry, 1979). Responses to six categories of behavioural events were analysed: partner behaviours and own behaviours that were rated positive, neutral and negative in impact. For each behaviour respondents wrote down the most important cause on the internal-external, stable-unstable and global-specific causal dimensions. Once again there was support for the view that the discrepancy between self and partner attributions is related to marital distress, although, because of missing data, these results were strongest for female respondents. Distressed wives exhibited a negative attributional bias by making more benign attributions for their own behaviour than for their partners' behaviour. In contrast, non-distressed wives made 'spouse-enhancing' attributions. This effect was most evident for the global-specific dimension. For positive behaviours, non-distressed wives were more likely to see the cause of their partners' behaviour as global than were distressed wives. For negative behaviours, the distressed wives saw the causes of partner behaviour as more global than the causes of their own behaviour, whereas the reverse was true in the non-distressed group. Also, the causes of partner behaviour were seen as more global in the distressed than in the non-distressed group (see figure 9).

In addition to the research on attributional activity, or 'spontaneous' attributions, in marriage, one can extend research by means of additional measures of attribution. For example, Madden and Janoff-Bulman (1981) investigated the relationship between self-*blame* and marital satisfaction. Married females rated how much they would blame themselves and their partners for hypothetical and actual conflicts. Relative self-blame was clearly associated with satisfaction: women who blamed themselves more than their husbands for marital conflict reported higher levels of marital satisfaction than women who blamed their husbands more than themselves. Fincham et al. (1987a, Study 2) went a stage further by investigating both causal and responsibility attributions. They asked happily married and distressed persons to imagine the occurrence of certain positive and negative behaviours in their relationships and to make attributions for the same behaviours performed (a) by their partners and (b) by themselves. After writing down the major cause of each behaviour, respondents made three judgements related to causal attribution dimensions (locus, stability and globality) and three judgements related to responsibility

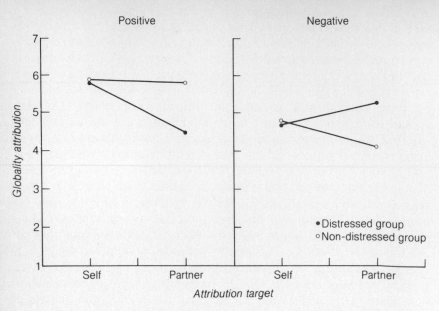

FIGURE 9   *Mean globality attribution as a function of type of behaviour, attribution, target and marital distress (data from Fincham et al., 1987a, Study 1, © 1987 by the American Psychological Association, reprinted by permission of the publisher and author)*

dimensions (blame/praise, intent and motivation). The only causal dimension on which self-partner differences were obtained was the global-specific dimension in the distressed group. Attributions for partner behaviour were seen as more global than self-attributions, but this difference was found only for negative behaviours. The results were stronger for responsibility attributions. Distressed respondents considered their own behaviour, relative to that of their partners, to reflect more positive intentions and unselfish motivation. Non-distressed respondents, in contrast, viewed their partners' behaviour as more unselfishly motivated and more praiseworthy than their own.

Fincham et al. (1987b) also reported strong effects for measures of responsibility attribution in their replication and extension of Fincham and O'Leary's (1983) study. Distressed spouses inferred more negative intentions and selfish motivations and judged negative spouse behaviour as more blameworthy than did non-distressed spouses. Fincham et al. also reported that only responsibility attributions, and not causal attributions, predicted the affective impact of and intended responses to the behaviour. Clearly, there is now strong evidence that both causal and responsibility attributions are important in marriage. Their relative importance, however, is best considered in the context of the little available research to date that has investigated the direction of causation between attributions and marital satisfaction.

The relationship between attributions and marital satisfaction. The results of research considered so far provide support for the view that people involved in non-distressed and distressed relationships (i.e., people who differ in marital satisfaction) tend to offer different explanations for events, and especially difficulties, within their relationships. This evidence suggests that attributions may serve to maintain, or even initiate, current levels of marital distress (e.g., Arias and Beach, 1987; Baucom, 1986; Berley and Jacobson, 1984), but it does not tell us how, if at all, the two variables are *causally* related.

As there are only two published longitudinal studies to answer this question, one of which deals with dating rather than marital relationships, I will review them both in some detail. In the first study, Fletcher et al. (1987) investigated the impact of attributions over a two-month period in the dating relationships of a sample of undergraduates. The main measure of attribution for the longitudinal component of the research assessed 'Actor versus partner causal attribution for relationship maintenance'. This measure required respondents to divide 100 into two parts, reflecting how responsible each partner was perceived to be in maintaining the relationship (Fletcher et al. refer to this as a measure of 'causal responsibility', p. 485, but thereafter refer to the partners' 'causal inputs', e.g., p. 486; I will therefore treat this as a measure of causal attribution). For this measure the authors expected a curvilinear relation: respondents who reported high relationship happiness, commitment and love would be more likely to perceive each partner as contributing equal causal inputs for relationship maintenance; whereas unequal attribution would be associated with lower levels of happiness, commitment and love. Fletcher et al. tested the relations for the presence of quadratic components, using multiple regression techniques. The regression equations for each variable – happiness, commitment and love – were used to plot regression lines, and the curves obtained did approximate the expected curvilinear relation (see figure 10).

This study also tested for significant curvilinear relations over time, between actor vs partner attributions at Time 1 and relationship happiness and love at Time 2 (partialling out the effect of relationship happiness or love for partner at Time 1). For relationship happiness

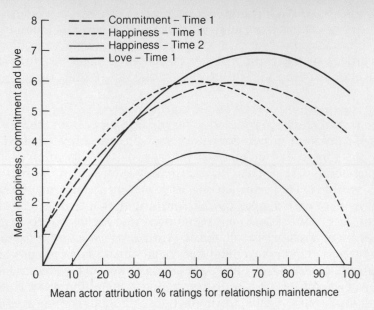

FIGURE 10   *Mean actor-attribution percentage ratings for relationship maintenance plotted against relationship happiness, commitment and love for partner, including the quadratic components; the curve for relationship happiness at Time 2 was calculated with relationship happiness at Time 1 partialled out (from Fletcher et al., 1987, © 1987 by the American Psychological Association, reprinted by permission of the publisher and author)*

there was a significant curvilinear relation: respondents who perceived both partners as providing equal causal inputs for relationship maintenance at Time 1 were happier two months later (see figure 10). Of particular importance to the overall argument, there was no effect of happiness and love at Time 1 on attributions at Time 2. This pattern of data suggests that attributions may have more influence on relationship happiness than vice versa.

The second, more ambitious, longitudinal study was carried out by Fincham and Bradbury (1987), who assessed both perceptions of what produced an event or behaviour (causal attributions) and perceptions of accountability or answerability for the event or behaviour (responsibility attributions). As these authors pointed out, the two types of attribution are closely related; responsibility judgements are said to 'entail' judgements of causation, because persons are normally held responsible only for outcomes that they cause. The two measures are not, however, always highly correlated, because they are made according to different criteria (see Fincham and Jaspars, 1980; Shaver, 1985). On the basis of previous research (e.g., Fincham et al., 1987b), Fincham and Bradbury argued that responsibility attributions, rather than causal attributions, would be central in marriage and would therefore be more prominent in their longitudinal analysis.

This study, which provided the first data relevant to the causal relation between attributions and *marital* satisfaction, assessed respondents' attributions at two points in time, separated by 10–12 months. Data were collected from 39 couples (31 of which responded to an advertisement in the newspaper and eight of which were seeking marital counseling), including measures of causal and responsibility attributions for marital difficulties and for hypothetical negative behaviours performed by a spouse (e.g., 'Your spouse criticizes something you do'). For both difficulties and behaviours spouses wrote down what they considered the major cause of the stimulus event. They then rated the cause on dimensions of locus, globality and stability. In addition, they made three responsibility judgements concerning blame, intentionality and selfish motivation.

The six ratings yielded two indices, of causal and responsibility attribution. The causal attribution index was scored to indicate the extent to which spouses viewed the causes in a manner likely to maximize the impact of the negative event (i.e., located the cause in the spouse and saw it as stable and global). The responsibility index was scored to indicate the extent to which spouses made less benign attributions (i.e., saw the behaviour as intentional, worthy of blame and reflective of selfish concerns). Marital satisfaction was measured using the Marital Adjustment Test (Locke and Wallace, 1959).

Both causal and responsibility indices were related to marital satisfaction in both phases of the study. Contrary to predictions, there was no evidence to suggest that responsibility attributions were more strongly related to marital satisfaction than were causal attributions. Both types of attribution were also quite stable over the course of a year and showed approximately the same degree of variation as did marital satisfaction scores. To test the main longitudinal hypothesis, causal and responsibility indices obtained in phase 1 were entered into a hierarchical regression analysis to predict marital satisfaction one year later. A significant increase in R^2 associated with the inclusion of the attribution indices was, however, obtained only in the regression analysis conducted using data for wives. Beta weights associated with both causal and responsibility attributions were also significant.

Regarding the possible causal role of attributions in marital satisfaction, these results were strengthened by two further findings. First, because marital satisfaction scores obtained in the two phases of the study were strongly related, it is noteworthy that attributions accounted for any significant portion of the variance in this measure. Second, marital satisfaction at phase 1 did not predict attributions at phase 2. This latter result is consistent with the view that wives' attributions, at least, are causally related to their future marital satisfaction.

There are three main findings of this important study. First, the correlations between measures of attribution and marital satisfaction are important because prior research (reviewed above) demonstrated the existence of attributional differences between extreme groups (i.e., non-distressed vs distressed spouses). Second, the unexpected finding of no difference in the predictive power of measures of causal and responsibility attribution may be due to the samples used. The majority of spouses in this study were not in marital therapy, and their scores on the Locke-Wallace Marital Adjustment Test were quite high. Fincham and Bradbury (1987) suggested that perhaps attributions of responsibility were more important than attributions of causality in previous studies only because the couples were severely distressed and in marital therapy; precisely such couples, of course, would be expected to be concerned about issues of accountability and blame (Jacobson and Margolin, 1979). Finally, although there was a strong association between attributions and concurrent marital satisfaction for husbands and wives, only wives' attributions predicted future marital satisfaction. The authors suggested the possibility that husbands' attributions might simply *reflect* their marital satisfaction, whereas wives' attributions may *influence* it. They also noted the fit between their data and the view that women may be the 'barometers' of marital functioning (e.g., Gottman, 1979; Ickes, 1985), because in our society they are more concerned with issues such as attachment, intimacy and caring than men are.

This last conclusion seems, however, the opposite of that put forward by Holtzworth-Munroe and Jacobson (1985). They suggested that distressed husbands were the barometers of relationship satisfaction, because only they were more inclined towards attributional activity than their non-distressed counterparts. Conclusions should be cautious in view of the different designs, samples and measures of the two studies. One possibility is that wives are the barometers of normal or relatively non-distressed relationships, and husbands are the barometers of distressed relationships.

In a critical review of marital attributions Bradbury and Fincham (in press, a) show exemplary caution with reference to these longitudinal studies. They acknowledge that longitudinal data cannot be used to infer causality, although both these studies did yield findings that are consistent with a causal direction *from* attributions *to* relationship quality or satisfaction. The evidence for this direction of influence is, however, promising rather than definite. As Fincham and Bradbury (1987) themselves concluded, more research is needed, with at least three waves of data, to investigate different lag times and to rule out influence in the opposite direction. Bradbury and Fincham (in press – a) have also considered the possibility that any relation between attribution and marital satisfaction, whether concurrent or predictive, may be an artefact of their non-independence. Having inspected the items on standard measures of relationship satisfaction, they admit that the strong effects found on the global-specific dimension may be, in part, due to overlapping item content (i.e., the measure of marital satisfaction includes items that themselves may reflect general attributional tendencies). Overall, however, Bradbury and Fincham contend that the association may be inflated by the item overlap, but is not simply an artefact.

Relationship termination. The final area of research linking attributions and relationships is concerned with the termination of relationships, as in separation and divorce. Some of the research deals with attributions, and other studies are concerned with more general 'accounts'. I will deal with the two approaches in turn and then consider how they are related.

One intuitively important role of attributions in relationship termination is to help the individual to come to terms with such a significant life event. Thus Newman and Langer (1981) investigated whether particular patterns of attribution were associated with post-divorce adaptation. They asked a sample of divorced females (of whom only 14 out of 66 were recently divorced) to 'explain the main reason why they had become divorced' (p. 226). Two major types of attribution identified were 'person' and 'interactive' attributions. As person attributions referred, in every case, to characteristics of the spouse, rather than of the respondent herself (e.g., the spouse's emotional immaturity, psychological problems or selfishness), I shall hereafter refer to them as spouse attributions. Interactive attributions referred to such things as changing lifestyles or values, a lack of closeness and love, and financial problems.

The main comparison in Newman and Langer's paper is between

those respondents who were rated as having made spouse attributions for their divorces and those who made interactive attributions. Significantly more women who made spouse attributions for their divorces were unhappy and saw themselves as socially inactive, and significantly fewer of them were optimistic, than those who made interactive attributions. On absolute scores, there were three differences between the groups: people who made spouse attributions judged themselves significantly less active and less socially skilled, and felt that they had less strong personalities, than did the interactive group. Finally, in a six-month follow-up with 48 of the respondents (made by telephone), those who made interactive attributions reported that they were happier than did their counterparts who made spouse attributions. In addition, significantly more people who said they had asked for their divorces made spouse attributions than did those who said they were asked for a divorce.

Although interesting, this study is subject to two interpretive qualifications. First, the authors never state the respective numbers of respondents who gave the two types of attributions. Second, as the authors themselves are aware, it is not clear whether interactive explanations lead to better post-divorce adjustment or whether people who make interactive attributions in general view themselves more positively.

Fletcher (1983) has also examined the structure and content of attributions for separation. He asked people to explain their recent marriage break-down and separation and then coded attributions from verbal protocols. As predicted, respondents saw their ex-spouses as more responsible for the causes of the break-up than they were themselves.[5] Interestingly, the decision to leave a relationship also had a significant influence on attributions. Respondents who made the decision to leave made higher attributions to themselves, but lower attributions to external factors acting on their ex-spouses, than did those who were left. Given procedural differences between the studies, it is unclear whether this result is really inconsistent with Newman and Langer's (1981) finding that those who asked for the divorce made more spouse attributions. One possible explanation lies in the fact that most of Newman and Langer's (female) respondents had been divorced for between one and three years, whereas Fletcher's (male and female) respondents had been separated for less than 18 months. It is conceivable that those who have quite recently asked for a divorce see themselves as responsible, in the sense of having taken the decision, and that those temporally separated from their decision to divorce are more concerned with rationalization and justification on the grounds of their spouses' obnoxious behaviour. A final interesting feature of Fletcher's study was that a large number of his respondents did not stop at dispositional attributions, but went beyond dispositions to background factors (e.g., upbringing) to explain the origin of personal characteristics. This realization that attributions can be arranged in some sort of 'perceived causal structure' (Kelley, 1983; see chapter 3) forges a link with the study of more general accounts given for relationship termination.

The link between attributions and accounts is made explicit by Harvey et al. (in press), who approach accounts from the framework of attribution theory. They define accounts as: 'people's explanations for past actions and events and characterizations of self and significant others that are presented in story-like fashion' (see also Harvey et al., 1978b, 1986; Lloyd and Cate, 1985; Weber et al., 1987). Accounts, according to these authors, represent more than collections of disparate attributions; they are meanings organized into a story. These stories are especially likely to be 'told', and developed, after the loss of close relationships. They may help people make sense of the loss of these relationships, release emotions and provide a greater sense of psychological control concerning the loss (see Weiss, 1975). Weber et al. (1987) emphasize that accounts do sometimes explain events, but their focus is much broader, including rationalization, justification and working through grief. Weber et al. list six general motives for making accounts: self-esteem, emotional purging, establishing a sense of control, the search for closure, the search for understanding, and accounts as ends in themselves. Presumably all these motives would help to explain why Weiss's (1975) respondents indicated that their most pronounced period of trying to make sense out of their marital troubles was immediately prior to, and for months or even years after, actual separation.

Some of the functions of accounts were revealed in a study by Harvey et al. (1986). They asked male and female students to provide as many explanations as they could for why their most recent significant close relationship had broken up and then to list their most important expectations about how their current or future relationships would develop. Of particular interest were the degrees of association between the different categories of explanations and expectations. The results suggested that if one can develop an explanation that identifies a solvable problem within a past failed relationship (e.g., 'communication problems'), then one's expectations for future relationships might be influenced by these accounts. For example, a commitment to 'open communication' would be an optimistic expectation based on one's account of a previous failed relationship.

Another study by Harvey (Harvey et al., 1978b, Study 2) followed a case-study approach. Ten separated persons were interviewed on two to four different occasions for a period of about six months. Harvey et al. found that these respondents continued to go over the causes of the relationship conflict long after it had ended (see also Stephen, 1987). Indeed, these researchers proposed that profound analysis of a relationship lags somewhat behind the critical behaviour in the sequence from conflict to separation. The focus of such accounts, furthermore, was on fixing blame and adjusting (generally lowering) evaluations of the partner.

Relationship termination is evidently an important phase of close relationships for anyone interested in the richness and diversity of naturally occurring attributions. As Harvey et al. (1978b) pointed out, however, researchers need to rule out artefactual explanations, such as the need for separating spouses to develop a 'story' that will facilitate the legal and psychological dissolution of their relationship. Researchers also must attempt to do justice to what can be detailed stories, while not losing sight of the need for valid and reliable measurement instruments that are closely allied to a testable theory. New techniques for the analysis of accounts continue to evolve (see Antaki, 1988), but they are still some way behind the rigour of attributional methods. The attributional approach is nonetheless complemented by, and sometimes merges into, the work on accounts, especially where issues of accountability are at stake. The major strength of the attributional approach, however, is precisely in its theoretical breadth and sophistication, characteristics not yet achieved by the work on accounts.[6]

Summary

The research on attributions in close relationships has advanced the literature both theoretically and methodologically. Theoretically, there is some evidence of generalization from phenomena such as actor-observer differences and the self-serving bias, but both effects are transformed in the context of close relationships, where the partners know each other well and are interdependent. The informational-perceptual flavour of actor-observer differences is overtaken by the importance of evaluation, and the internal-external focus of the self-serving bias is extended to dimensions of stability and especially globality in the form of relationship-enhancing and distress-maintaining attributions. Methodologically, most of the studies in this area have identified the shortcomings of the dispositional vs situational dichotomy and have explored new categories, such as interpersonal and relationship attributions.

The research within three broad areas – interpersonal conflict, marital satisfaction and relationship termination – yields quite consistent support for the importance of attributions in close relationships. On interpersonal conflict, there is evidence that attributions are linked to relationship satisfaction and to behaviour in the form of conflict-resolution strategies. On marital satisfaction there is now a large body of research, much of it highly sophisticated, showing how distressed and non-distressed couples make differing attributions for events in their relationships. There is particularly strong evidence that distressed spouses make causal and responsibility attributions that minimize the impact of positive behaviour by their partners and maximize the impact of negative behaviour, whereas non-distressed spouses do the reverse. Furthermore, these patterns of attribution, which serve to maintain marital distress, may actually determine, and not merely reflect, marital satisfaction. Finally, on relationship termination, the research suggests that attributions may help those involved to come to terms with such a devastating event and to plan their future. At this stage of relationships, attributions seem especially to be part of more detailed accounts, whose functions go beyond explanation to include rationalization, justification and the working through of grief.

CONCLUSION

My reaction on reviewing the burgeoning literature on interpersonal attribution is both positive and optimistic; much has been done already, but more will surely follow. When we reflect back and look ahead, four main themes emerge, and these can serve as conclusions to this chapter.

First, one cannot simply extrapolate from more basic social-psychological work to interpersonal attributions. There is evidence for actor-observer differences and self-serving biases in interpersonal attribution, and attributions have demonstrable interpersonal consequences. When, however, people interact with detailed knowledge of and emotions towards each other, and in order to discuss important issues, the attribution process is infused with evaluation and not merely cognition. Research on interpersonal attributions can, then, help to develop a more ecologically valid approach to social cognition (Fincham, 1985a).

Second, what are at present implicit links between attribution and communication need to be made explicit. As Newman (1981b) has argued, attributions need to reflect more realistically the dynamism of interpersonal interactions and intimate relationships (cf. Miller and Steinberg, 1975). Communication research proposes that when strangers first meet, their primary concern is with reducing uncertainty and increasing predictability about the behaviour of themselves and others (Berger and Calabrese, 1975). Over time, however, concerns change, topics become more intimate and communication itself changes. Attribution, like communication, is a circular process. Actors and observers, like speakers and listeners, change roles; one person's attribution can be both stimulus and response; and attributions both follow and lead to behaviour, as we see in expectancy-confirmation processes. At present, however, we know very little about how attributions change in the course of both interactions and relationships. A more communication-oriented approach would emphasize how, as well as what, attributions are made.

Third, although for theoretical and pragmatic reasons I have tried to keep separate attributions of cause and responsibility (and to focus on the former), this distinction breaks down at the level of interpersonal attribution. As I have noted at several points in this chapter, the concern with causal explanation merges with, and is sometimes supplanted by, the concern with accountability. As researchers study more intimate relationships they must ask not only whether attributions are internal, stable or global, but also whether they reflect blame, intentionality and selfish motivation. In short, explanation gives way to justification and retribution.

Fourth, and finally, the research on attributions in close relationships has implications for the use of attributions in clinical interventions. This is neither my focus nor my speciality, but it should be noted that some interventions now assume that attributions influence marital satisfaction (e.g., Baucom and Lester, 1986; Wright and Fichten, 1976). One implication of the reported research is that marital therapists should not stop when spouses begin to engage in positive behaviours. Rather, therapy should then focus on attributional processes in order to ensure that the spouses' attributions do not undermine the potentially reinforcing impact of positive changes (Holtzworth-Munroe and Jacobson, 1985). An alternative interpretation is that attributions themselves may reflect an undesirable concern with *quid pro quo* exchanges that should be extinguished completely (Fincham, 1985a). Finally, and more realistically, therapy might try to help spouses to make more benign attributions (Baucom, 1986; Berley and Jacobson, 1984; Epstein, 1982) and to make equally benign attributions for their own and their partner's behaviour (Fincham et al., 1987a). We are taught in Western as well as Eastern cultures to 'do unto others as we would have them do to us'; now that we have looked at the pervasive and sometimes pernicious nature of interpersonal attributions, it may be of no little significance to admonish people to 'attribute others' behaviour as you would wish them to attribute your own'.[7]

6 Intergroup Attribution: Social Categorization and its Consequences

> We live in a social environment which is in constant flux. Much of what happens to us is related to the activities of groups to which we do or do not belong; and the changing relations between these groups require constant readjustments of our understanding of what happens and constant causal attributions about the why and the how of the changing conditions of our life.
>
> (Tajfel, 1969)

INTRODUCTION

The transition from the preceding chapter to the present one can be understood in the light of the distinction between interpersonal and intergroup behaviour. To convey the differences between these two forms of behaviour, Tajfel (1978) proposed a hypothetical continuum, with end-points of 'pure' interpersonal and 'pure' intergroup behaviour. At the interpersonal end, we deal with relations that are purely determined by interpersonal characteristics of those involved; for example, the intimate relationship between room-mates. At the intergroup extreme, we are concerned with relations that are defined completely by people's memberships in social groups; for example, a Jew and an Arab discussing the Palestinian uprising. Tajfel acknowledged that both end-points were pure, or idealized, in that, for example, even an intimate heterosexual relationship could shift from the interpersonal to the intergroup end of the continuum as a result of the topic being discussed. Thus Deaux and Major (1987) proposed that the salience of gender schemata can be triggered by particular life events or specific actions of a perceiver towards a target (see Spence, 1984, 1985). In this manner an interpersonal interaction between husband and wife, as studied in the previous chapter, could develop into a gender-based intergroup interaction when a division of labour is discussed. Notwithstanding the deliberately dynamic nature of this interpersonal–intergroup continuum, it has proved useful to distinguish between the two types of behaviour and to ensure that research is directed as much towards intergroup as to interpersonal relations.

This chapter deals with attributional phenomena nearer the intergroup end of Tajfel's continuum. As he suggested, three main criteria distinguish between the two extremes. First, the presence or absence of at least two clearly identifiable social categories – for example, black and white or male and female. Second, whether there is low or high *inter*subject variability of behaviour or attitude within each group (intergroup behaviour is typically homogeneous or uniform, whereas interpersonal behaviour shows the normal range of individual differences). Third, whether there is low or high *intra*subject variability in relation to other group members (i.e., whether a person reacts similarly to a wide range of different others from the same category, as in the case of stereotyping). Thus, in summary, as Sherif (1966) observed, intergroup behaviour occurs 'whenever individuals belonging to one group interact, collectively or individually, with another group or its members *in terms of their group identification*' (p. 12). Interpersonal behaviour, in contrast, refers to interaction that is determined by the individual characteristics of, and personal relationships between, participants (Brown and Turner, 1981; Tajfel, 1978).

The psychological components of intergroup behaviour have been discussed by Turner (1982; Turner et al., 1987), who has argued that a transition from personal to social identity underlies the shift from interpersonal to intergroup behaviour. Personal identity refers to self-definitions in terms of personal or idiosyncratic characteristics; social identity denotes definitions based on group or category memberships. Along with these self-definitions go self-assignments of the common or critical attributes of group membership. So not only can people see outgroup members in stereotyped ways, they can also see themselves as relatively interchangeable with ingroup members. Thus intergroup behaviour is more uniform both within the group and towards outgroups, because people develop their attitudes and actions on the basis of those common attributes. It should be clear, therefore, that it is not simply a matter of numbers of people that distinguishes the two kinds of behaviour. Both interpersonal and intergroup behaviour are the actions of individuals 'acting in terms of self' (Turner et al., 1987, p. ix), but in one case they are the actions of individuals *as* individuals and in the other they are actions of individuals *as* group members.

From this perspective, *intergroup attribution* refers to the ways members of different social groups explain the behaviour (as well as the outcomes and consequences of behaviour) of members of their own and other social groups. A person attributes the behaviour of another person not simply to individual characteristics, but to characteristics associated with the group to which the other person belongs. In addition, the perceiver or attributor is also conceived of as a group member, which constitutes a further influence on the intergroup attribution process. As we will see, intergroup attributions are often ethnocentric, in the sense that members of a particular group favour members of their own group, rather than members of outgroups (see LeVine and Campbell, 1972; Sumner, 1906).

This chapter begins with theoretical contributions to intergroup attribution, that are borrowed from the literature on both intergroup relations and attribution theory. I then provide a systematic and critical review of the available empirical research, followed by a discussion of its cognitive and motivational bases, and its possible emotional consequences. Finally, I illustrate the importance and applicability of this research with reference to the attributional bases of intergroup conflict, especially attempts to reduce conflict between groups. Ironically, Heider began his monograph on *The Psychology of Interpersonal Relations* with the statement that 'social psychologists have been mainly interested in the relations between people when larger groups play a role' (1958, p. 3). In subsequent years this claim has certainly not been true, but thanks to a recent growth of interest in the social psychology of intergroup relations (e.g., Billig, 1976; Brewer and Kramer, 1985; Messick and Mackie, in press; Tajfel, 1982) there is now an impressive body of evidence that social categorization constitutes a fundamental influence on causal attributions.

THEORETICAL CONTRIBUTIONS TO INTERGROUP ATTRIBUTION

One outcome of the distinction between interpersonal and intergroup behaviour has been the discussion of whether social units require a new level of theory differing from that which is appropriate to the study of individuals (Campbell, 1958). Taylor and Brown (1979) argued against simple extrapolations from the individual to the group; but they maintained that an acceptance of the individual as the unit of analysis need not result in an ignorance of social processes and, moreover, was a prerequisite for a psychological approach to intergroup phenomena. Tajfel, however, rejoined that there was a fundamental distinction between 'individualistic' theories and those concerned with 'socially shared patterns of individual behaviour' (1979, p. 187). There is merit in both theoretical positions and some rapprochement is necessary. As Turner et al. (1987) have recently concluded, psychological processes belong only to individuals, but there is a psychological discontinuity between individuals acting as 'individuals' and as 'group members'. Group behaviour cannot be reduced to interpersonal relationships.

This section reviews theoretical contributions of two different sorts: from intergroup relations to intergroup attributions, and from interpersonal to intergroup attributions. In view of the distinction between interpersonal and intergroup behaviour, and the debate concerning whether a new level of theory is required, extrapolations of the latter type should be made cautiously. But together these literatures provide a rich theoretical background to the investigation of intergroup attributions.

From intergroup relations to intergroup attributions

Several major theorists of intergroup relations acknowledged the attributional component of intergroup perceptions, whether in terms of causality, responsibility or blame (all of which have been used interchangeably).

Allport's classic analysis of prejudice drew out a number of attributional implications of scapegoating, usually directed at a weak but identifiable minority: 'It is not we ourselves who are responsible for our misfortunes, but other people' (1954, p. 244). Allport also discussed 'cause and effect thinking' and built on to Heider's (1944) work on over-attribution to persons. Allport pointed out that the propensity for person attributions had an important consequence for group relations – the person, or group, seen as the cause was attacked. As he quoted from Tertullian:

> They take the Christians to be the cause of every disaster to the state, of every misfortune to the people. If the Tiber reaches the wall, if the Nile does not reach the fields, if the sky does not move or if the earth does, if there is a famine, or if there is a plague, the cry is at once, 'The Christians to the Lions'. (quoted by Allport, 1954, p. 243)

Sherif's (1966) study of intergroup relations also included a number of fascinating aspects of intergroup attribution. He saw the role of stereotypes in relation to blaming the outgroup and vindicating the ingroup and he noted that 'the assignment of blame is conducted almost entirely from the ingroup's point of view' (pp. 109–10).

Campbell (1967) also approached intergroup attribution from the study of stereotypes and he saw 'erroneous causal perception' as one of the undesirable aspects of stereotypes, whereby characteristics of the outgroup are seen as the cause of the hostility felt by the ingroup. He also noted the tendency to perceive racial rather than environmental causes for group differences. Environmental causes are complex and diffuse, whereas skin colour and facial characteristics are highly visible (see also LeVine and Campbell, 1972).

Tajfel's (1969) cognitive analysis of prejudice referred most specifically to some of the functions of intergroup attributional bias. He argued that a perceiver's system of causes must provide, as far as possible, a positive self-image (see discussion of social identity, below). Tajfel was especially interested in the way people ascribed changes in the world to characteristics and actions of the ingroup or outgroup. He suggested (after Jones and Davis, 1965) that person rather than situation attributions would predominate. There would also be an even greater need for simplification and predictability in the case of intergroup, as compared to interpersonal, attributions. These group attributions would involve the 'personalizing' of large-scale groups and a preference for explanations focused on inherent group charac-teristics, rather than transient situational factors.

A more recent and detailed theory of intergroup attribution has been developed in a series of publications by Deschamps (1973–4, 1977, 1983; Deschamps and Clémence, 1987). His theoretical framework is constructed from research in two areas – social categorization and social representations. It is now well known that categorization of the social world serves a cognitive-organizational function (e.g., Rosch, 1978); although information regarding individual differences within a category may be lost, the complex social environment must be reduced to manageable units. The main role played by categorization is that, in a situation of less than complete information, perceivers infer character-istics of an object from the category to which it belongs (see Billig, 1976; Tajfel, 1972, 1978). From this perspective a perceiver attributes the behaviour of another person not simply to individual character-istics, but to characteristics associated with the group to which the other belongs. Thus attributions vary as a function of the social categorization of the actor or target. This fact was demonstrated in the early experiments by Thibaut and Riecken (1955). Experimental subjects met two stimulus persons (confederates of the experimenter), one of whom was of considerably higher status than the other. During the experiment the subject repeatedly tried to influence the behaviour of the two confederates, both of whom eventually complied at the same moment. Both studies reported that the perceived locus of causality was internal for compliance by the higher-status person and external for compliance by the lower-status person.[1] These studies did not, however, manipulate the social categorization of the perceiver, a person who is also located within a system of categories. The social categorization of the perceiver constitutes a further influence on the process of intergroup attribution, one that must be investigated in interaction with the social categorization of the actor.

Deschamps's use of social representations was an attempt to introduce the shared systems of beliefs that group members hold about their own and other groups. These representations are dealt with in detail in the following chapter, but Deschamps focused on a more conventional type of representation, namely social stereotypes. He seemed, however, to attach major importance to the fact that stereotypes are essentially characteristics or traits 'attributed' to members of one group by members of another group. As I have argued earlier, however, trait attribution (description) is not synonymous with causal attribution (explanation). Nonetheless, stereotypes should form an essential part of a theory of intergroup attribution. Thus the content of stereotypes may provide easily available or accessible causes of outgroup (or indeed ingroup) behaviour. As Bruner (1957b) noted, accessible categories tend to preclude the operation of other causal categories, which is exactly what seems to happen in many of the studies reviewed below.

It should now be clear that several scholars of intergroup relations identified the phenomena of intergroup attribution. They did not, however, make very precise predictions, unlike scholars who approached intergroup attribution from some of the well-established attributional phenomena.

From interpersonal to intergroup attributions

Phenomenal causality. Although Heider (1958) was primarily concerned with interpersonal relations, he did offer some interesting insights into the intergroup attribution process. As noted above in chapter 2, Heider (1944) proposed that if two events are similar to each other, or proximate, then the one is likely to be seen as the cause of the other. For example, a 'bad' act is easily connected with a 'bad' person (see Zillig, 1928). Heider seemed to acknowledge, here, the impact of social categorization on attribution. A further consequence of the unit-formation of actor and act is their mutual influence. Heider claimed that acts become infused with the characteristics of the person to whom they are attributed, and thus the same act performed by quite different actors is often not seen as the same act at all. Finally, in the same paper, Heider noted that 'Scapegoat behaviour often is not simply release of aggression but includes blaming others for changes which, if attributed to the person, would lower the self-esteem' (p. 245). Heider was thus clearly aware of the role of categorization and its related biases, and he drew attention to some of the functions fulfilled by what I call intergroup attributions.

Correspondent inference.   Jones and Davis (1965) applied their theory only to interpersonal attribution, but Cooper and Fazio (1979) used it as the basis of their attempt to analyse the 'outrageous logic' of people acting as group members, who try to 'convince themselves of the evil inherent in out-group members' (p. 150). They argued that 'personalism' (a perceiver's belief that an actor intended to benefit or harm the perceiver specifically), although not a frequent occurrence when we act as individuals, might be more typical of intergroup encounters. Cooper and Fazio introduced a new term, 'vicarious personalism', to convey the perception by members of one group that another group's actions were aimed at and intended for them. The result of this perception, they argued, is that ingroup members make a simplistic correspondent inference about the evil nature of the outgroup.

As noted earlier, Jones and McGillis's (1976) revision of Correspondent Inference Theory also acknowledged that group memberships could have an impact on attributions. They emphasized the impact of expectancies on dispositional attribution, including category-based expectancies that could dominate individual characteristics.

Actor-observer differences.   Jones and Nisbett (1972) hypothesized that observers' attributions are both more dispositional and less situational than those of actors. Stephan (1977) drew an analogy between this actor-observer difference and ingroup-outgroup differences in attribution. He suggested that an observer, when observing the behaviour of an ingroup rather than an outgroup member (particularly in the case of different cultural groups) would have more information on the antecedents of the observed behaviour; would be more likely to empathize; and would be more likely to analyse the situation in terms similar to those of the actor.

The main problem with Stephan's analogy is that, as noted in previous chapters, the actor-observer hypothesis ignores the observer's evaluation of the actor and his or her behaviour. As Regan (1978), for example, has shown, when we like or dislike other people, we may attribute their behaviour in a manner relatively consistent with our view of them. The effect of liking, or evaluation, interacts with the main effect implied by the Jones-Nisbett hypothesis. Thus positive behaviour by a liked other is attributed more to internal causes than the same behaviour by a disliked other. Given that acts themselves, as well as our prior knowledge of actors, may have an evaluative dimension, the actor-observer hypothesis would not seem to provide a promising basis for intergroup attributions (see Jaspars and Hewstone, 1982).

From self-serving to group-serving attributions. Research on interpersonal attributions for success and failure has documented a tendency for perceivers to make more flattering self-attributions following success than following failure outcomes. More generally, Kelley (1973) identified a tendency for perceivers to attribute to themselves events with positive outcomes and to attribute to another person events with negative outcomes (Kelley called this bias 'egocentric' but it is, strictly speaking, 'egotistic'; see chapter 5). Taylor and Jaggi (1974) proposed that the same bias applied at the group level (labelled 'ethnocentric' attribution), with people attributing positive events to their own group and negative events to other groups. They therefore predicted that perceivers would make more internal attributions for other ingroup members performing socially desirable acts, and external attributions for undesirable acts. They predicted the reverse for attributions to outgroup members (see table 6).

Taylor and Jaggi's model has been extended by Pettigrew, who referred to an 'ultimate attribution error', defined as a 'systematic patterning of intergroup misattributions shaped in part by prejudice' (1979, p. 464). Strictly speaking, this 'error' is a *bias*, given the absence

TABLE 6 Ethnocentric attributions

Type of behaviour	Type of actor	
	Ingroup	Outgroup
Positive	Internal	External
Negative	External	Internal

Source: after Taylor and Jaggi, 1974.

of any criteria for accuracy (see chapter 3). It focuses on the explanation of outgroup behaviour and extends the fundamental attribution error (L. Ross, 1977), the tendency to underestimate situational factors and overestimate personal factors as causes of an actor's behaviour.

Pettigrew extrapolated from the positivity bias for intimate others (their positive actions are attributed internally and their negative actions externally) and the negativity bias for disliked others (their negative actions are attributed internally and their positive actions externally; see Regan et al., 1974; Taylor and Koivumaki, 1976). The basis of the 'ultimate attribution error' is a negativity bias for attributions of outgroup behaviour, because a negatively stereotyped view of the outgroup needs to be protected from a positive outgroup evaluation. If an outgroup member is seen as performing a negative act consistent with a negative view, the tendency to make a dispositional attribution will be enhanced. A problem arises, however, when the outgroup member is seen as performing a single positive act, inconsistent with the prejudiced perceiver's negative view of the outgroup. Assuming that the positive act cannot be denied altogether, or reevaluated, it must be 'explained away'. Pettigrew crossed degree of controllability of the act by the perceiver (High/Low) with the perceived locus of control of the act (Internal/External to the actor) to yield four main possibilities for explaining away positive behaviour by a member of a disliked outgroup (see table 7). These attributional possibilities illustrate some of the variety of ways in which outgroup members' positive acts can be explained away.[2]

Pettigrew specified the ultimate attribution error in the form of two main predictions:

> Across-group perceptions are more likely than within-group perceptions, especially for prejudiced individuals, to include the following:
> 1 For acts perceived as negative (antisocial or undesirable), behaviour will be attributed to personal, dispositional causes. Often these internal causes will be seen as innate characteristics, and role requirements will be overlooked.
> 2 For acts perceived as positive (prosocial or desirable), behaviour will be attributed to any one of the combination of the following: A. to the exceptional, even exaggerated, special case individual who is contrasted with his/her group; B. to luck or special advantage and often seen as unfair; C. to high motivation and effort; and/or D. to manipulable situational context. (Pettigrew, 1979, p. 469)

There is an obvious similarity between Pettigrew's classification scheme and the one proposed by Weiner et al. (1972) for attributions of achievement behaviour. Pettigrew acknowledged this resemblance, but argued that the goals and the underlying dimensions of the two

TABLE 7 Classification scheme for 'explaining away' positive behaviour by a member of a disliked outgroup

		Perceived locus of control of act	
		Internal	External
Perceived degree of controllability of act by the perceiver	Low	A. The exceptional case	B. Luck or special advantage
	High	C. High motivation and effort	D. Manipulable situational context

Source: Pettigrew, 1979, © by the Society for Personality and Social Psychology, Inc.

schemes were different (notably, for Weiner controllability refers to the actor, whereas for Pettigrew it refers, less convincingly, to the perceiver). Nonetheless, the success with which Weiner's work has been applied to interpersonal achievement situations suggests that it would also be applicable to intergroup attributions, especially in the sphere of achievement (see Hewstone, 1988a). Weiner's three dimensions – locus (internal/external), stability (stable/unstable) and controllability (controllable/uncontrollable) – have been used to classify four main causes of success and failure: ability, effort, luck and the task. Although I have warned, earlier, that the perceived causes may vary along Weiner's dimensions (e.g., luck may be seen as an internal and stable characteristic of some people), this taxonomy provides an interesting set of possibilities for ingroup-serving and outgroup-derogating attributions in achievement contexts. In particular, there would appear to be multiple possibilities for explaining away outgroup success and ingroup failure in group-serving terms (see table 8).

These possibilities broadly support Taylor and Jaggi's (1974) predictions of internal attribution for ingroup positive and outgroup negative acts, but external attribution for ingroup negative and outgroup positive acts, with one exception. Both outgroup success and ingroup failure can be attributed to effort, derogating the outgroup and favouring the ingroup, respectively. Effort is, in fact, a somewhat ambiguous attribution, because although most of us value perseverance, we can explain away the success of a disliked person by claiming that he or she had to try very hard (as Pettigrew noted). My predictions, based on Weiner's classification, also include three out of four of Pettigrew's attributions for positive outgroup behaviour (only 'the

TABLE 8   Ingroup-serving and outgroup-derogating attributions in achievement contexts

	Type of actor	
Type of outcome	Ingroup	Outgroup
Success		*Effort* (internal, unstable, controllable)
	Ability (internal, stable, uncontrollable)	*Luck* (external, unstable, uncontrollable)
		Task (external, stable, uncontrollable)
Failure	*Effort* (internal, unstable, controllable)	
	Luck (external, unstable, uncontrollable)	*Ability* (internal, stable, uncontrollable)
	Task (external, stable, uncontrollable)	

Source: Hewstone, 1988a.

exceptional case' is excluded) *as well as* making predictions for outgroup failure and both ingroup outcomes. More generally, the true value of Weiner's approach may lie in the underlying dimensions, rather than the perceived causes. Different perceived causes attain prominence in different situations, but according to Weiner (e.g., 1986) the three basic dimensions have wide-ranging applicability. Thus from the parentheses in table 8, one can predict the type, if not the content, of causes for intergroup attributions in general.

Summary

There is obviously no dearth of theoretical contributions to intergroup attribution. Some of these ideas are to be found in the literature on intergroup relations and others are extrapolated from theories of interpersonal attribution. The most promising integrations of these two perspectives extend our research horizons from self-serving to group-serving attributions and make quite specific predictions. In the following section I review the available literature on intergroup attributions.

EMPIRICAL EVIDENCE FOR INTERGROUP ATTRIBUTION

This section provides a selective, rather than exhaustive, review of the literature on intergroup attribution, grouped under three headings –

attributions for positive and negative outcomes, success and failure and group differences (see Hewstone, 1988b, for a comprehensive review). Although the number of published articles is quite small, some include multiple studies and nearly all of them test predictions for more than one social group, thus providing a respectable data base for conclusions about the consistency of effects.[3] There is clear evidence of intergroup attribution in all three types of study reviewed and, indeed, in most studies, but intergroup attributional bias is typically limited to specific dimensions, rather than ubiquitous.

Positive and negative outcomes

The first empirical investigation of intergroup attributions was carried out by Taylor and Jaggi (1974) in Southern India, against the background of conflict between Hindu and Muslim groups. Subjects (Hindu adults) first rated the concepts 'Hindu' and 'Muslim' on 12 evaluative traits, then read 16 one-paragraph descriptions. They were asked to imagine themselves in a given situation, being acted towards in a certain manner by another Hindu (ingroup member) or a Muslim (outgroup member). Some situations described socially desirable behaviour (e.g., being sheltered from the rain) and other situations described undesirable behaviour (e.g., being refused shelter). Subjects had to explain the behaviour of the other person involved by choosing one of a number of explanations. In each case one explanation was internal and the remainder were external. The basic hypothesis of the study was that perceivers would make internal attributions for other Hindus performing socially desirable acts, and external attributions for undesirable acts. Attributions for Muslim outgroup members, in contrast, would be external for socially desirable acts, but internal for socially undesirable ones.

In all four stories used, Hindu subjects were more likely to make internal attributions for socially desirable than socially undesirable behaviour performed by Hindus. In only two of the four stories with a Muslim actor, however, were attributions more internal for socially undesirable, compared with desirable, behaviours. Taylor and Jaggi did not directly compare the attributions for ingroup and outgroup members performing socially desirable and undesirable behaviours; from their results, however, very strong differences emerged. For socially desirable behaviours, internal attribution was higher for ingroup than outgroup actors; and for socially undesirable behaviours, internal attribution was lower for ingroup than outgroup actors.

Given the importance of this first study, Hewstone and Ward (1985) carried out a conceptual replication with four main refinements: (1) there were no ratings of ingroup and outgroup on evaluative traits before the causal attributions, which might induce a competitive response set; (2) there was one internal and one external attribution for each behaviour; (3) the data were transformed to allow for a standard analysis of variance, exploring all main effects and interactions; and (4) respondents from two groups were used, so that reciprocal intergroup attributions could be investigated.

Our first study involved Malay (majority) and Chinese (minority) groups in Malaysia. Malays behaved as expected, by making more internal attributions for a positive than a negative act by a Malay actor, although they did not reverse this pattern when judging a Chinese actor. When the two actors were compared directly, the Malays attributed a positive act by a Malay actor more to internal factors than a similar act by a Chinese actor, and they attributed a negative act by an ingroup member less to internal factors than a similar act by an outgroup actor. Thus there was clear evidence of ethnocentric attribution, with the effect of ingroup favouritism far stronger than that of outgroup derogation.[4] Contrary to predictions, the Chinese also favoured the Malay actors, at the expense of their own group; they showed no trace of ethnocentric attribution (see figure 11).

We then carried out a second study in Singapore, using the same ethnic groups and design, except that Malays were now the minority and Chinese the majority. The only effect was that Malays made more internal attributions for the positive than the negative behaviour of a Malay. The Chinese did not significantly favour either group (see figure 12). Overall, this set of studies indicated that ethnocentric attribution is not a universal tendency and can be reversed, in the case of low-status groups, against the background of political and cultural tension.

There are many differences between Malaysia and Singapore, but these different sets of results may reflect the different levels of inter-ethnic group conflict in the two countries, with more conflict in the politically tense and potentially assimilationist culture of Malaysia, than in relatively multicultural Singapore. These attributional data were backed up by ethnic stereotypes. In Malaysia, Malays saw themselves positively, but viewed the Chinese predominantly negatively (as did the Chinese themselves). In Singapore there was a striking overall decrease in stereotyping. The responses of the Chinese in Malaysia may also be due to the distinctive role many of them enact in Malaysian society. They constitute a prototypical 'middle man minority' (Blalock, 1967), occupying a marginal role between producer and consumer as a response to hostile reactions from the

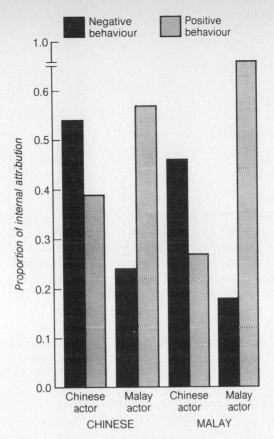

FIGURE 11 *Proportion of internal attribution as a function of ethnic group of perceiver, ethnic group of actor, and outcome (Malaysia) (after Hewstone and Ward, 1985, © 1985 by the American Psychological Association, reprinted by permission of the publisher and author)*

surrounding community (Bonacich, 1973). Bonacich argued that despite their undeniable economic successes, which should engender pride in group membership, 'Discrimination and hostility against minorities usually has the effect of hurting group solidarity and pride, driving a group to the bottom rather than the middle of the social structure' (p. 584). Our results are therefore consistent with a large sociological literature.

Stephan (1977) used a similar method to study 5th and 6th graders

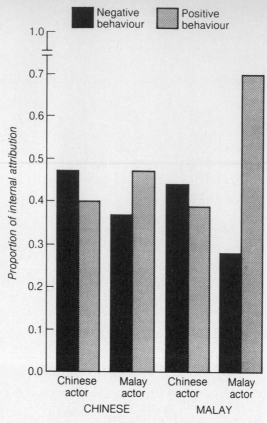

FIGURE 12   *Proportion of internal attribution as a function of ethnic group of perceiver, ethnic group of actor, and outcome (Singapore) (after Hewstone and Ward, 1985, © 1985 by the American Psychological Association, reprinted by permission of the publisher and author)*

in segregated and integrated schools in the South West of the United States. Children from three ethnic groups (blacks, Chicanos and Anglos) chose between internal and external attributions for positive and negative behaviours by another student from each group. Stephan analysed the data separately for the stimulus person, as a function of ethnicity, and reported ingroup-serving attributions for both Anglos and Chicanos. The Anglos made slightly more dispositional attributions for the positive behaviour of an Anglo than did blacks; the

Chicanos attributed the positive behaviour of Chicanos more dispositionally, and the negative behaviour of Chicanos less dispositionally, than did blacks. With this limited analysis, blacks revealed no ingroup-serving attributions, because Stephan failed to analyse how members of each group judged the ingroup in comparison with outgroups. If one examines the data more closely, in all three groups there was a strong tendency to give more internal attributions for positive than negative actions, irrespective of the group member-ship of the actor. Aside from this main effect, however, there appeared to be no differences in the Anglos' attributions for positive or negative behaviour by the ingroup and outgroups. The Chicanos gave slightly more dispositional attributions for positive behaviour by the ingroup, and slightly fewer dispositional attributions for negative behaviour by the ingroup, than for outgroups. The blacks showed the strongest tendency to be ingroup-serving: they gave more dispositional attributions for ingroup-positive than outgroup-positive behaviours, but did not differentiate between groups in attributing negative behaviours. This reinterpretation of Stephan's data suggests rather different evidence for intergroup attribution than he reported and underlines the importance of a full analysis of data, including main effects for the perceiver's group, the target group and the type of behaviour, as well as all interactions.

In a more realistic study of inter-racial attributions, Duncan (1976) asked white American college students to view a videotaped interaction of an increasingly violent argument in which, finally, one participant pushed the other. The major independent variables were the race (black/white) of the 'protagonist' and 'victim' of the push shown on the videotape. The attribution part of the study required subjects to indicate the extent to which the target behaviour should be attributed to situational forces, personal factors, the issue discussed or some combination of these causes. There were significant intergroup effects for both situational and personal attributions. When the protagonist was black, the subjects perceived his violent behaviour to be due less to situational, and more to personal, factors than when the protagonist was white. Although there were no tests comparing the two types of attribution, there appeared to be more person than situation attribution in the black protagonist conditions, and more situation than person attribution in the white protagonist conditions.[5]

Finally, intergroup attributions have been demonstrated in the sphere of international conflict. Rosenberg and Wolfsfeld (1977) analysed attributions made for five Israeli and five Arab behaviours during the Middle East conflict. The actions were all major events reported in the news and were classified as successes, failures, moral acts, immoral acts and neutral acts. Attributions were open-ended and coded as situational or dispositional. The strongest effects were found for two groups of students studying in the U.S. who were closely involved with the conflict – pro-Israeli and Israeli students vs Arab students. The first group ('Israelis') gave more dispositional attributions for Israeli success and moral acts, and fewer dispositional attributions for Israeli immoral acts, than did Arab students. They also gave fewer dispositional attributions for Arab success, and more dispositional attributions for Arab immoral acts, than did Arab students.

To summarize, it is clear that, using a variety of subject groups, in different countries, although predominantly using a within-subjects design (discussed below), ingroup-serving attributions have been found in studies investigating positive and negative outcomes. Two types of effect can be distinguished: 'categorization' effects compare the attributions made for ingroup and outgroup members, separately for positive and negative behaviours; 'outcome' effects compare the attributions made for positive and negative behaviours, separately for ingroup and outgroup actors. Overall, categorization effects are found for both types of behaviour in about half the groups tested; there is also a consistent favourable outcome effect for ingroup actors (more dispositional attribution for positive than negative behaviour), but the reverse, contrary to predictions, is not generally found for outgroup actors (i.e., there is *not* more dispositional attribution for negative than positive outgroup behaviour).

Despite consistent results, these studies have obvious limitations. First, with one exception (Duncan, 1976), they rely on within-subjects designs. These designs have the advantage of removing subject variance from error terms used to test treatment effects. But they may also have disadvantages: context effects that limit generalization of results and hypotheses (e.g., the assessment of intergroup biases) that are transparent to subjects (Greenwald, 1976). To some extent these disadvantages can be dealt with by appropriate counterbalancing, but we might expect stronger intergroup attributional bias in within-subjects designs, because the literature on salience shows that social categorization becomes more salient when two or more categories appear simultaneously, than when not (see Oakes, 1987). On the other hand, Greenwald argued that the within-subjects design can have greater external validity, because it contains confounds that are actually found in real life (e.g., sequential judgements of ingroup and outgroup actors). Future research should pay closer attention to these issues and should compare within- and between-subjects designs within the same study. Second, all these studies rely on the distinction between internal and external attributions, objections to which have already been discussed (see chapter 3; Miller et al., 1981). Both limitations are less serious in the case of achievement attributions, as shown below.

Success and failure

Weiner's (e.g., 1986) multi-dimensional approach to the structure of perceived causality provides for a sophisticated analysis of self-serving attributions that can be extrapolated to the intergroup level. The available research has dealt mainly, but not exclusively, with categorization based on ethnicity and gender.

Greenberg and Rosenfield (1979), after a review of some of the studies cited above, questioned whether intergroup attributions were based simply on dislike for outgroup members (ethnocentrism), or whether instead they were always founded on cultural stereotypes. To examine this question with respect to inter-racial (black-white) attributions, they used a task for which there appeared to be no race-based cultural assumptions (extra-sensory perception). They had white subjects of varying degrees of ethnocentrism (upper or lower third of the sample) watch four videotapes portraying success and failure for black and white actors, and then attribute each performance to Weiner's four causes. The three-way interaction between ethnocentrism, outcome and race of actor was highly significant for attributions to ability and marginally significant for attributions to luck. In the success conditions, highly ethnocentric subjects tended to attribute black success less to ability and more to luck than they did white success. Low-ethnocentrism subjects tended to attribute black success more to ability and less to luck than they did white success. In the failure conditions, highly ethnocentric subjects tended to attribute black failure more to lack of ability than they did white failure, but the reverse was true for low-ethnocentrism subjects. In addition, highly ethnocentric subjects attributed black failure more to lack of ability than did low-ethnocentrism subjects. These results were interpreted as evidence of intergroup attribution biases based on ethnocentrism alone, although it should be noted that the highly ethnocentric subjects may have endorsed the stereotype that blacks and whites did differ in ESP ability, whereas low-ethnocentrism subjects did not.

Whitehead et al., (1982) investigated attributions for success and failure on a task for which the relevant trait was either part of a positive stereotype or not part of any stereotype about the other. In pre-testing they found that white students perceived blacks to be more athletic, and slightly less intelligent, than whites. They therefore investigated separately black and white high school students' attributions for success and failure on these two tasks, as a function of race of the actor. For the academic task, there were intergroup effects for both sets of subjects. Black students attributed failure significantly more to lack of ability when the other was white than black; for white students there was a marginally significant tendency to attribute failure more to lack of ability when the other was black. Results were stronger on the athletic task. Black students attributed failure more to lack of ability when the other was white rather than black, whereas white students attributed failure more to lack of ability when the other was black. Finally, there was an interaction between race of perceiver and race of subject for task attributions, which the authors interpreted as an intergroup effect. On athletic tasks, blacks attributed the successful performance of whites more to the ease of the task than they did for blacks, and they attributed a white student's failure more to task difficulty than they did for blacks (i.e., the athletic task was seen as more difficult for white students). The ambiguity of these attributions is obvious, because the conventional interpretation of a task attribution for failure would be that it is self-serving for the actor. The authors' interpretation is, however, more plausible in the context of their other findings.

In a final study on ethnic groups, Hewstone et al. (in press) investigated self-, ingroup- and outgroup-attributions for hypothetical success and failure in a school exam. We classified the subjects, 15–year-old West German and Turkish (guestworker) children, as high or low in prejudice by means of a median-split procedure based on a single scale. They then made attributions to all four of Weiner's causes. The only intergroup effects were found for luck attributions. German students attributed ingroup failure more to bad luck than they did outgroup failure (ingroup-protecting) and Turkish students attributed ingroup success more to good luck than they did outgroup success. This latter effect seems to reflect an internalization of the prejudice that Turkish children are less able academically than German children.

Similar studies have been based on gender groups. Deaux and Emswiller (1974) had male and female students listen to the successful performance of either a male or female who performed well on an object-identification task. They also manipulated the sex-linkage of the task, by depicting the objects as either mechanical tools (masculine) or household utensils (feminine). The main dependent variable, unfortunately, confounded ability and luck attributions, by presenting subjects with a scale anchored by skill at one end and luck at the other end. For the masculine task, a male's success was attributed more to ability than was the female's equally successful performance. When the task was feminine, however, there was no difference. These results appear to be ingroup-favouring for the males, but ingroup-derogating for the females.

Feldman-Summers and Kiesler (1974, Experiment 2) followed up this study by investigating male and female students' attributions for a highly successful male or female physician, whose speciality was either paediatrics or surgery, and who did/did not take on his or her father's practice. Attributions again included all four causes, but these judgements were made ipsatively (i.e., 'more' of one attribution implied 'less' of another). All subjects attributed higher motivation to females than males, but there were also intergroup effects in the form of significant interactions between sex of subject and sex of stimulus person. First, male subjects attributed more ability to the male than the female physician; they also attributed the female's success relatively more to either her greater motivation or her having had an easier task. When the physician did not have a helpful father, the male subjects perceived the female physician as more motivated than the male physician. When the physician had taken over the practice from his/her father, male subjects perceived the female to have had an easier task than the male physician. Second, female subjects displayed an awareness of unfairness. They perceived the male physician as having had an easier task than the female, and they also attributed greater motivation to the female than the male physician. These results illustrate the ambiguity of effort attributions, which can be derogatory ('look how hard she had to try') or congratulatory ('with effort we can overcome sex discrimination'). This problem is discussed in more detail below.

Intergroup attributions based on gender have also been found in other studies (e.g., Feather and Simon, 1975), although not always (e.g., Stephan and Woolridge, 1977). One possible mediating variable may be more general attitudes towards women. Garland and Price (1977) had male students complete the 'Women as Manager Scale' (WAMS; Peters, Terborg and Taynor, 1974) and then attribute a woman's success or failure in a management position to Weiner's four causes. For the success condition, as predicted, there were significant positive correlations between the WAMS and attributions to both ability and hard work, and there were significant negative correlations with both luck and task attributions.

Finally, in a very different context, Hewstone et al. (1982) studied attributions given for success and failure in school examinations by schoolboys from British 'public' (private) and 'comprehensive' (state) schools. Categorization of stimulus person and outcome of the exam were both manipulated in a within-subjects design, including attributions to all four causes. The boys from public schools showed clear group-serving attributions only for failure. They attributed failure by an ingroup member less to lack of ability and more to lack of effort compared with failure by an outgroup member. The boys from comprehensive schools showed only a marginally significant tendency to attribute their failure more to bad luck than they did outgroup failure (see figure 13). These attributions fitted quite well with previously-collected data, from different samples, based on a content-analysis of open-ended essays by the two groups of pupils. Public schoolboys emphasized their intellectual ability and higher academic standards, whereas comprehensive boys drew attention to the privileges of a public school education. These findings support Deschamps's (1973–4) suggestion that intergroup representations provide a basis for intergroup attributions.

To summarize, from studies that used a variety of different groups and between- as well as within-subjects designs, there is consistent evidence for intergroup attributions in achievement contexts. Effects are stronger for failure than success and strongest for attributions of failure to ability (outgroup failure is attributed more to lack of ability than is ingroup failure). Thus ingroup-protection, instigated by the threatening implications of failure, appears to be stronger than ingroup-enhancement. Outgroup-favouring or ingroup-derogating attributions have also been reported in several studies, but predominantly for lower status/dominated groups (e.g., migrant labour populations and females).

Empirical support notwithstanding, this research could be improved and extended in four main ways:

1   As noted earlier, some of the results are ambiguous because we do not know how perceivers interpreted their causal attributions. Russell's (1982) Causal Dimension Scale deals with exactly this problem of translating the perceiver's causal *attributions* into causal *dimensions* (e.g., Weiner's locus, stability and controllability dimensions; see chapter 3). After making their attributions, respondents are asked to rate their perceived causes on a set of scales to assess separately each of Weiner's three dimensions. In this manner researchers can ascertain, for example, whether effort was used as an unstable or stable cause, and whether this view varied as a function of the social categorization of the target.

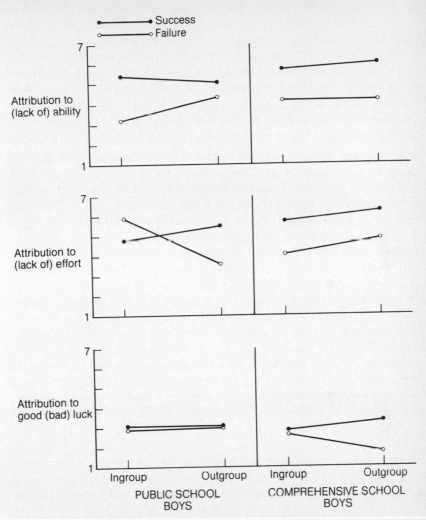

FIGURE 13 *Public and comprehensive schoolboys' attributions for ingroup and outgroup failure (Hewstone et al., 1982, © 1982 John Wiley & Sons Ltd, reprinted by permission of John Wiley & Sons Ltd and the author)*
Note   *Task attributions are not shown*

2   Not only can the meaning of perceived causes vary across perceivers and situations, but they can be interdependent (Heider, 1958; Weiner, 1983). For this reason researchers may have lost valuable information by computing separate analyses for each of the four main attributions. By including type of attribution as a repeated-measures factor in the analysis, one can test for differences between the ratings of the four causes. This information is ignored in every one of the published studies, yet this kind of analysis would indicate how subjects explain group members' outcomes in terms of a configuration of causes (see Hewstone et al., 1988, Study 1).

3   Researchers could analyse open-ended responses and expand the ecological validity of intergroup attribution, as has been done in interpersonal studies (e.g., Cooper and Burger, 1980; Frieze, 1976). Although open-ended procedures are time-consuming and weaker according to psychometric criteria (Elig and Frieze, 1979), they may lead to the identification of new perceived causes and new theoretical ideas, as has been shown in two recent studies.

Sousa and Leyens (1987) compared two methods for analysing open-ended achievement attributions for the success or failure of a male or female, viewed by males or females. When responses were classified according to four categories based on Weiner's scheme (internal/external × stable/unstable), both males and females attributed male success to stable, but female success to unstable, factors (cf. Deaux and Emswiller, 1974). In an alternative analysis, Sousa and Leyens used factorial correspondence analysis (Benzécri, 1982) to establish eight 'dictionaries of lexical units' (one for each outcome by a male or female actor, viewed by males or females). They then compared the similarities between the 'dictionaries' and found that male and female subjects shared a similar view of male, but not female, success. Thus when a different analysis was used, female subjects did *not* internalize the negative view of ingroup success.

Hewstone et al. (1988, Study 2) also reported a content-analysis of intergroup achievement attributions, based on 'public' schoolboys' explanations for ingroup and outgroup success and failure. We found that effort and ability were most frequently used, but that luck and task attributions were negligible. In addition, we found that 'school' was quite often given as a cause, especially in the case of outgroup failure (e.g., 'he received a bad education because he went to a comprehensive school'). As effort and ability attributions were clearly the most prominent, we then distinguished single cause (ability *or* effort) from joint cause (ability *and* effort) explanations to explore whether different causal schemata seemed to underlie the attributions made in different conditions. Although the results could not be compared across conditions (because of the nature of the design and the categorical data), some trends in the data were apparent. For success conditions ingroup success was dominated by explanations in terms of the presence of ability. The greatest number of responses occurred in the ability present/effort absent cell, suggesting that ability is the most important single perceived cause of ingroup academic success. In contrast, outgroup success was explained primarily by the presence of ability and effort, with the highest number of attributions in the ability present/effort present cell. This pattern of responses suggests a Multiple Necessary Cause schema (Kelley, 1972a): to succeed, a comprehensive schoolboy must be clever *and* hard-working.

For failure, the pattern was quite similar when explaining the performance of ingroup and outgroup pupils. The favoured explanation was lack of effort, with the highest number of attributions in the lack of ability absent/lack of effort present cell (although this trend was weaker for outgroup failure). These are the first data to suggest, tentatively, that different causal schemata may underlie attributions for the same outcome by ingroup and outgroup members. If corroborated in future research, these group-serving causal schemata would represent a rather subtle form of intergroup attribution that integrates Levels I and III.

4   Finally, given the impressive body of research on the affective consequences of interpersonal achievement attributions (see Weiner, 1986), it is surprising that no such research exists at the intergroup level. I return to this topic, below, under the heading of the emotional consequences of intergroup attributions.

Group differences

As final evidence for intergroup attribution, three studies have investigated people's attributions about differences between groups and social positions occupied by groups.

Hewstone and Jaspars (1982b) compared the explanations for institutional racism given by black (West Indian) and white adolescents. Accurate information was provided concerning four specific racial differences between black and white people in Britain (rates of arrest, unemployment, educational achievement and occupational status). Respondents read each item and rated two attributions referring to negative dispositions of black people and discrimination by white authority figures, respectively. For example, 'The unemployment rate among young *black* people is 17 per cent, among young *white* people it is 9 per cent. (a) Is this because *black* people are too lazy to work? (b) Is this because *white* bosses discriminate against black people?' (Hewstone and Jaspars, 1982b, p. 5). Black respondents attributed discrimination less to personal characteristics of blacks than did white respondents on all four items; and they attributed discrimination more to white authority figures than did white respondents on two items. When they had an opportunity to discuss their attributions with another ingroup member, black respondents further polarized their low attributions of the cause to personal characteristics of blacks (see figure 14). This pattern of attributions for group differences that reflect negatively on the ingroup can be seen as a further instance of group-serving causal attributions. Gurin et al. (1969) reported that young blacks in the U.S. who made similar attributions (judging economic or discriminatory factors more important causes of their social position than individual skill and personal qualities) often aspired to jobs that were non-traditional for blacks and were more ready to engage in collective action.[6]

The realism of the previous study did not allow for the examination of attributions concerning intergroup differences that were favourable and unfavourable to each group of respondents. Yet, when realistic differences between groups are to be explained, these differences might favour the ingroup or outgroup. Thus, while attributions might serve the interests of the ingroup or outgroup, social facts or intergroup differences to be explained may themselves favour either group. Hewstone et al. (1983) clarified this distinction by referring to group-*serving* attributions and group-*favouring* facts. They asked students from two rival universities (the higher status Hong Kong University, H.K.U., and the lower status Chinese University, C.U., in Hong Kong) to explain eight social facts relating to differences between the two groups; of the two available attributions for each fact, both were internal, but one was ingroup-serving and the other was outgroup-serving. Both open-ended and rating-scale dependent measures revealed group-serving attributions, that were clearest on the rating-scale attributions. There were, in fact, two group-serving effects, which were found in the presence of an ingroup or outgroup experimenter and for facts favouring either group. First, the lower status C.U. students gave higher ratings on the C.U.-serving attributions than did students from the other group. Second, both groups of students gave higher ratings on ingroup-serving than outgroup-serving attributions. It is apparently not necessary that an intergroup difference favours the ingroup rather than the outgroup, because unwelcome aspects of reality can be avoided by an appropriate choice of explanation.

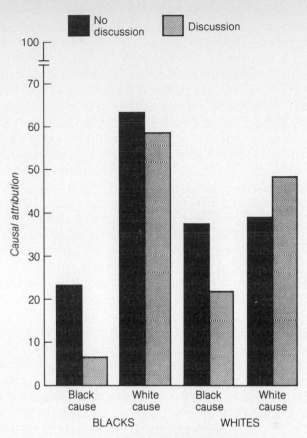

FIGURE 14   *Explanations for racial discrimination as a function of ethnic group of perceiver, type of cause, and discussion (after Hewstone and Jaspars, 1982b, © 1982 John Wiley &Sons Ltd, reprinted by permission of John Wiley &Sons Ltd and the author)*

The third, and final, study returned to gender-linked attributions. Bond et al. (1985, Experiment 1) examined males' and females' attributions for sex-typed behaviours when faced with an interviewer of the same or opposite sex, and in the presence or absence of a same-sex audience. Hong Kong-Chinese students were asked to make attributions for three male-typed and three female-typed behaviours; of the two available attributions for each behaviour, one was ingroup-serving and the other was outgroup-serving. Pre-testing ensured that the facts were perceived as being both equally true and equally desirable by both males and females, and that explanatory traits were rated equally positive by both groups. For male behaviours, there were no significant interaction effects involving sex of subjects. Instead, there was a strong tendency for males and females to endorse the male-serving attributions more strongly than the female-serving attributions. For female behaviours, however, females rated female-serving attributions higher than did males, and higher than they did male-serving attributions, but only when the same-sex audience was absent. Males rated male-serving attributions similarly to females, but their ratings were higher for male-serving than female-serving attributions, again in the audience-absent condition. Overall, then, both groups showed some evidence of group-serving bias (they rated ingroup-serving attributions higher than outgroup-serving attributions), but this tendency was weakened in front of an ingroup audience. Bond et al. (1985, Experiment 2) then carried out a conceptual replication of this study in the U.S., where the women's liberation movement has been stronger historically (cf. Kalmuss, Gurin and Townsend, 1981). As expected, this study yielded stronger intergroup effects. American students showed a group-serving bias across both male as well as female facts, and when the same-sex audience was absent or present.

From the results of the three published articles on intergroup attributions for group differences two types of effect can be distinguished: higher ratings of ingroup-serving vs outgroup-serving attributions; and higher ratings of ingroup-serving attributions by the ingroup compared with the outgroup. Both effects are found in all studies, but the first appears to be the stronger and more consistent one.

Summary

There is clear evidence for intergroup attribution, that supports the predictions by both Pettigrew (1979) and Hewstone (1988a), but only partially supports Taylor and Jaggi's (1974) predictions:

1   There is a tendency to attribute negative outgroup behaviour to personal causes within the actor. When found, this tendency takes the form of a categorization effect (there is more internal attribution for a negative act by an outgroup than an ingroup member), rather than an outcome effect for outgroup actors. Contrary to Taylor and Jaggi's hypothesis, there is generally *not* more internal attribution for negative than positive acts by an outgroup member. There is also a tendency for outgroup failure to be attributed more to lack of ability than is ingroup failure.

2 For positive acts, Pettigrew's predictions cannot be tested precisely, because none of the available studies has included attributions to 'the exceptional case'. For the remaining three causes, there is some support. Studies on attributions for positive outcomes have sometimes reported less internal attributions for a positive act by an outgroup than an ingroup member. There is also evidence that outgroup success is sometimes explained away as good luck, high effort or an easy task. These latter findings support my own model based on Weiner, but the use of high effort (internal) for a positive outcome contradicts Taylor and Jaggi.

In spite of the general empirical support, future work should take a broader approach to the problem. Pettigrew (1979) argued that future studies should include his complete set of potential attributions for positive outgroup behaviour. More generally, research should avoid forced-choice measures and the limited distinction between internal and external attribution. It should also undertake more detailed pilot work and content-analysis of open-ended responses to identify what attributions are relevant to a particular domain. Pettigrew also criticized the stimulus materials used and he noted that subjects in most experiments were 'removed from the behaviour itself' (p. 473). The vast majority of the research reviewed used simple printed materials and it is high time to move from vignettes to videotapes (e.g., Duncan, 1976). More important still, we need direct tests of the 'ultimate attribution error' in face-to-face interactions between perceiver and actor.

FOUNDATIONS AND CONSEQUENCES OF INTERGROUP ATTRIBUTION

Although intergroup attribution has been demonstrated empirically, we are still some way from a complete understanding of it. In this section I examine, first, cognitive and motivational bases of intergroup attribution, given that both types of factor have received detailed attention in discussion of interpersonal, self-serving attribution (e.g., Weary Bradley, 1978; Miller and Ross, 1975). I then consider, speculatively, some of the emotional consequences of group-based attributions.

Cognitive bases

Although the cognitive approach to attribution has already been reviewed (see chapter 4), this section deals with the application of this approach to intergroup relations. As recent reviews of the intergroup

literature show, an increasing amount of theory and research on intergroup relations has come to be influenced by this cognitive perspective
(see Brewer and Kramer, 1985; Messick and Mackie, 1989).

Salience. The most basic cognitive factor is the salience of social
categorization; social categorization must be noted, consciously or
unconsciously, in order to affect causal attributions. Once perceived,
perceptually salient information concerning group memberships may
be over-represented in causal explanations. For example, a single black
person in a small group of otherwise white people was perceived as distinctive and disproportionately causal in the group's performance
(Taylor et al., 1978). Given that attention to these salient stimuli also
leads perceivers to mistake members of a different group for each other
(Malpass and Kravitz, 1969; Taylor et al., 1978), it is easy to envisage
how outgroup members are assumed to be similar to one another and,
in turn, how that similarity may be used as a basis for causal reasoning
(Read, 1983, 1984). Although salience effects are intuitively compelling, empirical support has been mixed. For example, in different studies a novel or salient person's behaviour has been viewed both more
and less situationally than that of a nonsalient person (McArthur and
Post, 1977).
   Oakes (1987) has challenged this analysis of salience effects from a
different perspective, because she found no evidence of an automatic
tendency to focus on distinctive category memberships, or novel stimuli. She put forward a more complex, and functional, approach to salience, based on Bruner's (1957b) work. From this perspective, salience
is not an 'attention-grabbing' property of a stimulus, but rather an indication of current psychological significance. A salient group membership refers, then, 'to one which is *functioning psychologically* to
increase the influence of one's membership in that group on perception
and behaviour, and/or the influence of another person's identity as a
group member on one's impression of and hence behaviour towards
that person' (Oakes, 1987, p. 118). This conception of salience can be
further illustrated using the principle of meta-contrast (Turner et al.,
1987). According to this principle, within any given frame of reference,
any collection of stimuli is more likely to be categorized together to the
degree that the differences between those stimuli on relevant dimensions of comparison ('intra-class differences') are perceived as *less*
than the differences between that collection and other stimuli ('inter-
class differences'). The *meta-contrast ratio* (cf. D. T. Campbell, 1958)
is the mean inter-category difference divided by the mean intra-cate-
gory difference. Given a situation in which various categories could

become salient, Turner argues that the category associated with the largest meta-contrast ratio will become salient. This analysis of category salience may help us to predict which social categories in a particular situation will form the basis for intergroup attributions.

Expectancies and schemata. Once a particular category becomes salient, it is likely to evoke associated category-relevant knowledge in the form of expectancies (Deaux, 1976) or schemata (e.g., Fiske and Taylor, 1984). Several studies have shown that behaviour in line with expectancies is attributed to internal and stable causes, whereas behaviour discrepant with expectancies is attributed to unstable or situational factors (e.g., Bell et al., 1976; Hayden and Mischel, 1976; Regan et al., 1974; Rosenfield and Stephan, 1977; Weiner et al., 1972). It appears that, when perceivers explain expectancy-confirming or schema-congruent behaviour, they may simply rely on dispositions implied by a stereotype, without even bothering to consider additional factors (Pyszczynski and Greenberg, 1981).

Perhaps the most automatic kind of explanation is an attribution to group membership (e.g., 'she failed because she's a woman'). This kind of attribution has been demonstrated by Oakes (1987, Experiment 1), who reported strongest attributions to a target's male identity, when three men disagreed with three women (as opposed to one man disagreeing with five women, as would be predicted by the distinctiveness approach to salience; see also Wilder, 1978). Recall also that Hewstone et al. (1988, Study 2) reported quite frequent open-ended attributions to group membership ('school') in the case of public schoolboys' explanations for outgroup failure.

Expectancy-consistent attributions should also be viewed in the light of stereotypes. Stephan (1985) used the Bayesian notion of the diagnostic ratio to propose a model of how perceivers combine information about group membership and particular behaviours to give an explanation of stereotypical behaviour. Stephan suggested (after Ajzen and Fishbein, 1975) that a set of hypotheses could be generated, each with its respective diagnostic ratio (i.e., the subjective probability of an explanation being used to explain *a* given behaviour, divided by the probability of that explanation being used to explain *any* behaviour). A fairly simple rule for the selection of one hypothesis or explanation would be to 'map' the set of hypotheses (e.g., 'lack of ability', 'task difficulty' and 'bad luck' as explanations for failure) onto the set of stereotypical traits (e.g., 'aggressive', 'stupid', 'rude' etc.). Overlapping items, in this case lack of ability/stupid, would be obvious causal candidates. This kind of model also receives some support from Hewstone et al.'s

(1982) study of schoolboys' attributions for success and failure, which identified correspondence between intergroup representations and intergroup attributions. As a descriptive model of common-sense attribution, however, the diagnostic ratio is not compelling.

According to Pyszczynski and Greenberg (1981), perceivers engage in more thorough attributional processing of behaviours that disconfirm expectancies or are schema-incongruent. Kulik (1983) found that substantial situational pressures had almost no influence on attributions for confirming behaviours, but his subjects were very sensitive to potential situational causes of behaviour that disconfirmed their prior beliefs. As several authors have pointed out, this process would protect stereotypes from change. Because stereotypes refer to perceiver's assumptions about the dispositional attributes of ingroup and outgroup members, any behaviour violating the stereotype could be avoided on the basis that it reflected situational influences and thus did not derive from the personal characteristics of the actor (see Cooper and Fazio, 1979; D. L. Hamilton, 1979; Stephan and Rosenfield, 1982). A further consequence of this preference for situational attribution of unexpected behaviour is that counterstereotypical behaviour may not be stored in memory. As Crocker et al. (1983) showed, an incongruent act was most likely to be recalled only if it was explained in terms of the actor's disposition. On the other hand, if the behaviour was attributed to a situational cause, it was equally likely to be recalled whether it was congruent or incongruent.

The outcome of these, and other, biases is, as at the interpersonal level, pernicious. As Deaux and Major (1987) argued, processes of cognitive confirmation (e.g., Darley and Gross, 1983) operate to maintain perceivers' initial expectancies of a target and processes of behavioural confirmation (e.g., Snyder et al., 1977) induce a self-fulfilling prophecy. Cooper and Fazio (1979), in fact, contended that self-fulfilling prophecies were even more likely to occur in intergroup interaction; because groups are almost never totally homogeneous, but rather consist of a distribution of persons with certain traits, it becomes more likely that some evidence can be found to support one's preconceptions. Attributions, specifically, seem to influence whether behavioural confirmation perseveres beyond a specific context (Snyder, 1984; see chapter 5). For example, consider an ingroup member who interacts with a member of an outgroup perceived as hostile. The ingroup member acts on these beliefs and treats the outgroup member as hostile, as a result of which the latter actually behaves in a manner consistent with this label. If the outgroup member is led to believe that this hostile behaviour reflects something about his or her corresponding personal disposition, then the behaviour will extend to future interactions with members of the other group.

Although the cognitive bases of intergroup attribution are compelling, more research is required. Future research should measure expectancies more systematically and correlate them with attributions. Researchers should also collect measures such as processing time and memory for consistent and inconsistent behaviours and relate them to attributions. This kind of integration of Level I and Level III analyses should not, however, proceed without attention to motivational issues.

Motivational bases

The most obvious motivational basis for intergroup attributions is the desire to view one's own group positively, thus achieving, maintaining or defending one's self-esteem. Intergroup biases in attribution can, therefore, be seen as part of a much wider process – the search for positive social identity (or group self-esteem). According to social identity theory (Tajfel and Turner, 1979), people define themselves to a large extent in terms of their social group memberships and tend to seek a positive social identity (or self-definition as a group member). This identity is achieved by intergroup comparisons focused on the establishment of positively valued distinctiveness between one's own and other groups. From this perspective group members could use their attributions to achieve or enhance a positive social identity (e.g., by attributing positive ingroup, or negative outgroup, acts to internal, stable and/or controllable causes), or to protect that identity (e.g., by attributing negative ingroup, or positive outgroup, acts to external, unstable and/or uncontrollable causes). Indeed, Tajfel (1969, 1981) emphasized the role of stereotypes in explaining and justifying actions, and in providing a positive group image.

Although social identity theory provides a plausible account of intergroup attribution results, Messick and Mackie (1989) have argued that the theory's interpretation of intergroup bias is difficult to test. They pointed out that although people may want to maintain positive self-esteem, and they view membership groups positively, it remains to be shown that these are the motives for intergroup bias, in whatever form. Oakes and Turner (1980) did report that the act of intergroup discrimination increased actors' self-esteem (cf. Wagner et al., 1986), but Lemyre and Smith (1985), in a more controlled study, suggested that intergroup discrimination did not enhance self-esteem, but rather restored it in response to a threat to self-esteem posed by social categorization. Recently, Turner et al. (1987) have tried to clarify some misunderstandings concerning social identity theory's prediction with respect to self-esteem. They point out that the theory does *not* suggest that people always have a positive social identity but that, under particular circumstances, negative social identity is 'psychologically aversive' (p. 30). The theory also does *not* state that people always discriminate in favour of ingroups over outgroups, or that there will be a simple positive correlation between social identity and ingroup favouritism. Notwithstanding these qualifications to the relationship between social identity and ingroup favouritism, future work should investigate the relationship between ingroup-serving (or outgroup-derogating) attributions, on the one hand, and variables like self-esteem, and ingroup identification, on the other hand (see Brown et al., 1986; Lemyre and Smith, 1985).

Social identity theory also makes predictions about the variables that influence when subordinate groups will challenge dominant groups – when they perceive the *status quo* to be illegitimate and unstable (Turner and Brown, 1978). Some consistent evidence concerning the relationship between these perceptions and attributions has been reported (Bond et al., 1985; Hewstone et al., 1983), but it is still not clear what, if any, causal relationship exists between them.

Taylor and McKirnan (1984) have put forward a general five-stage model of intergroup relations that identifies causal attributions as one of the key processes affecting how disadvantaged groups respond to social inequality.[7] At Stage 1 ('Clearly stratified intergroup relations'), subordinate group members' attributions are useful in understanding why they accept their inferior status. Members of disadvantaged groups are led to attribute their status to ascribed (negative) character-istics, rather than external factors like discrimination by the dominant group. At Stage 2 ('Emerging individualistic social ideology'), group membership is seen as increasingly less important, and individual characteristics (such as ability and effort) as more important, causes of the status alignment. This ideology denies a causal role for the high status group in either the creation of, or change in, group inequality. At Stage 3 ('Social mobility'), group and individual attributions conflict, as individual members of the subordinate group attempt to 'pass' into the dominant group. Subordinate group membership is seen as the cause of disadvantaged social position, but individual efforts are seen as necessary to escape that position. Stage 4 ('Consciousness raising') is the result of failed attempts at social mobility. As at Stage 1, group membership (rather than individual factors) is seen as the cause of minority group status, but discrimination by the dominant group is highlighted (rather than inherent characteristics of the subordinate group). Thus attributions are used to persuade other subordinate group members that collective action is the appropriate response to injustice. Finally at Stage 5 ('Competitive intergroup relations') the subordinate group's disadvantaged position in the *past* is attributed to the dominant group, but their *future* position is perceived in terms of internal, controllable characteristics linked to a collective response. This ambitious theory could provide the basis for future research (using experimental and correlational techniques) to determine whether causal attributions merely reflect intergroup relations or may actually help to create them.

Emotional consequences

One of the ambiguities to emerge from this review is whether self-esteem should be viewed as a motivational determinant, or an emotional consequence, of attribution (the same question arose concerning the functions vs consequences of self-serving attributions; see chapter 3). According to Weiner, the locus dimension is of central importance for affective consequences: success attributed internally results in greater self-esteem (pride) than success attributed externally; failure attributed internally results in lower self-esteem than failure attributed externally. Although Weiner acknowledged that pride can be felt vicariously (when one sees a relative, friend or fellow countryman succeed for internal reasons), he did not discuss 'instances of affective experience mediated by personal identification' (Weiner, 1982, p. 191). This identification of oneself as a group member, and social identification with other group members, is, of course, fundamental to intergroup behaviour (Turner, 1982). One can then ask what, if any, affective consequences follow from ingroup-favouring or outgroup-derogating attributions? Although the role of emotions has, generally, been rather neglected in studies of intergroup behaviour (see Dijker, 1987; Pettigrew, 1986), the attributional approach offers a promising avenue for future research.

Although members of dominant (majority) groups might be expected to enhance their self-esteem by giving internal attributions for positive outcomes by ingroup members, this strategy may be difficult for members of subordinate (minority) groups. Their inferior social position can, in extreme circumstances, result in a pattern of attributional 'self-hate' (Lewin, 1948), whereby members of minority groups make group-serving attributions for the outgroup, but group-derogating attributions for the ingroup (e.g., Deaux and Emswiller, 1974; Hewstone and Ward, 1985, Experiment 1). When attributions are dysfunctional for the ingroup (e.g., negative outcomes are attributed to internal, stable causes), the resulting emotional consequences are likely to be helplessness and resignation (Weiner, 1982).

Other emotional consequences of attributions may, however, also be found. For example, anger may be experienced when a negative, self-related outcome or event is attributed to factors controllable by others (Weiner, 1982). An attributional approach could, then, contribute to the neglected analysis of the experience of discrimination. As Strenta and Kleck (1984) pointed out, it has been noted that people with stigmatizing physical characteristics often attribute their treatment by others to these causes. The consequences of these attributions have been demonstrated in experimental work by Dion and colleagues (Dion and Earn, 1975; Dion et al., 1978). Lone minority group members (e.g., Jews) who attributed their failure in a group task to religious discrimination by other group members (all gentiles), reported feeling more aggression (as well as sadness, anxiety and egotism) than did subjects who had not made these attributions. The subjects who ascribed their failure to discrimination also, however, rated themselves more favourably on positive traits underlying the Jewish stereotype (e.g., 'love of traditions', 'industrious', 'clever'). Thus failing, *if* one's failure is ascribed to discrimination by members of another group, can lead to a strengthened commitment to the ingroup.

Relatedly, Turner et al. (1984) have explored the relationship between attributions and group cohesion, although they found it was *not* necessary to explain failure in external terms. Turner et al. found that under conditions of high commitment to group membership, negative outcomes were attributed more to causes internal to the group than were positive outcomes (the opposite was true under conditions of low commitment to group membership). Furthermore, for these high-commitment groups, failure or defeat produced more cohesion than success or failure. In other words an appropriate choice of attributions can snatch some sort of victory out of the jaws of defeat. This kind of mechanism has obvious external validity, especially for groups that experience repeated negative outcomes (see Taylor et al., 1983). As Turner et al. concluded: 'a group which tended to disintegrate whenever it faced a real setback would not be a very useful form of association; it is precisely at these moments that some psychological mechanism is required to bolster solidarity and morale to meet the challenge' (1984, p. 110).

Summary

As Tetlock and Levi (1982) concluded, it is impossible, at present, to choose between cognitive and motivational explanations of attributional bias. The fact that so many potential determinants and associated emotional consequences exist simply underlines how pervasive intergroup attributions are and hence how important it is to understand them. In the wake of so many studies on pre-existing social categories (e.g., ethnicity and gender), it may now be time for a return to the laboratory in order to disentangle variables and specify directions of causal influence, while also making use of the variety of techniques for measuring both social cognitions and affective responses.

IMPLICATIONS FOR THE REDUCTION OF INTERGROUP CONFLICT

The material reviewed so far demonstrates the empirical and theoretical bases of an attributional approach to intergroup conflict (see Hewstone, 1988a). Rather than attempt to explain when and how intergroup conflict develops, an attributional approach seems most valuable in underlining how conflict is maintained, or even escalated, by giving different attributions for the same performance by ingroup and outgroup members and by explaining away outgroup achievements. In this section I focus on the role of attributions in attempts to reduce intergroup conflict.

A key issue for the reduction of intergroup conflict is how perceivers react to situational information about the outgroup that disconfirms their negative expectancies. For example, the 'contact hypothesis' – the belief that positive association with persons from a disliked outgroup will lead to the growth of liking and respect for that group (Cook, 1978) – appears to be based, in part at least, on the value of disconfirming negative expectancies about the outgroup. Yet, as was seen in the previous section, attributional bias conspires against the acceptance of disconfirming information at face value and supports the perseverance of negative beliefs about the outgroup. An attributional analysis of intergroup contact points to some of its pitfalls, that become clear when one examines available models of how schemata (in this case outgroup schemata or stereotypes) change in response to new, incongruent, information.

An attributional analysis of schema change

Weber and Crocker (1983) have compared three models of how beliefs such as stereotypes change in response to disconfirming information. The 'bookkeeping' model (Rothbart, 1981) views stereotype change as a gradual process in which each new instance of stereotype-discrepant information modifies the existing stereotype. Any single piece of disconfirming evidence elicits only a minor change; substantial changes occur incrementally with the accumulation of evidence that disconfirms the stereotype. The 'conversion' model (Rothbart, 1981) is more dramatic, because it predicts that a single, salient, incongruent instance can bring about schema change (as in a religious 'conversion'). According to this second model, schema change is all-or-none and is not brought about by minor disconfirmations. Support for this model was claimed by Gurwitz and Dodge (1977), who reported that stereotype change was greater when disconfirming information was concentrated in a description of one outgroup member than when it was dispersed across three people (each of whom only partly disconfirmed the stereotype). The third model, 'subtyping', contends that when all the disconfirming information is concentrated within a few persons, they will be subtyped (seen as a separate subcategory). This model predicts more change when incongruent information is dispersed across persons than when it is concentrated in a few.

Weber and Crocker's (1983) four studies provided partial support for two of the models. The bookkeeping model may describe how stereotypes change when incongruent information is dispersed across multiple outgroup members (because in this condition individuals could not easily be subtyped and the stereotype changed with each new piece of incongruent information). The subtyping model may be the best description of stereotype change when incongruent information is concentrated in a few outgroup members (the small number of persons in whom information is concentrated are easily subtyped). Finally, although unsupported in this research, the conversion model might apply when a perceiver is unsure of a stereotype and hence easily swayed by available information.

An attributional analysis of this research points to the likelihood that discrepant information will be explained away. If the perceiver attributes discrepant information to, for example, some special personal characteristic of the target, then there is no reason to expect generalization across other outgroup members. As Hewstone and Brown (1986) have argued, this failure to generalize attitude change is one of the central weaknesses of the traditional contact hypothesis. It is for this reason that we emphasized the interpersonal-intergroup continuum in our model of intergroup contact. The intergroup level of contact refers to behaviour between individuals that is determined by their identity as group representatives, rather than by their individual characteristics and personal relationships. If positive interaction with a member of the outgroup takes place on an intergroup basis, then there is a real chance that any positive change in attitude will be seen to apply not just to that person, but to others in the same group. In a parallel analysis, Rothbart and John (1985) argued for contact with a 'prototypical' outgroup member.

Two experimental studies support the argument above. Weber and Crocker (1983) found that people's stereotypes about occupational groups changed most when they were presented with counter-stereotypical information about *representative* members of those groups. The same information, when associated with atypical members of the category in question, had much less effect in modifying attitudes to the group as a whole. As Weber and Crocker noted, it was apparently more difficult for subjects to dismiss instances as 'exceptions' when the information was dispersed across group members (in complete contrast, Gurwitz and Dodge [1977] argued that it would be relatively easy to discount disconfirming behaviours when each person was described as demonstrating just one of them). Wilder (1984) systematically varied the prototypicality of the outgroup member in a contact situation and found, as he predicted, that there was a significant improvement in the evaluation of the outgroup only after a pleasant encounter with a typical outgroup member. He also provided support for the idea that typicality works by making it easier for subjects to generalize from the behaviour of a target to the behaviour of other outgroup members.

On the basis of the preceding evidence, researchers must ensure that counterstereotypic behaviour cannot be 'explained away' with reference to situational demands or individual exceptions to the rule (cf. Pettigrew, 1979).

An attributional model of conflict maintenance and reduction

The implications of the present analysis are summarized in figure 15 in the form of a schematic model. The model is based on, but extends, previous work reported earlier in this chapter (especially Cooper and Fazio, 1979; Deaux, 1976; Hewstone and Brown, 1986; Pettigrew, 1979; Stephan and Rosenfield, 1982). In previous versions of the

| Expectancies | Outgroup behaviour | Attribution | Outgroup member | Consequence |

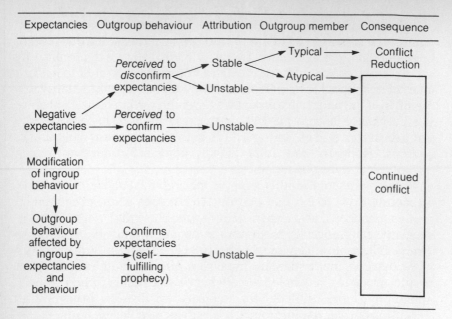

FIGURE 15   *Attribution of outgroup behaviour and the continuation or reduction of intergroup conflict (after Hewstone, 1988a)*

model (Hewstone, 1988a; Hewstone, 1988c), I focussed on internal vs external attributions of outgroup behaviour. Weiner's (1986) position is, however, clear that the *stability* of a perceived cause, rather than its locus, determines expectancy shifts (in this case, changes in beliefs about the characteristics of the outgroup). The most crucial attributional determinant of whether conflict is maintained or reduced is, therefore, whether outgroup behaviour is attributed to stable or unstable factors.[8]

The model assumes that there exist negative expectancies for outgroup behaviour in a situation of intergroup conflict. These negative expectancies can be confirmed by one of two routes. First, outgroup behaviour may be *perceived* to confirm expectancies and is thus attributed to stable causes, which maintains conflict. Second, negative expectancies may lead to modifications of the behaviour of ingroup members, outgroup behaviour that is affected by the ingroup's expectancies and outgroup behaviour that *actually confirms* ingroup expectancies (a self-fulfilling prophecy). This behaviour is again attributed to stable causes, so that conflict is maintained.

The model also allows for outgroup behaviour that does, or is perceived to, *disconfirm* expectancies. Unexpected behaviour can be explained in various ways. First, it can be attributed to unstable causes, which again maintains conflict. Alternatively, the unexpected behaviour can be attributed to stable causes, with different consequences depending on how the individual outgroup member is perceived. If perceived as atypical, the behaviour can be 'explained away' and the individual treated as a 'special case'. This attribution means that the behaviour has little impact on the outgroup stereotype. If, and only if, the individual is seen as a typical outgroup member, is there a real chance of generalized change of outgroup attitudes and a reduction of conflict.

Overall, the model helps to explain why intergroup conflict often persists despite information that disconfirms negative expectancies about the outgroup. As the model shows, in two out of three cases where outgroup behaviour is perceived to disconfirm negative expectancies, conflict-maintaining attributions can be given.

CONCLUSION

This chapter has taken issue with the individualistic bias of attribution research and shown that attributions can be analysed not only as intrapersonal and interpersonal phenomena, but also at an intergroup level. The theoretical bases of intergroup attribution are derived from both attribution theory and intergroup relations, and have received ample empirical confirmation. It is clear from the studies reviewed that in some cases attributions of behaviour by individuals are made not as a function of their unique individuality, but as a function of the social group or category to which they belong and to which the perceiver belongs. Thus social categorization provides an obvious method for refining attributions or what Mackie referred to as 'the progressive localization of a cause' (1974, p. 320; see Jaspars and Hewstone, in press). There is, moreover, a general tendency to make more favourable attributions for ingroup than outgroup behaviour. This tendency is found in explanations for positive and negative outcomes, successes and failures and intergroup differences, and appears to have a variety of cognitive and motivational determinants as well as emotional consequences.

Although I have cautioned against naive extrapolations from the interpersonal to the intergroup level of analysis, intergroup attribution seems to be one case in which extrapolation is justifiable. As has been seen, the most convincing theoretical analyses of intergroup attribution extend ideas from self-serving (egotistic) to group-serving (ethnocentric) attributions. This last claim does not, however, deny that there are differences between interpersonal and intergroup behaviour (Tajfel, 1978) or that there is a psychological discontinuity between acting as an individual and acting as a group member (Turner et al., 1987).

Finally, in view of the body of research on intergroup attribution, it is disappointing to note that this topic (which tries to integrate attribution theory and intergroup relations) is often ignored by theorists who focus on either attribution or intergroup relations. The investigation of intergroup attribution extends attribution theory from a predominantly intra-personal and interpersonal approach to a more general theory of social understanding, surely the aim of any major theoretical approach in social psychology. In addition, an attributional approach can be applied to some of the central topics in intergroup relations, such as the persistence of social stereotypes and the repeated failure to reduce intergroup conflict through contact between groups. Thus the relationship between attribution theory and intergroup relations can be mutually beneficial, although the potential of this relationship has yet to be fully exploited.

7 Societal Attribution: Collective Beliefs and the Explanation of Societal Events

Any causal explanation must be viewed within the context of social representations and is determined thereby.

(Moscovici, 1981)

INTRODUCTION

The aim of this chapter is, first, to consider explanations alongside the beliefs that are shared by large numbers of people within and between societies. The study of these beliefs brings attribution theory back to the issue of common-sense psychology with which Heider (1958) was originally concerned and deals with the rather neglected question of *where* attributions come from (Pepitone, 1981). The fact that attributions appear to be culturally and sub-culturally shared suggests the examination of wider social beliefs as bodies of knowledge that provide the basis, even the vocabulary, for social attributions. There are various constructs with which one could attempt an analysis of this knowledge – ideologies, attitudes, beliefs and so on. I prefer the concept of social representations as a genuinely societal knowledge structure that can further our understanding of common-sense causal explanation.

The second section of this chapter gives some illustrations of what might be called an 'attributing society', with reference to individualism and, more dramatically, the attributional components of witchcraft, persecution and conspiracy theories. The third section of the chapter moves from societal beliefs to the societal nature of what is to be explained – poverty and wealth, unemployment, urban riots and racial inequality. These four examples reveal that an important part of lay explanation has to do with the explanation of events that cannot be classified as intra-personal, interpersonal or intergroup. Finally, I consider the cultural component of attribution with reference to cross-cultural studies comparing Western and non-Western patterns of attribution, and more recent work that investigates the cultural basis of causal explanations by drawing on both psychology and anthropology.

SOCIETAL BELIEFS AND CAUSAL EXPLANATIONS

Common sense

Despite its widespread reference in the attribution literature, common sense has received little detailed attention until quite recently. Fletcher defined common sense as 'a cultural group's body of shared beliefs about the world' (1984, p. 204). He then considered three aspects of common sense, each of which emphasizes the shared nature of knowledge:

1 'Common sense as a set of shared fundamental assumptions about the nature of the social and physical world', knowledge that is universalistic and tacitly held. Fletcher means here those beliefs that are necessary for maintaining an intelligible and explicable view of the world, although his examples (e.g., the assumption that the world exists independently of our perception of it) do not include beliefs that play any major role in social life.

2 'Common sense as a set of cultural maxims and shared beliefs about the social and physical world', knowledge that is relativistic and explicitly known. Fletcher includes here proverbs and stock phrases that may vary widely both within and between cultures (e.g., beliefs about whether punishment deters criminals or whether the unemployed are lazy).

3 'Common sense as a shared way of thinking about the social and physical world', knowledge that is almost always tacitly known. Here Fletcher is less interested in the truth value of people's beliefs than in the cognitive processes by which people make their judgements and the type of concepts they use.

This broad conception of common sense highlights the lacunae of contemporary attributional approaches. These gaps in our knowledge are also identified by Kassin's (1981) heuristic conception of attribution principles according to the amount and complexity of information that an observer must encode in order to make an attribution. 'First-order' principles involve a single observation (e.g., causal schemata), whereas 'second-order' principles concern multiple observations of cause-effect relations (e.g., the covariation principle); both principles have stimulated a great deal of experimental work (see chapters 2 and 4), but what has been neglected are 'third-order' principles that deal with *theories* that guide inferences about how causes combine and operate. One approach to common sense that seems to complement attribution theory is that of social representations (see Hewstone, 1989).

Social representations

The term *social representations* has its origins in Durkheim's (1898) concept of *représentations collectives*, which he used to refer to characteristics of social thinking as distinct from individual thinking (later Moscovici, 1981, 1984, was even to refer to a 'thinking society'). From Durkheim's point of view, collective representations described a whole range of intellectual forms that included science, religion and myth. Durkheim also emphasized that a collective representation was not reducible to individual representations – it constituted a social reality *sui generis*. Moscovici (1976) replaced Durkheim's *représentation collective* with his own *représentation sociale* in order to acknowledge his intellectual ancestor, but also to make explicit his own conception of the way knowledge is represented in society and shared by its members in the form of common-sense 'theories' about all aspects of life and society. His view of social representations was more dynamic than Durkheim's and he saw them as created by individuals in interaction with each other and in the course of everyday conversations.

Definitions of social representations abound in the literature, of which two are most useful from an attributional perspective:

> [A] set of concepts, statements, and explanations originating in daily life in the course of inter-individual communications. They are the equivalent, in our society, of the myths and belief systems in traditional societies; they might even be said to be the contemporary version of common sense. (Moscovici, 1981, p. 181)

> Social representations ... concern the contents of everyday thinking and the stock of ideas that gives coherence to our religious beliefs, political ideas and the [mental] connections we create ... They make it possible for us to classify persons and objects, to compare and explain behaviours and to objectify them as parts of our social setting. (Moscovici, 1988, p. 214)

However social representations are defined, I wish to emphasize that, like Fletcher's (1984) definition of common sense, they are *shared* by many individuals (see Jaspars and Fraser, 1984) and can refer to a range of phenomena. For example, Sperber (1985) has distinguished between widely-distributed, long-lasting representations (culture), representations that are slowly transmitted over generations (traditions) and representations, typical of modern cultures, that spread rapidly throughout a whole population, but have a short life-span (fashions). I would argue that, and will try to illustrate how, all these kinds of beliefs form the backdrop against which social attributions are made. The present focus is less on the processes underlying social representations (see Jodelet, 1984; Moscovici, 1984; Moscovici and Hewstone, 1983) than on how they classify information and provide the contents of social cognition. Indeed social representations are considered, in the present context, as frames of reference that classify and select information as well as suggest explanations. As McGuire (1986) pointed out, most writers on the topic of representational constructs describe how representations serve as categories that guide, or misguide, oversimplified perception of complex situations.

Where social representations differ from other representational constructs is in their emphasis on the *transformation* of social knowledge. As its name implies, representation refers to a re-presentation, a mental reproduction of something else. Yet, a representation is not merely a reproduction but, rather, a construction or transformation. This aspect of social representations is central: the idea that the transformation of specialized knowledge (whether in science, economics or any other domain) is a fundamental aspect of common sense. Moscovici (1976) argued that specialized knowledge would only influence daily life *if* it passed from specialists to society. A complete analysis of social representations involves the study of how knowledge is transformed and represented, which may take the form of interviews with respondents, content-analyses of the mass media and comparisons between specialized and lay knowledge.

This transformation process is obvious when one considers the interface between science and common sense; as Moscovici noted, 'common sense is continually being created in our societies, especially where science and technical knowledge is popularized' (1984, p. 57). Thus scientific ideas and findings are often widely dispersed through society (see Roqueplo, 1974), as is currently seen in the growth of (mis)understanding about AIDS (see Markova and Wilkie, 1987). To capture this transformation process, and to distinguish it from attribution theory's model of the 'naive scientist', Moscovici offered the view of the layperson as an 'amateur scientist' – consuming, digesting and transforming scientific knowledge, rather than merely trying (and failing) to follow scientific rules of inference (see Moscovici, 1976,

1984; Moscovici and Hewstone, 1983). From this conception of the layperson, one might, for example, expect to find that some free-response explanations for the dissolution of personal relationships would be based on 'second-hand' knowledge of various psycho-therapies and theories of intimate relationships, sometimes filtered through the personal columns of newspapers. Kelley (1980) himself discussed how adults learn numerous theories about causality at a distance – theories involving agents such as bacteria, genes and atomic particles. Yet, we still know very little about how these technical terms become part of the layperson's repertoire of explanations.

Moscovici's (1976) book, *La Psychanalyse: son image et son public*, is still the classic study of social representations. It consists of a systematic analysis (using attitudinal measures and content-analysis of French newspapers) of how ideas about psychoanalysis spread through French society and were transformed into a social representa-tion. Most interesting from an attributional perspective was the evidence that some of Moscovici's respondents used their version of psychoanalysis as a basis for explaining their own and other people's behaviour. For example, 22 per cent of the school pupils and 45 per cent of the students in his sample reported having tried to analyse and interpret the reactions of others using terms like a 'complex' (see Moscovici, 1976, pp. 75, 187, 243, 358). Moscovici has also given other examples of social representations that might be expected to affect attributions, ranging from the effect of training in a particular 'school' of psychotherapy on the perceived cause, and recommended treatment, of mental illness (see Farina et al., 1978; Fisher and Farina, 1979), to the influence of Marxism once it has become a 'shared reference point for interpreting events' (Moscovici, 1988, p. 227).

The challenge posed by the social representations approach has already sparked curiosity and controversy. Potter and Litton (1985a), for example, have asked what are the 'groups' whose social representa-tions we should study; how large or small should they be; and how much consensus should they show to be accorded a social representa-tion? They worry that Moscovici provides no explicit procedure for identifying the groups independently of the data themselves and thus he risks circularity. These questions have led to a lively debate (see Hewstone, 1985; Moscovici, 1985; Potter and Litton, 1985b; Semin, 1985) that is not central here. Suffice to say that since we look at attitudes and stereotypes within and between 'groups', then why not do the same for social representations, while acknowledging, of course, that some social representations may be much more widely shared than others?

Although there remain theoretical and methodological questions about the social representations approach, it does provide a welcome, broader conception of social psychology than characterizes the discipline as a whole. Whether it should be seen as a critique of more individualistic approaches (Farr, 1987), or as different from, but complementary to, them (Moscovici, 1981) is a matter of personal preference. I am certainly not part of any movement to propose a new non-experimental social psychology (cf. Parker, 1987), and I am more interested in integrating the social representations approach with topics like social cognition and intergroup relations. The need for a social representations approach to attribution is made clear if one considers Wells's (1981) distinction between two ways in which people come to think about causal forces in their environment. 'Original processing' refers to the direct observation of relationships, like the covariation between events, and has been studied in detail at the intra-personal level of attribution. 'Socialized processing' concerns how people learn about causes and adopt cultural hypotheses through language-based communications; it has been relatively ignored in attribution theory, and more work at the societal level is clearly needed. This kind of research need not ignore within-group variation in beliefs or attributions (see McGuire, 1986), but it does shift attention to the neglected influence of collective beliefs on causal attributions.

The link between representations and explanations was made long ago by Fauconnet (1928) who, as a former student of Durkheim, understood that responsibility was part of the system of collective representations. More recently Moscovici (1981) argued that social representations determine *when* we seek explanations, because we are challenged to find an explanation, primarily, when events are inconsistent with our representations. This view parallels the philosophical conclusions of Hart and Honoré (1959) and the psychological work of Weiner (1985a). When we do explain events, however, especially societal events, wider social beliefs must often be taken into account, as Moscovici illustrated with explanations for unemployment:

> Some think of the unemployed person as lazy, unlucky or as incompetent in looking for work; others consider him to be a victim of economic downturn, of social injustice and the contradictions of the capitalist regime. The former attribute the cause of unemployment to the individual, to his way of facing the world, and the latter to the general situation, to the individual's class affiliation and to the way in which the world treats him. Obviously this divergence is due altogether to their respective social representations. One representation gives precedence, under all circumstances, to personal responsibility, individual effort and individual solutions to the problems of society; the other leads to sharp

awareness of social injustice and social responsibility, contemplating collective
solutions to individual problems. (Moscovici, 1981, pp. 207–8)

Summary

The concept of social representations offers a means by which
common sense can be reinstated into attribution theory, with a focus on
shared social beliefs and knowledge. Like other representations, social
representations serve as categories that influence the perception of
social information; unlike other representations, they focus on the
process by which specialized knowledge is transformed into common
sense and can be used in everyday thinking. The framework offered by
social representations is spelled out in the following two sections of this
chapter. The next section gives some examples of attribution at a wider,
societal level and introduces the historical dimension of attributions;
the third section then illustrates how social representations may prove
useful in interpreting the findings of research on lay explanations of
societal events.

FROM THE 'THINKING' TO THE 'ATTRIBUTING' SOCIETY?

In his book *Madness and Civilization* Michel Foucault (1967) noted
that in the later part of the eighteenth century the English were thought
to be especially prone to madness and melancholia, a predisposition
that was attributed to the fact that they were a nation of merchants
whose anxiety about their financial speculations led to more tyrannical
families and to a state in which 'man is dispossessed of his desires by the
laws of interest' (p. 214). To the extent that these explanations of
madness were widely shared by members of a society, then one can
reasonably talk of a societal attribution. But can one, or should one,
talk of an 'attributing society'?

The choice of heading for this section is deliberately provocative and
plays on Moscovici's own notion of the thinking society. If, however,
explanations circulate in society and are widely shared at a societal
level, then the notion of an attributing society is not, perhaps, that far-
fetched. Although G. Jahoda (1988) has attacked Moscovici for
resuscitating the notion of the 'group mind' in this manner, I recognize,
of course, that it is ultimately the individuals, not the groups or
societies, who do the thinking and the attributing. They do so, however,
on the basis of widely circulating information (e.g., attributions about
stock market fluctuations that appeared in the newspapers; see

Andreassen, 1987). My implied meaning of the attributing society is similar to D'Andrade's reference to a 'cultural information pool' (1981, p. 180), and can be illustrated with the topics of individualism, witchcraft, persecution and conspiracy.

Individualism

Ichheiser (1943) was interested in 'collectively (ideologically) conditioned patterns of misinterpretations' (p. 145) that he took to be characteristic of more or less everybody within a given group or society. He argued that these collective interpretations were not influenced by individual attitudes and experiences and, indeed, were more important than individual mechanisms in creating the social-psychological atmosphere of everyday life. In stark contrast to the contemporary 'errors and biases' approach to attribution, Ichheiser saw these misinterpretations not as errors, but as indispensable to the working system of a given culture and society.

As I noted in chapter 1, it was Ichheiser who first identified the 'fundamental attribution error', when he referred to the fact that concepts like 'success' and 'failure', 'merit' and 'blame' were based on the belief in personal determination of behaviour and were built into the ideology of our society. He viewed these collectively conditioned misinterpretations as an inevitable consequence of the ideology of the nineteenth century (see Lukes, 1973). Yet, beliefs change over time and Ichheiser (1949) noted that this social representation of individualism had already become misleading, as he illustrated with the case of unemployment, which he saw as a consequence of existing social conditions, rather than a matter of personal blame. It is precisely the analysis of such representations that has been missing from contemporary attribution research, which has preferred to analyse the 'fundamental attribution error' in cognitive terms.

Of witches, persecutions and conspiracies

A more societal perspective on attribution also turns attention to some less traditional topics for social psychological interpretation. Witchcraft, persecution and conspiracy all direct attention to the social, as well as psychological, functions of attribution. As Fauconnet (1928) noted, one of the major motives in responsibility attribution is to punish the cause of the crime and to prevent its reoccurrence or increase. This led Fauconnet to the notion of the person as a first cause (an idea taken up by Heider, 1944) and to the societal functions of attribution (see his chapter 6). Fauconnet also included the phenomena of scapegoating – from Nero, who blamed the Christians for the great fire of Rome, to Christians through the ages who have vented their wrath on witches, heretics and Jews. Bains (1983) has argued that these vivid examples of persecution illustrate the control function of attributions at a societal level. He suggested that one can interpret the existence of superstitious beliefs about causation (both in Third World countries today and in the West, historically) as arising, in large part, from the need to avoid feelings of passivity in the face of natural and social calamities. Thus witchcraft served as a theory of causality in medieval Europe for a variety of mundane as well as catastrophic events (Cohn, 1975). As Bains pointed out, the belief that finding the witch responsible would resolve the problem was central to the whole notion of witchcraft. The problem would be brought under *control* and Bains contended that almost all magical and superstitious beliefs attributed negative events to controllable causes. These beliefs almost all implied a straightforward course of action to, first, prevent an unwanted situation from occurring; and, if it had already occurred, to provide remedies to restore the world to its previous state. According to Thomas, an authority on magic and witchcraft, these causal theories were popular because 'they held out the possibility of redress. They did not merely offer the intellectual satisfaction of identifying the cause of the mishap' (1971, p. 545). In a similar vein, Willey (1934) characterized the nature of explanation in the seventeenth century as the desire to be rid of mystery and to remove fear and dependence (cf. Wolpert, 1987).

The treatment of witches was but one example of the more general phenomenon of persecution. According to Moore (1987), it was as early as the eleventh and twelfth centuries that deliberately and socially sanctioned violence was directed against groups of people defined by characteristics such as race, religion and way of life, whose membership of these groups was itself seen to justify their oppression. The victims included heretics, lepers and Jews and, as seen in the case of witches, there was often an attributional component to the persecution. Moore highlighted leprosy as a particularly interesting case because its cause (the bacillus *microbacterium leprae*) was only identified in 1874. There was therefore considerable freedom to ascribe the cause of leprosy to a wide variety of circumstances, from a lascivious temperament to an excess of bad fish in the diet.

Moore also noted that certain parallels were imposed on persecuted groups: Jews were held to resemble heretics and lepers in being 'unclean', sexually promiscuous and in presenting a menace to the wives and children of 'honest Christians'. The logical consequence of treating these groups as interchangeable was that they should be, and were, treated similarly (e.g., made to dress in a distinctive way, and forced to live apart from the community). This forced interchangeability provided the background for perceived collusion between the groups, for example the alleged conspiracy by Jews and lepers to poison the wells of France in 1321.

There was, of course, a close connection between the occurrence of crises and conspiracy-theory explanations. As Groh (1987a) relates, the search for an explanation of the catastrophic plague that swept Europe in the mid-fourteenth century led to an immediate confrontation with the Jews, Christianity's 'classical outsider group' (p. 16). Since the middle of the twelfth century the Jews had been accused of diabolical conspiracy against Christianity (see Poliakov, 1966)[1] and Zukier has conveyed the link between a calamitous event and the perceived conspiracy:

> [F]rom 1348 to 1350, Europe was ravaged by a bubonic epidemic, or Black Death plague. Over a third of the European population was decimated, and in many places more than half the inhabitants perished. People were stunned by the dimensions of the calamity, and groping for some understanding of what was happening, and for a measure of control over the events. Pope Clement VI declared the pestilence an act of God. But to many people, the Jews soon came to *embody the explanation*: the plague was but the monstrous unfolding of a Jewish plot to poison Christianity . . . (Zukier, 1987, pp. 96–7; emphases added).

As Zukier also pointed out, this adoption of the conspiracy theory is an example of the resemblance criterion at the societal level – the need to perceive some similarity between the consequences of an event and its causes (see chapter 4). Major negative consequences (whether the plague or the French Revolution) must have major, i.e. conspiratorial, causes (see also Roberts, 1974).

Conspiracy theory: social representation and societal attribution

Poliakov (1980) has labelled the fascination of human beings for an elementary and exhaustive causality a '*causalité diabolique*'. The 'demons' blamed for catastrophes vary over historical periods (and include witches, Jews, Jesuits, freemasons and Marxists) but all have been seen as protagonists of a world conspiracy and none more so than the Jews. Their persecution is based on the belief that all Jews everywhere 'form a conspiratorial body set on ruining and then dominating the rest of mankind' (Cohn, 1966, p. 16).

The historical background to the myth of a Jewish world conspiracy has been more than adequately documented elsewhere (see Cohn, 1966; Poliakov, 1968); what is interesting for the social psychologist is to examine the extent to which these ideas were shared, what social functions they served, and how they were transmitted. The best-known example of a conspiracy theory involving the Jews is, of course, the virulent anti-semitism of the Third Reich. Some indication of the extent to which these ideas were shared is given by Merkl's (1975) analysis of the autobiographies of 581 Nazis, 16 per cent of whom were found to believe in a Jewish world conspiracy. Merkl seems to have found evidence for a particular kind of obsessional causality that made Nazis especially receptive to plot theories. To the extent that this conspiracy theory was widely shared, one can characterize it as a social representation (Moscovici, 1987). This interpretation does not deny that there are individual differences in the espousal of such explanations and in the tendency to see 'persons as origins' (see De Charms et al., 1965; Maselli and Altrocchi, 1969), but it would surely be a mistake to confuse socially shared perceptions of conspiracy with individual paranoid delusions (Groh, 1987b). Similarly Zukier (1987) has argued that conspiracies are distinctly social phenomena, the collective nature of which is clear from their etymology.

Billig (1978) has provided a detailed analysis of the conspiracy theory from an attributional perspective and he noted that the skilled conspiracy theorist can explain all, even puzzling, events in terms of the sometimes inscrutable schemes of hidden conspirators. In the language of attribution theory, Billig argued, the conspiracy theorist could be said to make personal, rather than situational, attributions, and he demonstrated that these simplistic patterns of attribution are still to be found among the ranks of contemporary fascists (e.g., the British National Front Party). It is also useful to view the conspiracy theory in the light of the functions of attributions. This view of the world makes it easier to reduce dissonant perceptions (puzzling events can be attributed to invisible machinations) and allows the perceiver to reduce complexity (events are not allowed to have multiple causes).

The conspiracy theory also provides a sense of control over events. As Bains (1983) pointed out, crises are attributed to controllable causes – the activities of small groups of highly visible people. Control is also provided in the form of the remedy implied by such simplistic explanations. This is nowhere more evident than in Nazi ideology and propaganda. For example, Cohn (1966) reported that Hitler referred to the Jews as 'bacilli' and remarked to Himmler that, 'The discovery of the Jewish virus is one of the greatest revolutions that have taken place in the world. The battle in which we are engaged today is of the same sort as the battle waged, during the last century, by Pasteur and Koch. How many diseases have their origin in the Jewish virus! . . . We shall regain our health only by eliminating the Jews.'[2] The 'remedy' or treatment is premised on the explanation (the idea of millions of Jews as bearers of an imaginary plague). This explanation was picked up in the propaganda supplied by the anti-semitic newspaper, *Der Stürmer* (edited by the notorious Julius Streicher), which had a circulation of nearly half a million and was displayed on special notice-boards in towns and villages. By the end of 1936, *Der Stürmer* prescribed the treatment: 'The mobilization of the German people's will to destroy the bacillus lodged in its body is a declaration of war on all Jews throughout the world.'[3] This example highlights the unexplored question of how metaphors are used in causal explanations (see Hilton, 1982). Metaphors help us to understand one kind of experience, thing or object in terms of another (see Lakoff and Johnson, 1980); they might therefore be expected to guide explanations and to be used especially in the explanation of novel and bizarre events. It is perhaps no coincidence that the author Thomas Keneally used the same metaphor to explain the exceptional behaviour of Oskar Schindler, who risked his life to protect Jews in Nazi-occupied Poland:

> Old drinking friends of Oskar's . . . had sometimes thought of him as the victim of a Jewish virus. It was no metaphor. They believed it in literal terms . . . Some area of the brain fell under a thrall that was half bacterium, half magic. (Keneally, 1983, p. 350)

Although the Third Reich provides the most infamous example of a conspiracy theory at work, my illustrations have ranged from the twelfth to the twentieth century. If nothing else, this lineage should attest to the powerful appeal of simple causal explanations that are ubiquitous, timeless, spread easily 'from above' and passed on 'below' (Groh, 1987b). This ubiquity notwithstanding, conspiracy theories, like other patterns of explanation, have experienced peaks and troughs in influence and popularity. Wood (1982) has provided a fascinating historical analysis of the popularity of this perspective (see also Davis, 1969, 1971; Hofstadter, 1966). According to Wood, the century or so following the Restoration was *the* great era of conspiratorial fears: 'Everywhere people sensed designs within designs, cabals within cabals; there were court conspiracies, backstairs conspiracies, ministerial conspiracies, factional conspiracies, aristocratic con-spiracies, and by the last half of the eighteenth century even conspira-cies of gigantic secret societies that cut across national boundaries and spanned the Atlantic.' (Wood, 1982, p. 407). But it would be wrong, he warns, to see conspiratorial explanations as bizarre, rare or lower forms of explanation. They were often espoused by educated people and represented an enlightened view of the world, influenced by new scientific and philosophical developments, rather than the traditional Protestant conception of 'providence'. In short, Wood has provided a compelling illustration of the manner in which explanations are ideas of their time and vary with time (cf. Passmore, 1962; see chapter 1). Our interpretation of archival data must therefore be cautious:

> In our post-industrial, scientifically saturated society, those who continue to attribute combinations of events to deliberate human design may well be peculiar sorts of persons – marginal people, perhaps, removed from the centers of power, unable to grasp the conceptions of complicated causal linkages offered by sophisticated social scientists, and unwilling to abandon the desire to make simple and clear moral judgments of events. But people with such conspiratorial beliefs have not always been either marginal or irrational. Living in this complicated modern world, where the very notion of causality is in doubt, should not prevent us from seeing that at another time and in another culture most enlightened people accounted for events in just this particular way.' (Wood, 1982, p. 441)

This historical dimension of attribution is one that rarely emerges from the first three levels of analysis considered in this volume, but it is clearly fundamental to the societal level.

Summary

The tendentious, anthropomorphic notion of an attributing society has been illustrated with reference to individualism, witchcraft, persecution and conspiracy theory. The examples reveal the extent to which attributional ideas have been widely shared throughout societies at different historical periods, with awful consequences for the victims. All these collective beliefs, however, can be viewed as providing the attributor with an increased sense of control over threatening, sometimes calamitous, events. It is perhaps this control function of conspiracy theories that accounts for their importance historically, although the extent to which such ideas have been popular has varied over time and exemplifies the need to understand the temporal dimension of societal attributions.

EXPLANATIONS FOR SOCIETAL EVENTS

One consequence of the desire to explore attributions in a more social context is that the nature of what is to be explained may change dramatically. In particular, at the societal level, we are often interested in social conditions and events that are the outcomes of behaviour, rather than in behaviour itself. The explanation of these societal events may be considerably more complex than the explanation of behaviour, the focus of more traditional attribution research. The explanation of political and social events would, however, appear to be a quite common occurrence, an attribution we are called upon to make as citizens in a society, as well as a topic of research that will broaden the scope and context of attribution research. Most of the research to be reviewed below has not been based explicitly on a social representations approach; it does, however, invite an interpretation in these terms as can be seen in four main areas: attributions for poverty and wealth, unemployment, riots and racial inequality.[4]

Poverty and wealth

Feagin (1972) investigated explanations for poverty by asking a large sample of Americans to rate 11 common explanations of poverty. He divided the scales into three main categories: 'individualistic' (poverty is ascribed to the behaviour of poor people), 'societal' (poverty is ascribed to external, societal and economic forces) and 'fatalistic' (poverty is ascribed to luck and fate). Feagin's major finding was that half his sample of American adults explained poverty mainly in individualistic terms. There were, however, differences between racial, educational, income, religious and age groups, not all of which explained poverty mainly in individualistic terms. Later, factor-analytic studies confirmed Feagin's three categories, as well as his finding of the predominance of individualistic explanations and the effects of various demographic and attitudinal measures (e.g., Caplan and Nelson, 1973; Feather, 1974; Singh and Vasudeva, 1977). Townsend's (1979) survey on poverty revealed the same trend: around 30 per cent of 'the poor' in his sample blamed individuals for poverty, 22 per cent blamed the government and only 3 per cent blamed industry.

More recently, Furnham (1982a) studied explanations of poverty in Britain, using a sample of 120 adults and adding four additional explanations, based on pilot interviews, to Feagin's 11 explanations. For purposes of comparison, I focus just on Furnham's analysis of explanations 'for poverty in England' (he also assessed explanations for poverty in specific social groups), where he reported differences between Conservative and Labour voters.[5] Conservative voters rated individualistic explanations for poverty more important than did

Labour voters, and Labour voters rated two societal explanations more important than did Conservatives. In addition, Conservatives rated individualistic explanations more important than societal explanations, but the opposite was true for Labour voters.

These effects of political ideology were replicated by Pandey et al. (1982) in a small study of causal attributions for poverty in India, using a different, eight-item questionnaire with two explanations for each of four types of causes of poverty: 'self', 'fate', 'governmental policies' and 'economic dominance of a few in society'. Activists on the political left attributed significantly more to the government and economic causes, and significantly less to self and fate, than those on the right and neutrals. All groups, however, attributed more importance to the system causes than to the personal causes.

These studies indicate only a weak tendency towards individualistic attributions of poverty, but this tendency is reversed for respondents on the political left and in India (where poverty is much more widespread). Tyler and Rasinski (1983), from their studies on judgements of causality for political and social events and problems, reported that items assessing individual causality across problems, and individualistic causes of poverty, were much more highly inter-correlated than were items assessing social-structural causality. They suggested that judgements of individual causality may be more determined by ideology, whereas social-structural causes may be more responsive to the problems involved. This finding tends to support the idea of a social representation of individualism, at least for explanations of poverty, that is worthy of more detailed research. These results can also be interpreted using the 'Just World' hypothesis (Lerner, 1980; Lerner and Miller, 1978), according to which people derogate victims, holding them at least partly responsible for having been victimized, in order to perceive the world as just and a place in which misfortune occurs only to those who deserve it. Martin (1967) has argued that this magical kind of belief is shared by vast numbers of people. It is a view of the world that can serve an obvious adaptive function; people can confront the world as stable and orderly and orient themselves towards long-term goals. In particular, if other people's fates are seen as just, then the implication is that their own fate will be just too.

In contrast to the studies on poverty, Lewis (1981) reported that perceptions of the determinants of wealth were viewed as primarily societal in nature, or fatalistic. Furnham (1983), however, noted that comparisons between individualistic and societal explanations were meaningless if one ignored their evaluative nature. He asked 172 adults to rate 15 explanations for the existence of wealth in England. Conservatives rated *positive* individualistic explanations for wealth more important than did Labour voters (e.g., thrift and hard work), but Labour voters rated *negative* individualistic explanations for wealth more important (e.g., 'The rich are ruthless and determined'), as well as societal factors that maximize inequality (e.g., the taxation system). Finally, explanations for an outcome like wealth may be expected to vary cross-culturally; for example, Furnham and Bond (1986) reported especially high endorsement of individualistic explanations in Hong Kong (see also research in Australia by Forgas et al., 1982; and in Canada by Younger et al., 1977). More will be said about culture and attribution in the final section of this chapter.

Unemployment

In any society with high, or rising, unemployment the threat of jobless-ness may be expected to instigate causal attributions, especially among those closely concerned, because of their age, occupation or geographic location (e.g., Feather and Davenport, 1981; Gurney, 1981). Furnham (1982b) asked 284 British adults to rate 20 commonly offered explanations for unemployment, based on pilot interviews and content-analysis of the mass media. He categorized these explanations using the three categories suggested by Feagin (1972) for explanations of poverty: 'individualistic' (the unemployed were seen as being responsible for their plight), 'societal' (factors such as government, management and Trades Unions) and 'fatalistic' (unemployment seen as caused by fate, chance or uncontrollable factors). Furnham found that the explanations rated most important referred to present and past governments' actions and world-wide recession. The classification of these causes is, however, problematic. A factor analysis computed by Furnham yielded five, not three, factors and several inconsistencies (e.g., Factor 1 included eight individualistic and two societal items and was labelled 'individualistic'; yet the two societal items were Trades Unions and overmanning in industry). In view of this problem, it is perhaps most instructive to focus on the means and the nine explanations that revealed significant ($p < .01$) differences between employed and unemployed respondents (see table 9).[6]

For individualistic explanations, the employed saw two causes as significantly more important than did the unemployed ('Unemployed people don't try hard enough to get jobs' and 'Unwillingness of unemployed to move to places of work') and the unemployed saw two

TABLE 9 Mean explanations for unemployment offered by the employed and unemployed

Explanations	Employed	Unemployed
A Individualistic		
Unemployed people can earn more money on social security	5.21	5.31
Lack of effort and laziness among unemployed people	5.13	4.81
Unemployed people don't try hard enough to get jobs	3.15	4.21[a]
Unemployed people are too fussy and proud to accept some jobs	4.89	4.57
Poor education and qualifications among unemployed people	4.40	3.55[a]
Unwillingness of unemployed to move to places of work	4.32	5.51[a]
Inability of unemployed people to adapt to new conditions	4.77	4.38
Lack of intelligence or ability among the unemployed	5.46	4.76[a]
B Societal		
The policies and strategies of the present government	2.05	2.33
The policies and strategies of previous British governments	2.82	2.85
Inefficient and less competitive industries that go bankrupt	3.38	3.45
An influx of immigrants have taken up all available jobs	5.32	3.92[a]
Trace unions have priced their members out of a job	4.37	3.85
Overmanning in industry which has occurred for too long	3.53	3.93
Incompetent industrial management with poor planning	2.94	3.46[a]
Weak trace unions that do not fight to keep jobs	4.80	3.58[a]
C Fatalistic		
Sickness and physical handicap among unemployed people	5.14	3.74[a]
Just bad luck	5.73	5.27
World-wide recession and inflation	2.19	2.57
The introduction of widespread automation	3.70	3.09[a]

[a] p < .01 Numbers represent the mean on the following scale:
Important 1 2 3 4 5 6 7 Unimportant
Source: after Furnham, 1982b, © 1982 John Wiley & Sons Ltd, reprinted by permission of John Wiley & Sons Ltd and the author.

causes as significantly more important than did the employed ('Poor education and qualifications among unemployed people' and 'Lack of intelligence or ability among the unemployed'). For societal explanations, the employed saw one cause as significantly more important than did the unemployed ('Incompetent industrial management with poor planning') and the unemployed saw two causes as significantly more important than did the employed ('An influx of immigrants have taken up all available jobs' and 'Weak trade unions that do not fight to keep jobs'). Finally, for fatalistic explanations, the unemployed saw two causes as significantly more important than did the employed ('Sickness and physical handicap among unemployed people' and 'The introduction of widespread automation'). On the basis of these effects, broad conclusions about the relationship between employment status and preferred *type* of explanation are unwarranted. A more convincing characteristic of these data is that the employed and the unemployed *agree* on three out of four of the most important explanations (those explanations given an importance rating of less than three in table 9). There is thus evidence of a shared social representation (notwithstanding some differences between sub-groups), according to which the major, consensual explanations of unemployment are government policies and strategies and world-wide recession and inflation. There is, then, less evidence of the impact of individualism in the case of explanations of unemployment compared with explanations of poverty. This interpretation receives strong support from two additional studies. Lewis et al. (1987) investigated free-response explanations for unemployment, based on a larger sample. Using Feagin's (1972) classification scheme, they found far more societal (71 per cent) than fatalistic (22 per cent) or indi-vidualistic (7 per cent) attributions, although there were no effects for employment status. Gaskell and Smith (1985) interviewed a random sample of school leavers from London and obtained open-ended causal attributions as well as structured ratings of internal and external responsibility ascribed for reducing unemployment. External attribu-tions were found to be significantly more important than internal attributions for unemployment. As Gaskell and Smith pointed out, people predominantly hear and read about societal, rather than individualistic, causes of unemployment. Thus societal attributions should be conceived as, or at least as related to, social representations that are often contained in and transmitted via the mass media.

Feather (1985) has studied the relationship between wider belief and value systems and attributions for unemployment in a more explicit way. In a first study he had Australian students complete measures of conservatism (voting preference and Wilson and Patterson's, 1968, 'C' scale) and then rate 27 possible explanations for youth unemployment. Factor analysis yielded eight factors, seven of which formed the basis for derived scales indicating a type of attribution. These students rated explanations that referred to societal conditions ('Defective government', 'Social change' and 'Economic recession') as more important causes for youth unemployment than were explanations based on individualistic factors ('Lack of motivation' and 'Personal handicap', although 'Competence deficiency' was seen as important (see also Feather and Barber, 1983; Feather and Davenport, 1981). Conservative attitudes clearly influenced the way respondents rated explanations, as shown by positive correlations (between conservatism/voting conservative and attribution) with some scales ('Lack of motivation', 'Personal handicap', 'Social change' and 'Specific competition') and negative correlations with others ('Defective government' and 'Economic recession'). A second study confirmed the preference for societal over individualistic explanations and revealed small, but significant, correlations between Rokeach's (1973) Value Survey and attributions. Overall, these two studies support the general thrust of this chapter, that societal-level attributions need to be considered in the light of wider social beliefs; as Feather concluded: 'The explanations that people hold for events are not neutral beliefs that are the end products of unbiased, rational information processing. They are linked to other beliefs, attitudes, and values within the total belief system in ways that give meaning and consistency to the events that occur.' (1985, p. 885).

Although these studies do converge on some common findings, Schaufeli (1988) has raised a critical point concerning the different numbers of factors that emerge in different studies. He suggested the application of the Causal Dimension Scale (CDS, Russell, 1982; see chapter 3) because respondents might perceive many of the available attributions in different ways. Schaufeli analysed attributions for unemployment given by over 600 Dutch students and questioned the internal structure of the CDS, but he did report a parallel between explanations of employment-unemployment and success-failure. Generally, causal attributions for employment were more internal, stable and controllable and attributions for unemployment were more external, unstable and uncontrollable. This pattern of results suggested a process similar to the self-serving attributional bias, with the unemployed (especially) tending to attribute their condition to external rather than internal factors.

Finally it must be acknowledged that all these studies (with the

exception of Schaufeli, 1988) are cross-sectional. Changes in explanations for unemployment over time have, however, received some
attention. It has been suggested that people out of work for long periods of time tend to offer fatalistic explanations for the causes of their
own and other people's unemployment (Haynes and Nutman, 1981;
O'Brien and Kabanoff, 1979), although M. Jahoda (1979) noted that
the unemployed of the 1930s tended to end up blaming themselves. It
has, however, also been claimed that those out of work for long periods
of time are more externally oriented (they tend to attribute to social
and chance factors; Tiffany et al., 1970). Once again, caution is in order
here, because researchers have generally ignored the evaluative nature
of available attributions and it should not be assumed that any type of
attribution is, *a priori*, functional or dysfunctional (cf. Gurin et al.,
1969), although attributions do appear to moderate the psychosocial
effects of unemployment (Warr, 1984). In addition to longitudinal
effects, one should expect cohort effects. Kelvin (1980, 1984) has
argued that social psychologists, like economists, should collect data
over time, with a view to the future as well as to the present. As he
noted, it would be fascinating to have records of data such as explanations for unemployment from the early nineteenth through the twentieth century. Kelvin proposed that as the perceived probability of
unemployment increased, one would expect to see greater attention to
societal, and less to individualistic, factors (as shown, cross-sectionally,
by the data reported above). In addition, Warr (1984) has noted that a
higher local level of unemployment increases external causal attributions for unemployment (see also Honess, 1989). If, as I have argued,
explanations for societal outcomes such as unemployment are complex, then they must be matched by adequately complex designs (e.g.,
cross-sequential designs that include statistical controls for local levels
of unemployment). Public opinion poll data, collected over a long time
series, may provide an archival basis for this kind of research, although
this source has not yet been tapped by attribution researchers (see
Himmelweit, in press).

Riots

Recent examples of societal events that called for an explanation were
the 'riots', or civil disturbances, in Britain that involved police and,
predominantly, black youths. Newspaper reports following the
disturbances were primarily concerned with ascertaining their causes.[7]
It was, however, quite evident that there were no simple causal
explanations. The riots seemed to have a number of possible (and not

mutually exclusive) causes, some more proximal to the event, others more distal. Thus one cause for the disturbance in Bristol was given as the raid on a café by plain-clothes policemen, and the Brixton riot was seen as partly caused by police questioning of a black taxi driver on the evening before the trouble started. Clearly, these incidents might each have been necessary conditions for the riot, but they can hardly be seen as sufficient. As almost all reputable media sources reported at the time, the causes lay in part in less tangible aspects of the social environment – poor relations between police and young blacks, allegations concerning racial discrimination and appalling levels of unemployment in the black community.

These examples demonstrate just how complex causal attributions for social conditions can be. They also show how shared attributions can vary across groups. Thus the blacks themselves attributed the uprisings to discriminatory practices of the police, the local white population said that high unemployment was the key, the police (for a time) pointed to *agents provocateurs*, and the government (through the Prime Minister, Mrs Thatcher) was mainly concerned to deny that high unemployment was the cause. It is obvious from these examples that a diversity of explanations may abound for societal events. Similarly Campbell and Schuman (1969) reported that more blacks attributed the ghetto riots in the U.S. to discrimination and unemployment than did whites, and more whites gave explanations that referred to black power beliefs and the looters themselves than did blacks.

Two studies I wish to highlight here used more innovative methodology that illustrated the rich possibilities for research on societal attributions. Schmidt (1972) studied explanations of the civil disturbances that took place in many U.S. cities in the summer of 1967. He obtained explanations from the editorial pages of a range of newspapers and magazines published during the period June-October 1967. The major question behind his study was: what is the relation between the evaluation or perceived legitimacy of the riots and the type of explanation proposed?

Student judges sorted 76 explanations from the printed media into categories, then rated them on three properties that were felt to be related to the dimensions identified by a multidimensional scaling solution: (a) legitimacy-illegitimacy, (b) internal-external cause and (c) institutional-environmental cause. The two-dimensional representation yielded by non-metric scaling is shown in figure 16, for which Schmidt summarized the type of explanations that appear in different sections of the space (the numbers used below refer to the numbering of explanations in the figure).

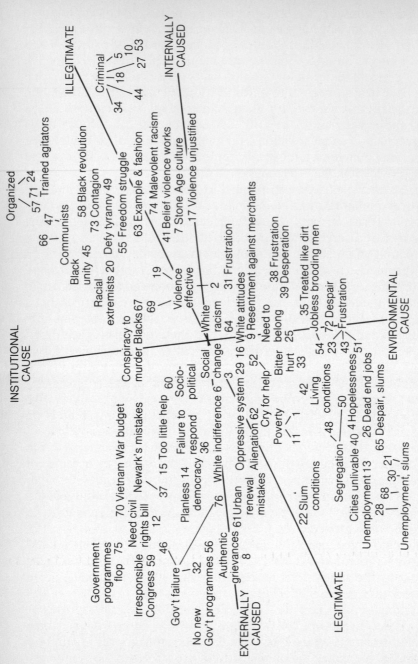

FIGURE 16 *Two-dimensional configuration of the 76 explanations showing the best-fitting axes of the properties internally caused–externally caused, institutional cause–environmental cause and legitimate–illegitimate (from Schmidt, 1972, © 1972 by the American Psychological Association, reprinted by permission of the publisher and author)*

On the right side of the space, three types of explanation can be seen. At the extreme right there are 'criminal' statements, close to the illegitimate pole; at the upper right there are explanations referring to 'communists', seen as organized, trained agitators. In the right-centre region, explanations are more heterogeneous, but there appear to be two related types of explanation: (1) statements that describe the rioters as people engaged in revolutionary and political action, but action that is precipitated by societal conditions (e.g., 49, 55); (2) statements that emphasize the effectiveness of the violence, but do not see the riots as a political act (e.g., 19).

Explanations that appear on the left side of the space all tend to play down the role of the actor as a cause of the riots and focus on external forces. Explanations in the lower left quadrant point to the physical conditions surrounding the actors – slums, unlivable cities and unemployment (e.g., 13, 22, 28, 40). The statements in the left-centre area highlight the failure of social institutions to improve the rioters' conditions (e.g., 46). Statements in the lower central region focus on the psychological conditions of the participants – hopelessness (4), despair (72) and frustration (43).

The internal-external and legitimate-illegitimate dimensions, which are of obvious theoretical importance, fitted well with the multi-dimensional space (using a multiple regression analysis). They were also highly intercorrelated, as seen in figure 16. Those statements seen as implying an internal cause were also seen as implying that the riot was illegitimate, whereas statements that focused on external causes were seen as implying that the riot was more legitimate. A third dimension contrasted institutional causes with environmental causes.

Schmidt also analysed the relation between the political position of the newspaper source of each statement and the type of explanation given for the riot. He found that sources on the political right and far left were both located on the right side of the space (i.e., they implied that the riot was internally caused). Media sources classified as 'left centre' tended to ascribe the rioting to external causes. These findings suggest, however, that the analysis missed out an important evaluative dimension, that could differentiate between explanations as distinct as 'freedom struggle' and 'criminal'.

Finally, Schmidt's data again highlighted the temporal dimension of societal attributions. He found that explanations published later in the summer and autumn focused more on external causes of the rioting and implied that it was more legitimate than those explanations that were published earlier. In sum, this study provides an original method for investigating societal attributions and one that has yet to receive the attention it deserves.

More recently, Litton and Potter (1985) made explicit use of the framework of social representations to study explanations of the St Paul's riot that took place in Bristol in 1980. Again the method was innovative, involving transcription of radio and television programmes, newspaper reports and editorials, and the testimony of six respondents who were involved in, or present during, the riot. The analysis of this 80,000 word corpus identified two main types of explanation – 'race' and 'the effects of government cuts and amenities' – but Litton and Potter emphasized that within each type of explanation there was considerable diversity. Their article suggests that a limited number of shared explanations were drawn upon to make sense of, and evaluate, this riot, but more convincing data will be required to demonstrate the full value of the social representations approach in this area.

Racial inequality

The final piece of research to review in this section provides a more detailed analysis of how attributions may fit together with other inferences, and feelings, to influence complex social judgements (how people work out their own positions on policy issues). Sniderman et al. (1986) studied the issue of whether or not the U.S. government should assist blacks and other minorities. They argued that when people are faced with a decision to help someone, their decision to help is based on their causal attributions (why does the need exist?) as well as on other information (including ideology and affect); all these elements might fit together into a 'chain of reasoning'. Using data from a national U.S. sample (white respondents only, 1972), Sniderman et al. estimated models of how the following five measures were interrelated (models were also estimated separately for three categories of education – failure to complete high school, high school but no college and at least some college):

1 Opposition to various government policies intended to promote racial equality (high scores indicate prejudice).
2 Causal attributions for racial inequality (high scores indicate prejudice).
3 Affect towards blacks (negative scores indicate prejudice).
4 Political ideology (from liberal [1] to conservative [7]).
5 Causal attributions for poverty (high scores on the first principal component indicate a 'lack of equal opportunities'

explanation; high scores on the second principal component indicate a 'lack of effort' explanation).

The most provocative issue addressed by Sniderman et al. was whether policy reasoning is 'affect driven' or 'cognition driven'. For the present discussion, the key question concerns the role of attributions in each model. In an affect-driven model, people start with their feelings towards blacks; if they dislike blacks, they can attribute the problems of blacks to the latter's own failings and then conclude that the government should not help blacks. Sniderman et al. suggested that these kinds of respondents pass quickly from their dislike of blacks to their opposition to government assistance for them, no intervening step is necessary. At the end of this process, they then 'double back' and complete the intermediate steps in the chain of reasoning. The results suggested that less educated people reasoned according to this kind of model; note that explanations for inequality had a very small (non-significant) impact on policy preferences (see figure 17).

The better educated, in contrast, reasoned according to a cognition-driven model. They based their policy preferences about government assistance for blacks partly on their explanation of why blacks were worse off than whites; in addition, they based their explanation of why blacks are worse off on their policy preference. They reasoned forwards *and* backwards (see figure 18). In view of the fact that both less- and well-educated groups reasoned 'backwards', we must clarify

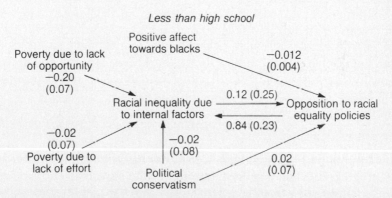

FIGURE 17   *Non-recursive model of racial policy preferences (affect driven) (after Sniderman et al., 1986, reprinted by permission of Cambridge University Press)*
   Note   *Unstandardized regression coefficients appear outside the parentheses, their standard errors inside them*

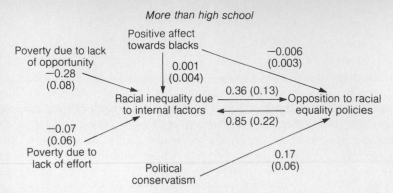

FIGURE 18   *Non-recursive model of racial policy preferences (cognition driven) (after Sniderman et al., 1986, reprinted by permission of Cambridge University Press)*
     Note   *Unstandardized regression coefficients appear outside the parentheses, their standard errors inside them*

Sniderman et al.'s distinction between reasoning backwards and rationalization. As they noted, rationalization usually implies, pejoratively, that a person produced his or her answers to conceal true beliefs or motives. Reasoning backwards suggests, without evaluation, only that people 'complete missing links in their chain of reasoning' (Sniderman et al., 1986, p. 429).

Sniderman et al. included appropriate caveats concerning the limitations of their cross-sectional methodology and the specific issue of race; this kind of research, however, makes a valuable contribution both in applying attributions to political decision-making and in honestly appraising the role of causal attributions alongside other (sometimes obviously more influential) measures.

Summary

This sampling of research from four areas has shown that attribution research can be, and has been, applied to the explanation of societal events. Three general points emerge. First, when explaining these kinds of events, wider social and collective beliefs do come into play and the concept of social representation proved useful in interpreting the results of research. It was, for example, noted that whereas attributions tended to be individualistic for poverty, they had become societal for unemployment. This first point merges with the second, namely that there is a temporal dimension to societal attributions. This dimension was seen most clearly in the case of explanations for unemployment and for riots. Third, and finally, explanations for complex societal events require more complex and sophisticated research. Attributions need to be investigated with other cognitive and affective measures, with an open mind as to whether attributions determine, or can be determined by, other judgements.

CULTURE AND ATTRIBUTION

Semin (1980) has made the point that the ANOVA model (Kelley, 1967; see chapter 2) may be of very little relevance to the attributions of someone from a different (i.e., non-Western) cultural background. There are at least two ways in which research has followed up this criticism. First, there have been straightforward comparisons between attributions made in different cultures (a *cross-cultural* approach). Second, without dispensing with cultural comparisons, scholars have begun to provide a richer analysis of the cultural basis of attribution (a *cultural* approach).

Cross-cultural research

Bond (1983) defined the cross-cultural approach to attribution as one that compares the extent and type of attributional activity across different cultures. His review found that members of various cultures can make reliable and functionally meaningful attributions, as shown by research in countries as different as Nigeria (e.g., Boski, 1983), Hong Kong (e.g., Bond et al., 1985), India (e.g., Singh et al., 1979) and Japan (e.g., Shaw and Iwawaki, 1972). But Bond emphasized that these studies show only that members of non-Western cultures can make attributions *when asked*; we have learned nothing about how frequently they undertake this activity in everyday life (see also Fletcher and Ward, 1988). An additional problem discussed by Bond is that studies have often merely imposed a Western (North American) attributional approach, at the level of constructs, questionnaires and individual items. Thus a narrowly cross-cultural approach does not even ask the questions, let alone provide the answers, that might lead to a broader approach to attribution theory.

Cultural attribution research

Work by Triandis and colleagues on 'subjective culture' (Triandis, 1976; Triandis et al., 1972) has found that persons from different cultural groups often make different causal attributions for the same behaviour, with interpersonal misunderstandings as the result. To understand such different attributions, we must delve deeper into 'culture', what D'Andrade has defined as 'the shared information – the cognitive content – upon which cognitive processes operate' (1981, p. 182).

Agar (1981) has proposed an integration of ethnographic and attributional perspectives. Rich examples of 'primitive' forms of causal attribution occur throughout the writing of ethnographers, some of which are both entertaining and instructive. Thus Lévy-Bruhl (1925) reported that the natives of Motumotu in New Guinea ascribed a kind of pleurisy epidemic, in turn, to the presence of a missionary, his sheep, two goats and, finally, a portrait of Queen Victoria. This, at first bizarre, attribution is more understandable in the light of collective beliefs or cultural representations. Fauconnet (1928) explained that in so-called primitive societies the infirm, magicians and foreigners were held responsible with great ease. In the religious classification of society, these people were regarded as impure and this impurity associated them with crime. Fauconnet illustrated this process with explicit reference to early European explorers who were often held responsible for inclement weather, the failure of hunting and fishing expeditions and so on.

Examples like this, although instructive, do not bear directly on the psychological processes or behavioural consequences derived directly from any part of attribution theory (G. Jahoda, 1979). Yet Jahoda has also argued that concepts drawn from theories that originate from within a particular culture cannot necessarily be operationalized in different cultures. He gives as an example the Zande 'theory' of dual causation, where witchcraft (as a distant cause) often operates in connection with a common-sense explanation (as an immediate cause) (see Evans-Pritchard, 1937). For the Azande people, Jahoda contended, the distinction between internal and external attributions would make little sense. This crucial distinction lies behind a paradigmatic example of cultural attribution research.

Miller (1984) was interested in the influence of 'cultural meaning systems' (D'Andrade, 1984), as opposed to either cognitive capacities or different experiences, on age and cultural variation in attribution. In particular, she studied the development of dispositional attributions, following the suggestion that there were different 'cultural conceptions of the person' in the cultures of North America and India (see Carrithers et al., 1986). Previous research on Western populations had found a significant increase over development in references to general dispositions of the agent (e.g., Livesley and Bromley, 1973; Peevers and Secord, 1973). In contrast, Shweder and Bourne (1982) found that adults from non-Western cultures generally placed less emphasis on dispositional properties of the agent (they used more contextual qualifiers and behavioural descriptions) than did American and Western European adults; this non-Western concept of the 'person' was not distinguishable from social roles and social relationships. Fletcher and Ward (1988) pointed out that this holistic, versus individualistic, conception of the person in non-Western cultures may have a realistic basis in that external roles and norms have a greater impact on the individual's behaviour in collectivist, compared to non-collectivist, cultures (G. Jahoda, 1982).

The purpose of Miller's research was to tease apart three explanations for cultural differences in the development of attributions: (1) in terms of children's cognitive capacities (e.g., Livesley and Bromley, 1973); (2) in terms of different cross-cultural and developmental experiences (e.g., lack of exposure to a more complex environment associated with modernization; Scribner and Cole, 1973); and (3) in terms of the different cultural conceptions of the person acquired by developing individuals in Western (individualistic) and non-Western (holistic) cultures.

In her first study Miller tested comparable numbers of Indian Hindus and North Americans (both middle-class) in each of four age groups (adults, 15-, 11- and 8-year olds). Rather than impose materials on her respondents, she used a coding scheme for exhaustive classification of their responses. She asked respondents to narrate two pro-social and two deviant behaviours and to explain why the behaviour was undertaken. As predicted, at older ages Americans used more general dispositions in their explanations than did Hindus (especially for deviant behaviours). There was little difference between the responses of Americans and Hindus at the youngest ages (8 and 11), but Miller reported a significant linear age increase in references to general dispositions among the American sample (see figure 19). For context attributions (e.g., reference to social roles and patterns of interpersonal relationships) the results were reversed. At older ages Hindus made significantly greater reference to contextual factors in their explanations than did Americans. Again, there was only a small cross-cultural difference between children, but there was a significant

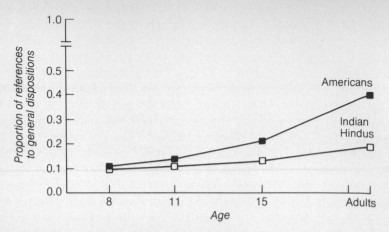

FIGURE 19   *Cultural and developmental patterns of dispositional attribution (data from Miller, 1984, © 1984 by the American Psychological Association, adapted by permission of the publisher and author)*

linear age increase in references to the context among the Hindus (see also Dalal, Sharma and Bisht, 1983).

By testing cognitive abilities, Miller ruled out a purely cognitive account of her findings – all respondents were capable of some abstract cognitive orientation. By comparing the Indian sample with Indian control groups, Miller also ruled out variation in reference to general dispositions as a function of attributors' socioeconomic status (i.e., experiential factors), although she did find that Anglo-Indians (with semi-Westernized cultural orientations) made more use of dispositions in explaining deviant behaviour than did other Indian groups. Finally, to rule out any explanation based on differences in the behaviours generated and explained by the two cultural groups, Miller carried out a second study. She had a new sample of American adults explain a set of deviant behaviours generated by Hindu adults and, as predicted, the Americans explained the events with many more dispositional, and fewer, contextual, references than did the Hindus.

In sum, this unique research provides evidence of the independent impact of cultural meaning systems on attribution and the need for future research to pay more attention to the social aspects of knowledge acquisition. Miller's findings also provide a persuasive societal-cultural account for the fundamental attribution error (L. Ross, 1977), but one that does not rule out other influences. The most likely explanation is that cognitive mechanisms (such as availability) exaggerate cultural tendencies, but we should be careful not to emphasize cognition to the exclusion of culture.

Summary

Attribution has been studied from cross-cultural and cultural perspectives. It has been useful to learn that members of various, sometimes strikingly different, cultures can make attributions, but we have also had to learn not to impose a Western attributional approach on indigenous psychologies (see Heelas and Lock, 1981). The nascent area of cultural attribution research has been less Procrustean and has taken culture more seriously. In doing so it has demonstrated that an understanding of culture is a sometimes invaluable aid to understanding causal attributions.

CONCLUSION

This chapter has probably gone further than some social psychologists would wish, in exploring attributions at the societal level. It has, however, explored some explanations that are shared by many members of a society or culture and demonstrated that attributional ideas do have a wider currency than some of their critics may argue.

The general notion that integrates much of this research is that of social representations. Some social psychologists will doubtless prefer ideologies, attitudes, beliefs or other representational constructs, but social representations have the unique virtue of both emphasizing *shared* knowledge structures and allowing us to remain at a *social-psychological* level of analysis. The present application of social representations led to topics such as individualism and conspiracy theory, as well as providing a novel *post hoc* interpretation of a disparate set of studies on attributions for poverty, unemployment and other societal conditions.

This review of research also identified some similarities and differences with research at the three other levels of analysis. For example, *evaluation* was shown to be as crucial to attributions for unemployment and riots as it was for actor-observer and husband-wife attributions at the interpersonal level. A new dimension to emerge was the *historical-temporal* dimension of attributions (without denying its relevance at other levels), as seen, again, in explanations for unemployment and riots. There is clearly a need for more longitudinal research on attributions, especially at this societal level.

Finally, it is encouraging to note that a focus on societal attribution has already brought together the perspectives of social psychologists, sociologists, political scientists and historians. This is a significant step in the pursuit of what has been called 'societal social psychology'; as Himmelweit et al. have argued:

> Social psychology, through its methodologies and theories, has a substantial contribution to make to the explanation of social phenomena, provided that researchers develop a sensitivity for the problems they investigate at the societal as well as the psychological level . . . This involves more use of the insights of the other social sciences and of historical and comparative data than is currently the practice. (1981, pp. 187–8)

I hope to have shown that attribution research has already made a contribution at this societal level, although there is obviously potential for much future research.

8 Conclusion

An adequate understanding of either a phenomenon or a theory requires that it can be investigated through a program of research planned to reveal the wide range of circumstances that affect the phenomenon and the rich set of implicit assumptions that limit the theory, thus making explicit the contexts in which one or another relationship obtains.

(McGuire, 1983)

Instead of adding to [the] proliferation of minitheories, researchers should focus on those fundamental principles of psychological functioning that have the potential to unify and organize the sprawling mass of research findings within one theoretical framework.

(Tetlock and Manstead, 1985)

This book began with the acknowledgement that explanations have long been grist to the mill of philosophers and psychologists (see chapter 1). Attribution theorists are notable, however, for their interest in common-sense explanations – what people think and believe about the causes of behaviour – which can be traced back, in psychology, to Michotte (1946) and, in sociology, to Ichheiser (1943). The central character is, of course, Fritz Heider (1944, 1958) whose 'naive psychology' provided the draft for the succeeding, and eminently more testable, theories of Jones and Davis (1965) and Kelley (1967, 1973). These latter theories have each made unique contributions to the development of the field and each offers insights into specific attributional problems (see chapter 2).

As research proceeded on the basis of these theories, it confronted fundamental questions concerning causal attribution – such as what exactly attributions are, how to measure them, when they are instigated, to what extent they are systematically biased, what functions they serve and what consequences they entail (see chapter 3). The sophistication of much of this work and the ingenuity with which researchers have sought to answer complex questions is exemplary. As ideas emerged they have been enthusiastically applied to a variety of psychological and social problems and the overall scope of the attribution research enterprise is striking. Yet despite these eulogies, critics have pointed to the limited perspective of much attribution research from the 1970s onwards. This book has tried to chart the progress of attribution research in terms of Doise's (1986) four levels of analysis and thus to explore causal attributions in the context of four major fields of social psychology.

At the *intra-personal* level (Level I; see chapter 4), causal attribution has been investigated from a cognitive or 'social cognition' viewpoint, with a focus on the mechanisms by which perceivers process information in causal analysis. Three major lines of research were identified: causal logic refers to the formal concepts that are thought to underlie attributions (e.g., covariation, causal schemata); causal process refers specifically to cognitive processes and advocates a more detailed analysis of causal information- processing (e.g., salience effects via availability); causal content refers to the knowledge people use to make causal attributions (e.g., scripts, schemata). Each of these approaches, which vary considerably in their information-processing demands, can claim some support in specific experimental contexts. Research at this level has supplied the concepts and methods for a more detailed analysis of causal attributions, but it is limited by a heavy reliance on laboratory research.

At the *interpersonal* level (Level II; see chapter 5) attribution research can be organized into two main parts, with reference to social interaction and close relationships. At this level of analysis there is evidence for attributional biases (actor-observer and self-serving effects), but one has to consider roles and perspectives as well as how apparently-cognitive attributions are related to evaluation, attraction and behavioural consequences. In close relationships the importance of evaluation is even more evident, especially in the areas of interpersonal conflict, marital satisfaction and relationship termination. There is evidence that attributions are linked to relationship-satisfaction and conflict-resolution strategies, that attributions differentiate distressed and non-distressed spouses and maintain marital distress, and that attributions (often as part of more detailed accounts) may help those affected to come to terms with the devastating breakup of a close relationship.

At the intergroup level (Level III; see chapter 6), social categorization has a clear impact on attribution and intergroup attributions are often ethnocentric; identical behaviours or outcomes are explained differently for members of in- and outgroups, with the tendency being to favour the ingroup. An attributional approach to intergroup conflict emphasizes how conflict is maintained, or even escalated, and contributes to our understanding of how best to reduce conflict through interventions such as intergroup contact.

Finally, at the *societal* level (Level IV; see chapter 7) attributions are considered alongside the beliefs that are shared by large numbers of people within and between societies. The concept of social representations provides a tool for analysing societal patterns of attribution (e.g., conspiracy theories), investigating attributions for societal events (e.g., poverty, unemployment) and exploring attributions in different cultures.

What picture of the field emerges from this review of the literature? In a widely-cited critique of social psychology, Steiner (1974) appeared to blame attribution theory in particular for drawing social perception away from the 'social'. Referring to the work of Jones and Davis (1965) and Kelley (1967), Steiner argued: 'On reading these models the overworked man from Mars might conclude that earthlings never converse with one another, never listen to another's judgment, and never accept the prefabricated verdict of social reality' (1974, p. 103). One conclusion at the end of this book is that the sprawling area of attribution research has now eschewed Steiner's criticism. His words certainly rang true 15 years ago, but in the light of attributional research on personal relationships, intergroup relations and collective beliefs the literature has arguably provided an answer to Steiner's subsequent question: 'How do attributions affect the collective enterprise that is our way of life?' (1974, p. 103).

To the extent that attribution theory and research have answered Steiner's critique, they have done so by focusing more attention on Doise's (1986) Levels II, III and IV, without abandoning analyses at Level I. Doise (1980) applied his levels model to experimental social psychology, rather than attribution research, and found that a large proportion of published research provided explanations in terms of intra-personal or interpersonal processes (Levels I and II). Many fewer studies explained experimental outcomes in terms of intergroup or societal concepts (Levels III and IV) and, where they did so, they tended to invoke one of these levels in association with one of the first two levels. My conception of both attribution research and Doise's analysis suggests that the integration (or 'articulation', as Doise calls it) of different levels represents the next major challenge to workers in this area. As Doise wrote, 'If there is a case for distinguishing four levels of analysis, it is in order to unite them better in future research' (1986, p. 28; see also Doise, 1984).

If integration is limited, for conceptual simplicity, to cases involving two levels, Doise's four levels of analysis provide for six types of integration. Table 10 gives examples for each combination, drawn from studies reviewed in more detail in previous chapters. None of these studies was carried out with reference to Doise's work, however, and some of the types of integration are suggestive at best. For these reasons a detailed discussion is inappropriate at this stage. Nonetheless, the possibilities for future work are apparent and the potential for a less fragmented approach to attribution should be clear. For example, interpersonal and intergroup analyses can and should address issues of intra-personal information-processing, while analyses of interpersonal accounts are situated in the framework of societal beliefs, as communicated by the mass media.

The advantages of a multi-level approach to attribution are several and obvious. First, the use of a levels model can be thought of in terms of D. T. Campbell's (1969) concept of 'triangulation', the idea that

TABLE 10   Research integrating Doise's levels of analysis

Type of integration	Study	Illustration
Levels I–II (intrapersonal-interpersonal)	Ross and Sicoly, 1979	Significant correlation between the tendency of marital partners to recall self-relevant behaviours ('availability') and the tendency to overestimate own perceived responsibility (egocentrism).
Levels I–III (intrapersonal-intergroup)	Hewstone, Gale and Purkhardt, 1988	Tendency to explain outgroup vs ingroup success using a Multiple Necessary Cause schema.
Levels I–IV (intrapersonal-societal)	J. G. Miller, 1984	Preference for dispositional attribution due to interaction of cultural and cognitive factors.
Levels II–III (interpersonal-intergroup)	Duncan, 1976	Outcome of a social interaction involving two individuals is explained differently as a function of their respective group memberships.
Levels II–IV[a] (interpersonal-societal)	Harvey, 1987	Interpersonal attributions given for the termination of close relationships must usually accord with, and may be influenced by, prevailing cultural values.
Levels III–IV (intergroup-societal)	Hewstone, Jaspars and Lalljee, 1982	Social representations provide a basis for intergroup attributions of success and failure.

[a] In this case there is no empirical evidence to support the type of integration.

multiple vantage points enable the researcher to 'fix' on a common object in a way that would be impossible from a single point (Brewer and Collins, 1981). Thus the topic of attributional biases looks quite different when a purely information-processing · perspective is supplanted with interpersonal, intergroup and societal levels of analysis.

Second, the pursuit of a social psychology in this mould encourages methodological diversity. In particular, the extremes of Level I and Level IV analyses will tend to capitalize on the respective strengths of laboratory and field research, although the overall research programme is best seen as a process of coming and going between the laboratory and the outside world (cf. Festinger, 1953).

Third, although I have no wish to revive the debate over the extent to which social psychology is 'social', the present approach does, at least in places, satisfy the criteria of social psychology laid down by Carlson (1984): (1) Subjects were chosen so as to represent or to compare meaningfully defined social groups (cf. chapters 6, 7); (2) Subjects were observed in genuine social interaction with real people (cf. chapter 5); (3) Social structural variables (e.g., socioeconomic status, ethnicity, occupation) were related to psychological measures (cf. chapters 6, 7); (4) Social influences on psychological functioning were observed (e.g., group atmosphere, language community, dyadic relationships, social class; cf. chapters 5, 6, 7); (5) Subjects were asked about social issues meaningful to them (cf. chapters 5, 6, 7).

These criteria, as Kenrick (1986) has pointed out, favour research done in the 'real world' with people engaging in social interaction. Carlson's approach is limited, however, in its exclusion of social cognition research from the field of social psychology. As van Dijk (1988) has argued, social psychology needs to be both more cognitive and more social than it has traditionally been if we are to understand social information-processing as well as society and its members. This fact is obvious as soon as one begins to think about the articulation between Doise's levels and about the new possibilities for research that emerge from their synthesis. I have tried to explore attribution at both cognitive and social extremes.

What, then, of the future of attribution research; is this book a requiem or an overture? Olson and Ross (1985) have referred to some of the main reasons for dissatisfaction with attribution research. Too many studies have tested theoretical derivations using pencil-and-paper methodologies, laboratory experimentation and undergraduate subjects, raising serious questions about the vitality of the field and the validity of its findings. These familiar criticisms are, of course, not limited to attribution theory and research, although this qualification does nothing to counter the limitations of social psychology's narrow data base (see Sears, 1986). The scope of attribution research, however, has been shown to be considerably broader than most of its critics realize. Although I have no wish to impose an attributional 'hegemony' on other researchers (see Semin, 1980), it is only fair to judge the field on its true extent, achievements and limitations. In these terms, I am optimistic about the future. Although the field is still unbalanced, with far more work at the intra-personal and interpersonal levels, there is substantial evidence for intergroup attribution and for the application of attributional ideas at the societal level. If attribution research is pursued on all four levels of analysis, bridges will be built between such broad, typically separate, areas as social cognition, social interaction, intergroup relations and social representations; we will no longer have what Moscovici called 'an archipelago of lonely paradigms' (1985, p. 91).

The quotation from McGuire (1983) at the head of this chapter argues eloquently for the need to study social-psychological phenomena across varying contexts and at different levels; the passage quoted from Tetlock and Manstead (1985) propounds the importance of fundamental principles over 'minitheories'. On the basis of reviews presented in the preceding chapters, I submit that the field (notwith-standing its limitations) *has* achieved a remarkable breadth and diversity. It also deals with what is undeniably a fundamental principle – the way people understand their world and explain events in it (as Kelley, 1973, argued, attribution theory is related to the more general field of 'psychological epistemology', the processes by which people 'know', and know that they know, the world). My view, then, is that attribution theory is not only a worthwhile intellectual pursuit, but one that has been pursued in a worthwhile manner. My conclusion is that the study of causal attribution – from cognitive processes to collective beliefs – should be, and can be, as broad as the study of social psychology itself.

Notes

1 This chapter draws heavily on the historical and philosophical work cited in an excellent chapter by Fischhoff (1976).
2 For a more comprehensive treatment, see Hart and Honoré (1959); for a philosophical extension of their work, see Gorowitz (1965).
3 Experimental research in the tradition of Michotte continues, but it occupies a place in general or perceptual, rather than social, psychology (e.g., Todd and Warren, 1982; Weir, 1978).
4 Other sociologists have also written on the attribution or imputation of motives (e.g. MacIver, 1940; Mills, 1940; M. Weber, 1947), but there is no obvious connection between this work and attribution theory.
5 See Rudmin et al. (1987) for a complete bibliography of Ichheiser's work which indicates that some of these most influential ideas appeared first in earlier papers, published in Polish or German.
6 My nomenclature for the four levels differs slightly from Doise's, but the structure is essentially identical. I disagree, however, with his classification of Kelley's (1967) work at Level II; in my opinion it is a quintessential Level 1 model. Doise (personal communication) is flexible about how the levels should be labelled, and now agrees with the present classification of Kelley's (1967) work.

CHAPTER 2 CLASSIC THEORIES OF CAUSAL ATTRIBUTION

1 Gergen and Jones (1963) did include two attributional measures, but neither of them was affected by the experimental variables.
2 On a historical note, P. A. White (1989) has traced this covariation principle back to William of Ockham, who wrote during the fourteenth century (see Grant, 1971, p. 30).
3 Logically it may be argued that the augmentation principle applies to what Kelley (1972a) called the schema for 'compensatory causes', rather than to the MSC and MNC schemata. The compensatory causal schema incorporates the ideas that (a) attributors can distinguish the degree of strength,

and not only the presence or absence, of cause and effect; and (b) the absence, or low level, of one cause can be compensated for by an increase in the other (see also Hull and West, 1982).

4   Although the names for these schemata are now widely used, Hilton (in press) has argued that the MNC schema would be better termed a Multiple Necessary *Conditions* schema. This is because it is the combined sum of necessary conditions that constitute the *single* cause. In the MSC case, in contrast, each factor is sufficient to produce the effect and thus there are two causes.

CHAPTER 3   ATTRIBUTION THEORY AND RESEARCH: FUNDAMENTAL QUESTIONS

1   Ipsative measures are those in which the score of one attribution must influence the score of other attributions, as when the 'total cause' of an event (100 per cent) must be accounted for from the given number of particular causes (e.g., Feldman-Summers and Kiesler, 1974).

2   Interestingly, Jones et al. (1972) hypothesized that 'adults function at different levels of attributional complexity at different times and under different conditions' (p. xii).

3   This study was not included in Weiner's (1985a) review.

4   Ross (personal communication) chose the name to imply 'fundamental' in the sense of important, and not, as has been assumed, in the sense of ubiquitous. This point is made clearly by Quattrone (1982b): 'Because the distinction between personal and situational causal factors is fundamental to all major theories of attribution, the bias is no ordinary attributional error. It is the *fundamental* attribution error.' (p. 376).

5   Wright and Wells (1988) have argued that the attitude attribution paradigm overestimates the dispositional bias by leading attributors to believe that their task is to infer attitude information from the speech *in spite of* the author's lack of choice.

6   As Miller and Ross (1975) noted, the self-serving bias has been described and illustrated in a variety of ways. Consistent with the emphasis on causal attributions, the present treatment excludes self-serving biases in the attribution of responsibility (e.g., 'defensive attribution'; Burger, 1981; Thornton, 1984; Walster, 1966).

7   Although Tetlock and Levi (1982) included the 'belief in a just world' as a fourth major function, it seems economical to include this under the rubric of 'control'.

CHAPTER 4   INTRA-PERSONAL ATTRIBUTION: CAUSAL LOGIC, COGNITIVE PROCESSES AND KNOWLEDGE STRUCTURES

1   I have termed this cognitive approach to attribution an 'intra-personal' one, in line with Doise's (1986) levels of analyses. It should be dis-

tinguished, however, from a single-subject, intra-subject or idiographic approach to causal attribution, which eschews aggregated data in favour of a detailed study of the judgemental strategies used by perceivers in causal analysis (e.g., Arkkelin et al., 1979; Tukey and Borgida, 1983).

2 According to *Current Contents* (No. 18, 2 May 1983) McArthur's study had been cited in over 180 publications.

3 Only the results for the complete information condition are reported; Orvis et al. (1975) also presented subjects with 'incomplete' information configurations, to see how they would 'fill in' missing information.

4 Hilton and Slugoski (1986) refer to it as a 'Natural Logic' model, but I prefer the term Logical Model (see Hewstone and Jaspars, 1987).

5 In addition to the studies reported below, Burleson (1986) has analysed a single motive-seeking conversation that provides some evidence that people use consensus, distinctiveness and consistency information in ordinary conversations; the reliability of this finding is, however, unclear.

6 Most of Taylor and Fiske's work involved salience manipulations on an interpersonal interaction. I include this work at Level I, rather than II, because its primary focus was attributional information processing, not attribution in social interaction.

7 It should be emphasized that the automatic vs controlled distinction refers to cognitive processes, not to awareness of such processes. Nisbett and Wilson (1977; Wilson and Nisbett, 1978) have argued that people do not have direct access to their cognitive processes, a view that has been challenged (Ericsson and Simon, 1980; Smith and Miller, 1978; P. A. White, 1988b) and that is not relevant to the present issue.

CHAPTER 5   INTERPERSONAL ATTRIBUTION: FROM SOCIAL INTERACTION
TO CLOSE RELATIONSHIPS

1 Greenwald suggests the new designation 'beneffectance' as a compound of beneficence (doing good) and effectance (competence): 'Beneffectance is thus the tendency to take credit for success while denying responsibility for failure' (1980, p. 605).

2 The relevant dependent measures in Ross and Sicoly's (1979) five studies are as follows: Experiment 1–attribution of responsibility; Experiment 2–evaluations of whether a statement improved or lowered a group's score; Experiment 3–open-ended causal attribution; Experiment 4–judgements of who controlled the discussion; Experiment 5–estimates of percentage contribution to a piece of work.

3 M. Ross (1981) also acknowledged that the final product of joint work between A and B may represent unique contributions of each person *and* an 'emergent contribution' (p. 310) that would not have occurred in the absence of either A or B. If this were the case, then Ross and Sicoly's (1979) method for calculating the contribution bias would be invalid.

Ross's later data, however, suggest that group members do not fully appreciate the interactive nature of their joint endeavour.

4   It should be noted that, although Sillars (1981) uses the terms *blame* and *responsibility* interchangeably, a reading of his original studies reveals that the measures referred explicitly to responsibility, not blame (see Sillars, 1980a, b).

5   Fletcher (1983) actually uses the expression 'causal responsibility' (p. 152), which I take to mean responsibility for the causes of the marriage break-down.

6   A promising, but still nascent, development is the application of a knowledge-structure approach to explanation (see chapter 4) in the context of close relationships (Read and Miller, in press).

7   Interestingly, the Bible intones the positive form of this rule ('Therefore all things whatsoever ye would that men should do to you, do ye even so to them'; Matthew, 7:12); Confucius, perhaps with more insight, invoked the negative form ('What you do not want done to yourself, do not do unto others'; *The Confucian Analects*, Book 15:23).

CHAPTER 6   INTERGROUP ATTRIBUTION: SOCIAL CATEGORIZATION AND ITS CONSEQUENCES

1   It should be noted, however, that Thibaut and Riecken's (1955) first study forced a choice of internal attribution to either the higher status or the lower status person and only just over half the subjects in their second study made the predicted attributions.

2   Pettigrew (1979) classified 'High motivation and effort' as controllable by the perceiver, because motivated outgroup members are seen as responding to aspects of the situation that are under some control of others.

3   Studies that used responsibility or punishment, rather than causal, judgements are excluded (e.g., Wang and McKillip, 1978).

4   A more precise comparison of ingroup favouritism and outgroup derogation would be gained by including a control condition that contained neither group label nor information relating to ingroup or out-group membership (see Rosenbaum, 1986). This condition was included by Bornewasser (1985), but his dependent measure was responsibility attribution.

5   There is some doubt as to whether all Duncan's (1976) videotapes portrayed equivalent behaviour and whether black and white subjects would judge the behaviour differently. Studies in which subjects of only one group participate are always problematic in that there are multiple explanations for the results. Sagar and Schofield (1980) did use black and white subjects in an attempt to address these issues, but they did not include causal attributions among their dependent measures.

6   Because Hewstone and Jaspars's (1982b) study deals with the explanation

of *societal* phenomena, one could argue for its inclusion in chapter 7. As its main focus was on comparing attributions across groups, however, I have included it here. Strictly speaking, it is a piece of research that integrates Levels III and IV.

7   Although Taylor and McKirnan (1984) refer to attributions of both causality and responsibility, sometimes interchangeably, I focus here on causal attributions.

8   I am grateful to Bernard Weiner for making this correction to the model, during a colloquium I gave at the University of California, Los Angeles, in May 1988.

CHAPTER 7   SOCIETAL ATTRIBUTION: COLLECTIVE BELIEFS AND THE
EXPLANATION OF SOCIETAL EVENTS

1   Moore (1987) gave 1144 as the first appearance of what became the foundation of the myth of Jewish conspiracy – the accusation of ritual murder of a Christian boy by Jews.

2   Quoted by Cohn (1966, pp. 186–7) from H. R. Trevor-Roper (ed.), *Hitler's table talk* (London, 1953, p. 332).

3   Quoted by Cohn (1966, p. 201) from L. W. Bondy, *Racketeers of hatred. Julius Streicher and the Jew-baiters' international* (London, 1946, pp. 36–7).

4   This is, necessarily, a sampling of research topics. Other societal issues for which attributions have been studied include the social positions of groups (A. Campbell, 1971; Erskine, 1968), rape (e.g., Howard, 1984a, b), crime and police harassment (e.g., Tyler and Rasinski, 1983), immigration (Furnham, 1986) and delinquency (Furnham and Henderson, 1983; Hollin and Howells, 1987).

5   Furnham (1982a) reported no *post hoc* tests to compare Conservative, Labour and Liberal voters, but by inspection his interpretations are correct and can be followed with caution.

6   Furnham (1982b) also analysed effects of political affiliation, but as no means are reported, I will not discuss these data here.

7   See, for example, *The Times*, 3 April 1980 and *The Sunday Times*, 12 April 1981. A survey reported in *The Times*, 14 May 1981 revealed that different views were held by black and white respondents as to the main cause of the trouble in Brixton.

References

Abele, A. (1985). Thinking about thinking: causal, evaluative and finalistic cognitions about social situations. *European Journal of Social Psychology*, 15, 315–32.

Abelson, R. P. (1981). The psychological status of the script concept. *American Psychologist*, 36, 715–29.

Abelson, R. P. and Black, J. B. (1986). Introduction. In J. A. Galambos, R. P. Abelson and J. B. Black (eds), *Knowledge structures*. Hillsdale, N. J.: Erlbaum.

Abelson, R. P. and Lalljee, M. (1988). Knowledge structures and causal explanation. In D. Hilton (ed.), *Contemporary science and natural explanation: Commonsense conceptions of causality*. Brighton: Harvester Press.

Abrams, R. D. and Finesinger, J. E. (1953). Guilt reactions in patients with cancer. *Cancer*, 6, 474–82.

Abramson, L. Y., Seligman, M. E. P. and Teasdale, J. D. (1978). Learned helplessness in humans: Critique and reformulation. *Journal of Abnormal Psychology*, 87, 49–74.

Agar, A. H. (1981). Ethnography as an interdisciplinary campground. In J.H. Harvey (ed.), *Cognition, social behavior and the environment*. Hillsdale, N.J.: Erlbaum.

Ajzen, I., Dalton, C. A. and Blyth, D. P. (1979). Consistency and bias in the attribution of attitudes. *Journal of Personality and Social Psychology*, 37, 1871–6.

Ajzen, I. and Fishbein, M. (1975). A Bayesian analysis of attribution processes. *Psychological Bulletin*, 82, 261–77.

Ajzen, I. and Holmes, W. H. (1976). Uniqueness of behavioral effects in causal attribution. *Journal of Personality*, 44, 98–108.

Allington, R. (1980). Teacher interruption behaviors during primary grade oral reading. *Journal of Educational Psychology*, 72, 371–7.

Alloy, L. B. and Abramson, L. Y. (1979). Judgment of contingency in depressed and nondepressed students: Sadder but wiser? *Journal of Experimental Psychology: General*, 108, 441–85.

Alloy, L. B. and Abramson, L. Y. (1982). Learned helplessness, depression, and the illusion of control. *Journal of Personality and Social Psychology*, 42, 1114–26.

Alloy, L. B., Abramson, L. Y. and Viscusi, D. (1981). Induced mood and illusion of control. *Journal of Personality and Social Psychology*, 41, 1129–40.

Alloy, L. B. and Tabachnik, N. (1984). Assessment of covariation by humans and animals: The joint influence of prior expectations and current situational information. *Psychological Review*, 91, 112–49.

Allport, G. W. (1954/1979). *The nature of prejudice*. Reading, Mass.: Addison-Wesley.

Anderson, C. A. (1983). The causal structure of situations: The generation of plausible causal attributions as a function of type of event situation. *Journal of Experimental Social Psychology*, 19, 185 203.

Anderson, C. A. (1985). Actor and observer attributions for different types of situations: Causal-structure effects, individual differences, and the dimensionality of causes. *Social Cognition*, 3, 323–40.

Anderson, C. A., Lepper, M. R. and Ross, L. (1980). Perseverance of social theories: The role of explanation in the persistence of discredited information. *Journal of Personality and Social Psychology*, 39, 1037–49.

Anderson, J. (1938). The problem of causality. *Australasian Journal of Psychology and Philosophy*, 16, 127–42.

Andreassen, P. B. (1987). On the social psychology of the stock market: Aggregate attributional effects and the regressiveness of prediction. *Journal of Personality and Social Psychology*, 53, 490–6.

Antaki, C. (1984). Core concepts in attribution theory. In J. Nicholson and H. Beloff (eds), *Psychology Survey 5*. Leicester: The British Psychological Society.

Antaki, C. (1985). Attribution and evaluation in ordinary explanations of voting intention. *British Journal of Social Psychology*, 24, 141–52.

Antaki, C. (1986). Ordinary explanation in conversation: Causal structures and their defence. *European Journal of Social Psychology*, 15, 213–30.

Antaki, C. (ed.) (1988). *Analysing lay explanation: A casebook of methods*. London: Sage.

Antaki, C. and Brewin, C. (eds) (1982). *Attributions and psychological change: Applications of attributional theories to clinical and educational practice*. London: Academic Press.

Antaki, C. and Fielding, G. (1981). Research on ordinary explanations. In C. Antaki (ed.), *The psychology of ordinary explanations of social behaviour*. London: Academic Press.

Antaki, C. and Naji, S. (1987). Events explained in conversational 'because' statements. *British Journal of Social Psychology*, 26, 119–26.

Argyle, M. and Henderson, M. (1985). *The anatomy of relationships*. London: Penguin.

Arias, I. and Beach, S. R. H. (1987). The assessment of social cognition in the context of marriage. In K. D. O'Leary (ed.), *Assessment of marital discord*. Hillsdale, N.J.: Erlbaum.

Arkkelin, D., Oakley, T. and Mynatt, C. (1979). Effects of controllable versus uncontrollable factors on responsibility attributions: A single-subject approach. *Journal of Personality and Social Psychology*, 37, 110–15.

Arkin, R. M., Appelman, A. J. and Burger, J. M. (1980a). Social anxiety, self-presentation, and the self-serving bias in causal attributions. *Journal of Personality and Social Psychology*, 38, 23–35.

Arkin, R. M. and Baumgardner, A. H. (1985). Self-handicapping. In J. H. Harvey and G. Weary (eds), *Attribution: Basic issues and applications*. Orlando, Fla.: Academic Press.

Arkin, R. M., Cooper, H. and Kolditz, T. (1980b). A statistical review of the literature concerning the self-serving attribution bias in interpersonal influence situations. *Journal of Personality*, 48, 435–48.

Arkin, R. M. and Duval, S. (1975). Focus of attention and causal attribution of actors and observers. *Journal of Experimental Social Psychology*, 11, 427–38.

Arkin, R. M., Gabrenya, W. K., Jr. and McGarvey, B. (1978). The role of social perspective in perceiving the causes of success and failure. *Journal of Personality and Social Psychology*, 46, 762–77.

Arntz, A., Gerlsma, C. and Albersnagel, F. A. (1985). Attributional Style Questionnaire: Psychometric evaluation of the ASQ in Dutch adolescents. *Advances in Behavioral Research and Therapy*, 7, 55–89.

Au, T. K.-F. (1986). A verb is worth a thousand words: The causes and consequences of interpersonal events implicit in language. *Journal of Memory and Language*, 25, 104–22.

Austin, J. L. (1962). *How to do things with words*. Oxford: Clarendon Press.

Averill, J. A. (1982). *Anger and aggression*. New York: Springer Verlag.

Averill, J. A. (1983). Studies on anger and aggression. *American Psychologist*, 38, 1145–60.

Axelrod, R. (ed.) (1976). *Structure of decision: The cognitive maps of political elites*. Princeton: Princeton University Press.

Ayer, A. J. (1980). *Hume*. Oxford: Oxford University Press.

Bains, G. (1983). Explanations and the need for control. In M. Hewstone (ed.), *Attribution theory: Social and functional extensions*. Oxford: Basil Blackwell.

Bargh, J. A. (1984). Automatic and conscious processing of social information. In R. S. Wyer and T. K. Srull (eds), *Handbook of social cognition* (Vol. 3). Hillsdale, N. J.: Erlbaum.

Barjonet, P. E. (1980). L'influence sociale et des représentations des causes de l'accident de la route. *Le Travail Humain*, 43, 243–53.

Bartlett, F. (1932). *A study in experimental and social psychology*. Cambridge: Cambridge University Press.

Bassili, J. N. and Smith, M. C. (1986). On the spontaneity of trait attribution: Converging evidence for the role of cognitive strategy. *Journal of Personality and Social Psychology*, 50, 239–45.

Baucom, D. H. (1986). Attributions in distressed relations: How can we explain them? In D. Perlman and S. Duck (eds), *Intimate relationships: Development, dynamics, and deterioration*. London: Sage.

Baucom, D. H. and Lester, G. W. (1986). The usefulness of cognitive restructuring as an adjunct to behavioral marital therapy. *Behavior Therapy*, 17, 385–403.

Baumeister, R. F. (1982). A self-presentational view of social phenomena. *Psychological Bulletin*, 91, 3–26.

Beauvois, J. L. and Dubois, N. (1988). The norm of internality in the explanation of psychological events. *European Journal of Social Psychology*, 18, 299–316.

Bell, L. G., Wicklund, R. A., Manko, G. and Larkin, C. (1976). When unexpected behavior is attributed to the environment. *Journal of Research in Personality*, 10, 316–27.

Bellezza, F. S. and Bower, G. H. (1981). Person stereotypes and memory for people. *Journal of Personality and Social Psychology*, 41, 856–65.

Bem, D. J. (1967). Self-perception: An alternative interpretation of cognitive dissonance phenomena. *Psychological Review*, 74, 183–200.

Bem, D. J. (1972). Self-perception theory. In L. Berkowitz (ed.), *Advances in experimental social psychology* (Vol. 6). New York: Academic Press.

Benzécri, J.-P. (1982). *Histoire et pré-histoire de l'analyse des données*. Paris: Dunod.

Berger, C. R. and Calabrese, R. (1975). Some explorations in initial interactions and beyond. *Human Communication Research*, 1, 99–112.

Berglas, S. and Jones, E. E. (1978). Drug choice as a self-handicapping strategy in response to noncontingent success. *Journal of Personality and Social Psychology*, 36, 405–17.

Berley, R. A., and Jacobson, N. S. (1984). Causal attributions in intimate relationships: Toward a model of cognitive-behavioral marital therapy. In P. Kendall (ed.), *Advances in cognitive-behavioral research and therapy* (Vol. 3). New York: Academic Press.

Berscheid, E., Graziano, W., Monson, T. and Dermer, M. (1976). Outcome dependency: Attention, attribution and attraction. *Journal of Personality and Social Psychology*, 34, 978–89.

Billig, M. (1976). *Social psychology and intergroup relations*. London: Academic Press.

Billig, M. (1978). *Fascists: A social psychological view of the National Front*. London: Harcourt Brace Jovanovich.

Billig, M. (1982). *Ideology and social psychology*. Oxford: Basil Blackwell.

Blalock, H. M. (1967). *Toward a theory of minority group relations*. New York: Wiley.

Block, J. and Funder, D. C. (1986). Social roles and social perception: Individual differences in attribution and 'error'. *Journal of Personality and Social Psychology*, 51, 1200–7.

Bohner, G., Bless, H., Schwarz, N. and Strack, F. (1988). What triggers causal attributions? The impact of subjective probability. *European Journal of Social Psychology*, 18, 335–46.

Bonacich, E. (1973). A theory of middleman minorities. *American Sociological Review*, 38, 583–94.

Bond, M. H. (1972). Effect of an impression set on subsequent behavior. *Journal of Personality and Social Psychology*, 24, 301–5.

Bond, M. H. (1983). A proposal for cross-cultural studies of attribution. In M. Hewstone (ed.), *Attribution theory: Social and functional extensions*. Oxford: Basil Blackwell.

Bond, M. H., Hewstone, M., Wan, K.-C. and Chiu, C.-K. (1985). Group-serving attributions across intergroup contexts: Cultural differences in the explanation of sex-typed behaviours. *European Journal of Social Psychology*, 15, 435–52.

Borgida, E. and Brekke, N. (1981). The base rate fallacy in attribution and prediction. In J. H. Harvey, W. J. Ickes and R. F. Kidd (eds), *New directions in attribution research* (Vol. 3). Hillsdale, N. J.: Erlbaum.

Bornewasser, M. (1985). Verantwortlichkeitsattributionen im Intergruppen-Kontext am Beispiel deutscher Arbeiter und jugoslawischer Gastarbeiter. *Gruppendynamik*, 16, 19–33.

Boski, P. (1983). A study of person perception in Nigeria: Ethnicity and self versus other attributions for achievement related outcomes. *Journal of Cross-Cultural Psychology*, 14, 85–108.

Bottenberg, E. H. (1975). Phenomenological and operational characteristics of factor-analytically derived dimensions of emotion. *Psychological Reports*, 37, 1253–4.

Bower, G. H., Black, J. B. and Turner, T. J. (1979). Scripts in memory for text. *Cognitive Psychology*, 11, 177–220.

Bower, G. H. and Cohen, P. R. (1982). Emotional influences in memory and thinking: Data and theory. In M. S. Clark and S. T. Fiske (eds), *Affect and cognition: The 17th Annual Carnegie Symposium on Cognition*. Hillsdale, N. J.: Erlbaum.

Bradbury, T. N. and Fincham, F. D. (in press, a). Assessing spontaneous attributions in marital interactions: Methodological and conceptual considerations. *Journal of Social and Clinical Psychology*.

Bradbury, T. N. and Fincham, F. D. (in press, b). Attributions in marriage: Review and critique. *Psychological Bulletin*.

Brehm, S. S. (1985). *Intimate relationships*. New York: Random House.

Brehm, S. S. and Aderman, D. (1977). On the relationship between empathy and the actor versus observer hypothesis. *Journal of Research in Personality*, 11, 340–6.

Brewer, M. B. and Collins, B. E. (1981). Perspectives on knowing: Six themes from Donald T. Campbell. In M. B. Brewer and B. E. Collins (eds), *Scientific inquiry and the social sciences: A volume in honor of Donald T. Campbell*. San Francisco, Cal.: Jossey-Bass.

Brewer, M. B. and Kramer, R. M. (1985). The psychology of intergroup attitudes and behavior. *Annual Review of Psychology*, 36, 219–43.

Brewer, W. F. and Nakamura, G. V. (1984). The nature and functions of schemas. In R. S. Wyer and T. K. Srull (eds), *Handbook of social cognition* (Vol. 1). Hillsdale, N. J.: Erlbaum.

Brewin, C. R. (1985). Depression and causal attributions: What is their relation? *Psychological Bulletin*, 98, 297–309.

Brewin, C. R. and Furnham, A. (1986). Attributional versus preattributional variables in self-esteem and depression: A comparison and test of learned helplessness theory. *Journal of Personality and Social Psychology*, 50, 1013–20.

Brickman, P., Ryan, K. and Wortman, C. B. (1975). Causal chains: Attribution of responsibility as a function of immediate and prior causes. *Journal of Personality and Social Psychology*, 32, 1060–7.

Brophy, J. and Good, T. (1970). Teachers' communication of differential expectations for children's classroom performance: Some behavioral data. *Journal of Educational Psychology*, 61, 365–74.

Brown, J. (1984). Effects of induced mood on causal attributions for success and failure. *Motivation and Emotion*, 8, 343–54.

Brown, J. D. and Siegel, J. M. (1988). Attributions for negative life events and depression: The role of perceived control. *Journal of Personality and Social Psychology*, 54, 316–22.

Brown, R. and Fish, D. (1983). The psychological causality implicit in language. *Cognition*, 14, 237–73.

Brown, R. J., Condor, S., Matthews, A., Wade, G. and Williams, J. (1986). Explaining intergroup differentiation in an industrial organization. *Journal of Occupational Psychology*, 59, 273–86.

Brown, R. J. and Turner, J. C. (1981). Interpersonal and intergroup behaviour. In J. C. Turner and H. Giles (eds), *Intergroup behaviour*. Oxford: Basil Blackwell.

Bruner, J. S. (1957a). Going beyond the information given. In H. Gruber, G. Terrell and M. Wertheimer (eds), *Contemporary approaches to cognition*. Cambridge, Mass.: Harvard University Press.

Bruner, J. S. (1957b). On perceptual readiness. *Psychological Review*, 64, 123–51.

Brunswik, E. (1952). The conceptual framework of psychology. In *International encyclopaedia of unified science* (Vol. 1). Chicago: University of Chicago Press.

Bulman, R. J. and Wortman, C. B. (1977). Attributions of blame and coping in the 'real world': Severe accident victims react to their lot. *Journal of Personality and Social Psychology*, 35, 351–63.

Burger, J. M. (1981). Motivational biases in the attribution of responsibility for an accident: A meta-analysis of the defensive-attribution hypothesis. *Psychological Bulletin*, 90, 496–512.

Burger, J. M. and Rodman, J. L. (1983). Attributions of responsibility for group tasks: The egocentric bias and the actor-observer difference. *Journal of Personality and Social Psychology*, 45, 1232–42.

Burke, K. (1962). *A grammar of motives*. Cleveland: Meridian Books. (First published 1945.)

Burleson, B. R. (1986). Attribution schemes and causal inference in natural conversations. In D. G. Ellis and W. A. Donohue (eds), *Contemporary issues in language and discourse processes*. Hillsdale, N.J.: Erlbaum.

Buss, A. R. (1978). Causes and reasons in attribution theory: A conceptual critique. *Journal of Personality and Social Psychology*, 36, 1311–21.

Buss, A. R. (1979). On the relationship between causes and reasons. *Journal of Personality and Social Psychology*, 37, 1458–61.

Calder, B. J. (1977). Endogenous-exogenous versus internal-external attributions: Implications for the development of attribution theory. *Personality and Social Psychology Bulletin*, 3, 400–6.

Campbell, A. (1971). *White attitudes toward black people*. Ann Arbor, Mich.: Institute for Social Research.

Campbell, A. and Schuman, H. (1969). *Racial attitudes in fifteen American cities*. Ann Arbor, Mich.: Institute for Social Research.

Campbell, D. T. (1958). Common fate, similarity, and other indices of the status of aggregates of persons as social entities. *Behavioral Science*, 3, 14–25.

Campbell, D. T. (1967). Stereotypes and the perception of group differences. *American Psychologist*, 22, 817–29.

Campbell, D. T. (1969). Reforms as experiments. *American Psychologist*, 24, 409–29.

Camper, P. M., Jacobson, N. S., Holtzworth-Munroe, A. and Schmaling, K. B. (1988). Causal attributions for interactional behaviors in married couples. *Cognitive Therapy and Research*, 12, 195–209.

Caplan, N. and Nelson, S. D. (1973). On being useful: The nature and consequences of psychological research on social problems. *American Psychologist*, 28, 199–211.

Carlson, R. (1984). What's social about social psychology? Where's the person in personality research? *Journal of Personality and Social Psychology*, 47, 1304–9.

Carrithers, M., Collins, S. and Lukes, S. (eds) (1986). The *category of the person*. Cambridge: Cambridge University Press.

Carroll, J. S. and Payne, J. W. (1976). The psychology of the parole decision process: A joint application of attribution theory and information processing psychology. In J. S. Carroll and J. W. Payne (eds), *Cognition and social behaviour*. Hillsdale, N. J.: Erlbaum.

Carroll, J. S. and Payne, J. W. (1977). Crime seriousness, recidivism risk and causal attributions in judgments of prison term by students and experts. *Journal of Applied Psychology*, 62, 595–602.

Carroll, J. S., Perkowitz, W. T., Lurigio, A. J. and Weaver, F. M. (1987). Sentencing goals, causal attributions, ideology, and personality. *Journal of Personality and Social Psychology*, 52, 107–18.

Carroll, J. S. and Wiener, R. L. (1982). Cognitive social psychology in court and beyond. In A. H. Hastorf and A. M. Isen (eds), *Cognitive social psychology*. New York: Elsevier/North-Holland.

Chaiken, S. (1980). Heuristic versus systematic information processing and the use of source versus message cues in persuasion. *Journal of Personality and Social Psychology*, 39, 752–66.

Chaikin, A. L. and Cooper, J. (1973). Evaluation as a function of correspondence and hedonic relevance. *Journal of Experimental Social Psychology*, 9, 257–64.

Chapman, L. J. and Chapman, J. P. (1969). Illusory correlation as an obstacle to the use of valid diagnostic signs. *Journal of Abnormal Psychology*, 74, 271–80.

Chodoff, P., Friedman, S. and Hamburg, D. (1964). Stress defences and coping behavior: Observations in parents of children with malignant disease. *American Journal of Psychiatry*, 120, 743–9.

Christensen, A., Sullaway, M. and King, C. E. (1983). Systematic error in behavioral reports of dyadic interaction: Egocentric bias and content effects. *Behavioral Assessment*, 5, 129–40.

Clarey, E. G. and Tesser, A. (1983). Reactions to unexpected events: The naive scientist and interpretive activity. *Personality and Social Psychology Bulletin*, 9, 609–20.

Clark, L. F. and Woll, S. B. (1981). Stereotype bias: A reconstructive analysis of their role in reconstructive memory. *Journal of Personality and Social Psychology*, 41, 1064–72.

Clark, M. S. and Reis, H. T. (1988). Interpersonal processes in close relationships. *Annual Review of Psychology*, 39, 609–72.

Cohen, L., van den Bout, J., Kramer, W. and van Vliert, T. A. (1986). Dutch Attributional Style Questionnaire: Psychometric properties and findings of some Dutch-American differences. *Cognitive Therapy and Research*, 10, 665–9.

Cohn, N. (1966). *Warrant for genocide: The myth of the Jewish world conspiracy and the Protocol of the Elders of Zion*. New York and Evanston, Ill.: Harper and Row.

Cohn, N. (1975). *Europe's inner demons. An enquiry inspired by the Great Witch Hunt*. London: Chatto.

Collingwood, R. G. (1961). On the so-called idea of causation (first published 1938). In H. Morris (ed.), *Freedom and responsibility: Readings in philosophy and law*. Stanford: Stanford University Press.

Cook, S. W. (1978). Interpersonal and attitudinal outcomes in cooperating interracial groups. *Journal of Research and Development in Education*, 12, 97–113.

Cooley, C. H. (1902). *Human nature and social order*. New York: Scribner's.

Cooper, H. M. and Burger, J. M. (1980). How teachers explain students' academic performances: A categorization of free response academic attributions. *American Educational Research Journal*, 17, 95–109.

Cooper, J. and Fazio, R. H. (1979). The formation and persistence of attitudes that support intergroup conflict. In W. G. Austin and S. Worchel (eds), *The social psychology of intergroup relations*. Monterey, Cal.: Brooks/Cole.

Cordray, D. S. and Shaw, J. I. (1978). An empirical test of the covariation analysis in causal attribution. *Journal of Experimental Social Psychology*, 14, 280–90.

Coulthard, M. (1975). Discourse analysis in English a short review of the literature. *Language Teaching Abstracts*, 8, 73–89.

Cowie, B. (1976). The cardiac patient's perception of his heart attack. *Social Science and Medicine*, 10, 87–96.

Coyne, J. C. and Gotlib, I. H. (1983). The role of cognition in depression: A critical appraisal. *Psychological Bulletin*, 94, 472–505.

Crittenden, K. S. (1983). Sociological aspects of attribution. *Annual Review of Sociology*, 9, 425–46.

Crocker, J. (1981). Judgment of covariation by social perceivers. *Psychological Bulletin*, 90, 272–92.

Crocker, J., Fiske, S. T. and Taylor, S. E. (1984). Schematic bases of belief change. In J. R. Eiser (ed.), *Attitudinal judgment*. New York: Springer.

Crocker, J., Hannah, D. B. and Weber, R. (1983). Person memory and causal attributions. *Journal of Personality and Social Psychology*, 44, 55–66.

Cunningham, J. D. and Kelley, H. H. (1975). Causal attributions for interpersonal events of varying magnitude. *Journal of Personality*, 43, 74–93.

Cutrona, C. E., Russell, D. and Jones, R. D. (1985). Cross-situational consistency in causal attributions: Does attributional style exist? *Journal of Personality and Social Psychology*, 47, 1043–58.

Dalal, A. K., Sharma, R. and Bisht, S. (1983). Causal attributions of ex-criminal tribal and urban children in India. *Journal of Social Psychology*, 119, 163–71.

D'Andrade, R. G. (1981). The cultural part of cognition. *Cognitive Science*, 5, 179–95.

D'Andrade, R. G. (1984). Cultural meaning systems. In R. A. Shweder and R. A. LeVine (eds), *Culture theory: Essays on mind, self and emotion*. Cambridge: Cambridge University Press.

Darley, J. M. and Fazio, R. H. (1980). Expectancy confirmation processes in the social interaction sequence. *American Psychologist*, 35, 867–81.

Darley, J. M. and Goethals, G. R. (1980). People's analyses of the causes of ability-linked performances. In L. Berkowitz (ed.), *Advances in experimental social psychology* (Vol. 13). New York: Academic Press.

Darley, J. M. and Gross, P. H. (1983). A hypothesis-confirming bias in labeling effects. *Journal of Personality and Social Psychology*, 44, 20–33.

Darom, E. and Bar-Tal, D. (1981). Causal perception of pupils' success or failure by teachers and pupils: A comparison. *Journal of Educational Research*, 74, 233–9.

Davidson, D. (1963). Actions, reasons and causes. *Journal of Philosophy*, 60, 685–700.

Davidson, D. (1967). Causal relations. *Journal of Philosophy*, 64, 691–703.

Davies, M. F. (1985). Social roles and social perception biases: The questioner superiority effect revisited. *British Journal of Social Psychology*, 24, 239–48.

Davis, D. B. (1969). *The slave power conspiracy and the paranoid style*. Baton Rouge, La.: Louisiana State University Press.

Davis, D. B. (ed.) (1971). *Fear of conspiracy*. Ithaca, N.Y.: Cornell University Press.

Davitz, J. R. (1969). *The language of emotion*. New York: Academic Press.

Deaux, K. (1976). Sex: A perspective on the attribution process. In J. H. Harvey, W. J. Ickes and R. F. Kidd (eds), New *directions in attribution research* (Vol. 1). Hillsdale, N.J.: Erlbaum.

Deaux, K. and Emswiller, T. (1974). Explanations of successful performance on sex-linked tasks: What is skill for the male is luck for the female. *Journal of Personality and Social Psychology*, 29, 80–5.

Deaux, K. and Major, B. (1987). Putting gender into context: An interactive model of gender-related behavior. *Psychological Review*, 94, 369–89.

De Charms, R., Carpenter, V. and Kuperman, A. (1965). The 'origin-pawn' variable in person perception. *Sociometry*, 28, 241–58.

de Jong, P. F., Koomen, W. and Mellenbergh, G. J. (1988). Structure of causes for success and failure: A multidimensional analysis of preference judgments. *Journal of Personality and Social Psychology*, 55, 718–25.

Derry, P. A. and Kuiper, N. A. (1981). Schematic processing and self-reference in clinical depression. *Journal of Abnormal Psychology*, 90, 286–97.

Deschamps, J.-C. (1973–4). L'attribution, la catégorisation sociale et les représentations intergroupes. *Bulletin de Psychologie*, 27, 710–21.

Deschamps, J.-C. (1977). *L'attribution et la catégorisation sociale*. Berne: Peter Lang.

Deschamps, J.-C. (1983). Social attribution. In J. Jaspars, F. D. Fincham and M. Hewstone (eds), *Attribution theory and research: Conceptual, developmental and social dimensions*. London: Academic Press.

Deschamps, J.-C. and Clémence, A. (1987). *L'explication quotidienne*. Cousset: Del Val.

DeSoto, C. B. (1960). Learning a social structure. *Journal of Abnormal and Social Psychology*, 60, 417–21.

DeSoto, C. B., Henley, N. M. and London, M. (1968). Balance and the grouping schema. *Journal of Personality and Social Psychology*, 8, 1–7.

Diener, C. I. and Dweck, C. S. (1978). An analysis of learned helplessness: Continuous changes in performance, strategy and achievement cognitions following failure. *Journal of Personality and Social Psychology*, 36, 451–62.

Dijker, A. J. M. (1987). Emotional reactions to ethnic minorities. *European Journal of Social Psychology*, 17, 305–25.

Dion, K. L. and Earn, B. M. (1975). The phenomenology of being a target of prejudice. *Journal of Personality and Social Psychology*, 32, 944–50.

Dion, K. L., Earn, B. M. and Yee, P. H. N. (1978). The experience of being a victim of prejudice: An experimental approach. *International Journal of Psychology*, 13, 197–214.

Doise, W. (1980). Levels of explanation in the European Journal of Social Psychology. *European Journal of Social Psychology*, 10, 213–31.

Doise, W. (1984). Social representations, inter-group experiments and levels of analysis. In R. M. Farr and S. Moscovici (eds), *Social representations*. Cambridge/Paris: Cambridge University Press, Maison des Sciences de l'Homme.

Doise, W. (1986). *Levels of explanation in social psychology*. Cambridge/Paris: Cambridge University Press/Maison des Sciences de L'Homme.

Dretske, F. (1988). *Explaining behavior: Reasons in a world of causes*. Cambridge, Mass.: MIT Press.

Dreyfus, H. (1979). *What computers can't do*. New York: Harper and Row.

Druian, P. and Omessi, E. (1982). *A knowledge structure theory of attribution*. Unpublished manuscript, Grinnell College, Iowa.

Duck, S. W. (ed.) (1984). *Personal relationships* (Vol. 5). London: Academic Press.

Duncan, B. L. (1976). Differential social perception and attribution of intergroup violence: Testing the lower limits of stereotyping of blacks. *Journal of Personality and Social Psychology*, 34, 590–8.

Duncker, K. (1945). On problem-solving. *Psychological Monographs*, 58, (5, Whole No. 270).

Durkheim, E. (1898). Représentations individuelles et représentations collectives. *Revue de Métaphysique et de Morale*, 6, 273–302. (Translated as 'Individual and collective representations', in E. Durkheim, *Sociology and philosophy*. New York: The Free Press, 1974.)

Duval, S. and Duval, V. H. (1983). *Consistency and cognition: A theory of causal attribution*. Hillsdale, N. J.: Erlbaum.

Duval, S. and Wicklund, R. A. (1972). *A theory of objective self-awareness*. New York: Academic Press.

Duval, S. and Wicklund, R. A. (1973). Effects of objective self-awareness on attributions of causality. *Journal of Experimental Social Psychology*, 9, 17–31.

Dweck, C. S. (1975). The role of expectations and attributions in the alleviation of learned helplessness. *Journal of Personality and Social Psychology*, 31, 674–85.

Einhorn, H. J. and Hogarth, R. M. (1986). Judging probable cause. *Psychological Bulletin*, 99, 3–19.

Eiser, J. R. (1983a). Attribution theory and social cognition. In J. M. F. Jaspars, F. D. Fincham and M. Hewstone (eds), *Attribution theory and research: Conceptual, developmental and social dimensions*. London: Academic Press.

Eiser, J. R. (1983b). From attributions to behaviour. In M. Hewstone (ed.), *Attribution theory: Social and functional extensions*. Oxford: Basil Blackwell.

Elig, T. W. and Frieze, I. H. (1975). A multidimensional scheme for coding and interpreting perceived causality for success and failure events. *JSAS Catalog of Selected Documents in Psychology*, 5, 313 (MS. No. 1069).

Elig, T. W. and Frieze, I. H. (1979). Measuring causal attributions for success and failure. *Journal of Personality and Social Psychology*, 37, 621–34.

Enzle, M. E., Harvey, M. D. and Wright, E. F. (1980). Personalism and distinctiveness. *Journal of Personality and Social Psychology*, 39, 542–52.

Enzle, M. E. and Schopflocher, D. (1978). Instigation of attribution processes by attributional questions. *Personality and Social Psychology Bulletin*, 4, 595–9.

Epstein, N. (1982). Cognitive therapy with couples. *The American Journal of Family Therapy*, 10, 5–16.

Ericsson, K. A. and Simon, H. A. (1980). Verbal reports as data. *Psychological Review*, 87, 215–51.

Erskine, H. (1968). The polls: Recent opinion on racial problems. *Public Opinion Quarterly*, 32, 696–703.

Evans-Pritchard, E. E. (1937). *Witchcraft, oracles and magic among the Azande*. Oxford: Oxford University Press.

Farina, A., Fisher, J. D., Getter, H. and Fisher, E. H. (1978). Some consequences of changing people's views regarding the nature of mental illness. *Journal of Abnormal Psychology*, 87, 272–9.

Farr, R. M. (1987). Social representations: A French tradition of research. *Journal for the Theory of Social Behaviour*, 17, 343–70.

Farr, R. M. and Anderson, A. (1983). Beyond actor/observer differences in perspective: Extensions and applications. In M. Hewstone (ed.), *Attribution theory: Social and functional extensions*. Oxford: Basil Blackwell.

Fauconnet, P. (1928). *La responsabilité*. Paris: Alcan.

Fayol, M. and Monteil, J.-M. (1988). The notion of 'script': From general to developmental and social psychology. *Cahiers de Psychologie Sociale*, 8, 335–62.

Feagin, J. (1972). Poverty: We still believe that God helps them who help themselves. *Psychology Today*, 6, 101–29.

Feather, N. T. (1974). Explanations of poverty in Australian and American samples: The person, society and fate? *Australian Journal of Psychology*, 26, 199–216.

Feather, N. T. (1985). Attitudes, values, and attributions: Explanations of unemployment. *Journal of Personality and Social Psychology*, 48, 876–89.

Feather, N. T. and Barber, J. G. (1983). Depressive reactions and unemployment. *Journal of Abnormal Psychology*, 92, 185–95.

Feather, N. T. and Davenport, P. R. (1981). Unemployment and depressive affect: A motivational and attributional analysis. *Journal of Personality and Social Psychology*, 41, 422–36.

Feather, N. T. and Simon, J. G. (1973). Fear of success and causal attribution for outcome. *Journal of Personality*, 41, 525–42.

Feather, N. T. and Simon, J. G. (1975). Reactions to male and female success and failure in sex-linked occupations: Impressions of personality, causal attributions, and perceived likelihood of different consequences. *Journal of Personality and Social Psychology*, 31, 20–31.

Feather, N. T. and Tiggermann, M. (1984). A balanced measure of attributional style. *Australian Journal of Psychology*, 36, 267–83.

Feldman-Summers, S. and Kiesler, S. B. (1974). Those who are number two try harder: The effect of sex on attributions of causality. *Journal of Personality and Social Psychology*, 30, 846–55.

Felson, R. B. and Ribner, S. A. (1981). An attributional approach to accounts and sanctions for criminal violence. *Social Psychology Quarterly*, 44, 137–42.

Ferguson, T. J. and Wells, G. L. (1980). Priming of mediators in causal attribution. *Journal of Personality and Social Psychology*, 38, 461–70.

Festinger, L. (1953). Laboratory experiments. In L. Festinger and D. Katz (eds), *Research methods in the behavioral sciences*. New York: Holt.

Fiedler, K. (1978). Kausale und generalisierende Schlüsse aufgrund einfacher Sätze. *Zeitschrift für Sozialpsychologie*, 9, 37–49.

Fiedler, K. (1982). Causal schemata: Review and criticism of research on a popular construct. *Journal of Personality and Social Psychology*, 42, 1001–13.

Fiedler, K. and Semin, G. R. (1988). On the causal information conveyed by different interpersonal verbs: The role of implicit sentence context. *Social Cognition*, 6, 21–39.

Fincham, F. D. (1983). Developmental dimensions of attribution theory. In J. M. F. Jaspars, F. D. Fincham and M. Hewstone (eds), *Attribution theory and research: Conceptual, developmental and social dimensions*. London: Academic Press.

Fincham, F. D. (1985a). Attributions in close relationships. In J. H. Harvey and G. Weary (eds), *Attribution: Basic issues and applications*. Orlando, Fla.: Academic Press.

Fincham, F. D. (1985b). Attribution processes in distressed and nondistressed couples: 2. Responsibility for marital problems. *Journal of Abnormal Psychology*, 94, 183–90.

Fincham, F. D., Beach, S. R. and Baucom, D. H. (1987a). Attribution processes in distressed and nondistressed couples: 4. Self-partner attribution differences. *Journal of Personality and Social Psychology*, 52, 739–48.

Fincham, F. D., Beach, S. R. and Nelson, G. (1987b). Attribution processes in distressed and nondistressed couples: 3. Causal and responsibility attributions for spouse behavior. *Cognitive Therapy and Research*, 11, 71–86.

Fincham, F. D. and Bradbury, T. N. (1987). The impact of attributions in marriage: A longitudinal analysis. *Journal of Personality and Social Psychology*, 53, 510–17.

Fincham, F. D. and Bradbury, T. N. (in press). Perceived responsibility for marital events: Egocentric bias or partner-centric bias? *Journal of Marriage and the Family*.

Fincham, F. D., Bradbury, T. N. and Grych, J. H. (in press). Conflict in close relationships: The role of intrapersonal phenomena. In *Advances in Applied Social Psychology* (Vol. 5).

Fincham, F. D. and Jaspars, J. M. F. (1980). Attribution of responsibility:

From man-the-scientist to man-as-lawyer. In L. Berkowitz (ed.), *Advances in experimental social psychology* (Vol. 13). New York: Academic Press.

Fincham, F. D. and O'Leary, K. D. (1983). Causal inferences for spouse behavior in maritally distressed and nondistressed couples. *Journal of Social and Clinical Psychology*, 1, 42–57.

Fincham, F. D. and Shultz, T. R. (1981). Intervening causation and the mitigation of responsibility for harm. *British Journal of Social Psychology*, 20, 113–20.

Fischhoff, B. (1976). Attribution theory and judgment under uncertainty. In J. H. Harvey, W. J. Ickes and R. F. Kidd (eds), *New directions in attribution research* (Vol. 1). Hillsdale, N. J.: Erlbaum.

Fisher, J. D. and Farina, A. (1979). Consequences of beliefs about the nature of mental disorders. *Journal of Abnormal Psychology*, 88, 320–7.

Fiske, S. T. (1980). Attention and weight in person perception: The impact of extreme and negative behavior. *Journal of Personality and Social Psychology*, 38, 889–906.

Fiske, S. T. (1982). Schema-triggered affect: Applications to social perception. In M. S. Clark and S. T. Fiske (eds), *Affect and cognition: The 17th Annual Carnegie Symposium* on *Cognition*. Hillsdale, N. J.: Erlbaum.

Fiske, S. T., Kenny, D. A. and Taylor, S. E. (1982). Structural models for the mediation of salience effects on attribution. *Journal of Experimental Social Psychology*, 18, 105–27.

Fiske, S. T. and Taylor, S. E. (1984). *Social cognition*. New York: Random House.

Fletcher, G. J. O. (1983). The analysis of verbal explanations for marital separation: Implications for attribution theory. *Journal of Applied Social Psychology*, 13, 245–58.

Fletcher, G. J. O. (1984). Psychology and common sense. *American Psychologist*, 39, 203–13.

Fletcher, G. J. O., Danilovics, P., Fernandez, G., Peterson, D. and Reeder, G. D. (1986). Attributional complexity: An individual differences measure. *Journal of Personality and Social Psychology*, 51, 875–84.

Fletcher, G. J. O., Fincham, F. D., Cramer, L. and Heron, N. (1987). The role of attributions in the development of dating relationships. *Journal of Personality and Social Psychology*, 53, 481–9.

Fletcher, G. J. O., Fitness, J. T. and Blampied, N. M. (1988). The link between attributions and happiness in close relationships. Unpublished manuscript, University of Canterbury, New Zealand.

Fletcher, G. J. O., Grigg, F. and Bull, V. (in press). The organization and accuracy of personality impressions: Neophytes versus experts in trait attribution. *New Zealand Journal of Psychology*.

Fletcher, G. J. O. and Ward, C. (1988). Attribution theory and processes: A cross-cultural perspective. In M. H. Bond (ed.), *The cross-cultural challenge to social psychology*. Newbury Park, Cal.: Sage.

Floyd, F. J. and Markman, H. J. (1983). Observational biases in spouse observation: Toward a cognitive/behavioral model of marriage. *Journal of Consulting and Clinical Psychology*, 51, 450–7.

Forgas, J., Morris, S. and Furnham, A. (1982). Lay explanations of wealth: Attributions for economic success. *Journal of Applied Social Psychology*, 12, 381–97.

Försterling, F. (1985). Attributional retraining: A review. *Psychological Bulletin*, 98, 495–512.

Försterling, F. (1986). Attributional conceptions in clinical psychology. *American Psychologist*, 41, 275–85.

Försterling, F. (1988). *Attribution theory in clinical psychology*. Chichester: Wiley.

Forsyth, D. R. (1980). The functions of attributions. *Social Psychology Quarterly*, 43, 184–9.

Forsyth, D. R. and Schlenker, B. R. (1977). Attributing the causes of group performance: Effects of performance quality, task importance, and future testing. *Journal of Personality*, 45, 220–36.

Foucault, M. (1967). *Madness and civilization: A history of insanity in the age of reason*. London: Tavistock.

Frankel, A. and Snyder, M. L. (1978). Poor performance following unsolvable problems: Learned helplessness or egotism? *Journal of Social Psychology*, 36, 1415–23.

Frey, D. (1978). Reactions to success and failure in public and private conditions. *Journal of Experimental Social Psychology*, 14, 172–9.

Frey, D. and Rogner, O. (1987). The relevance of psychological factors in the convalescence of accident patients. In G. R. Semin and B. Krahé (eds), *Issues in contemporary German social psychology*. London: Sage.

Frieze, I. H. (1976). Causal attributions and information seeking to explain success and failure. *Journal of Research in Personality*, 10, 293–305.

Frieze, I. H. (1981). Children's attributions for success and failure. In S. S. Brehm, S. M. Kassin and F. S. Gibbons (eds), *Developmental social psychology: Theory and research*. New York: Oxford University Press.

Frieze, I. H., Bar-Tal, D. and Carroll, J. S. (eds) (1980). New *approaches to social problems: Applications of attribution theory*. San Francisco: Jossey-Bass.

Frisch, M. (1961). *Andorra*. London: Methuen.

Funder, D. C. (1982). On the accuracy of dispositional vs. situational attributions. *Social Cognition*, 1, 205–22.

Funder, D. C. (1987). Errors and mistakes: Evaluating the accuracy of social judgment. *Psychological Bulletin*, 101, 75–90.

Furnham, A. (1982a). Why are the poor always with us? Explanations for poverty in Britain. *British Journal of Social Psychology*, 21, 311–22.

Furnham, A. (1982b). Explanations for unemployment in Britain. *European Journal of Social Psychology*, 12, 335–52.

Furnham, A. (1983). Attributions for affluence. *Personality and Individual Differences*, 4, 31–40.

Furnham, A. (1986). Some explanations for immigration to, and emigration from, Britain. *New Community*, 13, 65–78.

Furnham, A. and Bond, M. H. (1986). Hong Kong Chinese explanations for wealth. *Journal of Economic Psychology*, 7, 447–60.

Furnham, A. and Henderson, M. (1983). Lay theories of delinquency. *European Journal of Social Psychology*, 13, 107–20.

Furnham, A., Jaspars, J. M. F. and Fincham, F. D. (1983). Professional and naive psychology: Two approaches to the explanation of social behaviour. In J. M. F. Jaspars, F. D. Fincham and M. Hewstone (eds), *Attribution theory and research: Conceptual, developmental and social dimensions*. London: Academic Press.

Galambos, J. A., Abelson, R. P. and Black, J. B. (eds) (1986). *Knowledge structures*. Hillsdale, N.J.: Erlbaum.

Garfinkel, H. (1967). *Studies in ethnomethodology*. Englewood Cliffs, N.J. : Prentice-Hall.

Garland, H., Hardy, A. and Stephenson, L. (1975). Information search as affected by attribution type and response category. *Personality and Social Psychology Bulletin*, 4, 612–15.

Garland, H. and Price, K. H. (1977). Attitudes towards women in management and attributions for their success and failure in a managerial position. *Journal of Applied Psychology*, 62, 29–33.

Garvey, C. and Caramazza, A. (1974). Implicit causality in verbs. *Linguistic Inquiry*, 5, 459–64.

Gaskell, G. and Smith, P. (1985). An investigation of youths' attributions for unemployment and their political attitudes. *Journal of Economic Psychology*, 6, 65–80.

Gergen, K. J. and Jones, E. E. (1963). Mental illness, predictability and affective consequences as stimulus factors in person perception. *Journal of Abnormal and Social Psychology*, 6, 95–104.

Gilbert, D. T. and Jones, E. E. (1986). Perceiver-induced constraint: Interpretations of self-generated reality. *Journal of Personality and Social Psychology*, 50, 269–80.

Gilovich, T. and Regan, D. T. (1986). The actor and the experiencer: Divergent patterns of causal attribution. *Social Cognition*, 4, 342–52.

Goffman, E. (1959). *The presentation of self in everyday life*. Garden City, N.Y.: Doubleday.

Goldberg, L. R. (1981). Unconfounding situational attributions from uncertain, neutral and ambiguous ones: A psychometric analysis of descriptions of oneself and various types of others. *Journal of Personality and Social Psychology*, 41, 517–52.

Golding, S. L. and Rorer, L. G. (1972). Illusory correlation and subjective judgment. *Journal of Abnormal Psychology*, 80, 249–60.

Gollwitzer, P. M., Earle, W. B. and Stephan, W. G. (1982). Affect as a determinant of egotism: Residual excitation and performance attributions. *Journal of Personality and Social Psychology*, 43, 702–9.

Gorowitz, S. (1965). Causal judgments and causal explanations. *Journal of Philosophy*, 62, 695–711.

Gottman, J. M. (1979). *Marital interaction: Experimental investigations*. New York: Academic Press.

Gould, R. and Sigall, H. (1977). The effects of empathy and outcome on attribution: An examination of the divergent-perspectives hypothesis. *Journal of Experimental Social Psychology*, 13, 480–91.

Grant, E. (1971). *Physical science in the Middle Ages*. London: Wiley.

Graumann, C. F. and Sommer, M. (1984). Schema and inference: Models in cognitive social psychology. In J. R. Royce and L. P. Mos (eds), *Annals of theoretical psychology* (Vol. 1). New York: Plenum Press.

Greenberg, J., Pyszczynski, T. and Solomon, S. (1982). The self-serving attributional bias: Beyond self-presentation. *Journal of Experimental Social Psychology*, 18, 56–67.

Greenberg, J. and Rosenfield, D. (1979). Whites' ethnocentrism and their attributions for the behaviour of blacks: A motivational bias. *Journal of Personality*, 47, 643–57.

Greenwald, A. G. (1976). Within-subjects designs: To use or not to use? *Psychological Bulletin*, 83, 314–20.

Greenwald, A. G. (1980). The totalitarian ego: Fabrication and revision of personal history. *American Psychologist*, 35, 603–18.

Grice, H. P. (1975). Logic in conversation. In P. Cole and J. L. Morgan (eds), *Syntax and semantics* (Vol. 3). New York: Academic Press.

Grigg, F., Fletcher, G. J. O. and Fitness, J. (in press). Spontaneous attributions in happy and unhappy dating relationships. *Journal of Social and Personal Relationships*.

Groh, D. (1987a). The temptation of conspiracy theory, or: Why do bad things happen to good people? Part I: Preliminary draft of a theory of conspiracy theories. In C. F. Graumann and S. Moscovici (eds), *Changing conceptions of conspiracy*. New York: Springer Verlag.

Groh, D. (1987b). The temptation of conspiracy theory, or: Why do bad things happen to good people? Part II: Case studies. In C. F. Graumann and S. Moscovici (eds), *Changing conceptions of conspiracy*. New York: Springer Verlag.

Gurin, P., Gurin, G., Lao, R. and Beattie, H. (1969). Internal-external control in the motivational dynamics of negro youth. *Journal of Social Issues*, 25, 29–53.

Gurney, R. (1981). Leaving school, facing unemployment and making attributions about the causes of unemployment. *Journal of Vocational Behaviour*, 18, 79–91.

Gurwitz, S. B. and Dodge, K. A. (1977). Effects of confirmations and disconfirmations on stereotype-based attributions. *Journal of Personality and Social Psychology*, 35, 495–500.

Gurwitz, S. B. and Topol, B. (1978). Determinants of confirming and disconfirming responses to negative social labels. *Journal of Experimental Social Psychology*, 14, 31–42.

Hamilton, D. L. (1979). A cognitive-attributional analysis of stereotyping. In L. Berkowitz (ed.), *Advances in experimental social psychology* (Vol. 12). New York: Academic Press.

Hamilton, D. L. (1988). Causal attribution viewed from an information processing perspective. In D. Bar-Tal and A. W. Kruglanski (eds), *The social psychology of knowledge*. Cambridge: Cambridge University Press.

Hamilton, D. L. and Trolier, T. K. (1986). Stereotypes and stereotyping: An overview of the cognitive approach. In J. F. Dovidio and S. L. Gaertner (eds), *Prejudice, discrimination and racism*. Orlando, Fla.: Academic Press.

Hamilton, V. L. (1980). Intuitive psychologist or intuitive lawyer? Alternative models of the attribution process. *Journal of Personality and Social Psychology*, 39, 767–72.

Hansen, R. D. (1980). Commonsense attribution. *Journal of Personality and Social Psychology*, 39, 996–1009.

Hansen, R. D. (1985). Cognitive economy and commonsense attribution processing. In J. H. Harvey and G. Weary (eds), *Attribution: Basic issues and applications*. Orlando, Fla.: Academic Press.

Harré, R. (1977). The ethogenic approach: Theory and practice. In L. Berkowitz (ed.), *Advances in experimental social psychology* (Vol.10). New York: Academic Press.

Harré, R. and Madden, E. H. (1975). *Causal powers: A theory of natural necessity*. Oxford: Basil Blackwell.

Hart, H. L. A. and Honoré, A. M. (1959). *Causation in the law*. Oxford: Clarendon Press.

Hart, H. L. A. and Honoré, A. M. (1961). Causation in the law. (First published 1956). In H. Morris (ed.), *Freedom and responsibility: Readings in philosophy and law*. Stanford: Stanford University Press.

Harvey, J. H. (1987). Attributions in close relationships: Research and theoretical developments. *Journal of Social and Clinical Psychology*, 5, 420–34.

Harvey, J. H., Agostinelli, G. and Weber, A. L. (in press). Account-making and the formation of expectations about close relationships. *Review of Personality and Social Psychology*.

Harvey, J. H. and Harris, B. (1983). On the continued vitality of the attributional approach. In M. Hewstone (ed.), *Attribution theory: Social and functional extensions*. Oxford: Basil Blackwell.

Harvey, J. H., Ickes, W. J. and Kidd, R. F. (eds) (1976). New *directions in attribution research* (Vol. 1). Hillsdale, N. J.: Erlbaum.

Harvey, J. H., Ickes, W. J. and Kidd, R. F. (eds) (1978a). New *directions in attribution research* (Vol. 2). Hillsdale, N. J.: Erlbaum.

Harvey, J. H., Ickes, W. J. and Kidd, R. F. (eds) (1981a). New *directions in attribution research* (Vol. 3). Hillsdale, N. J.: Erlbaum.

Harvey, J. H. and McGlynn, R. P. (1982). Matching words to phenomena: The case of the fundamental attribution error. *Journal of Personality and Social Psychology*, 43, 345–6.

Harvey, J. H., Town, J. P. and Yarkin, K. L. (1981b). How fundamental is 'The fundamental attribution error'? *Journal of Personality and Social Psychology*, 40, 346–9.

Harvey, J. H. and Tucker, J. A. (1979). On problems with the cause-reason distinction in attribution theory. *Journal of Personality and Social Psychology*, 37, 1441–6.

Harvey, J. H. and Weary, G. (1984). Current issues in attribution theory and research. *Annual Review of Psychology*, 35, 427–59.

Harvey, J. H. and Weary, G. (eds) (1985). *Attribution: Basic issues and applications*. Orlando, Fla.: Academic Press.

Harvey, J. H., Weber, A. L., Galvin, K. S., Huszti, H. and Garnick, N. (1986). Attribution and the termination of close relationships: A special focus on the account. In R. Gilmour and S. Duck (eds), *Personal relationships*. Hillsdale, N. J.: Erlbaum.

Harvey, J. H., Wells, G. L. and Alvarez, M. D. (1978b). Attribution in the context of conflict and separation in close relationships. In J. H. Harvey, W. J. Ickes and R. F. Kidd (eds), *New directions in attribution research* (Vol. 2). Hillsdale, N. J.: Erlbaum.

Harvey, J. H., Yarkin, K. L., Lightner, J. M. and Town, J. P. (1980). Unsolicited interpretation and recall of interpersonal events. *Journal of Personality and Social Psychology*, 38, 551–68.

Hastie, R. (1981). Schematic principles in human memory. In E. T. Higgins, C. P. Herman and M. P. Zanna (eds), *Social cognition: The Ontario Symposium*. (Vol. 1). Hillsdale, N.J.: Erlbaum.

Hastie, R. (1983). Social inference. *Annual Review of Psychology*, 34, 511–42.

Hastie, R. (1984). Causes and effects of causal attribution. *Journal of Personality and Social Psychology*, 46, 44–56.

Hastie, R. and Park, B. (1986). The relationship between memory and judgment depends on whether the judgment task is memory-based or on-line. *Psychological Review*, 93, 258–68.

Hayden, T. and Mischel, W. (1976). Maintaining trait consistency in the resolution of behavioral inconsistency: The wolf in sheep's clothing? *Journal of Personality*, 44, 109–32.

Haynes, J. and Nutman, P. (1981). *Understanding the unemployed*. London: Tavistock.

Hazlewood, J. D. and Olson, J. M. (1986). Covariation information, causal questioning, and interpersonal behavior. *Journal of Experimental Social Psychology*, 22, 276–91.

Head, H. (1920). *Studies in neurology*. New York: Oxford University Press.

Heelas, P. and Lock, A. (eds) (1981). *Indigenous psychologies: the anthropology of the self*. London: Academic Press.

Heider, F. (1944). Social perception and phenomenal causality. *Psychological Review*, 51, 358–74.

Heider, F. (1958). *The psychology of interpersonal relations*. New York: Wiley.

Heider, F. (1976). A conversation with Fritz Heider. In J. H. Harvey, W. J.

Ickes and R. F. Kidd (eds) *New directions in attribution research* (Vol. 1). Hillsdale, N.J : Erlbaum.

Heider, F. and Simmel, M. (1944). An experimental study of apparent behaviour. *American Journal of Psychology*, 57, 243–49.

Henderson, M. and Hewstone, M. (1984). Prison inmates' explanations for interpersonal violence: Accounts and attributions. *Journal of Consulting and Clinical Psychology*, 52, 789–94.

Hewstone, M. (ed.). (1983a). *Attribution theory: Social and functional extensions*. Oxford: Basil Blackwell.

Hewstone, M. (1983b). Attribution theory and common-sense explanations: An introductory overview. In M. Hewstone (ed.), *Attribution theory: Social and functional extensions*. Oxford: Basil Blackwell.

Hewstone, M. (1983c). The role of language in attribution processes. In J. M. F. Jaspars, F. D. Fincham and M. Hewstone (eds), *Attribution theory and research: Conceptual, developmental and social dimensions*. London: Academic Press.

Hewstone, M. (1985). On common sense and social representations: A reply to Potter and Litton. *British Journal of Social Psychology*, 24, 95–7.

Hewstone, M. (1988a). Attributional bases of intergroup conflict. In W. Stroebe, A. W. Kruglanski, D. Bar-Tal and M. Hewstone (eds), *The social psychology of intergroup conflict: Theory, research and applications*. New York: Springer.

Hewstone, M. (1988b). The 'ultimate attribution error': A review of the literature on intergroup causal attribution. Unpublished manuscript, University of Bristol.

Hewstone, M. (1988c). Causal attribution: From cognitive processes to collective beliefs. *The Psychologist: Bulletin of the British Psychological Society*, 1, 323–7.

Hewstone, M. (1989). Les représentations sociales et la causalité. In D. Jodelet (ed.), *Les représentations sociales*. Paris: Presses Universitaires de France.

Hewstone, M. and Antaki, C. (1988). Attribution theory and social explanations. In M. Hewstone, W. Stroebe, G. M. Stephenson and J.-P. Codol (eds), *Introduction to social psychology: A European perspective*. Oxford: Basil Blackwell.

Hewstone, M., Bond, M. H. and Wan, K.-C. (1983). Social facts and social attributions: The explanation of intergroup differences in Hong Kong. *Social Cognition*, 2, 142–57.

Hewstone, M. and Brown, R. J. (1986). Contact is not enough: An intergroup perspective on the 'contact hypothesis'. In M. Hewstone and R. J. Brown (eds), *Contact and Conflict in intergroup encounters*. Oxford: Basil Blackwell.

Hewstone, M., Gale, L. and Purkhardt, N. (1988). Intergroup attributions for success and failure: Group-serving bias and group-serving causal schemata. Unpublished manuscript, University of Bristol.

Hewstone, M. and Jaspars, J. M. F. (1982a). Intergroup relations and attribution processes. In H. Tajfel (ed.), *Social identity and intergroup relations*. Cambridge/Paris: Cambridge University Press, Maison des Sciences de l'Homme.

Hewstone, M. and Jaspars, J. M. F. (1982b). Explanations for racial discrimination: The effect of group discussion on intergroup attributions. *European Journal of Social Psychology*, 12, 1–16.

Hewstone, M. and Jaspars, J. M. F. (1983). A re-examination of the roles of consensus, consistency and distinctiveness: Kelley's cube revisited. *British Journal of Social Psychology*, 22, 41–50.

Hewstone, M. and Jaspars, J. M. F. (1984). Social dimensions of attribution. In H. Tajfel (ed.), *The social dimension: European developments in social psychology*. Cambridge/Paris: Cambridge University Press, Maison des Sciences de l'Homme.

Hewstone, M. and Jaspars, J. M. F. (1987). Covariation and causal attribution: A logical model of the intuitive analysis of variance. *Journal of Personality and Social Psychology*, 53, 663–72.

Hewstone, M. and Jaspars, J. M. F. (1988). Implicit and explicit consensus as determinants of causal attribution: Two experimental investigations. *European Journal of Social Psychology*, 18, 93–8.

Hewstone, M., Jaspars, J. and Lalljee, M. (1982). Social representations, social attribution and social identity: The intergroup images of 'public' and 'comprehensive' schoolboys. *European Journal of Social Psychology*, 12, 241–69.

Hewstone, M., Wagner, U. and Machleit, U. (in press). Self-, ingroup- and outgroup-achievement attributions of German and Turkish pupils in West Germany. *Journal of Social Psychology*.

Hewstone, M. and Ward, C. (1985). Ethnocentrism and causal attribution in Southeast Asia. *Journal of Personality and Social Psychology*, 48, 614–23.

Higgins, E. T. (1981). Role-taking and social judgment: Alternative developmental perspectives and processes. In J. H. Flavell and L. Ross (eds), *New directions in the study of social-cognitive development*. Cambridge: Cambridge University Press.

Higgins, E. T. and Bargh, J. A. (1987). Social cognition and perception. *Annual Review of Psychology*, 38, 369–425.

Higgins, E. T. and Bryant, S. L. (1982). Consensus information and the fundamental attribution error: The role of development and in-group versus out-group knowledge. *Journal of Personality and Social Psychology*, 43, 889–900.

Higgins, E. T., Fondacaro, R. and McCann, D. (1981). Rules and roles: The 'communication game' and speaker-listener processes. In W. P. Dickson (ed.), *Children's oral communication skills*. New York: Academic Press.

Hilton, D. J. (1982). The myth of economics: The influence of common-sense analogies on economic argument and reasoning. Unpublished manuscript, University of Oxford.

Hilton, D. J. (1988). Logic and causal attribution. In D. J. Hilton (ed.),

Contemporary science and natural explanation: Commonsense conceptions of causality. Brighton: Harvester Press.

Hilton, D. J. (in press). A conversational model of causal explanation. *Psychological Bulletin*.

Hilton, D. J. and Jaspars, J. M. F. (1987). The explanation of occurrences and non-occurrences: A test of the inductive logic model of causal attribution. *British Journal of Social Psychology*, 26, 189–202.

Hilton, D. J. and Knibbs, C. S. (1988). The knowledge-structure and inductivist strategies in causal attribution: A direct comparison. *European Journal of Social Psychology*, 18, 79–92.

Hilton, D. J. and Slugoski, B. R. (1986). Knowledge-based causal attribution: The Abnormal Conditions Focus model. *Psychological Review*, 93, 75–88.

Hilton, D. J., Smith, R. H. and Alicke, M. D. (1988). Knowledge-based information acquisition: Norms and the functions of consensus information. *Journal of Personality and Social Psychology*, 55, 530–40.

Hilton, J. L. and Darley, J. M. (1985). Constructing other persons: A limit on the effect. *Journal of Experimental Social Psychology*, 21, 1–18.

Himmelweit, H. T. (in press). The dynamics of public opinion or the life history of issues. In C. Fraser and G. Gaskell (eds), *Attitudes, opinions and representations: Social psychological analyses of widespread beliefs*. Oxford: Oxford University Press.

Himmelweit, H. T., Humphreys, P., Jaeger, M. and Katz, M. (1981). *How voters decide: A longitudinal study of political attitudes and voting extending over fifteen years*. London: Academic Press.

Hofstadter, R. (1966). *The paranoid style in American politics and other essays*. London: Jonathan Cape.

Hollin, C. R. and Howells, K. (1987). Lay explanations of delinquency: Global or offence-specific? *British Journal of Social Psychology*, 26, 203–10.

Holtzworth-Munroe, A. and Jacobson, N. S. (1985). Causal attributions of married couples: When do they search for causes? What do they conclude when they do? *Journal of Personality and Social Psychology*, 48, 1398–1412.

Honess, T. M. (1989). A longitudinal study of school leavers' employment experiences, time structuring and self-attributions as a function of local opportunity structure. *British Journal of Psychology*, 80, 45–77.

Horai, J. (1977). Attributional conflict. *Journal of Social Issues*, 33, 88–100.

Howard, J. A. (1984a). The 'normal' victim: The effects of gender stereotypes on reactions to victims. *Social Psychology Quarterly*, 47, 270–81.

Howard, J. A. (1984b). Societal influences on attribution: Blaming some victims more than others. *Journal of Personality and Social Psychology*, 47, 494–505.

Howard, J. A. (1985). Further appraisal of correspondent inference theory. *Personality and Social Psychology Bulletin*, 11, 467–77.

Howard, J. A. (1987). The conceptualization and measurement of attributions. *Journal of Experimental Social Psychology*, 23, 32–58.

Howard, J. A. and Levinson, R. (1985). The overdue courtship of attribution and labeling. *Social Psychology Quarterly*, 48, 191–202.

Howe, G. W. (1987). Attributions of complex cause and the perception of marital conflict. *Journal of Personality and Social Psychology*, 53, 1119–28.

Hui, C. H. and Ip, K.-C. (1989). The control of social role bias: Effects of question preparation and subsequent feedback in a quiz game. *British Journal of Social Psychology*, 28, 31–8.

Hull, J. G. and West, S. G. (1982). The discounting principle in attribution. *Personality and Social Psychology Bulletin*, 8, 208–13.

Hume, D. C. (1975 edn) *Enquiries concerning human understanding and concerning the principles of morals*. (Edited by L. A. Selby-Bigge, 3rd edn revised by P. H. Nidditch). Oxford: Oxford University Press. (Original work published 1748.)

Ichheiser, G. (1943). Misinterpretations of personality in everyday life and the psychologist's frame of reference. *Character and Personality*, 12, 145–60.

Ichheiser, G. (1949). Misunderstandings in human relations: A study of false social perception. *American Journal of Sociology*, 55, 1–70.

Ichheiser, G. (1970). *Appearances and realities: Misunderstandings in human relations*. San Francisco: Jossey-Bass.

Ickes, W. J. (1985). Sex-role influences on compatibility in relationships. In W. J. Ickes (ed.), *Compatible and incompatible relationships*. New York: Springer-Verlag.

Ickes, W. J., Patterson, M. L., Rajecki, D. W. and Tanford, S. (1982). Behavioral and cognitive consequences of reciprocal versus compensatory responses to pre-interaction expectancies. *Social Cognition*, 1, 160–90.

Ickes, W. J., Robertson, E., Tooke, W. and Teng, G. (1986). Naturalistic social cognition: Methodology, assessment, and validation. *Journal of Personality and Social Psychology*, 51, 66–82.

Isen, A. M. (1984). Toward understanding the role of affect in cognition. In R. S. Wyer and T. K. Srull (eds), *Handbook of social cognition* (Vol. 3). Hillsdale, N.J.: Erlbaum.

Isen, A. M., Means, B., Patrick, P. and Nowicki, G. (1982). Some factors influencing decision-making strategy and risk-taking. In M. S. Clark and S. T. Fiske (eds), *Affect and cognition: The 17th Annual Carnegie Symposium on Cognition*. Hillsdale, N.J.: Erlbaum.

Jacobson, N. S., McDonald, D. W., Follette, W. C. and Berley, R. A. (1985). Attribution processes in distressed and nondistressed married couples. *Cognitive Therapy and Research*, 9, 35–50.

Jacobson, N. S. and Margolin, G. (1979). *Marital therapy*. New York: Brunner/Mazel.

Jahoda, G. (1979). A cross-cultural perspective on experimental social psychology. *Personality and Social Psychology Bulletin*, 5, 142–8.

Jahoda, G. (1982). *Psychology and anthropology: A psychological perspective*. London: Academic Press.

Jahoda, G. (1988). Critical notes and reflections on 'social representations'. *European Journal of Social Psychology*, 18, 195–209.

Jahoda, M. (1979). The impact of unemployment in the 1930s and 1970s. *Bulletin of the British Psychological Society*, 32, 309–14.

Jahoda, M. (1983). The emergence of social psychology in Vienna: An exercise in long-term memory. *British Journal of Social Psychology*, 22, 343–9.

James, W. (1890). *Principles of psychology* (Vol. 1). New York: Holt.

Jaspars, J. M. F. (1983). The process of causal attribution in common sense. In M. Hewstone (ed.), *Attribution theory: Social and functional extensions*. Oxford: Basil Blackwell.

Jaspars, J. M. F. (1986). Forum and focus: A personal view of European social psychology. *European Journal of Social Psychology*, 16, 3–16.

Jaspars, J. M. F., Fincham, F. D. and Hewstone, M. (eds) (1983a). *Attribution theory and research: Conceptual, developmental and social dimensions*. London: Academic Press.

Jaspars, J. M. F. and Fraser, C. (1984). Attitudes and social representations. In R. M. Farr and S. Moscovici (eds), *Social representations*. Cambridge/Paris: Cambridge University Press, Maison des Sciences de l'Homme.

Jaspars, J. M. F. and Hewstone, M. (1982). Cross-cultural interaction, social attribution and inter-group relations. In S. Bochner (ed.), *Cultures in contact: Studies in cross-cultural interaction*. Oxford: Pergamon Press.

Jaspars, J. M. F. and Hewstone, M. (in press). Collective beliefs, social categorization and causal attribution. In C. Fraser and G. Gaskell (eds), *Attitudes, opinions and representations: Social psychological analyses of widespread beliefs*. Oxford: Oxford University Press.

Jaspars, J. M. F., Hewstone, M. and Fincham, F. D. (1983b). Attribution theory and research: The state of the art. In J. M. F. Jaspars, F. D. Fincham and M. Hewstone (eds), *Attribution theory and research: Conceptual, developmental and social dimensions*. London: Academic Press.

Jellison, J. M. and Green, J. (1981). A self-presentation approach to the fundamental attribution error: The norm of internality. *Journal of Personality and Social Psychology*, 40, 643–9.

Jervis, R. (1976). *Perception and misperception in international politics*. Princeton, N. J.: Princeton University Press.

Jodelet, D. (1984). Représentation sociale: phénomènes, concept et théorie. In S. Moscovici (ed.), *Psychologie sociale*. Paris: Presses Universitaires de France.

Jones, E. E. (1979). The rocky road from acts to dispositions. *American Psychologist*, 34, 107–17.

Jones, E. E. (1985a). Major developments in social psychology during the past five decades. In G. Lindzey and E. Aronson (eds), *Handbook of social psychology* (Vol. 1) (3rd edn). New York: Random House.

Jones, E. E. (1985b). Retrospective review [F. Heider, The *psychology of interpersonal relations*, 1958]: The seer who found attributional wisdom in naivety. *Contemporary Psychology*, 32, 213–16.

Jones, E. E. and Berglas, S. (1978). Control of attributions about the self through self-handicapping strategies: The appeal of alcohol and the role of underachievement. *Personality and Social Psychology Bulletin*, 4, 200–6.

Jones, E. E. and Davis, K. E. (1965). From acts to dispositions: The attribution process in person perception. In L. Berkowitz (ed.), *Advances in experimental social psychology* (Vol. 2). New York: Academic Press.

Jones, E. E., Davis, K. E. and Gergen, K. J. (1961). Role playing variations and their informational value for person perception. *Journal of Abnormal and Social Psychology*, 63, 302–10.

Jones, E. E. and De Charms, R. (1957). Changes in social perception as a function of the personal relevance of behaviour. *Sociometry*, 20, 75–85.

Jones, E. E., Farina, A., Hastorf, A. H., Markus, H., Miller, D. T. and Scott, R. A. (1984). *Social stigma: The psychology of marked relationships*. New York: Freeman.

Jones, E. E and Harris, V. A. (1967). The attribution of attitudes. *Journal of Experimental Social Psychology*, 3, 1–24.

Jones, E. E., Kanouse, D. E., Kelley, H. H., Nisbett, R. E., Valins, S. and Weiner, B. (1972). *Attribution: Perceiving the causes of behaviour*. Morristown, N.J.: General Learning Press.

Jones, E. E. and McGillis, D. (1976). Correspondent inferences and the attribution cube: A comparative reappraisal. In J. H. Harvey, W. J. Ickes and R. F. Kidd (eds), *New directions in attribution research* (Vol. 1). Hillsdale, N.J.: Erlbaum.

Jones, E. E. and Nisbett, R. E. (1972). The actor and the observer: Divergent perceptions of the causes of behaviour. In E. E. Jones, D. E. Kanouse, H. H. Kelley, R. E. Nisbett, S. Valins and B. Weiner (eds), *Attribution: Perceiving the causes of behaviour*. Morristown, N.J.: General Learning Press.

Jussim, L. (1986). Self-fulfilling prophecies: A theoretical and integrative review. *Psychological Review*, 93, 429–45.

Kahneman, D. and Tversky, A. (1972). Subjective probability: A judgment of representativeness. *Cognitive Psychology*, 3, 430–54.

Kahneman, D. and Tversky, A. (1973). On the psychology of prediction. *Psychological Review*, 80, 237–51.

Kalmuss, D., Gurin, P. and Townsend, A. L. (1981). Feminist and sympathetic feminist consciousness. *European Journal of Social Psychology*, 11, 131–47.

Kanouse, D. E. (1972). Language, labeling and attribution. In E. E. Jones, D. E. Kanouse, H. H. Kelley, R. E. Nisbett, S. Valins and B. Weiner, *Attribution: Perceiving the causes of behaviour*. Morristown, N.J.: General Learning Press.

Kassin, S. M. (1979). Consensus information, prediction and causal attribution: A review of the literature and issues. *Journal of Personality and Social Psychology*, 37, 1966–81.

Kassin, S. M. (1981). From laychild to 'layman': Developmental causal attribution. In S. S. Brehm, S. M. Kassin and F. X. Gibbons (eds), *Developmental social psychology*. New York: Oxford University Press.

Kassin, S. M. (1982). Heider and Simmel revisited: Causal attribution and the animated film technique. In L. Wheeler (ed.), *Review of Personality and Social Psychology* (Vol. 3). Beverly Hills, Cal.: Sage.

Kassin, S. M. and Hochreich, D. J. (1977). Instructional set: A neglected variable in attribution research? *Personality and Social Psychology Bulletin*, 3, 620–3.

Kassin, S. M., Lowe, C. A. and Gibbons, F. X. (1980). Children's use of the discounting principle: A perceptual approach. *Journal of Personality and Social Psychology*, 39, 719–8.

Kelley, H. H. (1967). Attribution theory in social psychology. In D. Levine (ed.), *Nebraska symposium on motivation* (Vol. 15). Lincoln: University of Nebraska Press.

Kelley, H. H. (1972a). Causal schemata and the attribution process. In E. E. Jones, D. E. Kanouse, H. H. Kelley, R. E. Nisbett, S. Valins and B. Weiner, *Attribution: Perceiving the causes of behaviour*. Morristown, N.J.: General Learning Press.

Kelley, H. H. (1972b). Attribution in social interaction. In E. E. Jones, D. E. Kanouse, H. H. Kelley, R. E. Nisbett, S. Valins and B. Weiner (eds), *Attribution: Perceiving the causes of behaviour*. Morristown, N. J.: General Learning Press.

Kelley, H. H. (1973). The processes of causal attribution. *American Psychologist*, 28, 107–28.

Kelley, H. H. (1977). An application of attribution theory to research methodology for close relationships. In G. Levinger and H. L. Raush (eds), *Close relationships: Perspectives on the meaning of intimacy*. Amherst, Mass.: University of Massachusetts Press.

Kelley, H. H. (1979). *Personal relationships: Their structures and processes*. Hillsdale, N. J.: Erlbaum.

Kelley, H. H. (1980). The causes of behavior: Their perception and regulation. In L. Festinger (ed.), *Retrospections on social psychology*. New York: Oxford University Press.

Kelley, H. H. (1983). Perceived causal structures. In J. M. F. Jaspars, F. D. Fincham and M. Hewstone (eds), *Attribution theory and research: Conceptual, developmental and social dimensions*. London: Academic Press.

Kelley, H. H., Berscheid, E., Christensen, A., Harvey, J. H., Huston, T. L., Levinger, G., McClintock, E., Peplau, L. A. and Peterson, D. R. (1983). *Close relationships*. New York: Freeman.

Kelley, H. H. and Michela, J. L. (1980). Attribution theory and research. *Annual Review of Psychology*, 31, 457–503.

Kelly, G. A. (1955). *The psychology of personal constructs*. (2 vols.) New York: Norton.

Kelman, H. C. (1958). Compliance, identification and internalization: Three processes of attitude change. *Journal of Conflict Resolution*, 2, 51–60.

Kelvin, P. (1980). Social psychology 2001: the social psychological bases and implications of structural unemployment. In R. Gilmour and S. Duck (eds), *The development of social psychology*. London: Academic Press.

Kelvin, P. (1984). The historical dimension of social psychology: the case of unemployment. In H. Tajfel (ed.), *The social dimension: European developments in social psychology* (Vol. 2). Cambridge/Paris: Cambridge: Cambridge University Press, Maison des Sciences de l'Homme.

Keneally, T. (1983). *Schindler's ark*. London: Coronet.

Kenny, D. A. (1985). Quantitative methods for social psychology. In G. Lindzey and E. Aronson (eds), *The handbook of social psychology* (3rd edn). New York: Random House.

Kenrick, D. T. (1986). How strong is the case against contemporary social and personality psychology? A response to Carlson. *Journal of Personality and Social Psychology*, 50, 839–44.

Kingdon, J. W. (1967). Politicians' beliefs about voters. *American Political Science Review*, 61, 137–45.

Kintsch, W. (1974). *The representation of meaning in memory*. Hillsdale, N. J.: Erlbaum.

Knight, J. A. and Vallacher, R. R. (1981). Interpersonal engagement in social perception: The consequences of getting into the action. *Journal of Personality and Social Psychology*, 40, 990–9.

Kruglanski, A. W. (1975). The endogenous-exogenous partition in attribution theory. *Psychological Review*, 82, 387–406.

Kruglanski, A. W. (1979). Causal explanation, teleological explanation: On radical particularism in attribution theory. *Journal of Personality and Social Psychology*, 37, 1447–57.

Kruglanski, A. W. (1988). *Basic processes in social cognition: A theory of lay epistemology*. New York: Plenum.

Kruglanski, A. W. and Ajzen, I. (1983). Bias and error in human judgment. *European Journal of Social Psychology*, 13, 1–44.

Kruglanski, A. W., Baldwin, M. W. and Towson, S. M. (1983). The lay-epistemic process in attribution-making. In M. Hewstone (ed.), *Attribution theory: Social and functional extensions*. Oxford: Basil Blackwell.

Kruglanski, A. W., Schwartz, J. M., Maides, S. and Hamel, I. Z. (1978). Covariation, discounting and augmentation: Towards a clarification of attributional principles. *Journal of Personality*, 46, 176–89.

Kuiper, N. A. (1978). Depression and causal attributions for success and failure. *Journal of Personality and Social Psychology*, 36, 236–46.

Kulik, J. A. (1983). Confirmatory attribution and the perpetuation of social beliefs. *Journal of Personality and Social Psychology*, 44, 1171–81.

Kun, A. and Weiner, B. (1973). Necessary versus sufficient causal schemata for success and failure. *Journal of Research in Personality*, 7, 197–207.

Lakoff, G. and Johnson, M. (1980). *Metaphors we live by*. Chicago: University of Chicago Press.

Lalljee, M. (1981). Attribution theory and the analysis of explanations. In C. Antaki (ed.), *The psychology of ordinary explanations of social behaviour*. London: Academic Press.

Lalljee, M. and Abelson, R. P. (1983). The organization of explanations. In M.

Hewstone (ed.), *Attribution theory: Social and functional extensions*. Oxford: Basil Blackwell.

Lalljee, M., Lamb, R., Furnham, A. and Jaspars, J. M. F. (1984). Explanations and information search: Inductive and hypothesis-testing approaches to arriving at an explanation. *British Journal of Social Psychology*, 23, 201–12.

Lalljee, M., Watson, M. and White, P. (1982). Explanations, attributions, and the social context of unexpected behaviour. *European Journal of Social Psychology*, 12, 17–29.

Lalljee, M., Watson, M. and White, P. (1983). Some aspects of the explanations of young children. In J. M. F. Jaspars, F. D. Fincham and M. Hewstone (eds), *Attribution theory and research: Conceptual, developmental and social dimensions*. London: Academic Press.

Lane, R. E. (1962). *Political ideology*. New York: Free Press.

Langer, E. J. (1975). The illusion of control. *Journal of Personality and Social Psychology*, 32, 311–28.

Langer, E. J. (1978). Rethinking the role of thought in social interaction. In J. H. Harvey, W. J. Ickes and R. F. Kidd (eds), *New directions in attribution research* (Vol. 2). Hillsdale, N.J.: Erlbaum.

Langer, E. J. and Abelson, R. P. (1972). The semantics of asking a favor: How to succeed in getting help without really dying. *Journal of Personality and Social Psychology*, 24, 26–32.

Langer, E. J., Taylor, S. E., Fiske, S. T. and Chanowitz, B. (1976). Stigma, staring, and discomfort: A novel stimulus hypothesis. *Journal of Experimental Social Psychology*, 12, 451–63.

Lau, R. R. and Russell, D. (1980). Attributions in the sports pages. *Journal of Personality and Social Psychology*, 39, 29–38.

Lay, C. H., Burron, B. F. and Jackson, D. N. (1973). Base rates and informational value in impression formation. *Journal of Personality and Social Psychology*, 28, 390–5.

Lay, C. H., Ziegler, M., Hershfield, L. and Miller, D. T. (1974). The perception of situational consistency in behaviour: Assessing the actor-observer bias. *Canadian Journal of Behavioural Science*, 6, 376–84.

Leddo, J. and Abelson, R. P. (1986). The nature of explanations. In J. A. Galambos, R. P. Abelson and J. B. Black (eds), *Knowledge structures*. Hillsdale, N. J.: Erlbaum.

Leddo, J., Abelson, R. P. and Gross, P. H. (1984). Conjunctive explanations: When two reasons are better than one. *Journal of Personality and Social Psychology*, 47, 933–43.

Lederer, W. J. and Jackson, D. D. (1968). *The mirages of marriage*. New York: Plenum.

Lefcourt, H. M. (1973). The functions of the illusions of control and freedom. *American Psychologist*, 28, 417–25.

Lemyre, L. and Smith, P. M. (1985). Intergroup discrimination and self-esteem in the minimal group paradigm. *Journal of Personality and Social Psychology*, 49, 660–70.

Lerner, M. J. (1980). *The belief in a just world*. New York: Plenum.

Lerner, M. J. and Miller, D. T. (1978). 'Just World' research and the attribution process: Looking back and ahead. *Psychological Bulletin*, 85, 1030–51.

LeVine, R. A. and Campbell, D. T. (1972). *Ethnocentrism: Theories of conflict, ethnic attitudes and group behavior*. New York: Wiley.

Levinger, G. (1980). Toward the analysis of close relationships. *Journal of Experimental Social Psychology*, 16, 510–44.

Levinson, S. (1983). *Pragmatics*. Cambridge: Cambridge University Press.

Lévy-Bruhl, L. (1925). *How natives think*. New York: Alfred A. Knopf.

Lewin, K. (1948). *Resolving social conflicts*. New York: Harper and Row.

Lewin, K. (1951). *Field theory in social science*. New York: Harper and Row.

Lewis, A. (1981). Attributions and politics. *Personality and Individual Differences*, 2, 1–4.

Lewis, A., Snell, M. and Furnham, A. (1987). Lay explanations for the causes of unemployment in Britain: Economic, individualistic, societal or fatalistic? *Political Psychology*, 8, 427–39.

Lichtenstein, E. H. and Brewer, W. F. (1980). Memory for goal-directed events. *Cognitive Psychology*, 12, 412–45.

Litton, I. and Potter, J. (1985). Social representations in the ordinary explanation of a 'riot'. *European Journal of Social Psychology*, 15, 371–88.

Liu, J. L. and Steele, C. M. (1986). Attributional analysis as self-affirmation. *Journal of Personality and Social Psychology*, 51, 531–40.

Livesley, W. J. and Bromley, D. B. (1973). *Person perception and adolescence*. London: Wiley.

Lloyd, S. A. and Cate, R. (1985). Attributions associated with significant turning points in premarital relationships. *Journal of Social and Personal Relationships*, 2, 419–36.

Locke, D. and Pennington, D. (1982). Reasons and other causes: Their role in attribution processes. *Journal of Personality and Social Psychology*, 42, 212–23.

Locke, H. J. and Wallace, K. M. (1959). Short marital adjustment and prediction tests: Their reliability and validity. *Marriage and Family Living*, 21, 251–5.

Locksley, A. and Stangor, C. (1984). Why versus how often: Causal reasoning and the incidence of judgmental bias. *Journal of Experimental Social Psychology*, 20, 470–83.

Lukes, S. (1973). *Individualism*. Oxford: Basil Blackwell.

Lukes, S. (1975). *Emile Durkheim: His life and work: A historical and critical study*. Harmondsworth: Penguin.

Lunt, P. (1988). The perceived causal structure of examination failure. *British Journal of Social Psychology*, 27, 171–180.

Lyman, S. M. and Scott, M. B. (1970). *A sociology of the absurd*. New York: Appleton-Century-Crofts.

McArthur, L. A. (1972). The how and what of why: Some determinants and consequences of causal attributions. *Journal of Personality and Social Psychology*, 22, 171–93.

McArthur, L. Z. and Post, D. L. (1977). Figural emphasis and person perception. *Journal of Experimental Social Psychology*, 13, 520–35.

McClure, J. (1984). On necessity and commonsense: A discussion of central axioms in new approaches to lay explanation. *European Journal of Social Psychology*, 14, 123–49.

McClure, J., Lalljee, M., Jaspars, J. M. F. and Abelson, R. P. (1989). Conjunctive explanations of success and failure: The effect of different types of causes. *Journal of Personality and Social Psychology*, 56, 19–26.

McFarland, C. and Ross, M. (1982). The impact of causal attributions on affective reactions to success and failure. *Journal of Personality and Social Psychology*, 43, 937–46.

McGuire, W. J. (1983). A contextualist theory of knowledge: Its implications for innovation and reform in psychological research. In L. Berkowitz (ed.), *Advances in experimental social psychology* (Vol. 16). Orlando, Fla.: Academic Press.

McGuire, W. J. (1986). The vicissitudes of attitudes and similar representational constructs in twentieth century psychology. *European Journal of Social Psychology*, 16, 89–130.

MacIver, R. M. (1940). The imputation of motives. *The American Journal of Sociology*, 46, 1–12.

Mackie, J. L. (1965). Causes and conditions. *American Philosophical Quarterly*, 2, 245–64.

Mackie, J. L. (1974). *The cement of the universe: A study of causation*. Oxford: Clarendon.

Madden, M. E. and Janoff-Bulman, R. (1981). Blame, control, and marital satisfaction: Wives' attributions for conflict in marriage. *Journal of Marriage and the Family*, 43, 663–74.

Major, B. (1980). Information acquisition and attribution processes. *Journal of Personality and Social Psychology*, 39, 1010–23.

Malpass, R. S. and Kravitz, J. (1969). Recognition for faces of own and other race. *Journal of Personality and Social Psychology*, 13, 330–4.

March, J. G. and Simon, H. A. (1958). *Organizations*. New York: Wiley.

Markova, I. and Wilkie, P. (1987). Representations, concepts and social change: The phenomenon of AIDS. *Journal for the Theory of Social Behaviour*, 17, 389–410.

Markus, H. and Zajonc, R. B. (1985). The cognitive perspective in social psychology. In G. Lindzey and E. Aronson (eds), *The handbook of social psychology* (Vol. 1). New York: Random House.

Martin, D. (1967). *A sociology of English religion*. London: SCM Press.

Martin, R. (1972). On weighting causes. *American Philosophical Quarterly*, 9, 291–9.

Maruyama, G. (1982). How should attributions be measured? A reanalysis of data from Elig and Frieze. *American Educational Research Journal*, 19, 552–8.

Maselli, M. D. and Altrocchi, J. (1969). Attribution of intent. *Psychological Bulletin*, 71, 445–54.

Mead, G. H. (1927). The objective reality of perspectives. In E. S. Brightman (ed.), *Proceedings of the sixth international congress of philosophy*. New York: Longmans, Green.

Mead, G. H. (1934). *Mind, self, and society*. Chicago: University of Chicago Press.

Medea, A. and Thompson, K. (1974). *Against rape*. New York: Farrar, Straus and Giroux.

Medcof, J. W. (in press). PEAT: An integrative model of attribution processes. In M. P. Zanna (ed.), *Advances in experimental social psychology* (Vol. 23). San Diego, Cal.: Academic Press.

Merkl, P. H. (1975). *Political violence under the Swastika*. Princeton: Princeton University Press.

Merton, R. K. (1948). The self-fulfilling prophecy. *Antioch Review*, 8, 193–210.

Merton, R. K. (1957). *Social theory and social structure*. Glencoe, Ill.: Free Press.

Messick, D. M. and Mackie, D. M. (1989). Intergroup relations. *Annual Review of Psychology*, 40, 45–82.

Messick, D. M. and Reeder, G. D. (1974). Roles, occupations, behaviors, and attributions. *Journal of Experimental Social Psychology*, 10, 126–32.

Metalsky, G. and Abramson, L. Y. (1981). Attributional style: Toward a framework for conceptualization and assessment. In P. Kendall and S. Hollon (eds.), *Assessment strategies for cognitive-behavioral interventions*. New York: Academic Press.

Meyer, C. B. and Taylor, S. E. (1986). Adjustment to rape. *Journal of Personality and Social Psychology*, 50, 1226–34.

Meyer, J. P. (1980). Causal attribution for success and failure: A multivariate investigation of dimensionality, formation and consequences. *Journal of Personality and Social Psychology*, 38, 704–18.

Michotte, A. E. (1946). *La perception de la causalité*. Paris: J. Vrin (translation: *The perception of causality*. New York: Basic Books, 1963).

Michotte, A. E. (1952). Albert Michotte van den Berck. In E. G. Boring, H. Werner, H. S. Langfeld and R. M. Yerkes (eds), A *history of psychology in autobiography* (Vol. 4). New York: Russell and Russell.

Mikula, G. and Schlamberger, K. (1985). What people think about an unjust event: Toward a better understanding of the phenomenology of experiences of injustice. *European Journal of Social Psychology*, 15, 37–49.

Mill, J. S. (1973 edn). System of logic (8th edn). In J. M. Robson (ed.), *Collected works of John Stuart Mill* (Vols 7 and 8). Toronto, Canada: University of Toronto Press. (Original work published 1872.)

Miller, A. G. and Rorer, L. G. (1982). Toward an understanding of the fundamental attribution error: Essay diagnosticity in the attitude attribution paradigm. *Journal of Research in Personality*, 16, 41–59.

Miller, D. T., Norman, S. A. and Wright, E. (1978). Distortion in person perception as a consequence of the need for effective control. *Journal of Personality and Social Psychology*, 36, 598–607.

Miller, D. T. and Porter, C. A. (1980). Effects of temporal perspective on the attribution process. *Journal of Personality and Social Psychology*, 39, 532–41.

Miller, D. T. and Ross, M. (1975). Self-serving biases in the attribution of causality: Fact or fiction? *Psychological Bulletin*, 82, 213–25.

Miller, D. T. and Turnbull, W. (1986). Expectancies and interpersonal processes. *Annual Review of Psychology*, 37, 233–56.

Miller, F. D., Smith, E. R. and Uleman, J. (1981). Measurement and interpretation of situational and dispositional attributions. *Journal of Experimental Social Psychology*, 17, 80–95.

Miller, G. R. and Steinberg, M. (1975). *Between people: A new analysis of interpersonal communication*. Chicago, Ill.: Science Research Associates.

Miller, J. G. (1984). Culture and the development of everyday social explanation. *Journal of Personality and Social Psychology*, 46, 961–78.

Mills, C. W. (1940). Situated actions and vocabularies of motive. *American Sociological Review*, 5, 904–13.

Minsky, M. (1975). A framework for representing knowledge. In P. H. Winston (ed.), *The psychology of computer vision*. New York: McGraw-Hill.

Monson, T. C. and Snyder, M. (1977). Actors, observers and the attribution process. *Journal of Experimental Social Psychology*, 13, 89–111.

Moore, B. S., Sherrod, D. R., Liu, T. J. and Underwood, B. (1979). The dispositional shift in attribution over time. *Journal of Experimental Social Psychology*, 15, 553–69.

Moore, R. I. (1987). *The formation of a persecuting society*. Oxford: Basil Blackwell.

Moscovici, S. (1976). *La psychanalyse, son image et son public*. Paris: Presses Universitaires de France (2nd edn, first published 1961).

Moscovici, S. (1981). On social representations. In J. P. Forgas (ed.), *Social cognition: Perspectives on everyday understanding*. London: Academic Press.

Moscovici, S. (1984). The phenomenon of social representations. In R. M. Farr and S. Moscovici (eds), *Social representations*. Cambridge/Paris: Cambridge University Press, Maison des Sciences de l'Homme.

Moscovici, S. (1985). Comment on Potter and Litton. *British Journal of Social Psychology*, 24, 91–2.

Moscovici, S. (1987). The conspiracy mentality. In C. F. Graumann and S. Moscovici (eds), *Changing conceptions of conspiracy*. New York: Springer Verlag.

Moscovici, S. (1988). Notes towards a description of social representations. *European Journal of Social Psychology*, 18, 211–50.

Moscovici, S. and Hewstone, M. (1983). Social representations and social explanations: from the 'naive' to the 'amateur' scientist. In M. Hewstone (ed.), *Attribution theory: Social and functional extensions*. Oxford: Basil Blackwell.

Murray, H. A. (1938). *Explorations in personality*. New York: Oxford University Press.

Mynatt, C. R., Doherty, M. E. and Tweney, R. D. (1977). Confirmation bias in a simulated research environment: An experimental study of scientific inference. *Quarterly Journal of Experimental Psychology*, 29, 85–95.

Neisser, U. (1980). On social knowing. *Personality and Social Psychology Bulletin*, 6, 601–5.

Nesdale, A. R. (1983). Effects of person and situation expectations on explanation seeking and causal attributions. *British Journal of Social Psychology*, 22, 93–9.

Newcombe, R. D. and Rutter, D. R. (1982a). Ten reasons why ANOVA theory and research fail to explain attribution processes: 1. Conceptual problems. *Current Psychological Reviews*, 2, 95–107.

Newcombe, R. D. and Rutter, D. R. (1982b). Ten reasons why ANOVA theory and research fail to explain attribution processes: 2. Methodological problems. *Current Psychological Reviews*, 2, 153–70.

Newman, H. M. (1981a). Communication within ongoing intimate relationships: An attributional perspective. *Personality and Social Psychology Bulletin*, 7, 59–70.

Newman, H. M. (1981b). Interpretation and explanation: Infuences on communicative exchanges within intimate relationships. *Communication Quarterly*, 29, 123–31.

Newman, H. M. and Langer, E. J. (1981). Post-divorce adaptation and the attribution of responsibility. *Sex Roles*, 7, 223–32.

Newtson, D. (1974). Dispositional inference from effects of actions: Effects chosen and effects foregone. *Journal of Experimental Social Psychology*, 10, 489–96.

Newtson, D. (1976). Foundations of attribution: The perception of ongoing behavior. In J. H. Harvey, W. J. Ickes and R. F. Kidd (eds), *New directions in attribution research* (Vol. 1). Hillsdale, N.J.: Erlbaum.

Nicholls, J. G. (1975). Causal attributions and other achievement-related cognitions: Effects of task outcome, attainment value, and sex. *Journal of Personality and Social Psychology*, 31, 379–89.

Nisbett, R. E. and Borgida, E. (1975). Attribution and the psychology of prediction. *Journal of Personality and Social Psychology*, 32, 932–43.

Nisbett, R. E., Caputo, C., Legant, P. and Maracek, J. (1973). Behaviour as seen by the actor and as seen by the observer. *Journal of Personality and Social Psychology*, 27, 154–64.

Nisbett, R. E. and Ross, L. (1980). *Human inference: Strategies and shortcomings of social judgment*. Englewood Cliffs, N.J.: Prentice-Hall.

Nisbett, R. E. and Wilson, T. D. (1977). Telling more than we can know: Verbal reports on mental processes. *Psychological Review*, 84, 231–59.

Oakes, P. J. (1987). Salience and categorization. In J. C. Turner et al., *Rediscovering the social group: A self-categorization theory*. Oxford: Basil Blackwell.

Oakes, P. J. and Turner, J. C. (1980). Social categorization and intergroup behaviour: does minimal intergroup discrimination make social identity more positive? *European Journal of Social Psychology*, 10, 295–301.

O'Brien, G. E. and Kabanoff, B. (1979). Comparison of unemployed and employed workers on work values, locus of control and health variables. *Australian Psychologist*, 14, 143–54.

Olson, J. M. and Ross, M. (1985). Attribution research: Past contributions, current trends, and future prospects. In J. H. Harvey and G. Weary (eds), *Attribution: Basic issues and applications*. Orlando, Fla.: Academic Press.

Orvis, B. R., Cunningham, J. D. and Kelley, H. H. (1975). A closer examination of causal inference: The roles of consensus, distinctiveness and consistency information. *Journal of Personality and Social Psychology*, 32, 605–16.

Orvis, B. R., Kelley, H. H. and Butler, D. (1976). Attributional conflicts in young couples. In J. H. Harvey, W. J. Ickes and R. F. Kidd (eds), *New directions in attribution research* (Vol. 1). Hillsdale, N.J.: Erlbaum.

Ostrom, T. M. (1981). Attribution theory: Whence and whither. In J. H. Harvey, W. J. Ickes and R. F. Kidd (eds), New *directions in attribution research* (Vol. 3). Hillsdale, N.J.: Erlbaum.

Ostrom, T. M. (1984). The sovereignty of social cognition. In R. S. Wyer and T. K. Srull (eds), *Handbook of social cognition* (Vol. 1). Hillsdale, N.J.: Erlbaum.

Overington, M. A. (1977). Kenneth Burke as social theorist. *Sociological Inquiry*, 47, 133–41.

Pachter, H. M. (1974). Defining an event: Prolegomenon to any future philosophy of history. *Social Research*, 44, 439–66.

Pandey, J., Sinha, Y., Prakash, A. and Tripathi, R. C. (1982). Right-Left political ideologies and attribution of the causes of poverty. *European Journal of Social Psychology*, 12, 327–31.

Parker, I. (1987). Social representations: Social psychology's (mis)use of sociology. *Journal for the Theory of Social Behaviour*, 17, 447–70.

Passer, M. W., Kelley, H. H. and Michela, J. L. (1978). Multidimensional scaling of the causes for negative interpersonal behaviour. *Journal of Personality and Social Psychology*, 36, 951–62.

Passmore, J. (1962). Explanation in everyday life, in science and in history. *History and Theory*, 2, 105–23.

Peevers, B. and Secord, P. (1973). Developmental changes in attribution of descriptive concepts to persons. *Journal of Personality and Social Psychology*, 27, 120–8.

Pepitone, A. (1981). Lessons from the history of social psychology. *American Psychologist*, 36, 972–85.

Peters, L. H., Terborg, J. R. and Taynor, J. (1974). Women as managers scale: A measure of attitudes toward women in management positions. *JSAS Catalog of Selected Documents in Psychology*, 4, 27. (MS. No. 585).

Peters, R. S. (1958). *The concept of motivation*. London: Routledge and Kegan Paul.

Peterson, C. (1980). Memory and the 'dispositional shift'. *Social Psychology Quarterly*, 43, 372–80.

Peterson, C. and Seligman, M. E. P. (1984). Causal explanations as a risk factor for depression: Theory and evidence. *Psychological Review*, 91, 347–74.

Peterson, C., Semmel, A., von Baeyer, C., Abramson, L. Y., Metalsky, G. I. and Seligman, M. E. P. (1982). The Attributional Style Questionnaire. *Cognitive Therapy and Research*, 6, 287–300.

Pettigrew, T. F. (1979). The ultimate attribution error: Extending Allport's cognitive analysis of prejudice. *Personality and Social Psychology Bulletin*, 5, 461–76.

Pettigrew, T. F. (1986). The intergroup contact hypothesis reconsidered. In M. Hewstone and R. J. Brown (eds), *Contact and conflict in intergroup encounters*. Oxford: Basil Blackwell.

Petty, R. E., Cacioppo, J. T. and Goldman, R. (1981). Personal involvement as a determinant of argument-based persuasion. *Journal of Personality and Social Psychology*, 41, 847–55.

Piaget, J. (1930). *The child's conception of physical causality*. London: Routledge.

Piaget, J. (1958). *The child's construction of reality*. London: Routledge and Kegan Paul.

Pittman, T. S. and D'Agostino, P. R. (1985). Motivation and attribution: The effects of control deprivation on subsequent information processing. In J. H. Harvey and G. Weary (eds), *Attribution: Basic issues and applications*. Orlando, Fla.: Academic Press.

Pittman, T. S. and Pittman, N. L. (1980). Deprivation of control and the attribution process. *Journal of Personality and Social Psychology*, 39, 377–89.

Pleban, R. and Richardson, D. C. (1979). Research and publication trends in social psychology: 1973–7. *Personality and Social Psychology Bulletin*, 5, 138–41.

Poliakov, L. (1966). *The history of anti-semitism* (Vol. 1). London: Elek Books.

Poliakov, L. (1968). *The history of anti-semitism* (Vol. 3). London: Routledge and Kegan Paul.

Poliakov, L. (1980). *La causalité diaboloque*. Paris: Calmann-Lévy.

Popper, K. (1959). *The logic of scientific discovery*. New York: Basic Books.

Posner, M. T. and Snyder, C. R. R. (1975). Attention and cognitive control. In R. L. Solso (ed.), *Information processing and cognition: The Loyola Symposium*. Hillsdale, N. J.: Erlbaum.

Potter, D. A. (1973). Personalism and interpersonal attraction. *Journal of Personality and Social Psychology*, 28, 192–8.

Potter, J. and Litton, I. (1985a). Some problems underlying the theory of social representations. *British Journal of Social Psychology*, 24, 81–90.

Potter, J. and Litton, I. (1985b). Representing representation: A reply to

Moscovici, Semin and Hewstone. *British Journal of Social Psychology*, 24, 99–100.

Pruitt, D. J. and Insko, C. A. (1980). Extension of the Kelley attribution model: The role of comparison-object consensus, target-object consensus, distinctiveness and consistency. *Journal of Personality and Social Psychology*, 39, 39–58.

Pryor, J. B., Gibbons, F. X., Wicklund, R. A., Fazio, R. H. and Hood, R. (1977). Self-focused attention and self-report validity. *Journal of Personality*, 45, 513–27.

Pryor, J. B. and Kriss, M. (1977). The cognitive dynamics of salience in the attribution process. *Journal of Personality and Social Psychology*, 35, 49–55.

Pyszczynski, T. A. and Greenberg, J. (1981). Role of disconfirmed expectancies in the instigation of attributional processing. *Journal of Personality and Social Psychology*, 40, 31–8.

Pyszczynski, T. A. and Greenberg, J. (1987). Toward an integration of cognitive and motivational perspectives on social inference: A biased hypothesis-testing model. In L. Berkowitz (ed.), *Advances in experimental social psychology* (Vol. 20). San Diego, Cal.: Academic Press.

Quattrone, G. A. (1982a). Overattribution and unit formation: When behavior engulfs the person. *Journal of Personality and Social Psychology*, 42, 593–607.

Quattrone, G. A. (1982b). Behavioral consequences of attributional bias. *Social Cognition*, 1, 358–78.

Raps, C. S., Peterson, C., Reinhard, K. E., Abramson, L. Y. and Seligman, M. E. P. (1982). Attributional style among depressed patients. *Journal of Abnormal Psychology*, 91, 102–8.

Read, S. J. (1983). Once is enough: Causal reasoning from a single instance. *Journal of Personality and Social Psychology*, 45, 323–34.

Read, S. J. (1984). Analogical reasoning in social judgment: The importance of causal theories. *Journal of Personality and Social Psychology*, 46, 14–25.

Read, S. J. (1987). Constructing causal scenarios: A knowledge structure approach to causal reasoning. *Journal of Personality and Social Psychology*, 52, 288–302.

Read, S. J., Druian, P. R. and Miller, L. C. (in press). The role of causal sequence in the meaning of actions. *British Journal of Social Psychology*.

Read, S. J. and Miller, L. C. (in press). Inter-personalism: Towards a goal-based theory of persons in relationships. In L. Pervin (ed.), *Goal concepts in personality and social psychology*. Hillsdale, N.J.: Erlbaum.

Reeder, G. D. (1982). Let's give the fundamental attribution error another chance. *Journal of Personality and Social Psychology*, 43, 341–4.

Reeder, G. D. and Brewer, M. B. (1979). A schematic model of dispositional attribution in interpersonal perception. *Psychological Review*, 86, 61–79.

Reeder, G. D., Fletcher, G. J. O. and Furman, K. (in press). The role of observers' expectations in attitude attribution. *Journal of Experimental Social Psychology*.

Reeder, G. D. and Fulks, J. L. (1980). When actions speak louder than words: Implicational schemata and the attribution of ability. *Journal of Experimental Social Psychology*, 16, 33–46.

Reeder, G. D., Messick, D. M. and van Avermaet, E. (1977). Dimensional asymmetry in attributional inference. *Journal of Experimental Social Psychology*, 13, 46–57.

Regan, D. T. (1978). Attributional aspects of interpersonal attraction. In J. H. Harvey, W. J. Ickes and R. F. Kidd (eds), *New directions in attribution research* (Vol. 2). Hillsdale, N. J.: Erlbaum.

Regan, D. T., Straus, E. and Fazio, R. H. (1974). Liking and the attribution process. *Journal of Experimental Social Psychology*, 10, 385–97.

Regan, D. T. and Totten, J. (1975). Empathy and attribution: Turning observers into actors. *Journal of Personality and Social Psychology*, 32, 850–6.

Rholes, W. S. and Pryor, J. B. (1982). Cognitive accessibility and causal attributions. *Personality and Social Psychology Bulletin*, 8, 719–27.

Riemer, B. S. (1975). Influence of causal beliefs on affect and expectancy. *Journal of Personality and Social Psychology*, 31, 1163–7.

Riess, M., Rosenfeld, P., Melburg, V. and Tedeschi, J. T. (1981). Self-serving attributions: Biased private perceptions and distorted public descriptions. *Journal of Personality and Social Psychology*, 41, 224–31.

Roberts, J. M. (1974). *The mythology of the secret societies*. St Albans: Paladin.

Robins, C. J. (1988). Attributions and depression: Why is the literature so inconsistent? *Journal of Personality and Social Psychology*, 54, 880–9.

Rokeach, M. (1973). *The nature of human values*. New York: Free Press.

Ronis, D. L., Hansen, R. D. and O'Leary, V. B. (1983). Understanding the meaning of achievement attributions: A test of derived locus and stability scores. *Journal of Personality and Social Psychology*, 44, 702–11.

Roqueplo, P. (1974). *Le partage du savoir*. Paris: Le Seuil.

Rosch, E. (1978). Principles of categorization. In E. Rosch and B. B. Lloyd (eds), *Cognition and categorization*. Hillsdale, N. J.: Erlbaum.

Rosenbaum, M. E. (1986). The repulsion hypothesis: On the nondevelopment of relationships. *Journal of Personality and Social Psychology*, 51, 1156–66.

Rosenberg, S. W. and Wolfsfeld, G. (1977). International conflict and the problem of attribution. *Journal of Conflict Resolution*, 21, 75–103.

Rosenfield, D. and Stephan, W. G. (1977). When discounting fails: An unexpected finding. *Memory and Cognition*, 5, 97–102.

Ross, L. (1977). The intuitive psychologist and his shortcomings: Distortions in the attribution process. In L. Berkowitz (ed.), *Advances in experimental social psychology* (Vol. 10). New York: Academic Press.

Ross, L. (1978). Some afterthoughts on the intuitive psychologist. In L. Berkowitz (ed.), *Cognitive theories in social psychology*. New York: Academic Press.

Ross, L., Amabile, T. M. and Steinmetz, J. L. (1977a). Social roles, social control and biases in social-perception processes. *Journal of Personality and Social Psychology*, 35, 485–94.

Ross, L. and Anderson, C. (1982). Shortcomings in the attribution process: On the origins and maintenance of erroneous social assessments. In A. Tversky, D. Kahneman and P. Slovic (eds), *Judgment under uncertainty: Heuristics and biases*. New York: Cambridge University Press.

Ross, L., Bierbrauer, G. and Polly, S. (1974). Attribution of educational outcomes by professional and nonprofessional instructors. *Journal of Personality and Social Psychology*, 29, 609–18.

Ross, L., Greene, D. and House, P. (1977b). The false consensus phenomenon: An attributional bias in self-perception and social perception processes. *Journal of Experimental Social Psychology*, 13, 279–301.

Ross, M. (1981). Self-centered biases in attributions of responsibility: Antecedents and consequences. In E. T. Higgins, C. P. Herman and M. P. Zanna (eds), *Social cognition: The Ontario Symposium* (Vol. 1). Hillsdale, N. J.: Erlbaum.

Ross, M. and Fletcher, G. J. O. (1985). Attribution and social perception. In G. Lindzey and E. Aronson (eds), *Handbook of social psychology* (Vol. 2) (3rd edn). New York: Random House.

Ross, M. and Sicoly, F. (1979). Egocentric biases in availability and attribution. *Journal of Personality and Social Psychology*, 37, 322–37.

Rothbart, M. (1981). Memory processes and social beliefs. In D. L. Hamilton (ed.), *Cognitive processes in stereotyping and intergroup behavior*. Hillsdale, N. J.: Erlbaum.

Rothbart, M., Evans, M. and Fulero, S. (1979). Recall for confirming events: Memory processes and the maintenance of social stereotypes. *Journal of Experimental Social Psychology*, 15, 343–55.

Rothbart, M. and John, O. P. (1985). Social categorization and behavioral episodes: A cognitive analysis of the effects of intergroup contact. *Journal of Social Issues*, 41, 81–104.

Rotter, J. B. (1954). *Social learning and clinical psychology*. New York: Prentice Hall.

Rotter, J. B. (1966). Generalized expectancies for internal versus external control of reinforcement. *Psychological Monographs*, 80, (1)(Whole No. 609).

Rozeboom, W. W. (1973). Dispositions revisited. *Philosophy of Science*, 40, 59–74.

Ruble, D. N. and Feldman, N. S. (1976). Order of consensus, distinctiveness and consistency information and causal attributions. *Journal of Personality and Social Psychology*, 34, 930–7.

Ruble, D. N., Feldman, N. S., Higgins, E. T. and Karlovac, M. (1979). Locus of causality and the use of information in the development of causal attributions. *Journal of Personality*, 47, 595–614.

Rudmin, F., Trimpop, R. M., Kryl, I.-P. and Boski, P. (1987). Gustav Ichheiser in the history of social psychology: An early phenomenology of social attribution. *British Journal of Social Psychology*, 26, 165–80.

Russell, D. W. (1982). The causal dimension scale: A measure of how individuals perceive causes. *Journal of Personality and Social Psychology*, 42, 1137–45.

Russell, D. W. and McAuley, E. (1986). Causal attributions, causal dimensions, and affective reactions to success and failure. *Journal of Personality and Social Psychology*, 50, 1174–85.

Russell, D. W., McAuley, E. and Tarico, V. (1987). Measuring causal attributions for success and failure: A comparison of methodologies for assessing causal dimensions. *Journal of Personality and Social Psychology*, 52, 1248–57.

Ryan, W. (1971). *Blaming the victim*. New York: Pantheon.

Sagar, H. A. and Schofield, J. W. (1980). Racial and behavioral cues in Black and White children's perceptions of ambiguously aggressive acts. *Journal of Personality and Social Psychology*, 39, 590–8.

Schachter, S. (1964). The interaction of cognitive and physiological determinants of emotional state. In L. Berkowitz (ed.), *Advances in experimental social psychology* (Vol. 1). New York: Academic Press.

Schank, R. and Abelson, R. (1977). *Scripts, plans, goals, and understanding*. Hillsdale, N. J.: Erlbaum.

Schaufeli, W. B. (1988). Perceiving the causes of unemployment: An evaluation of the causal dimensions scale in a real-life situation. *Journal of Personality and Social Psychology*, 54, 347–56.

Schlenker, B. R. (1975). Group members' attributions of responsibility for prior group performance. *Representative Research in Social Psychology*, 6, 96–108.

Schlenker, B. R. (1980). *Impression management: The self-concept, social identity and interpersonal relations*. Monterey, Cal.: Brooks/Cole.

Schlenker, B. R. and Miller, R. S. (1977a). Egocentrism in groups: Self-serving biases or logical information processing? *Journal of Personality and Social Psychology*, 35, 755–64.

Schlenker, B. R. and Miller, R. S. (1977b). Group cohesiveness as a determinant of egocentric perceptions in cooperative groups. *Human Relations*, 30, 1039–55.

Schlenker, B. R., Soraci, S. and McCarthy, B. (1976). Self-esteem and group performance as determinants of egocentric perceptions in cooperative groups. *Human Relations*, 29, 1163–76.

Schmidt, C. F. (1972). Multidimensional scaling of the printed media's explanations of the riot of the summer of 1967. *Journal of Personality and Social Psychology*, 24, 59–67.

Schneider, W. and Shiffrin, R. M. (1977). Controlled and automatic human information processing: I. Detection, search, and attention. *Psychological Review*, 84, 1–66.

Schwarz, N. (1987). *Stimmung als Information: Untersuchungen zum Einfluss von Stimmungen auf die Bewertung des eigenen Lebens*. Heidelberg: Springer-Verlag.

Schwarz, N. and Clore, G. (1983). Mood, misattribution, and judgments of subjective well-being: Informative and directive functions of affective states. *Journal of Personality and Social Psychology*, 45, 513–23.

Scott, M. B. and Lyman, S. (1968). Accounts. *American Sociological Review*, 33, 46–62.

Scribner, S. and Cole, M. (1973). Cognitive consequences of formal and informal education. *Science*, 183, 554–9.

Sears, D. O. (1986). College sophomores in the laboratory: Influences of a narrow data base on social psychology's view of human nature. *Journal of Personality and Social Psychology*, 51, 515–30.

Seligman, M. E. P., Abramson, L. Y., Semmel, A. and von Baeyer, C. (1979). Depressive attributional style. *Journal of Abnormal Psychology*, 88, 242–7.

Semin, G. R. (1980). A gloss on attribution theory. *British Journal of Social and Clinical Psychology*, 19, 291–300.

Semin, G. R. (1985). The 'phenomenon of social representations': A comment on Potter and Litton. *British Journal of Social Psychology*, 24, 93–5.

Semin, G. R. and Fiedler, K. Relocating attributional phenomena within a language-cognition interface: The case of actors' and observers' perspectives. Unpublished manuscript, University of Sussex.

Semin, G. R. and Manstead, A. S. (1983). *The accountability of conduct: A social psychological analysis*. London: Academic Press.

Shaklee, H. (1983). Causal schemata: Description or explanation of judgment process? A reply to Fiedler. *Journal of Personality and Social Psychology*, 45, 1010–12.

Shaklee, H. and Fischhoff, B. (1982). Strategies of information search in causal analysis. *Memory and Cognition*, 10, 520–30.

Shaver, K. G. (1975). *An introduction to attribution processes*. Cambridge, Mass.: Winthrop.

Shaver, K. G. (1981). Back to basics: On the role of theory in the attribution of causality. In J. H. Harvey, W. J. Ickes and R. F. Kidd (eds), *New directions in attribution research* (Vol. 3). Hillsdale, N.J.: Erlbaum.

Shaver, K. G. (1985). *The attribution of blame: Causality, responsibility and blameworthiness*. New York: Springer-Verlag.

Shaw, M. E. and Iwawaki, S. (1972). Attribution of responsibility by Japanese and Americans as a function of age. *Journal of Cross-Cultural Psychology*, 3, 71–82.

Sherif, M. (1966). *Group conflict and co-operation: Their social psychology*. London: Routledge and Kegan Paul.

Sherman, S. J. and Corty, E. (1984). Cognitive heuristics. In R. S. Wyer and T. K. Srull (eds), *Handbook of social cognition* (Vol. 1). Hillsdale, N. J.: Erlbaum.

Shields, N. M. and Hanneke, C. R. (1983). Attribution processes in violent relationships: Perceptions of violent husbands and their wives. *Journal of Applied Social Psychology*, 13, 515–27.

Shiffrin, R. M. and Schneider, W. (1977). Controlled and automatic human information processing: II. Perceptual learning, automatic attending and general theory. *Psychological Review*, 84, 127–90.

Showers, C. and Cantor, N. (1985). Social cognition: A look at motivated strategies. *Annual Review of Psychology*, 36, 275–306.

Shultz, T. R. and Ravinsky, R. B. (1977). Similarity as a principle of causal inference. *Child Development*, 48, 1552–8.

Shultz, T. R. and Schleifer, M. (1983). Towards a refinement of attribution concepts. In J. M. F. Jaspars, F. D. Fincham and M. Hewstone (eds), *Attribution theory and research: Conceptual, developmental and social dimensions*. London: Academic Press.

Shweder, R. A. and Bourne, E. J. (1982). Does the concept of the person vary cross-culturally? In A. J. Marsella and G. M. White (eds), *Cultural conceptions of mental health and therapy*. Dordrecht, Holland: D. Reidel.

Sillars, A. L. (1980a). Attributions and communication in roommate conflicts. *Communication Monographs*, 47, 180–200.

Sillars, A. L. (1980b). The sequential and distributional structure of conflict interactions as a function of attributions concerning the locus of responsibility and stability of conflicts. In D. Nimmo (ed.), *Communication Yearbook* (Vol. 4), Edison, N. J.: Transaction Books.

Sillars, A. L. (1981). Attributions and interpersonal conflict resolution. In J. H. Harvey, W. J. Ickes and R. F. Kidd (eds), *New directions in attribution research* (Vol. 3). Hillsdale, N. J.: Erlbaum.

Simon, H. A. (1968). Causation. *International Encyclopaedia of the Social Sciences* (Vol. 2), 350–56.

Singh, R., Gupta, M. and Dalal, A. K. (1979). Cultural difference in attribution of performance: an integration-theoretical analysis. *Journal of Personality and Social Psychology*, 37, 1342–51.

Singh, S. and Vasudeva, P. (1977). A factorial study of the perceived reasons for poverty. *Asian Journal of Psychology and Education*, 2, 51–6.

Slovic, P. and Lichtenstein, S. (1971). Comparison of Bayesian and regression approaches to the study of human information processing in judgment. *Organizational Behavior and Human Performance*, 6, 649–744.

Slugoski, B. R. (1983). Attribution in conversational context. Paper presented at the Annual Meeting of the British Psychological Society (Social Psychology Section), Sheffield, England.

Smith, E. R. and Miller, F. D. (1978). Limits on perception of cognitive processes: A reply to Nisbett and Wilson. *Psychological Review*, 85, 355–62.

Smith, E. R. and Miller, F. D. (1979a). Attributional information processing: A response time model of causal subtraction. *Journal of Personality and Social Psychology*, 37, 1723–31.

Smith, E. R. and Miller, F. D. (1979b). Salience and the cognitive mediation of attribution. *Journal of Personality and Social Psychology*, 37, 2240–52.

Smith, E. R. and Miller, F. D. (1982). Latent-variable models of attributional measurement. *Personality and Social Psychology Bulletin*, 8, 221–5.

Smith, E. R. and Miller, F. D. (1983). Mediation among attributional inferences and comprehension processes: Initial findings and a general method. *Journal of Personality and Social Psychology*, 44, 492–505.

Sniderman, P. M., Hagen, M. G., Tetlock, P. E. and Brady, H. E. (1986). Reasoning chains: Causal models of policy reasoning in mass publics. *British Journal of Political Science*, 16, 405–30.

Snyder, C. R., Higgins, R. L. and Stucky, R. J. (1983). *Excuses*. New York: Wiley.

Snyder, M. (1976). Attribution and behavior: Social perception and social causation. In J. H. Harvey, W. J. Ickes and R. F. Kidd (eds), *New directions in attribution research* (Vol. 1). Hillsdale, N. J.: Erlbaum.

Snyder, M. (1984). When belief creates reality. In L. Berkowitz (ed.), *Advances in experimental social psychology* (Vol. 18). New York: Academic Press.

Snyder, M. and Gangestad, S. (1981). Hypothesis-testing processes. In J. H. Harvey, W. J. Ickes and R. F. Kidd (eds), *New directions in attribution research* (Vol. 3). Hillsdale, N. J.: Erlbaum.

Snyder, M. and Jones, E. E. (1974). Attitude attribution when behavior is constrained. *Journal of Experimental Social Psychology*, 10, 585–600.

Snyder, M. and Swann, W. B. (1978a). Hypothesis-testing processes in social interaction. *Journal of Personality and Social Psychology*, 36, 1202–12.

Snyder, M. and Swann, W. B. (1978b). Behavioral confirmation in social interaction: From social perception to social reality. *Journal of Experimental Social Psychology*, 14, 148–62.

Snyder, M., Tanke, E. D. and Berscheid, E. (1977). Social perception and interpersonal behavior: On the self-fulfilling nature of social stereotypes. *Journal of Personality and Social Psychology*, 35, 656–66.

Snyder, M. and Uranowitz, S. (1978). Reconstructing the past: Some cognitive consequences of person perception. *Journal of Personality and Social Psychology*, 36, 941–50.

Snyder M. L., Smoller, B., Strenta, A. and Frankel, A. (1981). A comparison of egotism, negativity and learned helplessness as explanations for poor performances after unsolvable problems. *Journal of Personality and Social Psychology*, 40, 24–30.

Snyder, M. L., Stephan, W. G. and Rosenfield, D. (1976). Egotism and attribution. *Journal of Personality and Social Psychology*, 33, 435–41.

Snyder, M. L., Stephan, W. G. and Rosenfield, D. (1978). Attributional egotism. In J. H. Harvey, W. J. Ickes and R. F. Kidd (eds), *New directions in attribution research* (Vol. 2). Hillsdale, N.J.: Erlbaum.

Solomon, S. (1978). Measuring dispositional and situational attributions. *Personality and Social Psychology Bulletin*, 4, 589–94.

Sousa, F. and Leyens, J.-P. (1987). *A priori* vs. spontaneous models of attribution: The case of gender and achievement. *British Journal of Social Psychology*, 26, 281–92.

Spence, J. T. (1984). Masculinity, femininity, and gender-related traits: A conceptual analysis and critique of current research. *Progress in Experimental Personality Research*, 13, 1–97.

Spence, J. T. (1985). Gender identity and its implications for concepts of masculinity and femininity. In T. Sondregger (ed.), *Nebraska symposium on motivation*. Lincoln, Neb.: University of Nebraska Press.

Sperber, D. (1985). Anthropology and psychology: Towards an epidemiology of representations. *Man*, 20, 73–89.

Spurzheim, J. G. (1934). *Phrenology, in connexion with the study of physiognomy*. Boston: Marsh, Capen and Lyon (2nd American edn).

Srull, T. K. and Wyer, R. S. (1979). The role of category accessibility in the interpretation of information about persons: Some determinants and implications. *Journal of Personality and Social Psychology*, 37, 1660–72.

Steiner, I. D. (1974). Whatever happened to the group in social psychology? *Journal of Experimental Social Psychology*, 10, 94–108.

Steiner, I. D. and Field, W. L. (1960). Role assignment and interpersonal influence. *Journal of Abnormal and Social Psychology*, 61, 239–46.

Stephan, W. G. (1977). Stereotyping: Role of ingroup-outgroup differences in causal attribution of behaviour. *Journal of Social Psychology*, 101, 255–66.

Stephan, W. G. (1985). Intergroup relations. In G. Lindzey and E. Aronson (eds), *Handbook of social psychology* (Vol. 2). New York: Random House.

Stephan, W. G. and Rosenfield, D. (1982). Racial and ethnic stereotyping. In A. G. Millar (ed.), *In the eye of the beholder: Contemporary issues in stereotyping*. New York: Praeger.

Stephan, W. G., Rosenfield, D. and Stephan, C. (1976). Egotism in males and females. *Journal of Personality and Social Psychology*, 34, 1161–7.

Stephan, W. G. and Woolridge, D. W. (1977). Sex differences in attributions for the performance of women on a masculine task. *Sex Roles*, 3, 321–8.

Stephen, T. (1987). Attribution and the process of adjustment to relationship termination. *Journal of Social and Personal Relationships*, 4, 47–62.

Stevens, L. and Jones, E. E. (1976). Defensive attribution and the Kelley cube. *Journal of Personality and Social Psychology*, 34, 809–20.

Storms, M. D. (1973). Videotape and the attribution process: Reversing actors' and observers' points of view. *Journal of Personality and Social Psychology*, 27, 165–75.

Storms, M. D. and McCaul, K. D. (1976). Attribution processes and emotional exacerbation of dysfunctional behavior. In J. H. Harvey, W. J. Ickes and R. F. Kidd (eds), *New directions in attribution research* (Vol. 1). Hillsdale, N.J.: Erlbaum.

Strenta, A. C. and Kleck, R. E. (1984). Physical disability and the perception of social interaction: It's not what you look at but how you look at it. *Personality and Social Psychology Bulletin*, 10, 279–88.

Sumner, G. A. (1906). *Folkways*. New York: Ginn.

Surber, C. F. (1981). Necessary versus sufficient causal schemata: Attributions for achievement in difficult and easy tasks. *Journal of Experimental Social Psychology*, 17, 569–86.

Swann, W. B. (1983). Self-verification: Bringing social reality into harmony with the self. In J. Suls and A. G. Greenwald (eds), *Psychological perspectives on the self* (Vol. 2). Hillsdale, N. J.: Erlbaum.

Sweeney, P. D., Anderson, K. and Bailey, S. (1986). Attributional style in depression: A meta-analytic review. *Journal of Personality and Social Psychology*, 50, 974–91.

Tajfel, H. (1969). Cognitive aspects of prejudice. *Journal of Social Issues*, 25, 79–97.

Tajfel, H. (1972). La catégorisation sociale. In S. Moscovici (ed.). *Introduction à la psychologie sociale*. Paris: Larousse.

Tajfel, H. (ed.) (1978). *Differentiation between social groups*. London: Academic Press.

Tajfel, H. (1979). Individuals and groups in social psychology. *British Journal of Social and Clinical Psychology*, 18, 183–91.

Tajfel, H. (1981). Social stereotypes and social groups. In J. C. Turner and H. Giles (eds), *Intergroup behaviour*. Oxford: Basil Blackwell.

Tajfel, H. (1982). Social psychology of intergroup relations. *Annual Review of Psychology*, 33, 1–30.

Tajfel, H. and Turner, J. C. (1979). An integrative theory of intergroup conflict. In W. G. Austin and S. Worchel (eds), *The social psychology of intergroup relations*. Monterey, Cal.: Brooks/Cole.

Taylor, D. M. and Brown, R. J. (1979). Towards a more social social psychology. *British Journal of Social and Clinical Psychology*, 18, 173–81.

Taylor, D. M., Doria, J. and Tyler, J. K. (1983). Group performance and cohesiveness: An attribution analysis. *Journal of Social Psychology*, 119, 187–98.

Taylor, D. M. and Jaggi, V. (1974). Ethnocentrism and causal attribution in a South Indian context. *Journal of Cross-Cultural Psychology*, 5, 162–71.

Taylor, D. M. and McKirnan, D. J. (1984). A five-stage model of intergroup relations. *British Journal of Social Psychology*, 23, 291–300.

Taylor, S. E. (1981). The interface of cognitive and social psychology. In J. H. Harvey (ed.), *Cognition, social behavior and the environment*. Hillsdale, N. J.: Erlbaum.

Taylor, S. E. (1982). The availability bias in social perception and interaction. In D. Kahneman, P. Slovic and A. Tversky (eds), *Judgment under uncertainty: Heuristics and biases*. New York: Cambridge University Press.

Taylor, S. E. and Crocker, J. (1981). Schematic bases of social information processing. In E. T. Higgins, C. P. Herman and M. P. Zanna (eds), *Social cognition: The Ontario symposium on personality and social psychology*. Hillsdale, N. J.: Erlbaum.

Taylor, S. E., Crocker, J., Fiske, S. T., Sprinzen, M. and Winkler, J. D. (1979). The generalizability of salience effects. *Journal of Personality and Social Psychology*, 37, 357–68.

Taylor, S. E. and Fiske, S. T. (1975). Point of view and perceptions of causality. *Journal of Personality and Social Psychology*, 32, 439–45.

Taylor, S. E. and Fiske, S. T. (1978). Salience, attention and attribution: Top of the head phenomena. In L. Berkowitz (ed.), *Advances in experimental social psychology* (Vol. 11). New York: Academic Press.

Taylor, S. E. and Fiske, S. T. (1981). Getting inside the head: Methodologies for process analysis in attribution and social cognition. In J. H. Harvey, W. J.

Ickes and R. F. Kidd (eds), *New directions in attribution research* (Vol. 3). Hillsdale, N. J.: Erlbaum.

Taylor, S. E., Fiske, S. T., Etcoff, N. and Ruderman, A. (1978). The categorical and contextual bases of person memory and stereotyping. *Journal of Personality and Social Psychology*, 36, 778–93.

Taylor, S. E. and Koivumaki, J. H. (1976). The perception of self and others: Acquaintanceship, affect and actor-observer differences. *Journal of Personality and Social Psychology*, 33, 403–8.

Tedeschi, J. T. (ed.) (1981). *Impression management theory and social psychological research*. New York: Academic Press.

Tedeschi, J. T. and Reiss, M. (1981). Verbal strategies in impression management. In C. Antaki (ed.), *The psychology of ordinary explanations of social behaviour*. London: Academic Press.

Tetlock, P. E. (1980). Explaining teacher explanations of pupil performance: A self-presentational interpretation. *Social Psychology Quarterly*, 43, 283–290.

Tetlock, P. E. (1983). Accountability and complexity of thought. *Journal of Personality and Social Psychology*, 45, 74–83.

Tetlock, P. E. and Levi, A. (1982). Attribution bias: On the inconclusiveness of the cognition-motivation debate. *Journal of Experimental Social Psychology*, 18, 68–88.

Tetlock, P. E. and Manstead, A. S. R. (1985). Impression management versus intrapsychic explanations in social psychology: A useful dichotomy? *Psychological Review*, 92, 59–77.

Tetlock, P. E. and McGuire, C. B. Jr. (1986). Cognitive perspectives on foreign policy. In R. K. White (ed.), *Psychology and the prevention of nuclear war: A book of readings*. New York: New York University Press.

Thibaut, J. W. and Riecken, H. W. (1955). Some determinants and consequences of the perception of social causality. *Journal of Personality*, 24, 113–33.

Thomas, K. (1971). *Religion and the decline of magic*. Harmondsworth: Penguin.

Thompson, S. C. and Kelley, H. H. (1981). Judgments of responsibility for activities in close relationships. *Journal of Personality and Social Psychology*, 41, 469–77.

Thorngate, W. (1976). Must we always think before we act? *Personality and Social Psychology Bulletin*, 2, 31–5.

Thorngate, W. (1979). Memory, cognition and social performance. In L. H. Strickland (ed.), *Soviet and Western perspectives in social psychology*. Oxford: Pergamon Press.

Thornton, B. (1984). Defensive attribution of responsibility: Evidence for an arousal-based motivational bias. *Journal of Personality and Social Psychology*, 46, 721–34.

Tiffany, D. W., Cowan, J. R. and Tiffany, P. M. (1970). The *unemployed, a social-psychological portrait*. New York: Prentice-Hall.

Tillman, W. S. and Carver, C. S. (1980). Actors' and observers' attributions for success and failure: A comparative test of predictions from Kelley's cube, self-serving bias and positivity bias formulations. *Journal of Experimental Social Psychology*, 16, 18–32.

Todd, J. T. and Warren, W. H. (1982). Visual perception of relative mass in dynamic events. *Perception*, 11, 325–35.

Tomkins, S. S. (1981). The quest for primary motives: Biography and autobiography of an idea. *Journal of Personality and Social Psychology*, 41, 306–29.

Town, J. P. and Harvey, J. H. (1981). Self-disclosure, attribution, and social interaction. *Social Psychology Quarterly*, 44, 291–300.

Townsend, P. (1979). *Poverty in the United Kingdom: A survey of household resources and standards of living*. Harmondsworth: Penguin.

Trabasso, T., Rollins, H. and Shaughnessy, E. (1971). Storage and verification stages in processing concepts. *Cognitive Psychology*, 2, 239–89.

Trabasso, T., Secco, T. and van den Broek, P. (1984). Causal cohesion and story coherence. In H. Mandl, N. L. Stein and T. Trabasso (eds), *Learning and comprehension of text*. Hillsdale, N.J.: Erlbaum.

Triandis, H. C. (ed.) (1976). *Variations in black and white perceptions of the social environment*. Champaign, Ill.: University of Illinois Press.

Triandis, H. C., Vassiliou, V., Vassiliou, G., Tanaka, Y. and Shanmugam, A. (eds) (1972). *The analysis of subjective culture*. New York: Wiley.

Trolier, T. K. and Hamilton, D. L. (1986). Variables influencing judgments of correlational relations. *Journal of Personality and Social Psychology*, 50, 879–88.

Trope, Y. (1986). Identification and inferential processes in dispositional attribution. *Psychological Review*, 93, 239–57.

Tucker, J. A., Vuchinich, R. E. and Sobell, M. B. (1981). Seeking information about one's own ability as a determinant of choice among tasks. *Journal of Personality and Social Psychology*, 32, 1004–13.

Tukey, D. D. and Borgida, E. (1983). An intrasubject approach to causal attribution. *Journal of Personality*, 51, 137–51.

Tulving, E. and Pearlstone, Z. (1966). Availability versus accessibility of information in memory for words. *Journal of Verbal Learning and Verbal Behavior*, 5, 381–91.

Turnbull, W. (1986). Everyday explanation: The pragmatics of puzzle resolution. *Journal for the Theory of Social Behaviour*, 16, 141–60.

Turnbull, W. and Slugoski, B. (1988). Conversational and linguistic processes in causal attribution. In D. Hilton (ed.), *Contemporary science and natural explanation: Commonsense conceptions of causality*. Brighton: Harvester Press.

Turner, J. C. (1982). Towards a cognitive redefinition of the social group. In H. Tajfel (ed.), *Social identity and intergroup relations*. Cambridge/Paris: Cambridge University Press, Maison des Sciences de l'Homme.

Turner, J. C. and Brown, R. J. (1978). Social status, cognitive alternatives and intergroup relations. In H. Tajfel (ed.), *Differentiation between social groups*. London: Academic Press.

Turner, J. C., with Hogg, M. A., Oakes, P. J., Reicher, S. D. and Wetherell, M. S. (1987). *Rediscovering the social group: A self-categorization theory.* Oxford: Basil Blackwell.

Turner, J. C., Hogg, M. A., Oakes, P. J. and Smith, P. M. (1984). Failure and defeat as determinants of group cohesiveness. *British Journal of Social Psychology*, 23, 97–111.

Tversky, A. and Kahneman, D. (1971). Belief in the law of small numbers. *Psychological Bulletin*, 76, 105–10.

Tversky, A. and Kahneman, D. (1973). Availability: A heuristic for judging frequency and probability. *Cognitive Psychology*, 5, 207–32.

Tversky, A. and Kahneman, D. (1974). Judgment under uncertainty: Heuristics and biases. *Science*, 185, 1124–31.

Tversky, A. and Kahneman, D. (1983). Extensional versus intuitive reasoning: The conjunction fallacy in probability judgment. *Psychological Review*, 90, 293–315.

Tyler, T. R. and Rasinski, K. (1983). Explaining political events and problems: The relationship between personal and environmental causality. *Micropolitics*, 2, 401–22.

Valle, V. A. and Frieze, I. H. (1976). Stability of causal attributions as a mediator in changing expectations for success. *Journal of Personality and Social Psychology*, 33, 579–87.

van der Pligt, J. (1981). Actors' and observers' explanations: Divergent perspectives or divergent evaluations? In C. Antaki (ed.), *The psychology of ordinary explanations of social behaviour*. London: Academic Press.

van Dijk, T. (1988). Social cognition, social power and social discourse. *Text*, 8, 129–57.

Van Kleeck, M. H., Hillger, L. A. and Brown, R. (1988). Pitting verbal schemas against information variables in attribution. *Social Cognition*, 6, 89–106.

Vinokur, A. and Ajzen, I. (1982). Relative importance of prior and immediate events: A causal primacy effect. *Journal of Personality and Social Psychology*, 42, 820–9.

Wagner, U., Lampen, L. and Syllwasschy, J. (1986). In-group inferiority, social identity and out-group devaluation in a modified minimal group study. *British Journal of Social Psychology*, 25, 15–24.

Walster, E. (1966). Assignment of responsibility for an accident. *Journal of Personality and Social Psychology*, 3, 73–9.

Wang, G. and McKillip, J. (1978). Ethnic identification and judgements of an accident. *Personality and Social Psychology Bulletin*, 4, 296–9.

Warr, P. (1984). Work and unemployment. In P. J. D. Drenth, H. Thierry, P. J. Willems and C. J. de Wolff (eds), *Handbook of work and organization psychology*. London: Wiley.

Wason, P. C. and Johnson-Laird, P. N. (1972). *Psychology of reasoning: Structure and content*. Hillsdale, N. J.: Erlbaum.

Watson, D. (1982). The actor and the observer: How are their perceptions of causality divergent? *Psychological Bulletin*, 92, 682–700.

Watzlawick, P., Beavin, J. and Jackson, D. (1967). *Pragmatics of human communication: A study of interactional patterns, pathologies, and paradoxes*. New York: W. W. Norton.

Weary Bradley, G. (1978). Self-serving biases in the attribution process: A reexamination of the fact or fiction question. *Journal of Personality and Social Psychology*, 36, 56–71.

Weary, G. (1980). Examination of affect and egotism as mediators of bias in causal attributions. *Journal of Personality and Social Psychology*, 38, 348–57.

Weary, G. (1981). Role of cognitive, affective and social factors in attribution biases. In J. H. Harvey (ed.), *Cognition, social behavior and the environment*. Hillsdale, N.J.: Erlbaum.

Weary, G. and Arkin, R. M. (1981). Attributional self-presentation. In J. H. Harvey, W. J. Ickes and R. F. Kidd (eds), *New directions in attribution research* (Vol. 3). Hillsdale, N.J.: Erlbaum.

Weary, G., Harvey, J. H., Schwieger, P., Olson, C. T., Perloff, R. and Pritchard, S. (1982). Self-presentation and the moderation of self-serving attributional biases. *Social Cognition*, 1, 140–59.

Weary, G., Rich, M. C., Harvey, J. H. and Ickes, W. (1980). Heider's formulation of social perception and attributional processes: Toward further clarification. *Personality and Social Psychology Bulletin*, 6, 37–43.

Weber, A. L., Harvey, J. H. and Stanley, M. A. (1987). The nature and motivations of accounts for failed relationships. In R. Burnett, P. McGhee and D. D. Clarke (eds), *Accounting for relationships*. London: Methuen.

Weber, M. (1947). *Theory of social and economic organization*. Glencoe, Ill.: The Free Press.

Weber, R. and Crocker, J. (1983). Cognitive processes in the revision of stereotypic beliefs. *Journal of Personality and Social Psychology*, 45, 961–77.

Wegner, D. M. and Finstruen, K. (1977). Observers' focus of attention in the simulation of self-perception. *Journal of Personality and Social Psychology*, 35, 56–62.

Weiner, B. (1979). A theory of motivation for some classroom experiences. *Journal of Educational Psychology*, 71, 3–25.

Weiner, B. (1982). The emotional consequences of causal attributions. In M. Clark and S. T. Fiske (eds), *Affect and cognition: The 17th Annual Carnegie Symposium on Cognition*. Hillsdale, N.J.: Erlbaum.

Weiner, B. (1983). Some methodological pitfalls in attributional research. *Journal of Educational Psychology*, 75, 530–43.

Weiner, B. (1985a). 'Spontaneous' causal thinking. *Psychological Bulletin*, 97, 74–84.

Weiner, B. (1985b). An attributional theory of achievement motivation and emotion. *Psychological Review*, 92, 548–73.

Weiner, B. (1986). *An attributional theory of motivation and emotion*. New York: Springer Verlag.

Weiner, B., Amirkhan, J., Folkes, V. S. and Verette, J. A. (1987). An attributional analysis of excuse giving: Studies of a naive theory of emotion. *Journal of Personality and Social Psychology*, 52, 316–24.

Weiner, B., Frieze, I. H., Kukla, A., Reed, I., Rest, S. and Rosenbaum, R. M. (1972). Perceiving the causes of success and failure. In E. E. Jones, D. E. Kanouse, H. H. Kelley, R. E. Nisbett, S. Valins and B. Weiner, *Attribution: Perceiving the causes of behavior*. Morristown, N. J.: General Learning Press.

Weiner, B., Nierenberg, R. and Goldstein, M. (1976). Social learning (locus of control) versus attributional (causal stability) interpretations of expectancy of success. *Journal of Personality*, 44, 52–68.

Weiner, B., Russell, D. and Lerman, D. (1978). Affective consequences of causal ascriptions. In J. H. Harvey, W. J. Ickes and R. F. Kidd (eds), *New directions in attribution research* (Vol. 2). Hillsdale, N.J.: Erlbaum.

Weiner, B., Russell, D. and Lerman, D. (1979). The cognition-emotion process in achievement-related contexts. *Journal of Personality and Social Psychology*, 37, 1211–20.

Weir, S. (1978). The perception of motion: Michotte revisited. *Perception*, 7, 247–60.

Weiss, R. L. and Margolin, G. (1977). Assessment of marital conflict and accord. In A. R. Ciminero, K. D. Calhoun and H. E. Adams (eds), *Handbook of behavioral assessment*. New York: Wiley.

Weiss, R. L. and Perry, B. A. (1979). *Assessment and treatment of marital dysfunction*. Eugene, Oreg.: Oregon Marital Studies Program.

Weiss, R. S. (1975). *Marital separation*. New York: Basic Books.

Wells, G. L. (1981). Lay analyses of causal forces on behavior. In J. H. Harvey (ed.), *Cognition, social behavior and the environment*. Hillsdale, N.J.: Erlbaum.

Wells, G. L. (1982). Attribution and reconstructive memory. *Journal of Experimental Social Psychology*, 18, 447–63.

Wells, G. L. and Harvey, J. H. (1977). Do people use consensus information in making causal attributions? *Journal of Personality and Social Psychology*, 35, 279–93.

Wells, G. L., Petty, R. E., Harkins, S. G., Kagehiro, D. and Harvey, J. H. (1977). Anticipated discussion of interpretation eliminates actor-observer differences in attribution of causality. *Sociometry*, 40, 247–53.

Wertheimer, M. (1923). Untersuchungen zur Lehre von der Gestalt, II. *Psychologische Forschung*, 4, 301–50.

Wetzel, C. G. (1982). Self-serving biases in attribution: A Bayesian analysis. *Journal of Personality and Social Psychology*, 43, 197–209.

White, P. A. (1984). A model of the layperson as pragmatist. *Personality and Social Psychology Bulletin*, 10, 333–48.

White, P. A. (1988a). Causal processing: Origins and development. *Psychological Bulletin*, 104, 36–52.

White, P. A. (1988b). Knowing more about what we can tell: 'Introspective access' and causal report inaccuracy 10 years later. *British Journal of Psychology*, 79, 13–46.

White, P. A. (1989). Concepts of causation in philosophy and in psychology. Unpublished manuscript, University of Wales, College of Cardiff.

White, R. W. (1959). Motivation reconsidered: The concept of competence. *Psychological Review*, 66, 297–333.

Whitehead, G. I., Smith, S. H. and Eichhorn, J. A. (1982). The effect of subject's race and other's race on judgments of causality for success and failure. *Journal of Personality*, 50, 193–202.

Wilder, D. A. (1978). Perceiving persons as a group; effects on attributions of causality and beliefs. *Social Psychology*, 41, 13–23.

Wilder, D. A. (1984). Intergroup contact: The typical member and the exception to the rule. *Journal of Experimental Social Psychology*, 20, 177–94.

Wilensky, R. (1983). *Planning and understanding: A computational approach to human reasoning*. Reading, Mass.: Addison-Wesley.

Willey, B. (1934). *The seventeenth century background*. London: Chatto and Windus.

Wilson, G. D. and Patterson, J. R. (1968). A new measure of conservatism. *British Journal of Social and Clinical Psychology*, 7, 264–9.

Wilson, T. D. and Linville, P. W. (1985). Improving the performance of college freshmen with attributional techniques. *Journal of Personality and Social Psychology*, 49, 287–93.

Wilson, T. D. and Nisbett, R. E. (1978). The accuracy of verbal reports about the effects of stimuli on evaluations and behavior. *Social Psychology*, 41, 118–31.

Winch, P. (1958). *The idea of a social science*. London: Routledge and Kegan Paul.

Winter, L. and Uleman, J. S. (1984). When are social judgments made? Evidence for the spontaneousness of trait inferences. *Journal of Personality and Social Psychology*, 47, 237–52.

Winter, L., Uleman, J. S. and Cunniff, C. (1985). How automatic are social judgments? *Journal of Personality and Social Psychology*, 49, 904–17.

Wolosin, R. J., Sherman, S. J. and Till, A. (1973). Effects of cooperation and competition on responsibility attribution after success and failure. *Journal of Experimental Social Psychology*, 9, 220–35.

Wolpert, L. (1987). Science and anti-science: The Lloyd-Roberts lecture 1986. *Journal of the Royal College of Physicians of London*, 21, 159–65.

Wong, P. T. and Weiner, B. (1981). When people ask 'why' questions and the heuristics of attributional search. *Journal of Personality and Social Psychology*, 40, 650–63.

Wood, G. S. (1982). Conspiracy and the paranoid style: Causality and deceit in the eighteenth century. *William and Mary Quarterly*, 39, 401–41.

Wortman, C. (1976). Causal attributions and personal control. In J. H. Harvey, W. J. Ickes and R. F. Kidd (eds), New *directions in attribution research* (Vol. 1). Hillsdale, N.J.: Erlbaum.

Wortman, C. B., Costanzo, P. R. and Witt, T. R. (1973). Effect of anticipated performance on the attributions of causality to self and others. *Journal of Personality and Social Psychology*, 27, 372–81.

Wright, E. F. and Wells, G. L. (1988). Is the attitude-attribution paradigm suitable for investigating the dispositional bias? *Personality and Social Psychology Bulletin*, 14, 183–90.

Wright, J. and Fichten, C. (1976). Denial of responsibility, videotape feedback and attribution theory: Relevance for behavioral marital therapy. *Canadian Psychology Review*, 17, 219–30.

Wyer, R. S. (1981). An information-processing perspective on social attribution. In J. H. Harvey, W. J. Ickes and R. F. Kidd (eds), *New directions in attribution research* (Vol. 3). Hillsdale, N. J.: Erlbaum.

Wyer, R. S. and Carlston, D. E. (1979). *Social cognition, inference and attribution*. Hillsdale, N.J.: Erlbaum.

Wyer, R. S. and Srull, T. K. (1981). Category accessibility: Some theoretical and empirical issues concerning the processing of social stimulus information. In E. T. Higgins, C. P. Herman and M. P. Zanna (eds), *Social cognition: The Ontario symposium on personality and social psychology*. Hillsdale, N. J.: Erlbaum.

Wyer, R. S. and Srull, T. K. (eds) (1984). *Handbook of social cognition* (3 vols.). Hillsdale, N. J.: Erlbaum.

Yarkin, K. L., Harvey, J. H. and Bloxom, B. M. (1981). Cognitive sets, attribution, and social interaction. *Journal of Personality and Social Psychology*, 41, 243–52.

Yarkin-Levin, K. (1983). Anticipated interaction, attribution and social interaction. *Social Psychology Quarterly*, 46, 302–11.

Younger, J., Arrowood, A. and Hemsley, G. (1977). And the lucky shall inherit the earth: perceiving the causes of financial success and failure. *European Journal of Social Psychology*, 7, 509–15.

Zaccaro, S. J., Peterson, C. and Walker, S. (1987). Self-serving attributions for individual and group performance. *Social Psychology Quarterly*, 50, 257–63.

Zajonc, R. B. (1980). Cognition and social cognition: A historical perspective. In L. Festinger (ed.), *Retrospections on social psychology*. New York: Oxford University Press.

Zillig, M. (1928). Einstellung und Aussage. *Zeitschrift für Psychologie*, 106, 58–106.

Zuckerman, M. (1978). Actions and occurrences in Kelley's cube. *Journal of Personality and Social Psychology*, 36, 647–56.

Zuckerman, M. (1979). Attribution of success and failure revisited, or: The motivational bias is alive and well in attribution theory. *Journal of Personality*, 47, 245–87.

Zuckerman, M., Eghrari, H. and Lambrecht, M. R. (1986). Attributions as inferences and explanations: Conjunction effects. *Journal of Personality and Social Psychology*, 51, 1144–53.

Zuckerman, M., Koestner, R., Colella, M. J. and Alton, A. O. (1984).

Anchoring in the detection of deception and leakage. *Journal of Personality and Social Psychology*, 47, 301–11.

Zukier, H. (1986). The paradigmatic and narrative modes in goal-guided inference. In R. M. Sorrentino and E. T. Higgins (eds), *Handbook of motivation and cognition: Foundations of social behavior*. New York: Wiley.

Zukier, H. (1987). The conspiratorial imperative: Medieval Jewry in Western Europe. In C. F. Graumann and S. Moscovici (eds), *Changing conceptions of conspiracy*. New York: Springer Verlag.

Zullow, H. M., Oettingen, G., Peterson, C. and Seligman, M. E. P. (1988). Pessimistic explanatory style in the historical record: CAVing LBJ, presidential candidates, and East versus West Berlin. *American Psychologist*, 43, 673–82.

Index of Subjects

Index of Names